AMERICAN
BROADSIDE VERSE

AMS PRESS

NEW YORK

PUBLISHED ON THE FOUNDATION ESTABLISHED

IN MEMORY OF AMASA STONE MATHER

OF THE CLASS OF 1907 YALE COLLEGE

THE AMASA STONE MATHER MEMORIAL PUBLICATION FUND

The present volume is the twelfth work published by the Yale University Press on the Amasa Stone Mather Memorial Publication Fund. This Foundation was established August 25, 1922, by a gift to Yale University from Samuel Mather, Esq., of Cleveland, Ohio, in pursuance of a pledge made in June, 1922, on the fifteenth anniversary of the graduation of his son, Amasa Stone Mather, who was born in Cleveland on August 20, 1884, and was graduated from Yale College in the Class of 1907. Subsequently, after traveling abroad, he returned to Cleveland, where he soon won a recognized position in the business life of the city and where he actively interested himself also in the work of many organizations devoted to the betterment of the community and to the welfare of the nation. His death from pneumonia on February 9, 1920, was undoubtedly hastened by his characteristic unwillingness ever to spare himself, even when ill, in the discharge of his duties or in his efforts to protect and further the interests committed to his care by his associates.

The Ardent DESIRE,

and Sincere Cry, of a true Be-
liever in Jesus Christ.

PSAL. 38. 9. *Lord, all my Desire is before Thee.*

OH! that mine *Eye* might closed be,
  To what becomes me not to see!
That *Deafness* might possess my *Ear*,
To what concerns me not to hear.
That *Truth* my *Tongue* might always tye,
From ever speaking foolishly.
That no vain *Thought* beguile my rest,
Or be conceived in my *Breast.*
That by each *Word*, each *Deed*, each *Thought*,
Glory may to my GOD be brought.
  But what are Wishes, LORD, mine Eye
On thee is fix'd: To thee I cry;
O purge out all my Dross, my Tin,
Make me more White than Snow within.
Wash, Lord, and purify my Heart,
And make it clean in ev'ry Part;
And when 'tis clean, Lord, keep it too,
For that is more than I can do.

NEWPORT, Rhode-Island: Printed by J. FRANKLIN,
for *Reuben Packcom*, and sold by him in Newport. 1728.

AMERICAN BROADSIDE VERSE

From Imprints of the 17th & 18th Centuries

Selected & Edited, with an Introductory Note, by

OLA ELIZABETH WINSLOW

Associate Professor of English, Goucher College

New Haven, Connecticut, Yale University Press

London, Humphrey Milford, Oxford University Press

Mdccccxxx

Library of Congress Cataloging in Publication Data

Winslow, Ola Elizabeth, comp.
  American broadside verse from imprints of the 17th & 18th centuries.

  1. American poetry—Colonial period, ca. 1600-1775.
2. American poetry—Revolutionary period, 1775-1783.
3. Broadsides. I. Title.
PS601.W5 1974   821'.008   77-153361
ISBN 0-404-07000-0

To the Memory of My Father

WILLIAM DELOS WINSLOW

PREFACE

ANY student of broadside literature recognizes the appropriateness of the German words for this type of imprint—*Fliegende Blätter*, or the French translation of them, *feuilles volantes*. Flying leaves, indeed! He who would pursue them has set himself a chase.

This is especially true in America, where until recently the value of this fugitive material was but little known. In fact, much of it, now in safe-keeping in libraries or private collections, still remains uncatalogued, and is in part or wholly inaccessible to students. Fortunately, this is not true of all. The larger research libraries and the historical societies, notably the Massachusetts and the New York historical societies, have brought together sizable collections, not only of originals, but also of photostatic reproductions, so that study and evaluation of these early imprints now begin to be possible. Since 1922, new impetus, as well as invaluable guidance, has been given to such studies by Mr. Worthington C. Ford's *Check-List of Massachusetts Broadsides, Etc., 1639–1800*, "Massachusetts Historical Society Collections," Vol. LXXV.

Much of the broadside verse listed by Mr. Ford and other bibliographers of early Americana has been printed at some time or other in the publications of historical societies, in library bulletins, or in collections of early verse, but no considerable body of this material has ever been assembled. The specimens reproduced in this volume illustrate the several kinds of verse printed in broadside in America from about the middle of the seventeenth century, the date of the first extant imprints, to the end of the eighteenth century, when the newspaper had put an end to this type of imprint as a vital response to contemporary life. A few later imprints are included, but only of verses known to have been printed in broadside before the end of the eighteenth century. For convenience of reference and comparison, the broadsides included are grouped according to their general subject matter. The selections chosen represent the earliest available imprint in each of the several groups, and enough later specimens to indicate range and diversity of treatment. There are unfortunate omissions, as some of the rarest specimens, unique for the details they illustrate, are privately owned and have not been available for reproduction.

As nearly as possible, the arrangement is chronological within each group, the date on the sheet itself determining its place in the list. Usually these dates refer to the events which are the subject of the verses, rarely to the date of printing, and while in general the date of composition and the date of printing lie close together for broadside matter, there are many exceptions. Wherever possible, these have been traced, and an attempt made to determine the approximate date of printing, but unless the sheet has a colophon, such attempts are dangerously conjectural. All dates not appearing on the sheets themselves, are enclosed in square brackets. For convenience, in the Table of Contents and the Index, titles have sometimes been shortened, and punctuation modified. Measurements can be given only approximately, as most of the sheets have either been torn or cut. Many have been backed with cloth or cardboard and the margins trimmed to fit, so that the size of one original rarely corresponds exactly with the size of another original of the same broadside. The measurements given in this volume have reference only to the copy used for reproduction, and represent the extreme margin of the paper rather than merely the printed portion. So far as has been possible, the broadsides included have been reproduced from originals. The exceptions are noted. The location of each imprint reproduced is given, but no attempt is made to locate other copies of the same verses. Bibliographical references throughout are made to Mr. Ford's *Check-List* rather than to the Evans *Bibliography* or to any other of the earlier lists to which Mr. Ford had access. Explanatory notes have been limited to brief identification of authors and events, and occasional extracts from contemporary annals.

For access to the materials used, and for permission to reproduce the imprints selected for inclusion, thanks are due the many custodians of these widely scattered treasures. The list is long and includes many libraries, societies, and individuals not represented in the final selection. Broadsides are reproduced

Preface

from the collections of the following libraries and societies, separate acknowledgment being also made in connection with each reproduction: The American Antiquarian Society, The Boston Athenaeum, The Boston Public Library, The Bostonian Society, The Dedham Historical Society, The Essex Institute, The John Carter Brown Library, The John Hay Library, The Library Company of Philadelphia, The Library of Congress, The Massachusetts Historical Society, The Massachusetts Society of Mayflower Descendants, The New York Historical Society, The Rhode Island Historical Society, and the William L. Clements Library. Reproductions are also made from the private collections of Mr. Joseph Grafton Minot and Dr. A. S. W. Rosenbach. The kindness and courtesy of the custodians of these collections, and of the many others which have been examined, have made the assembling of these materials a pleasurable task. I wish also to record my appreciation of the many courtesies extended to me by the officials and staff of the Yale University Library during the final preparation of this volume.

Of course it must always be remembered that a study of so perishable a type of literature as broadside verse is necessarily based on mere fragments, and that these may not always be representative. Who knows what may have perished? Or for that matter, what may yet come to light, as the interest in popular literature in America continues to stretch farther back to the beginnings?

New Haven, May, 1930. O. E. W.

CONTENTS

Contents

INTRODUCTORY NOTE

AS defined by the *New English Diction-ary*, a "broadside" is "a sheet of paper printed on one side only, forming one large page." In early usage, the term "broadsheet" appears to have been identical.

Broadsides, or broadsheets, made their appearance soon after the invention of printing in 1450. In fact, the earliest dated specimen of printing from movable type was a broadside, the "Letter of Indulgence" granted by Pope Nicholas V, in aid of John II against the Turks, April 12, 1451. The sheet was issued, presumably by Gutenberg, at Mainz, in 1454. Records exist for other fifteenth-century imprints of similar character, and various specimens of these early issues are extant.*

English broadsides were slightly later, owing to the fact that Caxton's printing press was not set up at Westminster until 1476. Several imprints are extant from the last two decades of the fifteenth century, and from the first decade of the sixteenth. After the beginning of the reign of Henry VIII in 1509, such issues were more frequent.† Naturally, popular uses were not slow to follow. For England, these date from early in the sixteenth century, when the broadside became a medium for journalistic and even literary material.

Journalistically, its province was that of the lurid and the startling. Accounts of crimes, disasters, monstrosities, and other violations of nature so agreeable to a six-teenth-century taste, were hastily printed and hawked about the streets for a penny.

* Facsimiles of several interesting specimens of the early broadside are included in *Rariora*, edited by John Eliot Hodgkin (London, 1902), II, 243–250.

† Specimen titles for some of these early documents may be found in Robert Lemon's *Catalogue of a Collection of Printed Broadsides in the Possession of the Society of Antiquaries of London* (London, 1866).

This type of imprint, of which there are numerous survivals, supplies valuable data for the student of social history in sixteenth-century England.

The broadside ballad, which stands nearer to literature, is even better known through its sixteenth-century representatives. Volumes of these ballads have been collected and their relations to Elizabethan and seventeenth-century literature variously traced. Of the treasures that yet remain in this sort, the recent collections* edited by Mr. Hyder E. Rollins give encouraging testimony. Apparently the end of this story has not been reached, even at the present time.

It was of course natural that all these types of English imprint should reappear in colonial America with the introduction of printing. According to colonial records, the very first sheet of printed matter ever to issue from an American press was a broadside. The press was Stephen Daye's, set up at Cambridge in 1638, and the broadside, printed in 1639, was the "Freeman's Oath," an official document, and, in addition, the most poetic beginning on record for the literature of a republic.

Other official documents printed in broadside followed almost at once: colony laws, proclamations civil and religious, Harvard *Quaestiones* and *Theses*, and various other formal declarations. As in England, journal-

* *Old English Ballads, 1553–1625* (Cambridge: The University Press, 1920).

A Pepysian Garland, Black-Letter Broadside Ballads of the Years 1595–1639 (Cambridge: The University Press, 1922).

Cavalier & Puritan: Ballads and Broadsides Illustrating the Period of the Great Rebellion, 1640–1660 (The New York University Press, 1923).

The Pack of Autolycus, or, Strange and Terrible News of Ghosts, Apparitions, Monstrous Births, Showers of Wheat, Judgments of God, and other Prodigious and Fearful Happenings as told in Broadside Ballads of the Years 1624–1693 (Harvard University Press, 1927).

istic and literary issues also appeared. Among these, verse imprints were relatively infrequent throughout the whole history of the colonial press; for rhyme, in the beginning an inhibited desire in America, found favor but slowly.

After a few generations, however, all the familiar types of broadside imprint made their appearance: news stories, admonitions based upon disaster, marching songs, and, much more sparingly, romantic ballads. By comparison with their English prototypes, these colonial efforts were unoriginal. The same subjects had been treated before, and far less naïvely. Furthermore, an austere religious interpretation of life reduced any subject matter to an illustration of either God's wrath or favor, and the ballad accordingly became a sermon. Workmanship was often ridiculously crude.

But like other elements in a transplanted civilization, these harsh verses very soon came to have a distinctly American flavor. And as time went on, possibly because they were closer to the life of the moment than the more studied kinds of verse, they were less affected by English literary models than the more pretentious issues of the American press. In this fact lies their chief interest and value.

Literary historians have for the most part neglected these broadside imprints, and their neglect is understandable. The crudeness of the folk ballad is one thing; the crudeness of verses written by the descendants of Elizabethans is quite another. Such metrical compositions as came from the seventeenth-century presses of Samuel Green and John Foster would stand at the very nadir of literary creation in any age. And for that matter, by a strictly literary test, very few titles would survive from the eighteenth century, when rhymes had become slightly less obvious, and meters less jagged. For by a curious reversal of the usual order, America's balladry was to be created, not by her colonial patriots, but

by cowboys and lumberjacks and forty-niners in a far safer and more sophisticated age. The mood of Massachusetts pioneers and the perils of a new continent were not friendly to ballad making, and no amount of enthusiasm for colonial days can ever make American broadside verse into literature. Judged as meter, to say nothing of poetry, it deserves the neglect into which it has fallen. But viewed as an exhibit of indigenous American material, dating from the first generation of settlers, it has some claim to serious consideration.

For this body of unliterary material not only exposes certain awkward moments in the process of composition, which usually do not get themselves recorded in print, but it illuminates an important chapter in America's spiritual history, namely, the slow development of her national consciousness. Such a process does not lend itself well to analysis. It cannot be documented in any one example or score of examples. But somewhere between 1650 and 1800 America shifted her interest from heaven to the thirteen colonies, and began to regard her own landscape and her own heroes possessively. Until this had been accomplished, American literature could not begin. Pride had to be narrowly local before it could ever be national. It is this process in some of its more obvious stages that the penny sheets record.

Not that the record exists there alone. It can be similarly traced in early writings of various sorts: in descriptions of flora and fauna, in accounts of explorations, even in sermons. Broadside verse merely offers a somewhat more direct and immediate response to the life of the hour. Delayed for a week, or even a day, most of these verses would never have been written. There was a tribute to be paid, a warning to be sounded, and at once. Men spoke with the menace of disaster upon them, and they waited not to polish their words. Because of this directness and immediacy, broadside verses are somewhat more revealing than other colonial writings.

Authorship does not greatly matter. Sometimes the would-be poet signed his name; oftener he did not. Sometimes his name survives nowhere except on his penny verses, and in the records of the town where he died. But since he spoke less as an individual than as a member of the community, reflecting emotion and opinion rather than guiding them, his identity is less important than it might otherwise be.

Broadside verse is, of course, not a literary *genre*. The broadside was merely a medium of circulation, restricted to timely subjects of an urgent nature. Poetry of another sort might be quietly passed to one's friends in manuscript copies or await dignified publication in book form. Not so the message of the hour. It must be printed at once and was doubtless often forgotten as quickly.

The various situations which because of their urgency called forth these broadside issues, suggest a convenient classification by which they may be discussed.

First in point of time came the funeral verses and elegiac tributes, apologetically offered to the departed. Such verses, of course, had had a long history in England,* and their accepted conventions were thoroughly familiar to the early colonists. Moreover, the legitimacy of such a use of verse was unquestioned. Death was considered a safe subject for the exercise of one's powers of rhyming.

> Excuse me, though I Write in Verse,
> It's usual on a Dead mans Hearse,

wrote Nicholas Noyes,† a prolific elegist in his day. What had been done before, might still be done with impunity.

Just how these tributes were offered is a matter of some uncertainty, but they were

---

* For a representative collection of English broadside elegies, see John W. Draper, *A Century of Broadside Elegies* (London, 1928).

† In his *Poem* on James Bayley. Cf. p. 21, *infra*.

probably fastened to the pall covering the casket, as had long been the practice in England. There is an allusion in Samuel Sewall's *Diary* to such a custom in America. In recording his own attendance at the funeral of the Rev. Thomas Shephard, June 9, 1685, he wrote, "It seems there were some Verses; but none pinned on the Herse." Since early colonial burials were conducted with rigid simplicity as to ritual, it is probable that no ceremony attended the presentation of these memorials. They merely provided a silent outlet for the expression of grief, and an opportunity to honor the dead. Often one person was thus honored by numerous tributes.

The earliest extant American record of such verses is of the year 1647, nine years after the setting up of Stephen Daye's press at Cambridge. During this year Peter Bulkley and John Cotton lamented in verse the death of Thomas Hooker, and John Norton and Benjamin Wood in turn lamented the death of John Cotton. If these verses circulated in broadside, as is fairly likely, the imprints have not survived, but together with other similar tributes, they were included in Nathaniel Morton's *New-Englands Memoriall*, published in Cambridge in 1669.

The earliest funeral verses, of which a broadside imprint is known to be extant, appear to be those made by Perciful Lowle for John Winthrop, who died in 1649. According to the printer's note, however, these verses were not printed until many years later, and although it is probable that they appeared before the death of the author in 1665, there is no evidence to support such a conjecture. The verses were inclosed in heavy black borders, arched at the top to suggest a tombstone. It is possible that John Wilson's elegy for Joseph Brisco, who died in 1657, was issued before the Winthrop verses, although this sheet also bears no date other than that of the subject's death. These verses were likewise inclosed in black borders, less heavy and without the arch.

Probably scores of similar tributes were issued during the next decade, but only one appears to be extant, the anonymous verses on Mrs. Lydia Minot, who died in 1667. In the surviving imprint, which may be of later date, this tribute is adorned with the *Memento Mori* woodcut, so frequently in use after 1700, together with a crude representation of an hourglass and spade, which may have belonged to an earlier impression. The verses themselves take their theme from three clumsy anagrams which do little credit to the unknown author's ingenuity. But with or without ingenuity, anagram and acrostic were freely employed as forms of tribute, following a custom long sanctioned in English elegiac verse. Hardly an elegy survives which does not resort to one of these, or to some other form of word manipulation as labor fittingly expended upon such an occasion. Acrostic was usually easier to manage than anagram, but even that obstinate form of composition was less troublesome when the poet, like Mrs. Minot's elegist, scrupled not to misspell words when he found himself in too tight a place. Cross-word puzzlers of more recent years would probably feel superior to such unsportsmanlike liberties as *I di to Al myn', I di, not my Al, Dai in my Lot.* It may perhaps be said, in feeble extenuation, that as a name, *Lydia Minot*, and some others wrestled with by seventeenth-century elegists, offer scant resources for sentence structure.

Elegies appeared more frequently during the last two decades of the seventeenth century, and the first three decades of the eighteenth. These differed little, the one from the other, except in the list of services rendered, and virtues to be extolled. Elegiac sentiment came to be as stereotyped and repetitious as the heavy black borders and the death's head cuts. Occasionally there was a slight innovation in decoration, as in the "Words of Consolation" to the Stetsons in 1718,* in which the

* Cf. p. 33, *infra.*

printer attempted to illustrate the shipwreck which had caused the Stetson tragedy, but such attempts at realism were infrequent. There appears to have been very little incentive to originality either in decoration or in sentiment. Elegists were apparently satisfied with the accepted formula for both.

During the last half of the eighteenth century, the coffin cut replaced the *Memento Mori* as the usual heading. The mortuary borders were retained. If a disaster had involved more than one victim, there was a coffin for each, with initials for identification. The "Bloody Butchery" elegy of 1775 had forty coffins;* the "Elegiac Poem composed on the Never-to-be-Forgotten . . . Battle . . . on Bunker Hill," sixty coffins; "The Columbian Tragedy" of 1791, thirty-nine;† Jonathan Plummer's "Awful Malignant Fever" of 1796, forty-four. Various elegies issued on the death of Whitefield, in 1770, illustrate a more elaborate use of the coffin cut than was customary.‡ But of course the resources of the printer controlled such matters, many elegies being printed without cuts, and a few without even the mortuary borders.

A fresh contemporary view regarding elegiac composition was supplied by Benjamin Franklin's tart criticisms, printed in the *New-England Courant,* June 25, 1722. Under cover of the "Dogood" name, he reduced to absurdity an elegy on Mrs. Mehitebell Kitel, supposedly written by a Harvard student, whose unfortunate name provided opportunity for a mischievous anagram. Franklin's accompanying observation that the soil of America seldom produces any other sort of poetry than the elegy, was entirely true at that time, and his satiric "Receipt to make a New-England Funeral Elegy" was as appli-

* Cf. p. 57, *infra.* This sheet also contains a news account of the battle.

† Cf. p. 59, *infra.*

‡ See the two broadsides included, pp. 49 and 51, *infra.*

cable as it was merciless. For the subject, he says,

> Take one of your Neighbours who has lately departed this Life; it is no great matter at what Age the Party dy'd, but it will be best if he went away suddenly, being Kill'd, Drown'd, or Froze to Death.

To the ensuing compound of *"Virtues, Excellencies, Last Words,"* and *"Melancholly Expressions,"* he suggests that a scrap of Latin be added, as such *"will garnish it mightily."* If a *"Female"* is the subject, a larger quantity of *"Virtues, Excellencies,"* etc., will be necessary. No wonder such words occasioned angry rejoinders. Franklin was doubtless amused at the wrath of the brethren he had offended, but he or any other critic was powerless to change the taste in elegies at that date. Expressed in much the same idiom, they continued to be written in almost unbroken sequence for another fifty years.

Long practice smoothed out the crotchety rhymes somewhat, but as the bumptious Cotton Mather remarked, in his elegy upon Urian Oakes,

> Grief never made good poet.

Wrong as his verdict may be in terms of Dante, Milton, and others, it was true enough for the elegiac verse manufactured in America during the seventeenth and eighteenth centuries. The estimable clergymen who hammered it out lacked all worthy conceptions of poetry, and most of them knew it. Cotton Mather labelled himself "of all men the most unpoetical," and confessed that he essayed to go only

> So far as feet will carry me.

For the whole ministerial brotherhood with him, that was some furlongs short of immortal verse. Agony of composition was never less justified in its results, nor was the English language ever more tortured. Quarles and Sylvester and Herbert, and all the other "fantastic" poets would have had difficulty

in recognizing themselves on the pages of their American imitators, for colonial euphuism was an amateur product.

Judged as poetry, hardly a line from all these numerous elegies would survive. But as a record of personal bereavement, and an effort to comfort those that mourned, these tributes were unimpeachably sincere. Occasionally, when the author forgot his models sufficiently to be simple for a line or two, his emotion broke through the stiffly starched conventionalities and pulpit phraseology, but this was not often. Benjamin Tompson's "A Neighbour's Tears" is almost a classic among the elegies of all time for its tenderness and simplicity. But his "Grammarian's Funeral," which is a veritable triumph of labored ingenuity, is nearer the popular tradition of his day for a funeral piece. It might be assumed that the later elegies would be the best, but the reverse is true. By the time meters had been brought under control, and ministerial figures had gone out of fashion, funeral customs had changed, villages had grown into towns, and the elegy, once the shared lament of a whole community, had become a mere formal exercise. There is no better example of this change than any one of the scores of laments for Washington, printed at the close of the century. Such a device as putting a lament in the mouth of Lady Washington, as in the example included in this volume,* was only one of many artificialities. The elegy had become a mere survival.

The journalistic types of broadside verse had a similar history, becoming inevitably repetitious and stereotyped, but in their day they too constituted a vital record of contemporary life.

The earliest surviving narrative verses printed in broadside appear to be those entitled, "Some Meditations Concerning our Honourable Gentlemen and Fellow-Souldiers, in Pursuit of those Barbarous Natives

* P. 61, *infra.*

in the Narragansit-Country, December 28, 1675." These verses are not known through their original, which has not survived, but through a reprint made at New London, Connecticut, in 1721. Had they been printed for the first time in 1721, they would still constitute the earliest extant news ballad, for as yet, the extension of rhyme to subjects other than death had been timid indeed. There had been some secular verse, which may possibly have been printed in broadside, but record of such imprints has not come to light. In these 1675 verses the author recounts the story of one of the decisive battles of King Philip's War. For at least sixteen of the thirty-two stanzas, the poem is a true ballad. The narrative interest is uppermost, and the author tells his story with spirit. The second half is admonitory, the burden of the poet's thought being,

> O *New-England*, I understand,
> With thee God is offended.

The title suggests that the admonition was probably more important than the narrative.

Other ballads of Indian encounters survive from the decade of the 1720's. There is the Tilton ballad of 1722 which is entirely narrative. In his endeavor to tell "nor more nor less than truth," the poet threw parts of his story into dialogue, thereby following, perhaps unconsciously, an authentic ballad tradition. He naïvely states in the last lines that he has made

No alteration but in some expressions
Us'd other words; then pardon such digressions,
Since I us'd such only for sake of verse,
Which might not less nor more than truth rehearse.

He even retained broken idiom and patches of dialect. Literal transcription of fact was obviously his main intent.

Another broadside ballad having an Indian battle as its subject was advertised for sale in the *New-England Courant*, August 31, 1724. It had as its title, "The Rebels Rewards or, English Courage Displayed. Being a full and true Account of the Victory ob-

tained over the Indians at Norridgiwock, on the Twelfth of August last, by the English Forces under Command of Capt. Johnson Harmon. To the Tune of, All You that love Good Fellows, &c. Boston, Printed and Sold by J. Franklin, in Union Street 1724."* No copy of this imprint is known to be extant.

In the next year came the most famous of all the Indian ballads, spoken of a century later as the most beloved song in all New England. This was the Lovewell ballad of 1725, advertised for sale in the *New-England Courant* of May 31 under the title, "The Vountier's March."† Contemporary imprints of this ballad have not survived, but the verses so entitled are thought to be those printed by Farmer and Moore‡ in their *Collections, Historical and Miscellaneous; and Monthly Literary Journal*, Concord, New Hampshire, February, 1824. It is easy to understand the popularity of these verses. The balladist had a good story to tell, and he succeeded in telling it with something of breathlessness. His lines have a good swing, which would make them easy to memorize. Best of all, he let the story speak for itself. No one of the later treatments of this exploit possesses the simplicity and vigor of this ballad, and doubtless no one of them would have succeeded in making Captain Love-

---

* Ford, 515.   † Ford, 523.

‡ The relation between the Farmer and Moore version of this ballad and the news account of the battle printed in the *New-England Courant* of May 24, one week before the ballad was advertised for sale, has been minutely traced by Professor Kittredge in "The Battle of Lovewell's Pond," included in *Bibliographical Essays, A Tribute to Wilberforce Eames* (Cambridge, Mass., 1924). Professor Kittredge concludes that the correspondences between the ballad and the news account establish the authenticity of the Farmer and Moore ballad as the original version of this tale. The ballad as preserved by Farmer and Moore has been reprinted numerous times in modern anthologies. Cf. Burton E. Stevenson's *Poems of American History* (1908), pp. 106–108.

well's bravery the nursery tale it has continued to be even unto the present day. The importance of this one ballad in establishing a continuity of tradition, and laying a foundation for a common patriotism is perhaps incalculable. Should the original broadside issue yet come to light, it would be the most coveted treasure of its kind in America.

In the forties and fifties the French and Indian Wars supplied other subjects for tales of valor, among them the Cape Breton victories and the taking of Louisburg, the battle of Lake George, the expedition against Acadia, and finally the Siege of Quebec in 1759. The crusading spirit which animated the New England regiments engaging in the Canadian campaign, was reflected in these narrative accounts of the several battles. Victory became the occasion for appeals to even greater enthusiasm. Patriotism found its best material in the death of General Wolfe on the Plains of Abraham in 1759. His extreme youth, his brilliant military career, the paradox of his flaming spirit encased in so frail a body, the fact that he had engaged himself to be married immediately before setting sail for Quebec, and, above all, his death in the moment of victory, marked him the ideal ballad hero, and he inspired many songs.

As early as 1765, popular balladry began to serve a new cause—"Liberty, Property and No Stamps." In the next ten years more verse was printed in broadside than during any preceding decade in American history, and yet these many issues were representative neither in amount nor in quality of the verse written during the period of the Revolution. The chief reason was that the newspapers, by this time numerous in all the colonies, had greatly limited the broadside market. All of them were hospitable to verse, especially that of a political nature, and with their weekly and biweekly issues, they offered the poet almost as immediate a hearing as the penny sheet. For this reason, the chief

balladists, Philip Freneau, Francis Hopkinson, Thomas Paine, and various others, were seldom represented in broadside issues. They had their regular newspaper channels for reaching the public, and apparently preferred them. Sometimes, as was true of "The Battle of the Kegs," the broadside issue was a reprint of verses that had already appeared in a newspaper. Consequently, broadside verse of the Revolution must be considered a very partial record of popular rhyming during that time.

As might be expected, these verses were various in mood as in subject matter. Indignation, fear, flippancy, vituperation, light-heartedness, all were represented, for by 1770, rhymesters had learned that all verse in the service of a good cause need not be sober verse.

Songs were more numerous than narrative verses, since the balladist was no longer responsible for telling the news. He could now make marching songs on the basis of common knowledge of fact. The twentieth-century critic is likely to be impressed only with the crudity, even banality, of these jingles. But why admit the obvious? It is only necessary to recall that not so long ago a large portion of the world thrilled to "Tipperary" and "Over There," two clarion calls that can hardly stand the cool criticism of peace times. The truth is, war songs are not made for the printed page. If they are to be tested at all, it must be with reference to the enthusiasm they can inspire for a common cause when that cause is in jeopardy. Judged by such a standard, whatever may be the formula for a successful battle song, even such foolish doggerel as "Yankee Doodle" appears to meet the requirements.

But not all broadside verse up to the time of the Revolution had concerned fighting. There had been many issues of much slighter moment. Of the verses that survive in this sort, the most interesting are those that occur in sequence, as, for example, the execution ballads, of all types of penny versifying in America, the most prolific.

The first American criminal whose verses are extant was Richard Wilson, executed in 1732, and the first of a long procession of alleged penitents. The capitalizing of criminal punishment for the purpose of warning youth against evil ways had, like the funeral elegy, already enjoyed a long popularity in England, and the formula was well established. From crime to crime American imitators sounded the same lurid warnings, and put the same pious platitudes in the mouths of offenders. Except for details of the crime, it was always monotonously and inevitably the same ballad. For genius has nothing to do with such a type of composition, and left to the uninspired who can merely repeat, the *genre* changes not in the course of five centuries.

To a modern reader these dying confessions are chiefly interesting as social documents, throwing light as they do on the administration of a system of justice which could condemn a man to the scaffold for petty thievery. They are also interesting for the cuts which adorn them. Indeed, one suspects that the cuts had more to do with making these sheets salable than the pious confessions, for at least the cuts are refreshingly different the one from the other. The printer's ingenuity in adding or subtracting victims, increasing or decreasing the size of the crowd, or readjusting the dead cart, was a naïve piece of economy, suggesting that American illustrative art was still in the kindergarten stage. That these sheets were as popular as the number of imprints indicate, need occasion no surprise to readers of the present day whose memories go back as far as the "Ruth and Judd" extras of recent newspaper files. Last words continue to be salable, without the rhyme and at five times the price.

Another sequence of broadside titles concerned the portentous behaviors of nature,

the earthquakes, floods, tornadoes, as well as the disasters by fire and shipwreck. The balladist busied himself with the interpretation of these calamities as visitations of God's wrath, rather than with the narrating of attendant circumstances. Hence such issues, except for their cuts, were little more than rhymed sermons and urgent pleas for repentance. The earliest surviving broadside of this type seems to be that written on the 1744 earthquake, after which similar verses continued the story of disaster throughout the century. Some of the most interesting attempts at illustration appear on verses of this sort.

There is in addition to the verses of disaster a series of titles which concern neighborhood happenings of slighter moment. These are naturally less interesting to a later day than those which record events of significance. The drying up of the Merrimac River, the itinerary of a surveyor, or the symptoms of a suspected witch, are relatively unimportant except as they suggest the increasing extension of rhyme to secular subjects. There are a few stanzas in lighter vein, but it is to be feared that such have gained favor through their rarity rather than through any merits they possess. "Father Abbey's Will," for example, has been reprinted time after time as lonely evidence for the existence of a sense of humor as early as 1731, but this and the few other extant comic specimens are powerless to leaven the whole sober lump of American broadside rhyming prior to the Revolution. The best that can be said for them is that their presence was hopeful.

Admonitory verses, as might be expected, form one of the largest groups, and include injunctions to all ages and conditions. An exhibit of such verses loses its dulness if one examines it for the shifting emphasis in American thought which it reflects, and the changing basis for appeals to righteousness from decade to decade. As heaven lost its hold on the preacher's imagination, new motivations were found for the guidance of youth. The growth of a political conscience as well as an individual sense of wrong, and the concern for a national as well as a personal integrity are illuminating reflections of the time spirit in admonitory verse of post-Revolution times.

A new challenge to the printer's ingenuity, if not to the poet's imagination, came in the New Year's Greetings of the 1760's and afterward. These are of little interest in the specimens that survive, except for the improvement they show in workmanship from year to year. The printer made an effort to be artistic in his use of designs and cuts, and he sometimes succeeded. As for the verses, they were merely summaries of past events, and hopes for the future, with, of course, always the appeal of the printer's boy for donations, at the close. Presently enterprising servants of the public other than printers adopted the custom, and circulated rhymed appeals for patronage or holiday pennies. Such issues were very numerous. Modern handbills are their natural descendants.

The penny sheet was also an easy method of publicity for individual woes and grievances. Various amusing specimens are extant. There is, for example, a 1795 imprint called "The Virtuous, Faithful and Loving Wife's Garland,"* in which the "injur'd Hannah Sprout" details in rhyme the cruelties of Husband Sprout, and bids a blameless farewell to the world. There are two imprints of about 1800 in which Benjamin Fowler, who lost an eye "In Canada with Montgomery," and who now is about to lose a leg, makes out a good case for immediate relief.† And, most entertaining of all these personal broadsides, there are the twenty-five extant imprints of Jonathan Plummer of Newburyport, a traveling preacher and self-appointed accuser of the unrighteous. Any dereliction or calamity which came in his way was grist for his

mill, the more lurid the better. Nor did he stop to verify his accusations always, rumor being sufficient for his purpose. A typical example of his zeal as well as his method, is his attack on Parson Pidgin who was reputed to have kissed a young woman. Before his verses on this salable subject were in type, Jonathan Plummer found out that the parson had not kissed the young woman, but he had the verses printed anyway, possibly lest this parson or some other should be tempted to kiss this young woman or some other in the future.* Broadside history would certainly lose much of its sprightliness without the contributions of this loose-tongued fanatic, but to his fellow citizens in Newburyport, he must have been a supreme nuisance in his day.

After 1800 there were many broadside verses quite as entertaining as Plummer's, particularly the numerous tirades directed against women's fashions, and the other satiric and humorous verse which was concerned with current foibles. There were also a number of romantic ballads, many of them thinly disguised imitations of English issues. "The Babes in the Wood," of which there are ten Massachusetts imprints, is one example; "The Major's Only Son," of which there are also ten, is another. There are numerous other ballads of sailors, with variant titles, lovers' lamentations, maidens' laments, and the like.

But all this is a story by itself. With the close of the Revolution, broadside verse in America no longer had a vital relation to American life. The newspaper had crowded it out. And although all the old types persisted, they no longer had the authenticity of former days. America had broken with her colonial customs at almost every point, and post-Revolution balladry must accordingly be considered in connection with a whole

* Ford, 2765.   † Ford, 3114, 3206.

* Ford, 3297. See Ford's Index for other Plummer issues.

new set of conditions and interests. More-over, it is henceforth distinctly of minor importance.

To students of American culture, there is no detail of the everyday life of the past which is unimportant, and yet there is always a distinction to be made between that which is merely entertaining as a detail of quaintness, and that which is significant. Most of the body of earlier broadside verse possesses significance, in that it recorded beliefs and loyalties which were living gospel when they were uttered. In addition, the fact that these beliefs and loyalties belonged to the first century and a half of America's existence, vastly increases their importance. The corresponding period in the history of most of the nations of the world lies so far

back that all records perish. We make conjectures as to the early spiritual history of these nations. But since America has lived her entire life within the era of printing, every decade of her history is documented, not only by official decrees and state records, but by issues of popular poetry. These are fragmentary, and possibly unrepresentative here and there, but they make up an authentic record of how men interpreted the life of which they were a part, in the very hour in which they lived it. For this reason, these "flying leaves," frail waifs from America's provincial days, are not merely curiosities. To the discerning, they bring many hints in answer to that most interesting of all historical questions, how a nation comes to a realization of itself.

FUNERAL VERSES AND
MEMORIALS

A FUNERAL ELEGIE (WRITTEN MANY YEARS SINCE) ON THE DEATH OF THE MEMORABLE AND TRULY HONOURABLE JOHN WINTHROPE ESQ: . . . WHO DIED MAR. 26, 1649

BY PERCIFUL LOWLE

[The Massachusetts Historical Society]

SIZE, 8 by 12⅛ inches. Neither the writing nor the printing of these verses can be dated exactly. The "written many years since" of the heading, although ambiguous, probably means "written many years ago," perhaps at the time of Winthrop's death in 1649. If the verses were printed during the lifetime of the author, as is likely, they may have issued from the press of either Samuel Green or Marmaduke Johnson, both of whom were printing in Cambridge before 1665, the date of the author's death. But of course the sheet may have been printed much later. The elegy was reprinted in Robert C. Winthrop's *The Life and Letters of John Winthrop* (Boston, 1869), II, 465–467, and in Delmar R. Lowell's *The Historic Genealogy of the Lowells of America* (Rutland, Vermont, 1899), pp. 4–6.

John Winthrop was born January 12, 1588, in Suffolk County, England. After some years of practical experience as an attorney and magistrate, he joined in the Cambridge Agreement and removed to New England. He came as Governor of the Massachusetts colony, arriving at Salem in March, 1630, and bringing with him a large company of Puritan immigrants. His subsequent life was very closely bound up with the history of the Massachusetts colony, of which he was twelve times elected Governor. He died in office, March 26, 1649. His *Journal*, kept from the time the ship sailed until his death, constitutes an invaluable record of colonial life in Massachusetts during those years.

Percival Lowell (Perciful Lowle), the ancestor of the Lowell family in America, was a merchant of Bristol, England. He came to America in 1639 and settled in Newbury, Massachusetts, where he lived until his death, January 8, 1665. He was older than John Winthrop, having been born in 1571. No other verses of his appear to be extant.

who died in the 63d. Year of his Age.

It was rather his 62d. Winthrop was 61 years, 2 months, and 14 days old at the time of his death.

Conservator

One who preserves from injury. The term is well applied. Winthrop had repeatedly defended the colony from Parliamentary interference and coercion.

What goods he had he did not spare,

Cotton Mather's account of Winthrop in the *Magnalia* includes various instances of his generosity (Hartford ed., 1855), I, 121–122.

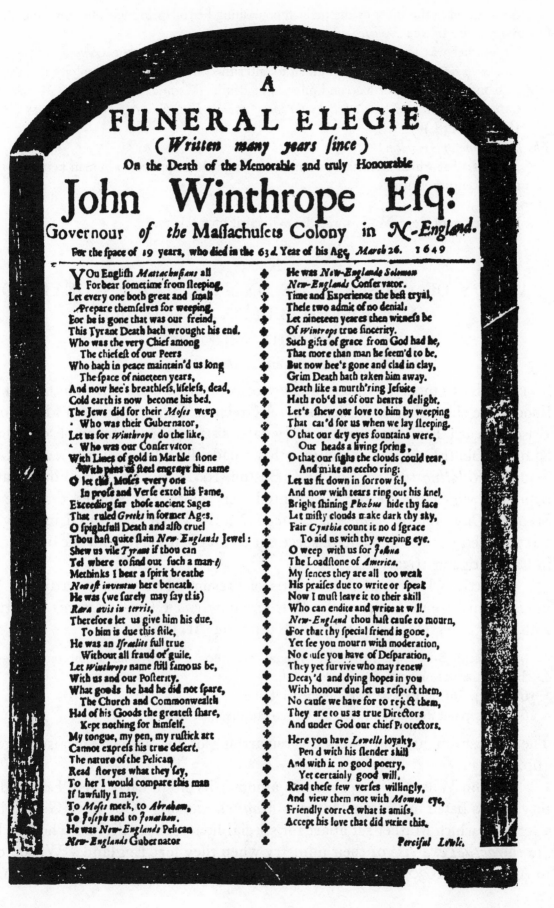

A
FUNERAL ELEGIE
(Written many years since)

On the Death of the Memorable and truly Honourable

John Winthrope Esq:

Governour *of the* Massachusets Colony in *N-England.*

For the space of 19 years, who died in the 63 d. Year of his Age, *March* 26. 1649

YOu English *Massachusians* all
　For bear sometime from sleeping,
Let every one both great and small
　Prepare themselves for weeping,
For he is gone that was our freind,
This Tyrant Death hath wrought his end.
Who was the very Chief among
　The chiefest of our Peers
Who hath in peace maintain'd us long
　The space of nineteen years,
And now hee's breathless, lifeless, dead,
Cold earth is now become his bed.
The Jews did for their *Moses* weep
　Who was their Gubernator,
Let us for *Winthrope* do the like,
　Who was our Conservator,
With Lines of gold in Marble stone
With pens of steel engrave his name
O let this *Moses* every one
　In prose and Verse extol his Fame,
Exceeding far those ancient Sages
That ruled *Greeks* in former Ages.
O spightfull Death and also cruel
Thou hast quite slain *New-Englands* Jewel:
Shew us vile *Tyrant* if thou can
Tel where to find out such a man—t/
Methinks I hear a spirit breathe
Non est inventus here beneath.
He was (we surely may say this)
Rara avis in terris,
Therefore let us give him his due,
　To him is due this stile,
He was an *Israelite* full true
　Without all fraud or guile.
Let *Winthrops* name still famous be,
With us and our Posterity.
What goods he had he did not spare,
　The Church and Commonwealth
Had of his Goods the greatest share,
　Kept nothing for himself.
My tongue, my pen, my rustick art
Cannot express his true desert.
The nature of the Pelican
Read storyes what they say,
To her I would compare this man
If lawfully I may.
To *Moses* meek, to *Abraham,*
To *Joseph* and to *Jonathan.*
He was *New-Englands* Pelican
New-Englands Gubernator

He was *New-Englands Solomon*
New-Englands Conservator.
Time and Experience the best tryal,
These two admit of no denial:
Let nineteen yeares then witness be
Of *Wintrops* true sincerity.
Such gifts of grace from God had he,
That more than man he seem'd to be.
But now hee's gone and clad in clay,
Grim Death hath taken him away.
Death like a murth'ring Jesuite
Hath rob'd us of our hearts delight.
Let's shew our love to him by weeping
That car'd for us when we lay sleeping.
O that our dry eyes fountains were,
　Our heads a living spring,
O that our sighs the clouds could tear,
　And make an eccho ring:
Let us sit down in sorrow set,
And now with tears ring out his knel,
Bright shining *Phœbus* hide thy face
Let misty clouds make dark thy sky,
Fair *Cynthia* count it no d sgrace
　To aid us with thy weeping eye.
O weep with us for *Joshua*
The Loadstone of *America.*
My sences they are all too weak
His praises due to write or speak
Now I must leave it to their skill
Who can endite and write at well.
New-England thou hast cause to mourn,
For that thy special friend is gone,
Yet see you mourn with moderation,
No cause you have of Desparation,
They yet survive who may renew
Decay'd and dying hopes in you
With honour due let us respect them,
No cause we have for to reject them,
They are to us as true Directors
And under God our chief Protectors.

Here you have *Lowells* loyalty,
　Pen'd with his slender skill
And with it no good poetry,
　Yet certainly good will.
Read these few verses willingly,
And view them not with *Momus* eye,
Friendly correct what is amiss,
Accept his love that did write this.

Perciual Lowle.

He was New-Englands Pelican
> An allusion to the fable of the pelican nourishing her offspring with her own blood.

Death like a murth'ring Jesuite
> No epithet was too harsh for the *Jesuite*, who, according to the *General Lawes of the Massachusetts Colony*, was forbidden to enter the jurisdiction of the colony upon penalty of banishment, and for a second offense, of death. (*General Lawes of the Massachusetts Colony, Revised and Published by Order of the General Court in October, 1658* [Boston, 1889], p. 158.)

The Loadstone of America.
> Magnet; that which attracts. A comparison frequently applied to human beings in seventeenth-century writings.

Momus eye
> In Greek mythology Momus was the evil spirit of mockery.

No. 3
A COPY OF VERSES MADE ON THE SUDDEN DEATH OF MR. JOSEPH BRISCO, JAN. 1, 1657
BY JOHN WILSON
[The Massachusetts Historical Society]

SIZE, 7½ by 12 inches. Printer and date of printing are unknown, but in all likelihood, the sheet was issued by Samuel Green of Cambridge, soon after Joseph Brisco's death. Evidence for this early date is strengthened by an observation of Samuel Abbott Green, who includes this broadside in his *Ten Fac-simile Reproductions Relating to New England* (Boston, 1902), pp. 30 ff. He notes that the paper on which the verses are printed very closely resembles that used by Stephen Daye for the *Harvard College Theses* which he printed in 1643 and 1647. Green was the immediate successor to Stephen Daye, and the only printer in Cambridge in 1657.

Little is known of Joseph Brisco. Presumably he was a native of England. Of his life in America, the *Boston Town and Church Records* supply the following items (Document 130, 1883, pp. 34, 61, 65):

1651. Joseph Brisco was married to Abigail Compton dau. of John Compton 30th—11th mo. by William Hibbins.

1657[/8]. Joseph Briscoe was drowned 1st Jan.

1658. Joseph of Joseph and Abigail Brisco born August 21st.

The baptism of his child and the remarriage of his widow are also recorded (pp. 67, 71).

John Wilson, his elegist, was a noted divine in early New England history. He is listed in Cotton Mather's *Magnalia* among "Our First Good Men," a term by which Mather set apart for special honor, those divines who had been "in the *actual exercise* of their ministry when they left England." Wilson came to America in 1630, and first preached under a great tree in Charlestown. He

A COPY OF VERSES

Made by that Reverend Man of God Mr. John Wilson, Pastor to the
first Church in Boston; On the sudden Death of

Mr. Joseph Brisco,

Who was translated from Earth to Heaven Jan. 1. 1657.

Not by a Fiery Chariot as Elisha was,
But by the Water, which was the outward cause :
And now at Rest with Christ his Saviour dear,
Though he hath left his dear Relations here.

Joseph Briscoe }
Job cries hopes. } Anagram.

THere is no *Job* but cries to God and hopes,
    And God his ear in Christ; to cries he opes,
    Out of the deeps to him I cry'd and hop'd,
    And unto me his gracious ear is op'd :
Doubt not of this ye that my death bewail,
What if it did so strangely me assail :
What if I was so soon in Waters drown'd,
And when I cry'd to men, no help I found :
There was a God in Heaven that heard my cry,
And lookt upon me with a gracious eye :
He that did pity *Joseph* in his grief,
Sent from above unto my soul relief :
He sent his Angels who did it conveigh
Into his Bosom, where poor *Laz'rus* lay :
Let none presume to censure my estate,
As *Job* his Friends did stumble at his Fate.
All things on Earth do fall alike to all,
To good Disciples, which on God that call ;
To those that do Blaspheme his Holy Name,
And unto those that reverence the same :
He that from nature drew me unto Grace,
And look'd upon me with a Fathers face :
When in my blood upheld me to the last,
And now I do of joyes eternal tast.
Remember how *Job's* precious children Dy'd,
As also what the Prophet *did* betide :   *Jonah*
What was the end of good *Josiah's* life,
And how it fared with *Ezekiels* Wife :
Remember what a Death it was that Christ
(Suffered for me) the Darling of the highest;
His Death of Deaths hath quite remov'd the sting,
No matter how or where the Lord doth bring
Us to our end; in Christ who live and die
And sure to live with Christ eternally.

took the "Freeman's Oath" in 1632, and in that same year became the first pastor of the Boston Church, a ministry which he continued until his death in 1667. He often wrote funeral and moralizing verses, and by them gained for himself some reputation as a poet. He was considered matchless in anagram. An account of his life is included in Mather's *Magnalia*, I, 302–321.

so soon in Waters drown'd,
 Apparently Joseph Brisco was a young man at the time of his death.
how Job's precious children Dy'd,
 They were killed by a great wind which caused the house to fall upon them. Job 1.19.
the end of good Josiah's life,
 He went to battle in disguise, and was killed by the archers. II Chron. 35.20–24.
how it fared with Ezekiels Wife;
 She died by the stroke of the Lord, and Ezekiel was forbidden to mourn for her. Ezek. 24.15–18.

No. 4
UPON THE DEATH OF THE VIRTUOUS AND RELIGIOUS MRS LYDIA MINOT, JAN. 27, 1667

[Reproduced through the kind permission of Mr. Joseph Grafton Minot]

SIZE, 8¼ by 13½ inches. Printer and date of printing are unknown. If the verses were printed at the time of Mrs. Minot's death, as is likely, they were presumably issued by Samuel Green of Cambridge, but it is not likely that the original issue bore the *Memento Mori* heading used on the present imprint. This cut does not appear again on any broadside issue thus far reported, until 1708, when it was used on the "Carmen Miserabile" for Jonathan Marsh. (See p. 23, *infra.*) After 1708 this heading appears more frequently than any other mortuary decoration on verses of this sort. It is possible that the present sheet is a reissue of the Minot verses, with only the *Memento Mori* heading added. The cruder hourglass and spade cuts probably belonged to the original issue. This broadside was reproduced by Mr. Joseph Grafton Minot in *A Genealogical Record of the Minot Family in America and England* (Boston, 1897).

 Lydia Minot was the daughter of Nicholas Butler of Dorchester. She married Captain John Minot, also of Dorchester, May 19, 1647, and as the elegy records, was the mother of five children. She died January 24, 1667, at the birth of her sixth child.

Each Branch, be't [Mercy or the Rod] when so it needs.
'Cause [now to God] and Christ I ever live.

Upon the DEATH of the Virtuous and Religious

Mrs. Lydia Minot,

(The wife of Mr. *John* Minot of *Dorchester*;)

The Mother of Five Children, who Died in CHILD-BED of the Sixth ; and together therewith was Interred *January* 27. 1 6 6 7.

> HEre lyes the Mother, & the Child, Interr'd in one ;
>   Both waiting for the same Bless'd Resurrection.
> She first to it was Life ; Then to't became a Grave,
> Dead in her Womb : To fetch it thence, Death to her gave.
> The Life and Death of both, his Sov'raignty Makes known,
> Who gives and takes at will, and no Controll can own.
> The Fruit and Tree together here lyes pluck't, yet sure
> That Root whence a Saint's All doth spring, must firm endure,
> Eternal Love, in which the Sap's the same, that feeds
> Each Branch, be't Mercy with Bad when so it needs.

ANAGRAMS.

∮LYDIA MINOT.∮

1. *I di to Al myn*'.

TO *All mine* Earthly Joys and Friends *I dy*,
  To whatsoe're below the Sun doth ly ;
To *All* that shadow cast, and hastes to change;
To *All* that is pursu'd within the Range
Of Sublunary Vain's, toss'd to and fro
Of sons of men that seek to th'Pit to go.
I dy to Husband, Children, Parents dear :
Mine they were once, I theirs; ('twixt hope and fear
No unmix'd Sweet I found) But now no more
These mine can be, as they were heretofore.
My Interest's translated up on High,
To things now mine, to which I ne're can dy.
Then happy Death, my welcome I'le thee give,
'Cause now to God and Christ I ever live.

2. *I di, not my Al*.

IDy, 'tis true, but yet it's *not my All*,
  That with this dust into the Grave doth fall.
Life hath my Better part ; which soon did post
By Angels Conduct, to the Heav'nly Host.
Life unto Life is gone, through th'Living way ;
But that which Mortal was, makes yet some stay.

When Breath expir'd, my Life came flowing in;
My Soul reviv'd, made free from th'death of Sin.
New Light, new Love, new Joy me now do fill,
New Robes I have, new Company, new Skill
To sing th'new Song: Sure this is Life indeed;
My All's alive in dying thus to speed.
Naked o'th'Body, my Soul in Bliss is sheath'd
My Garland of ne're-dying Flow'rs is wreath'd.
Then nought but Dust is dead; at Life's Return
This also shall be quickned from its Urn:
My Death, my Grave, shall then for ever dy,
And Life shall Triumph in the Victory.

3. *Dai in my Lot.*

L ight sown is for the Righteous; its full Crop
Y ields Glory's Harvest, Souls fill'd up to th'top
D ay *in my Lot* is now, still calm, still bright.
I n leaving your dark World, I left all Night ;
A scended where, nor Sun, nor Moon, we crave:
M y God,& th'Lamb's the light that here we have.
I n his Light we see light, and light'ned stay ;
N o light to that of th'Everlasting Day !
O pleasant Lines that thus are faln to me !
T o make that *Day my Lot* which aye shall be.

We'le wait (Blest Saint) till this Day break, and th'shadows flee :
So shall our wish be crown'd, to have One Lot with thee.

A FUNERAL ELEGY UPON THE DEATH OF THAT EXCELLENT AND MOST WORTHY GENTLEMAN JOHN WINTHROP ESQ., APRIL, 1676

[The Massachusetts Historical Society]

SIZE, 8 by 12 inches. The margins have been considerably trimmed. The sheet was probably issued by John Foster, the first Boston printer. It is included among the titles probably printed by him, in Samuel Abbott Green's *John Foster* (Boston, 1909), pp. 125–126. It is possible that Stephen Chester, by whom the present copy is inscribed, was the author. There are extant two of Stephen Chester's letters, written in the following year, mentioning the inclosure of lines on Governor Winthrop. These may be the lines to which reference is made. The letters are printed in the "Massachusetts Historical Society Collections" (6th series), V, 7–8. Benjamin Tompson was the author of another broadside elegy on John Winthrop. (Cf. Ford, 59.) This elegy was included by Tompson in his *New England's Tears for her Present Miseries* (1676). It is reprinted in the Appendix to *A Sketch of the Life of John Winthrop the Younger*, by Thomas Franklin Waters. ("Publications of the Ipswich Historical Society" [1899], VII.)

John Winthrop the Younger, son of the more famous John Winthrop of Massachusetts Bay, was born at Groton, England, February 12, 1606. He followed his father to America in 1631, and shortly after his arrival became one of the Assistants of the Massachusetts colony. He remained in Massachusetts for some years, dividing his time between civil duties and scientific pursuits. He later moved to Connecticut colony, of which he became governor in 1657. With the exception of one year, he continued in this office until his death in 1676. Major Fitz-John Winthrop, to whom these verses are inscribed in the present copy, was his son.

fatal year
This was the second year of King Philip's War, so costly in New England lives and property.

Extract
His descent from John Winthrop of Massachusetts Bay.

Whose travail's far into out-landish places,
The author may have in mind Winthrop's search for curious specimens of natural history. He was one of the early members of the Royal Society, and had brought together a considerable collection of rarities. Various communications from him relative to these are included in the early volumes of the "Philosophical Transactions and Collections of the Royal Society."

His Powders, Cordials and his [golden] Pills,
Winthrop gave free medical advice, and was much consulted. Cotton Mather spoke of his being furnished with "noble medicines, which he most charitably and generously gave

A

FUNERAL ELEGY

Upon the Death of that Excel'ont and most worthy Gentleman

John Winthrop Esq.

Late Governour of his Majestyes Colony of Conedicot·

who deceased April, 1 6 7 6.

Anagr. John Winthrop;
Oh Print Wenih:

Let woe be printed nigh unto our Land,
Since that Jehovahs formidable hand
Hath been bereaving us this fatal year,
Of such a Star within our Hemisphere.
A Star of such resplendent glorious Light,
Whose Fellow never yet approacht our sight,
Nor ever are we like his Peer to see
In all his comprehensive rarity.
A pretious Pillar in his earthly station,
A pious servant to his Generation,
Although his Extract was sublime and high,
Yet was he cloathed with humility.
His place of bearing Rule it was so sweet,
That Justice did with mercy in him meet.
His Learning was so grand that all may ghess
Our Winthrop's Master of the Languages,
Whose travail's far into out-landish places,
They did augment his other worthy graces.
And lest his Gallantry should seem to fall,
Behold his worth in matters Physical ;
My Pen can never fully it rehearse,
Whose Fame did overrun the Universe.
His Powders, Cordials, and his Green Pills,
O're flew the Mountains, and the lasting Hills.
So pregnant was his skill, none can discry,
And lofty Judgement into Chimistry.
Incomparable was the depth he had
In rare Inventions, sons of men to glad.
When Hartfords Charter was in some suspence
This worthy Heroe must away from hence.
Our Jurisdiction rightly to maintain,
And mediate before his Sovereign :
For which great Service who so fit as He,
One of th' Imperial Society.
A man of wisdome, Patience, Love, and Peace,
To Rich and poor his virtues did encrease,

His labour and his dealings were so free,
That none did more abound in Charity,
His Remedyes they did not only tend
Unto mens bodies, but a better end.
When Subdivisions in the Church did rise,
He had great skill to heal their Maladies.
Surcease my mournful Muse, further to add
Of this great Patriot, unless I had
Briarius hands to set his virtues forth,
And Argus Eyes to weep his golden worth.

ACCROSTICON.

INvironed with grief well be we may,
On every side in such a cloudy day,
He being gone who was our Countryes glory,
Not to return which make our hearts so sorry.

Woe and alass unto our Colonyes,
In middest of our other miseryes,
No mortal can express what dolour 'tis,
To be bereav'd of such a Gem as this.
Himself could only let us understand,
Rightly to value such a heavy hand ;
Oh may this dismal loss ne'r be forgot,
Per Plimouth, Boston, and Conedicot.

EPITAPH.

HEre lyes a Nont-such for all virtuous things,
Fittest to be discoursed of by Kings.

Mors omnibus communis.

FINIS

away upon all occasions; insomuch that where-ever he came, still the diseased flocked about him, as if the healing angel of Bethesda had appeared in the place." *Magnalia*, I, 159. For a modern physician's estimate of John Winthrop's skill in such matters, see Walter R. Steiner, "Governor John Winthrop, Jr., of Connecticut; as a Physician," *Johns Hopkins Hospital Bulletin*, Vol. XIV, No. 152, November, 1903.

In rare Inventions

Winthrop's practical interests ranged from the refining of gold and the building of American ships to the brewing of beer from Indian maize, and the inventing of a self-feeding lamp.

When Hartfords Charter was in some suspence

In 1661 Winthrop drew up a charter for Connecticut. His draft was accepted by the General Court, and Winthrop was appointed Agent for the colony in procuring the charter. He did so, completing his mission in the following year. His achievement was celebrated in a long narrative poem written by Roger Wolcott in 1725, entitled, *A Brief Account of the Agency of the Honourable John Winthrop*. ("Massachusetts Historical Society Collections" [1st series], IV, 262–298.)

th' Imperial Society

The Royal Society was organized in 1660. Winthrop became a member in 1661, on his third visit to England.

Surcease

Cease.

Briarius

Or *Aegaeon*, one of the three sons of Uranus and Gaea, known as the Uranidae. They were monsters, having a hundred arms and fifty heads.

Argus

The hundred-eyed son of Agenor, appointed by Juno to guard Io.

No. 6
LAMENTATIONS UPON THE NEVER ENOUGH BEWAILED DEATH OF THE REVEREND MR. JOHN REINER, DEC. 21, 1676

[The Boston Athenaeum]

SIZE, 9½ by 11¾ inches. Probably an imprint of John Foster. (Cf. Green, *John Foster*, pp. 128–129.) At least two lines are missing in the first column, and at least four in the second. No other copy is known, by which they may be supplied.

John Reiner (variously spelled) was a native of England. He was a graduate of Magdalen College, Cambridge, and according to Cotton Mather's list in the *Magnalia* had been engaged in the ministry before coming to America. He succeeded John Norton of Plymouth, and served the church there until 1654 when he moved to Dover, New Hampshire. He was minister at Dover until his death in 1676. For a contemporary estimate of his character, see *Plymouth Church Records*, I, 107–108 ("Publications of the Colonial Society of Massachusetts," XXII).

LAMENTATIONS

Upon the never enough bewailed Death of the Reverend

Mr. John Reiner,

Pastor of the Church of Christ at Dover who was gathered to his Father

DECEMBER, 21. 1676.

When *Heathen* first assail'd our peaceful Land
My Comfort was, ours is *Immanuels* Land.
When *Robbers* us impov'rish't thought I then
We may be poorer and not worser men.
I hope't when our young men i'th' field fell down
God brake our Arm of flesh to bare his own.
When treach'rous Foes did with success out-brave us
I said God meant to humble us, then save us.
But when that doleful word *REINER is dead*,
I heard, Lips quiver'd, Belly trembled,
My Spirits fail'd, Corruption seiz'd my Bones,
My Face grew pale, my heart as cold as Stones.
Mee thought I saw engraven on this Rod
Plain to be read that fatal *Ichabod.*
This single Death I count more wrath discovers
Then the removal of some hundred others.
Here's Anger great, Displeasure boiled up,
And that's the Gall and Wormwood in our Cup.
By former blasts our Leaves and Boughs did fall,
This terrible gust hath blown up Roots and all.
Some smarting Wounds we had receiv'd before,
This lays us welt'ring in our Blood and Gore,
Under the fifth Rib struck; you that pass by
Stand still and see, and sigh to see us dye.
Some of us saw of late our Houses burning,
Gods House lies waste now, High-way thither mourning,
Sanctuary-doors shut up, a Famine not
of Bread, but Bread of Life's our threatned Lot.
How many hath this Right'ous Mans Lips fed,
Who now must pine, 'cause no man breaks them Bread?
So much as Heav'n exceeds the Earth, so far
As Souls than Bodies more excelling are,
So much is this more then our former wo,
These Iron Bands our Souls have pierc't into.
What ever other ailes upon us were
Had God been pleased but to spare us here
Our Bread and Water of affliction would
Been less afflictive far, Oh that we could
Our Teacher see! but that sight of our eyes
Is gone, and He close in a corner lies,
Sure God a way for further Anger makes
When such a Man out of the way he takes.
In's latest Text too true a Prophet found, (*J...*
(Not one of *Samuels* Words fell to the gr...
      ...ow'd against us are

A precious Soul he was, not old but sage,
Grave, wise and prudent far above his age,
Chearful but serious, merry too but wise
(Sour Leven pleases not for Sacrifice)
His Courtesie obliged most and best,
His Innocence did stop the Mouths o'th'rest.
In Supplications mighty, fervent, bold
Like *Jacob* he with confidence took hold
Of God in Prayer, wrestling with him till
He wrestling got the name of *Israel*,
(Ah such a *Moses* we shall dearly miss
I'th Mount, when *Amalek* a fighting is)
His Sermons were Experiences, first wrought
On his own Heart, then lived what he taught.
He blameless was, unless you blame him shall
Because he was well spoken of by all.
His Life desir'd, his Death bewail'd you see
(Lord let our last end like the Righteous be)
A faithful Friend, plain-open-hearted he,
His words and heart in one did well agree,
Study what should or we would wish to be,
And say 'twas here, fear no Hyperbole.
Such pregnant young ones are but seldom found
Such pregnant young ones seldome stay w...
Not the Worlds field but Heavens Barn is th...
For forward Souls, so early ripe in Grace,
Though green in years, yet he was gather'd in
Like shock of Corn that fully rip'ned been.
My Brother *John*, I am distress'd for thee,
Thou very lovely, pleasant wert to me;
I thus bewail thee, but great sorrows will
Not drein themselves dry at a little quill.
Heart full, eyes full, too full themselves to vent
By words, a little taste is only meant.
I'le not attempt his worth, our loss to write,
Unless I had some Angel to indite,
To him that gav't the former's only known,
By sad effects the latter may be shown,
And best by him that's yet unborn be told,
But Lord while we thus weep our Foes grow...
We sigh, they sing, we mourn, Blasphem...
      ...of Vengeance and ther...

Samuel Sewall records John Reiner's death as follows ("Massachusetts Historical Society Collections" [5th series], *Sewall's Diary*, I, 31, 32, 34) :

Dec. 21 [1676] being Thorsday, Worthy Mr. Reyner fell asleep: was taken with a violent vomiting the Friday before, Lightheaded by Saturday, Lay speechless 24 hours, and then died on Thorsday even. We heard not that he was sick till Friday about 9 at night: on the Sabbath morn, comes William Furbur and brings the newes of Death. . . .

Dec. 28. Mr. Willard preaches. N.B. I got but just to hear the text. This day pleasant and smiling were it not the day of Mr. Reyner's funeral.

January 30. Sent a letter to Cousin Quinsey, which enclosed a piece of Gold that cost me 23s. Gave the letter to Mr. Josson. . . . Sent him a copy of verses made on Mr. Reyner.

This reference may be to the present verses. If Sewall had made verses of his own, he would probably have said so. The *Diary of John Hull* also records Reiner's death. ("Transactions and Collections of the American Antiquarian Society" [1857], III, 245.)

Dec. 21st. Mr. John Reynor, minister of Dover, died of a cold and fever that he took in the field among the soldiers.

I hope't when our young men i' th' field fell down
> An allusion to King Philip's War, which had ended only the preceding August. Over 600 young men had been killed, and there had been widespread ruin in the colonies, especially in Massachusetts.

Ichabod
> "The glory is departed from Israel," I Sam. 4.21.

Some of us saw of late our Houses burning,
> This fire is mentioned in Hull's *Diary*, p. 242: "Nov. 27th. 1676. A fire brake out two hours before day, and consumed about fifty dwelling-houses and the North Meeting-house. The Lord sent much rain, moderated the spreading of it."
>
> Allusion to this fire suggests that the elegist was probably a resident of Boston, and *of late* suggests that the elegy was probably written soon after Reiner's death.

ailes
> Afflictions. The substantive use of *ail* was common at this time.

Not one of Samuels Words fell to the g[round.]

Amalek
> An enemy of the Israelites. Exod. 17.8–16.

Such pregnant young ones seldome stay when [found.]
Not the Worlds field but Heavens Barn is t[he Place]
But Lord while we thus weep our Foes grow [bold,]

A

Small Testimony of that great HONOUR due to that Honourable Servant of GOD and his Generation

John Alden *Esq*;

Who changed this life for a better, *Sept.* 12*th. Anno Domini* 1687.

Annoq' Ætatis 89.

The memory of the just is blessed.

The just shall be had in everlasting remembrance.

GOD brought a *choice Vine* to this defart land;
And *here* did *plant* it with his own *right hand*,
And from the heathen's rage did it defend.
The which its root, from east to west did send.
This precious Saint who now is gone to rest,
And lie in Jesus bosom to be blest,
A branch was of this vine, God did remove,
Protect, defend, and water from above.
A man to God's commands that had respect,
And by His word he did his course direct.
A lover of God's Habitation.
A servant of his Generation.
He was according to the Will of God,
While in this lower world he had abode.
Sincere & faithful unto God was he,
True Vertue's friend, to Vice an enemy.
Holy and humble, full of Faith, & Love
To Saints on earth, to God & Christ above.
He many years did serve this Colony,
Administring Justice impartially.
He in this defart many changes saw,
Yet closely kept unto Jehovah's Law.
He Served God betimes, even from his youth,
And constantly did cleave unto his Truth.
On *Pisgah*'s mount he stood, and *Canaan* view'd
Which in his heart and life he most pursu'd.
On *Tabor*'s mount he saw transfigured
Blest Jesus, which within his bosom bred
That *love* that made him say, *'Tis good being here*,
Its good, yea *better* than to be elfe-where.
He lov'd on earth, to be with Christ on high:
He did on wings of Contemplation fly.
To God in heaven he sent up many a dart,
Which issued from a truly broken heart;

Which reach'd the ear of *God*, and such Return
From heaven brought which made his heart to
With *Enoch* he with God *on earth* did *walk* (burn.
With *Abram* he did with JEHOVAH talk.
With *Moses* he did on the mount ascend,
And to receive God's mind himself did bend
That he such meditations had divine,
Which in Saints eyes did cause his face to shine.
With *length of days* God did him satisfy,
He liv'd so long, that he desir'd to die.
He with old *Simeon* had of Christ a fight,
Who was prepar'd to be the Gentiles *Light*:
Which made him willing hence for to depart,
To be with Him that gained had his heart.
He with good *Jacob* in his aged state
Did earnestly for God's Salvation wait.
He with *Barzillai*, being near his end,
His thoughts 'bove *earthly* comforts did ascend.
He with St. *Paul*, his *course* now *finished*,
Unclothed, is quietly put to bed.
His Family and Christian friends he blest
Before he did betake himself to rest.
He to Religion was a real friend
And Justice, till death brought him to his end.
A man for God, and for his Countries Good,
In all Relations wherein he stood.

Let *ALDEN*'s all their Father imitate,
And follow him till they come to death's state:
And he will them most heartily embrace,
When he shall meet them in that blessed place.
And let *New-England* never want a Race
Of such as may be fill'd with *Alden*'s Grace.

Printed in the year, MDCLXXXVII.

A SMALL TESTIMONY OF THAT GREAT HONOUR DUE TO THAT HONOURABLE SERVANT OF GOD AND HIS GENERATION JOHN ALDEN ESQ; SEPT. 12, 1687

[The Massachusetts Society of Mayflower Descendants]

SIZE, 8 by 13⅜ inches. Printed in 1687, probably from the press of Samuel Green, in Cambridge. This sheet was reproduced in *The Mayflower Descendant*, Vol. IX, July, 1907, by Mr. George Ernest Bowman, who very kindly supplied another print from the same negative for the present reproduction. There is extant another broadside elegy on John Alden, entitled "Upon the Death of that Aged, Pious, Sincere-hearted Christian, John Alden Esq." A copy, owned by the Boston Athenaeum, was reproduced in *The Mayflower Descendant*, Vol. IX, October, 1907.

John Alden, at the time of his death, was the last male survivor of those who had signed the *Mayflower* compact. In 1620, when he embarked for America, he was the youngest of the Pilgrims. He was not of the Leyden Church, but according to William Bradford, had joined the company at Southampton. Bradford's entry concerning him, included in the Appendix to his *History of Plymouth Plantation* (1912 ed., II, 400), is as follows:

John Alden was hired for a cooper, at South-Hampton, wher the ship victuled; and being a hopefull yong man, was much desired, but left to his owne liking to go or stay when he came here; but he stayed and maryed here.

Bradford made two further entries concerning John Alden's marriage to Priscilla Mullins. (Pp. 406, 411.) The traditions surrounding this marriage have done more to make John Alden's name a household word than his very numerous and valuable services to the Plymouth colony. After 1633 he was almost constantly in the employ of the government, often to the very serious neglect of his own affairs. From 1633 to 1640 and from 1650 to 1686, he was Assistant to the Governor of the colony, and he was twice Deputy Governor. He was at various times Agent for the colony, Deputy to the General Court, and Member of the Council of War. In 1667 the sacrificial character of his services was recognized, and he was henceforth given a small gratuity. He died September 12, 1687, in Duxbury, of which he had been one of the founders.

with Barzillai
    A very aged man, a friend of David when he fled from Absalom. II Sam. 19.32.

UPON THE
DEATH of that Reverend and Aged Man of GOD,
Mr. SAMUEL ARNOLD,
Paſtor of the CHURCH at *Marſhfield*, who deceaſed in the 71ſt Year of
his Age, and of his Miniſtry the 36th, September 1693.

I.
WHEN Lights go out, Darkneſs ſucceas,
Is this ſad *Marſhfield's* Caſe
Ah! little, little, little know
We who ſucceeds in Place

II.
Of *Arnold* dead. This Star is ſet;
But where the next will riſe
With Amplitude, how long his Courſe,
Can't *Aſtrophil* deviſe.

III.
Thy Glory, *Marſhfield*, is eclipt'd,
Thy Sun hath run his Race:
Melpomene may traced be
By Tears on every Face.

IV.
Long has Heaven frown'd upon thy Coaſt
A *Trine* of Glory late,
Loſt them haſt now, thy fruitful Soul
Great *Winſlow*, thou didſt rate

V.
As peerleſs once: But he's removed
Thy *Bourn* is late drawn dry,
And brin ſh Tears now ſtain thy Face
At *Arnold's* mounting high.

VI.
This *Trine* in thee did lately ſhine;
Beams borrow'd from above
Did gild their *Viſibilia*,
darted from th' God of Love.

VII.
Concentrick were there Motions all,
Tho' fix'd in divers Spheres;
Each had both Head and Hands engag'd,
And *Sion's* Walls up rears.

VIII.
Theſe three tho' here a while depart,
Like Magnets ſtill did tend
To *them*, *Sion's* City, which
Remains when Time ſhall end.

IX.
And there are plac'd on Thrones moſt bright,
Shall in due Time return,
In Stately 'quirage to judge
All tha the Goſpel ſpurn.

X.
Arnold the laſt, but not the leaſt
Of theſe Three now aſcends,
Array'd with Robes of Righteouſneſs
Where Glory never ends.

XI.
True Faith, ſtrong Love in him did ſhine,
A Text-Man large and ready,

Sharp Eye, ſtrong Hand did ſteer his Courſe
In Piety moſt ſteady.

XII.
Strong Love to Chriſt, and to his Flock,
Did waſte this Shepherd's Life;
Zealous for Truth he did appear,
Yet was no Man of Strife.

XIII.
Except with Sin and Error's foul
Which felt his Heat and Flame,
A Flame Divine, which Lightning like;
Sin's Bones could p'arce and Tame.

XIV.
The proud aſpiring callous Braws
Of bold Enthuſiaſts,
Religiouſly Sarcaſtical,
The *Quakers* he oft blaſts

And ſtops their Mouths with Scripture Gag,
Makes them as mute as Sheep,
If in their ranging Circuit,
Into his Fold they peep.

XVI.
Peter and *John* were Fiſhermen,
Arnold was of that Trade;
Each had his Hooks and Nets, but at
Chriſt's Call aſide them laid.

XVII.
All Three much Fiſh did catch and kill,
But Men did catch and ſave;
Hence Crowns beſet with Gems do wait
Their Exit from the Grave.

XVIII.
Amos, an Herdman once, was call'd
To fill a Prophet's Place;
And he that ſate on *Iſrael's* Throne,
Was firſt old *Jeſſe's* Race.

XIX.
Arnold once hewing ſenſeleſs Blocks,
Wild Olives here did poliſh,
And fix'd them in *Jehovah't* Houſe,
Which Time ſhall ne'er aboliſh.

XX.
Arnold, a Man of heavenly Words;
An heavenly Man in Deeds,
In Heaven it ſelf full Chriſt enjoys,
No earthly Thing he needs.

XXI.
God grant this Candleſtick may hold
Another Star as bright,
Whoſe Riſing made our Midnight Noon,
Whoſe Setting brought our Night.

XXII.
Grant, Lord, the Widow his Relict
May not ſink down in Grief
Let her and hers from thee receive
Each Days Joys and Relief.

Samuel Arnold.
Anagram,
Lowe old Arm's.

OLD arm's leave, and new take up,
For you haſt drunk Death's bitter ſt Cup,
Death hath thee ſtung, Chriſt hath it ſlain,
And thou ſhalt ſurely riſe again,
In Robes and ſpirit, waſh'd in Chriſt's Blood,
Which is the Middeſt chiefeſt Good,

HOw ſolitary ſeems that Place
Which *Arnold's* Preſence late did grace?
What Echo from that Pulpit ſounds, (Wounds?
Whence *Arnold* preach'd Chriſt's bleeding
The Sov'rign Balm for Sinners great,
The Ruin of *Abaddon's* Seat.
Methinks I ſee, methinks I hear
That Puppy groan and drop a Tear
At *Arnold's* Exit, fearing, vext,
And with his Sorrows much perplext,
Who ſhall ſucceed; and of what Hair
The Man ſhall be that takes his Chair;
Whether a Text-man or a Drone,
Whether a Subſtantive alone,
Or one that is an Adjective,
Who doth by others Labours Thrive.
Grant, Lord, theſe Sheep may now unite
To beg of thee ſuch Beams of Light
Wherein they may unite, agree
To chuſe for them, and chuſe with Thee;
To chuſe a Man that can ſupply
The Place of *Arnold* mounted high.
Pour down thy Spirit on th' Fold,
And let that Candleſtick ſoon hold
A Star of the firſt Magnitude,
Endow'd with Grace's Plenitude.
Thy Throne, O God, do thou build up;
Soon take from them this bitter Cup,
Which they now drink. Let them rejoyce
To ſee and hear their Shepherd's Voice.

Ichabod Wiſwell.

Mr.
Samuel Arnold,
The late faithful Preacher of
the GOSPEL at *Marſh.fi.ld*,
Who left Earth for Heaven, *September* 1. 1693.
his laſt FAREWELL to the World.
Written by himſelf not long before his Death.

VAIN World wherein I for a Time did dwell,
I heartily unto thee bid Farewell.
My Time in thee draws near unto an End;
Jehovah to Thy Self O do Thou bend
My Soul, that it may ſoar and mount aloft,
With Eagle's wings, on high to thee as oft,
As with Nature's Sinkings am attended,
My ſtrong Deſire to Thee let be extended.
Thou art my Hope, my Help, my Joy, my Reſt,
My Sanctuary when with Grief oppreſt.
In all my Pilgrimage I have thee found
In Loving Kindneſs to me to abound.
In *England* old I firſt did draw my Breath,
And there I might have been a Man of Death;
But God me brought over the roaring Seas,
Into this Wilderneſs, where he did pleaſe
My ſtature, and to him draw my Heart
By his Grace, 'to chuſe him for my Part;
His Changes that with me
Will unchangeably to be.
My Salvation had upon the Sea,
When his Providence call'd there to be;
And by his Time appointed he did call
Me to leave the Ship, and Nets, and all
Employments ſecular, to ſerve his Name;
In catching Men, by lifting up the Fame
Of bleſſed JESUS, our *Immanuel*,
To draw poor Sinners with him for to dwell;
In which high Service he hath me ſuſtain'd;
His Power and Mercy have with me remain'd
Years Thirty Five, tho' Fleſh and Heart have fail'd
Oft Times, and Weakneſs hath on me prevail'd.
O Lord!
Let now my Sins by thee forgotten be;
Iniquity in me O do not ſee.
Let my poor Labours eke accepted be,
Which with my Heart I offer'd have to thee?
Let them not be forgot, but let them ſpring,
When I tranſlated am with thee to ſing.
Let my dear Fam'ly in thy Sight find Grace;
'Mong them that fear thee let them find a Place.
And let my Flock ſupplyed be by thee,
When I ſhall ceaſe them for to overſee.
Let God's *Jeruſalem* exalted be;
A Praiſe in th' Earth, O let them be to thee;
Let Sion full, and all thine Enemies
Let their Deſtruction them ſurprize.
When thou ſhalt call me hence, O let my Soul
Inable be it ſelf on thee to roll:
And ſo to launch into Eternity,
That I my Self in Chriſt may aye enjoy.
FINIS

UPON THE DEATH OF THAT REVEREND AND AGED MAN OF GOD, MR. SAMUEL ARNOLD, SEPT. 1, 1693

BY ICHABOD WISWELL

[The Library of Congress]

SIZE, 11½ by 15¼ inches. Printer and date of printing are unknown.

Samuel Arnold was the third minister in Marshfield. He had been admitted to be a freeman of the colony of New Plymouth in 1653, and had assumed the Marshfield pastorate in 1657. He is listed in the *Magnalia* as of the "Second Class," a term by which Mather designated those "young scholars" whose education was not complete when they arrived in America, and who had been obliged to perfect themselves without the aid of the college. Arnold not only had not been formally educated, but, if the statement in the elegy can be trusted, he had been a fisherman before he became a minister.

His elegist, the Rev. Ichabod Wiswall (spelled also Wiswell), was a resident of Duxbury, where he had been ordained minister in 1676, and where, in addition to his ministerial duties, he was a schoolmaster for many years. He had previously taught the school in Dorchester, which is thought to have been the town of his birth. According to the inscription on his Duxbury tombstone, he must have been born about 1637. He attended Harvard College for three years, but left without taking a degree. In colonial annals, his name figures chiefly in connection with his services as Town Agent for Duxbury, and in 1689, as Agent for Plymouth colony in the securing of a new charter. On his return to America after this mission, he resumed his pastorate, and died in Duxbury, July 23, 1700.

who succeeds in Place
Arnold was succeeded by Edward Tompson in 1696.

Astrophil
Probably in the very loose sense of one who knows the stars. Wiswall had some local reputation as an astrologist, and made various predictions. A poem of his, written on the comet of 1680, is preserved.

Melpomene
The muse of tragedy.

Trine
A group of three.

Like Garland fair, thy Head d[id wear,]

Great Winslow
Josiah Winslow, general in chief of the colonial forces in King Philip's War, and first native governor of Plymouth colony. He had died December 18, 1680.

Thy Bourn
Thomas Bourne, one of the earliest settlers of Marshfield. He had died May 11, 1664.

To Salem, Sion's City
Salem was a frequent abbreviation for Jerusalem.

Text-man
> One learned in scriptural texts, and apt at quoting them; also, an advocate of literal inter-
> pretation of the Bible. Obs. *NED.*

The Quakers he oft blasts;
> Quaker persecutions in Massachusetts were most severe from 1656 to 1660, when they
> were ended by order of the king, but Quakers were the target of ministerial scorn for some
> time afterward.

In Robes [m]ost white, wash'd in Christ's Blood,
Which [is our choice] and chiefest Good.
Abaddon's Seat
> The bottomless pit, of which Abaddon is the angel. Rev. 9.11.

of what Hair,
> Of what kind, or nature.

W[herein] in all my Changes he with me
Let [my poor Labours eke accepted] be,

No. 9
THRENODIA, OR A MOURNFULL REMEMBRANCE, OF THE MUCH TO BE LAMENTED DEATH OF THE WORTHY & PIOUS CAPT. ANTHONY COLLAMORE, DEC. 1693
BY DEODATE LAWSON

[*The Massachusetts Historical Society* (Photograph)]

SIZE, about 10⅜ by 13¼ inches. According to the colophon, printed in Boston, by Bartholomew Green, in 1694. The cut, which represents an interesting ar-rangement of mortuary symbols for this early date, reappears on "Poor Julle-youn's Warnings To Children and Servants" (Boston, 1732). The broadside was reproduced and reprinted in *The Mayflower Descendant*, XI (April, 1909), 65–69. The editor's note states that the original was at that time owned by Mrs. Bailey Hall Hitchcock, a member of the Massachusetts Society of Mayflower Descendants.

Anthony Collamore's story is more fully told in this elegy than in any other surviving record. He was a nephew and heir of Peter Collamore, an early resident of Scituate. His name also appears in connection with his marriage in 1666, and with an assignment of land in 1673. According to Samuel Deane, in *The History of Scituate* (Boston, 1831), the reef on which Collamore's ship was wrecked was henceforth known as Collamore's Ledge, in mournful memory of this tragedy. His daughter Mary lived to lament another tragedy of the sea, for she became the wife of Robert Stetson and the mother of Isaac Stetson, drowned off the cliffs of Scituate in 1718. (Cf. p. 33, *infra.*) Samuel Sewall's *Diary* (I, 387) contains brief mention of the earlier tragedy, as follows:

Dec. 20. . . . Capt. Cullimer and 5 others drown'd coming from Scituat last Satterday in a Boat. . . .

Deodate Lawson was minister of the Second Church of Scituate, from about 1693 to 1698, when his ministry was terminated by vote of the church. He had been absent a long time, and, according to the record, the members wished "a Pastor more spiritually and more fixedly disposed." (Deane's *History of Scituate*, p. 196.)

[Who together with Five] Persons more were Cast-away [in a] SLOOP going from [Scituate Harbour towards Boston,]
Some [Loaden Boats] to Boston bound away,
Some [Boats with Sailes] Expanded led the way,
None [did since that] alive on Shore appear;
Yet could not know [him for a] Certainty,
By any thing, but [by] the Cloaths he wore.
Prepare his Funeral to Sol[em]nize;
His Soldiers also at the [mou]rnfull call,
Gemebundus Composuit . . .
　　The sighing Deodate Lawson composed it.

No. 10
TO MY WORTHY FRIEND, MR. JAMES BAYLEY, MAY 28, 1706
BY NICHOLAS NOYES
[*The Boston Public Library*]

SIZE, 8¼ by 13¾ inches. These verses were apparently printed before July 29, 1707, as Sewall mentions having left a copy of them with Mrs. Champney on that date. John L. Sibley, in his *Biographical Sketches of Graduates of Harvard University* ([Cambridge, 1881], II, 245, 298), states that they were published July 30, 1707. He is probably thinking of the Sewall entry. The printer is not recorded.

　　The friendship which called forth this poem had doubtless been lifelong, as both James Bayley and Nicholas Noyes were natives of Newbury, Massachusetts. They had been born within three years of each other, and had attended Harvard at the same time. James Bayley, born September 12, 1650, and a graduate of Harvard in 1669, was the first minister at Salem village (now Danvers). While there he was the center of a prolonged and bitter controversy over his retention. Although by order of the General Court the matter was finally settled in his favor, Bayley moved, in 1680, to Killingworth, Connecticut, and thence to Roxbury, Massachusetts. At the time of his death, he had been a physician in Roxbury for some years. He was still living at the time this tribute was written, his death occurring January 18, 1706/7. Samuel Sewall delivered these verses to him and recorded his appreciation of them (*Diary*, II, 162; 171–172):

May 27, 1706.

. . . Got to Brother's in the night after nine a clock, Mr. Noyes had left his Verses for Mr. Bayley, which I carried with me next morning.

THRENODIA,

Or a Mournfull Remembrance, of the much to be Lamented Death of the Worthy & Pious
Capt. ANTHONY COLLAMORE,

with ____ Persons more were Cast away in a SLOOP, going from Scituate Harbor ____
On the 16. Day of December 1693

THE Great Jehovah is the Lord and King,
Both in the Heav'ns & on the Earth & Sea ;
What things Pleas Him in each to pass doth
Nor can He in His Will resisted be. (bring
He in His Fist rowines the Boist'rous Winds
And Raging Waters in a Garment binds.

'Tis but to Loose His Little Finger then,
And the most Furious blasts do lithe, thence ;
Enough to Terrisy the stoutest Men,
Nor can they find against it a Defence.
'Tis but to Slack the binding of the Seas,
And they will soon accomplish what He pleas.

December, last upon, the Sixteenth day,
Within the Harbour lay at Scituate
Some Loaden Boats to Boston bound away,
Which for Fair Wind and Weather there did wait,
Amongst the Rest was Captain Collamore,
Whose sad disaster, we must now Deplore.

These Boats with Sailes Expanded led the way,
Out of the Harbour ; and did fairly glide ;
Thus one by one stood out into the Bay,
With Wind at East North East and Flowing Tide,
The Captain in the Rere did Hoise up Saile,
And sailed after with a steddy Gale.

He did his best with speed to quit the Shore,
And seemed in his way to Prosper well ;
He Lufft up to the Wind and North ward bore,
For near an Hour as Spectators tell
That so he might be gaining of the Wind,
And to his Port the fairer Passage find.

But Dangers great did quickly him Surprize,
The Clouds did gather and obscure the Sun
Winds Whistled, Snow came thick and Seas did rise ;
And He was at a loss which way to run
As did appear to some that were before,
Who quickly after, saw the Boat no more.

With him Five Persons more Embarqued were,
Two Men, one Woman, and two Ladds beside :
Alas ! not one of them alive on Shore appear ;
But were all Drowned in the Ocean wide.
No more but two are yet to this day found,
Which doth the hearts of their Relations wound.

Whether some hidden Rock with fatal stroke,
At once gave Final stop unto their Course ;
By which the Masts and Yards and Boughs were
Not able to withstand so great a force. (Broke,
Thus some conceive who saw and view'd the Rack
Which quickly to the Shore was hurled back.

Or whether Laden deep with Wood,
The Swelling Waves did fill her by degrees,
When their Frozen Pump would do no good,
They soon became a Prey of the Seas :
Which Violently after them did go,
And bore them down into the deeps below.

What happ'ned to them, we can only guess,
Because none of them did Survive to tell ;
Nor can we think what Anguish did Posiess,
Their SOULS, when this Disaster them befell.
We humbly must Adore GOD'S Providence,
Who in the Deeps, His Judgments doth dispense.

One Ephraim Turner near the Fatal place,
Was cast upon the Shore and next day found ;
Most sorely batter'd on his Head and Face,
Who decently was Laid into the ground.
Relation of the Rest, in search the Shore,
For thirteen dayes but they could find no more.

But on the Fourteenth day one did espie,
A Corps he judg'd was Captain Collamore ;
Yet could not know it to a Certainty,
By any thing, but the Cloaths he wore.
His Form and Visage utterly was lost,
Having by Waves on Rocks been so long toss'd.

His Friends, his Neighbours and Relations all,
Prepare his Funeral to Solemnize ;
His Souldiers also at the unhappy call,
Appear with Drooping hearts and Dripping eyes.
With many Tears they laid him in the dust,
To wait the Resurrection of the Just.

And now although Relations of the Rest,
Know their own Sorrows and Distress of mind ;
While for the quieting their troubled Brest,
They in the Creature no relief can find.
Our Duty binds us all to Sympathize,
With such as Mourn in their Adversities.

But Publick Persons are a Publick loss,
Because more usefull, and more Eminent ;
They in their places went the greater cross,
And the more sad Occasion to Lament.
The Death of Collamore we must bewaile,
Our Glory's going when the Faithfull faile.

What Offices he bore of any kind,
He did adorn with Carriage full of Grace ;
His Modest, Humble, Condescending mind,
Could freely yield to any in their Place.
To all Degrees above him and below,
His rightly Order'd Courtesy did flow.

Unto this Province and the Government,
He was a Faithfull and a Constant Friend ;
In all the troubles which they under-went,
And what he had, was willing to Expend ;
For the Promotion of the Publick good,
At any time in what he understood.

In Scituate let each Inhabitant,
Greatly Lament this worthy Person's fall ;
Both Rich and Poor his Courtesy will want,
Who still was ready to oblige them all.
It was to many by Experience known,
He valu'd others good before his own.

He was the Captain of the Warlike train,
Love was his Banner, Love was his defence ;
Their Chearfull Service was return'd again,
His Acceptation was their Recompence ;
In that Great Company Commander he stood,
Where Mustered two hundred men and more.

In Judgment sound, in Life Upright within,
A Zealous Member of the Church was he ;
His Studies and Endeavours were not small,
That so CHRIST'S Kingdom might Enlarged be.
A Deacon also Faithfull to his trust,
To do that onely which was Right and Just.

The North Society in Scituate,
Hath lost a Leading Man and Loving Friend
Who ready was with them and ____
On ev'ry good Occasion ____
His Care and Cost was plainly ____
To settle and maintain GOD'S Worship ____

A Faithfull constant Husband to his Wife,
He also Tender was and Provident ;
True Peace they Chearish'd ____
Enjoying what they had, with good Content
GOD'S Blessing on their care and Industry
Did yield them Comfort and Prosperity.

A Father carefull of his Children too,
Whose Love to Souls and Bodies did Extend ;
He spared not the best that he could do,
In Warning them to mind their latter end.
He did his just Commands meekly Dispense,
And they did humbly yield Obedience.

He was a Master full of Gentleness,
Whose care it was, things honest to Provide ;
Obliging thus his Servants Faithfullness,
As he did in their diligence Confide.
So that to Serve him we may well Conclude
Was rather Freedom than a Servitude.

But GOD hath by his Sov'raign Providence,
Of such an Usefull Man this place bereft ;
A deep Affecting and Afflicting sense,
Is well becoming each one that is left,
We all in his remove a loss sustain,
Which sure GOD onely can make up again.

Since therefore All things come alike to all,
This Comfort in our Mourning doth remain,
Thorgh Duty binds us to lament his fall,
Yet in our Loss, He hath the greater Gain,
For Dying in the LORD, His Labours cease,
And of such Upright Men the end is Peace.

To Old and Young this Awfull Sudden stroke,
Doth Testify with loudest Vehemence ;
God tryes by others DEATH us to Provoke,
While it is Day to work with diligence.
Let then both High and Low the Rich and Poor,
Lament the DEATH of Captain Collamore.

Printed at Boston by Bartholomew Green, 1694.   Grinhildus Composuit Deodat Lawson.

I visited Mr. Bayley; find his sister Cheyny with him. He was very low at first; but after awhile revived and Spake freely; has been very ill this Moneth; especially last Satterday and Sabbath day night. Desired his service to Bro^r, Sister, Mr. Noyes, with much thanks for his verses which had been a great Comfort to him. . . .

Nicholas Noyes was born December 22, 1647. After his graduation from Harvard in 1667, he was for thirteen years minister at Haddam, Connecticut, but is chiefly known through his later ministry in Salem, which began in 1682 and continued until his death in 1717. During the Salem witch trials he was ardent in prosecution, and was in part responsible for the deaths which resulted, a fact which he later regretted bitterly. In addition to his ministerial services, he established for himself a reputation for learning, and found time to bring together the largest library of his day in Salem. As a composer of ingenious epitaphs and elegies he was, in the judgment of his day, unrivalled. Of these, in addition to the present specimen, the verses upon the Rev. Mr. John Higginson, and the Rev. Joseph Green, were the most celebrated. (Cf. also his verses on Mary Gerrish, p. 29, *infra*.)

And Elegies made of thine own.
 None appear to have survived.
[Groan,] Laugh, Sigh, Smile, [Cry,] Versifie?
Well! if this Stone should do its worst,
 The elegist's agile puns on the unfortunate disease of his friend call to mind another notorious exhibition of elegiac punning, Edward Bulkley's "Threnodia" on the Rev. Samuel Stone. (Included in Nathaniel Morton's *New-Englands Memoriall*, [1669].)
That rowl the Sisypean stone,
 Sisyphus, in Greek mythology, was punished by being made to roll a stone uphill in Hades.
Thy dust be s[af]e; for Christ shall find it,
And leave th[is] cruel Stone behind it.
Simeon's song
 When Jesus was presented in the temple. "Lord, now lettest thou thy servant depart in peace, according to thy word." Luke 2.29.

May 28th. 1706.

To my Worthy Friend,

Mr. James Bayley,

Living (if Living) in *Roxbury:* A POEM.

MY Old Companion ! and my Friend !
I cannot Come, and therefore send.
Some pity fhould be fhown to One
That's heavy laden with the Stone ;
That's wearied out with fits of pain
Returning like Clouds after Rain.
Alas ! my Brother, what can I
Do for thee, more than Pray and Cry,
To Counfel, and to comfort try,
And bear a part by Sympathy ?
Excufe me, though I Write in Verfe,
It's ufual on a Dead mans Hearfe :
Thou many a Death haft under-gone,
And Elegies made of thine own.

Our Saviours Funeral Obfequies,
One Celebrates before His eyes ;
And He the Oyntment kindly takes,
That for His Burial fhe makes.
Two Saints array'd in glorious drefs,
Appear, and talk of His Deceafe ;
Whofe Death from thine did take the Sting,
And wholfome make that Poyfon thing.
And I have feen thine hand, and Pen,
Play on that Cockatrices den
In meafur'd Lines, as if infpir'd,
And *Paroxifms* had only fir'd
An holy Soul with flaming zeal,
That flefh-pains it could fcarcely feel.
What ; in one breath, both Live and Dye,
Groan, Laugh, Sigh, Smile, cry, Verfifie ?
Is this the Stone ? are thefe the pains
Of that Difeafe, that plagues the Reins ?
That flyly fteals into the bladder ?
Then bites, and ftings like to the Adder.
Is this the Scourge of Studious men ?
That leaves unwhipt fcarce five of ten
And Whips them once, and over again.
In Chrifts School there's fmart Difcipline,
To make His Scholars more divine ;
Bleft they who do not take offence,
Whofe joy lyes in the Future Tenfe ;
Who when they are in moft diftrefs,
Love Chrift the more, and not the lefs.
His Yoke is eafy, burthen light,
To them that underftand things right ;
And none will afterward complain,
Who Hell efcape, and Heaven obtain.

Well ! if this Stone fhould do its worft,
It cannot make thee be accurft :
For if thou fhouldft be Ston'd to Death,
And this way Pelted out of Breath,
Thou wilt like *Stephen* fall afleep,
And free from pain for ever keep.

Great Pains, with as great Patience, may
Fall little fhort of *Martyrs* Pay :
For Chrifts Rewards are all of Grace,
No Merit but His, in either cafe.
Our Lord thee good Example offer'd,
Who learn'd Obedience while He fuffer'd,
Who for the joy was fet before Him,
Endur'd the Crofs He bore, and bore Him,
Who though He Pray'd it might be gone,
Yet alfo faid, Thy will be done.
That Stone which builders did refufe,
For thy Foundation choofe, and ufe.
Think alfo when thine Agonies
Are moft intenfe, and force loud cryes,

They are not worthy to compare
With thofe that Chrift for thee did bear :
Yea, think what Chrift for thee hath done,
Who took an harder, heavyer Stone
Out of thine *Heart* and it is gone.
Who did thy Wou d *Spirit* cure
Of Soul-pains, that none can endure,
And this is eafyer to be borne,
For in the *Flefh* abides this thorne ;
And if Chrift do not it remove,
Sufficient is His Grace, and Love,
To give thee comfort, and Support,
Becaufe this pain is light, and fhort ;
And works for thee the Glory great,
That doth exceed in length, and weight,
Befides, thefe Torments cant compare,
With Torments that *Eternal* are :
For they are utterly undone,
That rowl the *Sifyphean* Stone ;
Not they whofe pains are limited,
And are releas'd, as foon as dead.
Add one thought more ; that this diftrefs
Makes thee partake of *Holinefs* ;
The more the flefh is hack'd, and hew'd,
The more Corruption is fubdu'd.
Life is to thee the lefs endear'd,
And *Death* by thee is the lefs fear'd ;
For it's but once thou haft to dye,
And then Live to Eternity.
Thy weary Body fhall have Reft ;
Thy Soul from thence forth fhall be bleft ;
Thy duft be fafe ; for Chrift fhall find it,
And leave this cruel Stone behind it.
One Stone Gold's truth doth bring to light ;
Another makes Iron fharp, and bright :
A third our grain doth Pulverize,
And Separate the chaff likewife.
Thine, all thefe profits bring to thee,
In nobler fenfe than th' other three.
Thine proves thy Grace to be Sincere ;
Of ruft, and dulnefs, doth thee clear,
And makes thee Watch, and Pray, and long
To change thy groans, for *Simeons* Song.
Though grinding pains thy nature bruife,
They fit thee for thy Mafters ufe ;
And when thy duft fhall be refin'd ;
Thou fhalt be neither pain'd, nor pin'd ;
Nor full of petrifying juice,
Hard Studies, Heats, and Colds produce.
Then fhall hid Manna be thy fare,
In which no gritt, nor gravel are ;
Yea, Chrift will give thee a *White Stone*,
With a N w *Name* engrav'd thereon,
To the Enjoyer only Known.

Lord, once thou faidft, Arife and Walk ;
Thy Words were Works ; Mine are but Talk ;
Be pleas'd to bid thy fon, Good chear !
And fay, Thy Sins forgiven are !
Then, Sink, or Swim ; or Live, or Die,
He will thee greatly Glorifie.
Say fo to me too, fo will I.
A Man of Sorrow once Thou waft,
And ftill a fellow-feeling haft,
So to Thy Pity, I commend
My felf, and my afflicted Friend.

Nicholas Noyes.

CARMEN MISERABILE, A SOLEMN LACRYMATORY FOR THE GRAVE OF JONATHAN MARSH, JUNE 10, 1708

[The Boston Athenaeum]

SIZE, 8 by 12½ inches, with edges considerably trimmed. No other copy is known by which the missing portion in column two may be supplied. The sheet may have contained both signature and imprint. These verses present a curious specimen of elegiac language so tortured that clear elucidation of the author's thought is well-nigh impossible. The unwonted liberties which he takes with words would hardly seem to merit serious attention. He appears to be his own authority for his extraordinary usage.

Little is known of Jonathan Marsh aside from the facts recorded in the elegy. He was the son of Thomas Marsh of Hingham, and was born August 10, 1689.

hood-vail

To cover with a veil. The compound is not in *NED*.

The prest Elastick Heat cou'd not resay,

Meaning that the warmth of the body did not return.

Irall fire

The meaning is not clear. *Iral*, a rare word, means a precious stone.

rupt

To break. The author has wrongly used the word as a participle.

extillate

There is no such word.

The vast Eclipticks Oval

A reference to the ecliptic circle. *NED* cites Hobbes, 1662, "Does not the earth move in the ecliptic circle once a year?" In other words, Jonathan Marsh had attended Harvard almost two years.

since clouds Eclips'd our Light,

Probably a reference to the eclipse of May 1, 1706. Sewall has an entry concerning an eclipse on that date (*Diary*, II, 160): "Eclipse of the Sun, not seen by reason of the cloudy wether."

The staying Angel ne'r before

Possibly *ne'r before* in the author's memory. Harvard had been in existence since 1636, and there are records of other student deaths.

Qualis populea . . .

These lines, in which the present elegist found the title for his elegy, are taken from the Virgilian passage describing the mourning of Orpheus for Eurydice.

"Just as sorrowing Philomel, under the poplar shade, bemoans her lost young, which the clown, hard-hearted has stolen unfledged from the nest: but she throughout the night, seated upon a bough, renews her doleful lament, and fills all the place around with piteous wailings."

This quotation may have been continued in column two, and yet if so, why should the printer include the reference in column one?

CARMEN MISERABILE.
A Solemn Lacrymatory for the Grave of
Jonathan Marsh,

Junior-sophister : Who Deceas'd at *Harvard College* in *Cambridge* : *June* the 10th. 1708.
Born at *Hingham* : Aged Eighteen Years and Ten Months.

A Groaning Eccho tolleth in mine Ear,
A Ghastly Visage fill'd with *Panick* Fear
Draws nigh; desist th' approach, hood-vail your
And wave but the faint accent of your Cries. (Eyes
I feel the swifter Fate: forbear to tell,
Or copious tides of Grief will proudly swell
Beyond their stated Bounds, vie the command;
Recoil, nor dare transgress the sacred stand.
T'was known when first my vital Fumes were
Amazed Blood forgot to roll a-round, (bound,
Shrunk up for fear, congeal'd the *Springs* of Breath;
The true Effect declar'd the cause was Death:
The prest *Elastick* Heat cou'd not resay,
But the confining cold forc'd to obey,
Call'd in its Native power for support;
The hurrying Spirits to the midst resort.
Vacate the trembling Nerves to guide the Pen,
That else the raging Flouds of Tears wou'd spend,
Which now are Agonizing in the Fount
To fill the Deeps and burst th' Opposing Mount.
Ah! when regardless Death tears off the Branch,
It drives the flowing goar back with a stanch!
The venal course is stopt with furious Pain,
That else with liberal ease wou'd run a-main!
Humours and Words usurp'd by Passions will,
Leave empty strokes to exercise the quill!
Both Tears and Tones lick't up by Irall fire,
Lend dry rupt Sobs to extillate the Cryer!

The Gold-ray'd Nail near twice revolved round
The vast *Eclipticks* Oval, once had crown'd
The Candidates of Art with Diadems,
Textur'd with Laurels, while the plenteous Beams
Shone dazling joys, since clouds Eclips'd our Light,
But central Labours aggravate our Night.

The slaying Angel ne'r before did snatch
An Offspring while in the Maternal reach.
The Lion couchant Rampant now becomes,
Grown bold wrests from the *goddess swadling arms.*
Is it to scourge our past profusive spirit,
Or let us dearly know we do not merit
A double Jubilee to gain relief,
That Heaven succeeds the Instruments of grief?
Least we should surfeit with *Ambrosia* juice,
To learn us how to prize and how to use
Each grateful Worthy while his star allows :
Or by the Object of an humble thought,
As thro' a mournful *Optick* we are taught,
That high-bred Sons of men consist of clay;
Fevers may solve the bonds, then must they *crumb*
Extended feet, I haste to read his Grave; (away.
Too eager steps no curious Rank can save.

Acrostick-Epitaphium.

JONATHAN MARSH.
A man in Arts

I-N this void *Cenot*
O-ne that Inger
N-or less Ingeni
A Man in
T-H-A-

M-

R-o
S-e
P

Dolores

Qualis populea mærens Philomela sub umbra
Amissos queritur Fœtus, quos Durus arator
Observans, nido implumes detraxit : at illa
Flet noctem, ramoque sedens Miserabile Carmen
Integrat, et mæstis late loca questibus implet.

Virg. Lib. 4. Georg. Lin. 511.

THE GRAMMARIANS FUNERAL, AN ELEGY PUBLISHED UPON THE DEATH OF THE VENERABLE MR. EZEKIEL CHEVERS, AUG. 21, 1708

BY BENJAMIN TOMPSON

[*The Massachusetts Historical Society*]

SIZE, 8½ by 12 inches. As is stated in the heading, this is a reissue. Printer and date of printing are not known for either issue. The broadside was included in Green's *Ten Fac-simile Reproductions* (pp. 30 ff.).

Of John Woodmancy, for whom the verses were first penned, little is known. There is record of a John Woodmancy, who died in Boston in 1684, but the record does not state that he was a schoolmaster. Robert Woodmancy, a schoolmaster, had died in 1667. It is barely possible that the two names were confused by the printer.

Ezekiel Cheever, for whom the elegy was reissued in 1708, was the most famous of New England schoolmasters during colonial days. He died in his ninety-fourth year, having taught continuously for seventy years. During the last thirty-eight of these he had been headmaster of the Boston Latin School. He was the author of several books, of which the most famous was his *Latin Accidence, An Elementary Grammar*. This text passed through more than twenty editions, and was used for more than a century wherever Latin was taught in New England. A summary of Cheever's life is appended to Sewall's entry concerning his death, as follows (*Diary*, II, 231) :

Augᵗ. 21. Mr. Edward Oakes tells me Mr. Chiever died this last night.

Note. He was born January, 25, 1614. Came over to N-E. 1637. to Boston: To New-Haven 1638. Married in the Fall and began to teach School; which Work he was constant in till now. First, at New-Haven, then at Ipswich; then at Charlestown; then at Boston, whether he came 1670. So that he has Labour'd in that Calling Skillfully, diligently, constantly, Religiously, Seventy years. A rare Instance of Piety, Health, Strength, Serviceableness. The Wellfare of the Province was much upon his Spirit. He abominated Perriwigs.

In view of such a life story, the appropriateness of Sewall's next entry calls for no comment.

Augᵗ. 23, 1708. Mr. Chiever was buried from the School-house. . . .

To Benjamin Tompson, his elegist, belongs the distinction of being the first native American poet. He was born July 14, 1642, in Braintree. He attended Harvard and, after his graduation in 1662, became schoolmaster and physician as well as poet. The *Records of the Town of Braintree* (Randolph, Massachusetts, 1886, p. 693), under entry of his death, state that he was "Practitioner of Physick for above thirty years during which time hee kept a Gram. School in Boston, Charlestowne and Brantry." He had immediately preceded

The Grammarians Funeral,

OR,

An ELEGY composed upon the Death of Mr. *John Woodmancy*, formerly a School-Master in *Boston* : But now Published upon the DEATH of the Venerable

Mr. Ezekiel Chevers,

The late and famous School-Master of *Boston* in *New-England* ; Who Departed this Life the *Twenty-first* of *August* 1 7 0 8. Early in the Morning. In the Ninety-fourth Year of his Age.

EIght Parts of *Speech* this Day wear *Mourning Gowns*
Declin'd *Verbs, Pronouns, Participles, Nouns.*
And not declined, *Adverbs* and *Conjunctions,*
In *Lillies* Porch they stand to do their functions.
With *Preposition* ; but the most affection
Was still observed in the *Interjection.*
The *Substantive* seeming the limbed best,
Would set an hand to bear him to his Rest.
The *Adjective* with very grief did say,
Hold me by strength, or I shall faint away.
The Clouds of Tears did over-cast their faces,
Yea all were in most lamentable *Cases.*
The five *Declensions* did the Work decline,
And *Told* the *Pronoun Tu,* The work is thine ;
But in this case those have no call to go
That want the *Vocative,* and can't say O!
The *Pronoun* said that if the *Nouns* were there,
There was no need of them, they might them spare :
But for the sake of *Emphasis* they would,
In their Discretion do what ere they could.
Great honour was confer'd on *Conjugations,*
They were to follow next to the *Relations.*
Amo did love him best, and *Doceo* might
Alledge he was his Glory and Delight.
But *Lego* said by me he got his skill,
And therefore next the *Herse* I follow will.
Audio said little, hearing them so hot,
Yet knew by him much Learning he had got.
O *Verbs* the *Active* were, Or *Passive* sure,
Sum to be *Neuter* could not well endure.
But this was common to them all to Moan
Their load of grief they could not soon *Depone.*
A doleful Day for *Verbs,* they look so *moody,*
They drove Spectators to a Mournful Study.
The *Verbs* irregular, 'twas thought by some,
Would break no rule, if they were pleas'd to come.
Gaudeo could not be found ; fearing disgrace
He had with-drawn, sent *Mæreo* in his Place.
Possum did to the utmost he was able,
And bore as Stout as if he'd been A *Table.*

Volo was willing, *Nolo* some-what stout,
But *Malo* rather chose, not to stand out.
Possum and *Volo* wish'd all might afford
Their help, but had not an *Imperative Word.*
Edo from Service would by no means Swerve,
Rather than fail, he thought the *Cakes* to Serve.
Fio was taken in a fit, and said,
By him a Mournful *P O E M* should be made.
Fero was willing for to bear a part,
Altho' he did it with an aking heart.
Feror excus'd, with grief he was so Torn,
He could not bear, he needed to be born.
Such *Nouns* and *Verbs* as we defective find,
No *Grammar* Rule did their attendance bind
They were excepted, and exempted hence,
But *Supines,* all did blame for negligence.
Verbs Offspring, *Participles* hand-in-hand,
Follow, and by the same direction stand :
The rest Promiscuously did croud and cumber,
Such Multitudes of each, they wanted Number.
Next to the Corps to make th' attendance even,
Jove, Mercury, Apollo came from heaven.
And *Virgil, Cato,* gods, men, Rivers, Winds,
With *Elegies,* Tears, Sighs, came in their kinds.
Ovid from *Pontus* hast's Apparrell'd thus,
In Exile-weeds bringing *De Tristibus* :
And *Homer* sure had been among the Rout,
But that the Stories say his Eyes were out.
Queens, Cities, Countries, Islands, Come
All Trees, Birds, Fishes, and each Word in *Um.*
What *Syntax* here can you expect to find ?
Where each one bears such discomposed mind.
Figures of Diction and Construction,
Do little : Yet stand sadly looking on.
That such a Train may in their motion *chord,*
Prosodia gives the measure Word for Word.

Sic Mæstus Cecinit,

Benj. Tompson.

Ezekiel Cheever at the Boston Latin School. He died April 13, 1714, and as the record continues, "left behind him a weary world, eight Children 28 grand children." His tomb in Roxbury recognizes his threefold calling as follows:

> . . . Herse of Mr. Benj. Thomson
> Learned Schoolmaster,
> & Physician and y^e
> Renouned poet of N. Engl.

In addition to elegies and occasional pieces, Tompson was the author of *New England's Tears for her Present Miseries*, and *New England's Crisis* (1676). His poems were recently edited by Howard Judson Hall (Boston, 1924).

In Lillies Porch
> William Lilly (1468?–1522). English grammarian and author of a more famous *Latin Grammar* than Cheever's.

Sic Maestus Cecinit
> So sings the afflicted one.

No. 13
A NEIGHBOUR'S TEARS SPRINKLED ON THE DUST OF THE AMIABLE VIRGIN, MRS. REBEKAH SEWALL, AUG. 3, 1710
BY BENJAMIN TOMPSON
[The Boston Public Library]

Size, 8½ by 13 inches. Printer and date of printing are unknown. The Massachusetts Historical Society possesses a manuscript sheet containing two other Tompson elegies on Rebekah Sewall, although neither of them is written in his handwriting. The first is entitled, "A Neighbours Tears dropt on ye grave of an Amiable Virgin a pleasant plant cut downe in the blooming of her Spring Viz. m^rs Rebekah Sewal. Anno Aetatis 6. August ye 4th 1710. [Ben: Thompson.]" (Printed in "Massachusetts Historical Society Proceedings" [2d series], VIII, 388–389). The second of the two elegies very closely resembles the printed broadside here reproduced, and was obviously an earlier draft of the same verses. It is entitled, "A Clowde of Tears, sprinkled on the Dust of the Amiable Virgin m^rs Rebecka Sewel who Suddenly died August. 3 1710. Aetatis suae [B:T]." The present broadside was reproduced by Mr. Samuel Abbott Green in his *Ten Fac-simile Reproductions*, pp. 30 ff.

Rebekah Sewall was the eldest daughter of Samuel and Rebekah Sewall, and a granddaughter of Judge Sewall, whose *Diary* (II, 285) contains the following entry, written on the day of her death.

Our little Grand-Daughter Rebekah Sewall, born xr. 30. 1704. at Brooklin, died about Eight or Nine this morn. We knew not of her being Sick, till Dr. Noyes, as he returned, told us she was dead. The Lord effectually awaken us by these awfull Surprising Providences. My son

Memento **Mori.**

490. 107

A Neighbour's TEARS

Sprinkled on the Duſt of the Amiable Virgin,

Mrs. **Rebekah Sewall,**

Who was born **December** 30. 1704. and dyed
ſuddenly, **Auguſt** 3. 1710. Ætatis 6.

Heav'ns only, in dark hours, can Succour ſend;
And ſhew a Fountain, where the ciſterns end.
I ſaw this little One but t'other day
With a ſmall flock of Doves, juſt in my way:
What New-made Creature's this ſo bright? thought I
Ah! Pity 'tis ſuch Prettineſs ſhould die.
Madam, behold the Lamb of GOD; for there's
Your Pretty Lamb, while you diſſolve in Tears;
She lies infolded in her Shepherd's Arms,
Whoſe Boſom's always full of gracious Charms.
Great JESUS claim'd his own; never begrutch
Your Jewels rare into the Hands of Such.
He, with His Righteouſneſs, has better dreſs'd
Your Babe, than e're you did, when at your breaſt.
'Tis not your caſe alone: for thouſands have
Follow'd their ſweeteſt Comforts to the Grave.
Seeking the Plat of Immortality,
I ſaw no Place Secure; but all muſt dy.
Death, that ſtern Officer, takes no denial;
I'm griev'd he found your door, to make a trial.
Thus, be it on the Land, or Swelling Seas,
His Sov'raignty doth what His Wiſdom pleaſe.
Muſt then the Rulers of this World's affairs,
By Providence be brought thus into Tears?
It is a Leſſon hard, I muſt confeſs,
For our Proud Wills with Heav'ns to acquieſce.
But when Death goes before; Unſeen, behind,
There's ſuch a One, as may compoſe the Mind.
Pray, *Madam,* wipe the tears off your fair eyes;
With your tranſlated Damſel Sympathiſe:
Could She, from her New School, obtain the leave,
She'd tell you Things would make you ceaſe to grieve.

B. Tompſon

and daughter got thither before their Child dyed, and had Mr. Walter to pray with her. She was sensible to the last, catching her breath till she quite lost it.

The next entry reads:

Sixth-day, Augt 4th. Rebekah Sewall is buried in at Roxbury in the Governour's Tomb. . . .

Sewall's account of the procession suggests that even infant funerals were not without pomp.

For an account of Benjamin Tompson, see pp. 24–26, *supra*. He had himself lost a little girl, Mary, aged seven, March 28, 1700. There is a touching reference to her in the first of the manuscript elegies mentioned above. The lines, which end the piece, are as follows:

> Pleasant Rebecka, heres to thee a Tear
> Hugg my sweet Mary if you chance to see her
> Had you giv'n warning ere you pleasd to Die,
> You might have had a neater Elegy.

Mrs. Rebekah Sewall
By calling her *Mrs.* the author was paying a delicate tribute to this six-year-old child, since *Mrs.* was a title not usually applied to girls before they were in their teens. In colonial America, the title carried with it, in addition, a suggestion of such distinction as belonged to aristocratic birth or high office. Men and women in colonial records were more commonly referred to as *Goodman* and *Goodwife*.

I saw this little One . . .
In the first manuscript elegy, this line reads,
> *I saw this pretty Lamb . . .*
The next three lines are identical.

No. 14
UPON THE MUCH LAMENTED DEATH, OF THAT PIOUS AND HOPEFUL YOUNG GENTLEWOMAN, MRS. MARY GERRISH, NOV. 17, 1710

BY NICHOLAS NOYES

[*The Boston Public Library*]

SIZE, 8¼ by 13 inches. Printer and date of printing are unknown.

Mary Gerrish, born October 29, 1691, was the tenth child of Samuel and Hannah Sewall. She had given birth to a daughter (Hannah) on November 10. There are various details concerning her illness and death in Sewall's *Diary*, from November 10 to 18, 1710.

For an account of Nicholas Noyes, her elegist, see p. 20, *supra*. These verses show him in a different light than those written on James Bayley.

Relates
Relatives.
As sad, and Lonesome as the Pelican.
The alleged solitariness of the pelican in English tradition had no relation to the observa-

Upon the Much Lamented DEATH,

Of that Pious and Hopeful Young Gentlewoman,

Mrs. Mary Gerrish,

Wife of Mr. *Samuel Gerrish*; the Daughter of the Honourable
Samuel Sewall Efqr. Who Departed this Life *November* 17th. 1710.
Being the Night after Publick Thanksgiving.

FAIR Ladies fee, (if you can fee for Teares)
How Death regards not either Sex, or Years ;
Nor yet the beauty of the Mind, or Face,
Nor Pious Relates, Nor yet Perf'nal Grace.
That bare-bones Scithe Cuts with Impartial Stroke
The Tender Lily, and the Sturdy Oake ;
Parts Child, and Parents Mutually fond,
And Snaps in two the Matrimonial Bond ;
Quite Wifelefs, and half Lifelefs leaves the Man,
As fad, and Lonefome as the Pelican.
And rends the New-born Infant from the breaft,
And Bofome, where it fhould have Milk, and Reft.
It breaks in pieces by a fad Remove,
Brothers, and Sifters Bundled up in Love.
Don't it move Paffion, and Compaffion too ?
And yet alas ! we know not what to doe !
If we our Selves fhould of their Council make,
Its eafier to give Counfel, then to take.
Comforts, and Cordials won't be Relifhed ;
Rachel Refufed to be Comforted,
Unlefs they could have brought again her Dead.
Should we with Tears Commiferating Come,
Already there's too much of them at home :
And Breaftlefs Babes that are left Motherlefs,
By Sympathy partake in this Diftrefs ;
And with their Uptight Tears, and Sincere Cries
Condole the little *Hannah's* Miferies.
    If at the King of Terrots we fhould rail,
'Twere Sin and Folfy, and would not avail.
Such Courfe is void of all Religious fenfe,
And faults the Wife and Holy Providence,
Which all things Wifely doth, and well, and will
The Gracious Promife faithfully fulfill.
GOD's Works are Myfteries not underftood,
And yet His Truth will make them work for good.
Then let us Wait, and Pray, and all Combine
To Bend, and Bow *Our* Wills to the *DIVINE*.
Silence becomes us, and Submiffion ;
For we fhould come to this ; *Thy Will be Done* !
Relates, Refign to GOD your *Mary Gerrifh* ;
Believers tho' they Die, yet do not Perifh.
The Daughter, Sifter, Wife of Youth, and Mother
From one Thanksgiving went unto another ;
And left her Living Image ftill behind
With fuch as will to both in one be kind.

Pofuit, NICHOLAS NOYES.

tions of natural historians. It resulted from the Vulgate allusion, *pelicano solitudinis*, rendered in the King James version, Ps. 102.6, "I am like a pelican of the wilderness."

Condole the little Hannah's Miseries.

The child died the following April. Samuel Sewall speaks tenderly of her in the entries which record her illness, death, and burial. *Diary*, II, 307, entries of April 21, 22, 23, 24, 1711.

No. 15
GREATNESS & GOODNESS ELEGIZED, IN A POEM, UPON THE MUCH LAMENTED DECEASE OF THE HONOURABLE & VERTUOUS MADAM HANNAH SEWALL, OCT. 19, 1717

BY JOHN DANFORTH

[The Boston Public Library]

SIZE, 8 by 12½ inches. Printer and date of printing are unknown.

Hannah Sewall was the daughter of John Hull, mint-master in the colonies. She was born February 14, 1657/8, and became the wife of Samuel Sewall, February 28, 1675/6.

John Danforth, her elegist, was minister at Dorchester and the author of numerous elegies. He was born at Roxbury, November 8, 1660, was a graduate of Harvard in 1677, and minister at Dorchester from 1681 until his death May 26, 1730. James Blake's *Annals of the Town of Dorchester* (1750, p. 47) contains this mention of his poetizing.

. . . He took much pains to Eternize yᵉ Names of many of yᵉ good Christians of his own Flock; and yet yᵉ World is so ungratefull, that he has not a Line Written to preserue his memory, no not so much as upon his Tomb; he being buried in Lt. Govr. Stoughton's Tomb that was covered with writing before. And there also lyeth his Consort Mrs. Elizabeth Danforth.

Of John Danforth's seven elegies extant in broadside form, five were written to honor women. (In addition to the present specimen, cf. Ford, 326, 358, 368, 503.)

The PATRIOT
    Samuel Sewall.
Lucina's Dust
    In Roman mythology, Lucina was the goddess who presided over childbirth. The author may be confusing her with Juno or Diana, with whom she is sometimes identified.
Wilson Pronounc'd the Promis'd Blessing then;
    John Wilson, pastor of the First Church in Boston, observing that John Hull, as a young man, was extraordinarily dutiful toward his aged mother, declared that God would bless him, and make him to grow rich. (Cotton Mather's *Magnalia*, I, 314.) The prophecy was abundantly fulfilled.
Quitting New-England's Coasts
    John Hull died October 1, 1683.

Greatneſs & Goodneſs ELEGIZED,

In a POEM, Upon the much Lamented Deceaſe of the Honourable & Vertuous

Madam Hannah Sewall,

Late Conſort of the Honourable Judge SEWALL, in **Boſton**, in **New-England**.
She Exchanged *this* Life for a *Better*, *October*, 19th. *Anno Dom.* 1717. *Ætatis ſuæ.* 60.

A Mind *Serene* is only *fit* for Verſe,
Deſerved by this *Honourable Herſe :*
Our *Ruffled Mind* can ſcarcely Think, *for Tears* ;
Trembling Our Pen, at This Great Death, appears.
The PATRIOT, now in Sorrow almoſt Drown'd,
Merits *Condoleance* from the Country round.
Shall We adventure theſe Unpoliſh'd Lines ?
Lucina's Duſt deſerves far Richer Shrines.

To Name Her *Father* firſt We'll not think much ;
We knew Him well, & Wiſh there were *More Such.*
ChoiceHULL the fifthCommand obſerv'd ſo well
His Carriage to His Parent did Excell ;
Wilſon Pronounc'd the *Promis'd Bleſſing* then ;
The LORD of Providence too ſaid *AMEN.*
The *Hull*, ſoon *Built* upon, became an *Argo* ;
Deep fraighted with Terrene & Heav'nly *Cargo :*
Immortal *Vertue* gave Immortal *Name* ;
Long Life, Power, Honour, Added to His *Fame.*
Stretching his Courſe, Refreſh'd with Proſperous
[*Gales,*
Quitting*New-England's* Coaſts, to*Heav'n* He Sails.

This Precious Fragant *Flower* was, when he went,
Heir of's Vertues, Left in's Heavenly Tent :
A *Paragon,* upon *New-England's* Stage ;
Her *Piety* advancing with her *Age.*
Her Radiant *Graces,* of ſo Rich a *Worth,*
Pencils of *Angels* ſcarce can Paint 'em forth.

She was too Sparkling for *Plebæian* Eyes,
Heaven Bleſs'd SEWALL with this *Noble Prize* ;
Plac'd in the Chryſtal Sphere of Chaſteſt Love,
She Flow'r'd a *Race,* Devote to *Heav'n* above.
Full of *Contentment* and *Devoid* of Strife,
In Golden Characters She wrote her Life.
Her Mind, *Bright & Serene :* A Charming Sight :
No Saphire or Rich Ruby Shone ſo Bright.

Such was her *Courſe,* & *Choice,* & *Diſpoſition* ;
The Greateſt *Queens* may Envy her Condition.
Obſerving-*Ladys* muſt keep down their Vail,
'Till They're as *Full* of Grace, & *Free* from Gall,
As *Void* of Pride, as *High* in Vertue Rare,
As *much* in Reading, and as *much* in Prayer.
Wiſdom, with an *Inheritance,* She had :
Her *Charities* did make her Neighbours Glad.
When Darkned with Afflictions, in her Day,
Th' *Bright Cloudy Pillar* Guided ſtill her Way :
The Skie O'recaſt ; Yet in her *Cittadel*
The COMFORTER Vouchſaf'd to Shine, & Dwell.
Her Faith, Hope, Patience, Holineſs, and Love
(*Thank Heav'ns Free Grace,*) did All, moſt-ſted-
[faſt prove.
Up to the *Bleſſed-Seats,* Kind *Angels* bear
Her *'Parted-Soul* ; With *Hallelujahs* there :
To CHRIST, in Youth, drawn by His Saving
[charms,
Is now Incircled with His *Bleſſed Arms.*

The *Cares* of *State* & *Courts* are *Burdens* Great ;
Grief for her *Death* is a more *Preſſing Weight.*
Behold ! Our *Samuel* to the Utmoſt Try'd :
CHRIST's Alſufficient Grace, Ne're yet Deny'd.
Poor Borrowed Greatneſs dares not to Demur ;
Th' ALMIGHTY well Accepts your Offerings, SIR,
Whole *Hecatombs* you offer now in ONE ;
JESUS Remains ; You cannot be Undone ;
Exceſſive Grief, Saints well may Bluſh to own.
Long may You Stay, to Bleſs the Church & State !
KindHeav'n, We Hope, will large Years longer Wait.
Strong Conſolations from th' OMNIPOTENT,
Let *Fill* your Heart, in your thus *Emptied* Tent !
And may your *Progeny,* ſtill Left you, Stand
Sacred to GOD, and *Bleſſings* in the Land !

Ita humillime Precatur
JOHN DANFORTH, *V. D. M. Dorceſtria.*

Her Charities did make her Neighbours Glad.

Hannah Sewall was possessed of great wealth. The pleasant legend that at the time of her marriage, she had brought as a dowry her own weight in pine-tree shillings, does not do her fortune justice, even at that time. She was her father's only surviving child, and at his death, in 1683, inherited his large estate, subject to the widow's dower. Her mother died in 1695.

The Cares of State & Courts are Burdens Great;

At this time Sewall was a member of the Executive Council for the colony, and Judge of the Probate Court of the County of Suffolk. He was made Justice of the Superior Court in the following year, 1718.

Whole Hecatombs

Hundreds. Strictly, among the Greeks and Romans, a great public sacrifice (properly of a hundred oxen). *NED.*

And may your Progeny

Hannah had borne him fourteen children, of whom only five survived infancy. Four were living at the time of her death.

No. 16
WORDS OF CONSOLATION TO MR. ROBERT STETSON & MRS. MARY STETSON, HIS WIFE, ON THE DEATH OF THEIR SON ISAAC STETSON, NOV. 7, 1718
BY NATHANIEL PITCHER
[The Essex Institute]

SIZE, 7¾ by 10 inches. The margins have been trimmed. Printer and date of printing are unknown. The cut, which is interesting as an attempt to portray the disaster realistically, does not reappear on any imprint which has yet come to light. Mr. Ford suggests that it was probably copied from some English illustration. (Cf. Ford, 438.)

Isaac Stetson, as the title states, was the son of Robert Stetson. He was the great-grandson of Cornet Robert Stetson, one of the earliest settlers of Scituate and founder of the Stetson family in America. Isaac was born March 15, 1696, and died unmarried. He was drowned by the fourth cliff in Scituate. His grandfather, Anthony Collamore, had died in a shipwreck off the Scituate coast in 1693, and had been lamented in a broadside elegy. (Cf. p. 19, *supra.*)

Nathaniel Pitcher, the author of these verses, was minister in Scituate from 1707 until his death in 1723. He was born in 1685, and was a graduate of Harvard. He is credited with other occasional pieces, among them an elegy for Mrs. Hannah Robinson and her daughter, who, like the subject of the present elegy, "perished in the Mighty Deeps." This second elegy is preserved in Samuel Deane's *History of Scituate*, pp. 398–399.

Belov'd [as] Life, and to his Heart most Near;
Bright [Fa]ith, and Love, Obedience to prove
By a Friend

There is no clue to the authorship of the second tribute.

Words of Confolation to
Mr. *Robert Stetfon* & Mrs. *Mary Stetfon*, his Wife,
On the DEATH of their SON Ifaac Stetfon, Who Perifhed in the Mighty Waters,
November 7th. 1718.   Aged 22.

Ifaac Stetfon, Anagram.

'Tis Caft on Sea : --- A ! Son it's Ceaft.

On Sea being Caft, his Life is Caft away,
A ! Son it's Ceaft, Thou finifh'd haft thy day.

WHEN th' Famous Patriarch, *Abram* of Old
Was Call'd by GOD (who oft to him foretold,
Of Wondrous things, fhould be in future Times
And bleffings, that fhould Spring out of his Loines.)
To Sacrifice his Only *Ifaac* Dear,
Belov'd Life, and to his Heart moft Near,
Bright Faith, and Love, Obedience to prove
Unto his GOD the GOD of Heaven Above,
Refigningly he parts with his dear Son,
With Bright Devotion, LORD, *Thy Will be done.*

Hath GOD Remov'd from you your *Ifaac* Dear ?
Your Joy and Laughter, [*] turn'd into a Tear ?
Weeping in Floods, Orewhelm'd with Griefs, are got
Bewailing thus, Ah ! *Ifaac* he is not !
Yet offer him, with Spiritual Sacrifice
Such GOD Delights in, fuch He'l not defpife.
What though he's Dead ; T'was but a Mortal Son
That you begot ; Life's Thread is Quickly Spun.
What though he die i' th' Seas, and ne'er be found
To have a decent Burial in the Ground ;
Yet in the ORACLES Divine 'tis faid
The Mighty Sea fhall *Give up all her Dead.*
What though his Mortal Body Serve as Difhes
Inftead of Feeding Worms, to feed the Fifhes :
And all his duft be Scattered up and down,
As if the Windy Tempeft Swiftly blown ;
Yet GOD Thefe Scatter'd, Shatter'd *Atoms* all,
Into one Body, Eafily will call ;
And Re-unite them into Form Compleat,
When Soul and Body at the laft fhall Meet.

By Faith and Prayer, Submit ; Yea and Refign
Your dying *Ifaac* to the Will Divine.
Altho' you've loft a Son out of your Band
Yet blefs the Giving, and the Taking Hand :
Then fhall that Sacred Word be Underftood,
That All fhall work Together for your Good.
So Prays your Friend;

Nathaniel Pitcher.

[*] Ifaac, Signifies Laughter, or Joy.

A Sorrowful POEM *upon that Defirable Youth*
ISAAC STETSON *of Scituate, who was
Caft-away in a Sloop near the Mouth of the
North-River, in Scituate, the 7th day of No-
vember 1718. Anno Ætatis Suæ 22.*

YOU Mournful Poets once more Dip your Quill
And Wrack your Mufes to the height of Skill,
With peircing Lines reach every Generous Soul,
And Paint the Breafts that with Compaffion Rowl
Relate the Story of a Tender Youth,
And Trace your Paper with the Lines of Truth.
One Buried in the Brackifh Region where,
His Body Toil'd with anxious Grief and Care :
His Tender Father treads the fatal Shore,
Begging each Wave to Caft his Son afhore.
But cruel Waves difdain his Pitious Cries,
And Thundring Billows Drown the Weeping Eyes.
He wrings his hands, he weeps and Rends his Hair,
In all the Agonies of wild Defpair.
O Cruel Fate ! my Dolorous Groans fhall Drown
The Noife of Billows Rowling O're the Ground,
My Drooping Soul with forrows fore oppreft,
Grow's Unacquainted with the Joys of Reft,
He now Returns unto his Mournful Wife ;
Where he in Tears will weary out his Life :
And Pray to GOD, That when He fee's it Beft,
He'd take him to His Everlafting Reft.

By a Friend.

AN ELEGY UPON HIS EXCELLENCY WILLIAM BURNET, ESQ; WHO DEPARTED THIS LIFE SEPT. 7, 1729

[*The New York Public Library*]

SIZE, 8 by 13½ inches. Printed by Thomas Fleet of Boston, who at this time was doing a large business in ballads, pamphlets, and the like. The woodcuts which adorned these publications were made by a negro in his employ. This cut is probably his work.

William Burnet was born in Holland in 1688. He first came to America in 1720 as Governor of New York and New Jersey, but becoming unpopular, was transferred to Massachusetts and New Hampshire. On the occasion of his arrival in Boston, July, 1728, he was given a pompous welcome. Verses issued in his honor at that time are extant. (Cf. Ford, 554.) During his short term of office thereafter, enthusiasm cooled as the result of a controversy over his salary. The refusal of the colony to meet his demands had been upheld shortly before his death.

Burnet the Learn'd

The *Boston Weekly News-Letter* of September 11, 1729, in the article written on the occasion of Governor Burnet's death, mentions his library as his "chief Delight & Pride" and as "one of the noblest and richest *Collections* that *America* has seen."

With Manly Eloquence his Words were a[rm'd.]

Like Reverend Sarum

Governor Burnet's father, Gilbert Burnet, was Bishop of Salisbury. *Sarum* was the ecclesiastical name for Salisbury, as in *Sarum* missal, etc. The word had developed from a misunderstood abbreviation. *NED.*

AN
ELEGY
Upon His EXCELLENCY
William Burnet, Esq;

Who departed this Life *Sept.* 7th. 1729,   *Ætat.* 42.

IN mournful Lays let *Melpomene* sing,
  And griev'd & pensive touch the solemn String:
While all the Nine their gushing Sorrows shed,
To Mourn in decent sort the Mighty Dead.
BURNET the Great no more must bless our Eyes,
BURNET the Learn'd, the Gen'rous and the Wise;
Gone, gone for ever, that capacious Mind,
The vital Breath all scatter'd in the Wind.
His Eyes Majestick now no more must roll,
All mortal Thoughts are vanish'd from his Soul.

Ye Scholars who in Lib'ral Arts excel,
In correspondent Strains your Passions tell. (prov'd
Weep the bright Scholars who your Minds im-
Caress'd your Persons and your Converse lov'd.
Say in what Raptures fled the Hours away,
When his sweet Words beguil'd the live-long
                      (Day.
Say how he charm'd you with his fine Address,
While softest Airs the Gentleman confess :
But now no more you'l hear his charming Tongue
In flowing Eloquence glide smooth along.
No more expecting to his House you'l come,
Not fraught with Treasures go exulting home.
In the cold Grave lies that capacious Head
Where bright Ideas like the Sands were spread.
The Memory has lost its various Store,
And the' Invention shall instruct no more;

Ye who in high Authority are set
Lament of High Degrees the certain Fate.
To Death ev'n Kings and Princes are accurst,
Scepters and Crowns must mingle with the Dust.
Even BURNET dies, who so few Months before
Was hail'd Triumphant to the joyful Shore.
What Millions pour'd around his ratling Wheels,
While rising Dust smok'd o'er the distant Hills!
What Pomp, what Splendour glitter'd thro' the
                     Gates!
What Shouts arose in all the ecchoing Streets /
While Drums & Trumpets far were heard around,
And the arch'd Skies beat back the rolling Sound.
But Ah! No Greatness could secure his Breath,
BURNET the Great must yield to mightier Death.

From the chief Chair be carried to the Tomb,
And damp the Glory in the dismal Gloom.

Ye fairer Souls whom the gay Nine inspire
Mourn him who tun'd your Tongues and fed
                    (your Fire.
Well may the Muses hang their drooping Wing,
For him who sweetly like themselves could sing;
For him they rais'd the Voice & touch'd the Lyre,
Wound up the Strings, and bent the vocal Wyre
In alter'd Notes and solemn Sounds deplore,
The florid Fancy that must smile no more :
The Breath harmonious now for ever fled,
And the pale Lips silent among the Dead.

But chief in Anguish your sad Bosoms rend
To whom he gave the tender Name of *Friend*:
How kind, how free, how gen'rous and how just
He kept inviolate the sacred Trust.
Warm to defend, and eager still to praise,
His friendly Soul flow'd out ten thousand ways
But now no more his Friends shall hear his Voice,
Nor in his Conversation e're Rejoice.
His Wit no more shall charm, or Rhet'rick move,
Nor his free open Air enkindle Love.

Farewel great Soul, tho' thou away dost fly,
The faithful Muse shall raise thy Honours high;
In her just Lines thy Character be read,
And o'er thy Tomb this Epitaph be laid.

Beneath the sacred Honours of this Urn,
Round which the Muses and the Graces mourn,
Lies once the Owner of a Judgment clear,
A flowing Fancy and a tuneful Ear:
A Rich Invention fruitful as the Sea,
A Memory Capacious as the Sky.
With Manly Eloquence his Words were ar
And the fine Author every Reader charm'd
His Policy was deep, his Reason strong,
Like Reverend *Sarum* from whose Loins he sprung

F I N I S,

BOSTON: Printed and Sold by *T. Fleet* in *Pudding-Lane*, near the Town-House, where may be had His Excellency's Character.

AN ELEGY OCCASIONED BY THE SUDDEN AND AWFUL DEATH OF MR. NATHANAEL BAKER OF DEDHAM, MAY 7, 1733

[The Dedham Historical Society]

SIZE, 8¼ by 11½ inches. Printer and date of printing are unknown.

Nathanael Baker was the son of John Baker of Dedham. He was born April 4, 1706. An account of his death is included in the *Boston Weekly News-Letter*, May 10, 1733, as follows:

We hear from *Dedham*, That on Monday last one Mr. *Baker*, (Son of Mr *John Baker* Cornet of a Troop,) as he was riding home fell from off his Horse, and as 'tis tho't crack'd his Skull; he was soon after taken up, and dyed on Tuesday Night, not having spoke a Word after his Fall: He was a young Man, and just upon the point of being married.

This last detail may have supplied a hint to the elegist.

Come Melpomene, sing thou Tragi[c Muse,]
But [I] your mournful Subject now will [chuse]
In [doteful]! doleful Lays! [tu]ne up your [Lyre,]
O this our Son, in all his Strength and Pr[ime,]
When Youth and Beauty in their Lustre s[hine,]
How broken is the House, and desolate the [Wood,]
The Fields shall miss him, & the Herds that [rove,]
The Grass seems humble where he us'd to m[ove.]
But chiefly all his Friends with Anguish m[ourn,]
And have their Hearts with Grief and Sorrow [torn.]
Where are they now? where is he gone? ah [me,]
He feeds the Worms that can't be brib'd t[o flee.]
Young Marg'ret Fisher

If this be Margaret Fisher, the daughter of John Fisher of Dedham, as is likely, the prophecy of the elegist was fulfilled, for she died February 2, 1736/7, aged 25.

AN
ELEGY
Occasioned by the sudden and awful Death
OF
Mr. *Nathanael Baker*
Dedham:

A Young Man just upon the point of Marriage:
And Son to Lieutenant *JOHN BAKER.*

He fell from his Horse on Monday Night the 7th of *May*, 1733: and Died
the Wednesday following. Ætat. 27.

Come *Melpomene*, sing thou Tragi
Bu your mournulSt jeernow, will
In a refull doleful Lays! come up your
And raise in us a melancholy Fire.
Say, fainting Muse, how dreadful does it seem
That youthful, lovely, *Baker* is your Theme.
Assist ye N I N E, or else I cant relate,
In Strains of Woe, that shall be adequate ;
To the surprizing awful Accident.
Oh ! boundlefsGrief, Oh ! Tearsthat cant be pent
I tremble tho' I only mourn a Friend,
That came to a most unexpected End;
It seems to me, my Song would give relief,
If I could imitate his Parents Grief.
But that I know is far beyond the Pen,
Or Rhet'ric of the Sons of mortal Men ;
We can't express by Words, they can't reveal
The Floods of Grief, the Agonies they feel.
O this our Son, in all his Strength and Pri e
When Youth and Beauty in their Lustre s
Is hurl'd away to Shades of Death, and Gloc
How melancholy is the mournful Room ?
How broken is the House, and desolate the
And all the Places, where he frequented.
The Fields shall miss him, & the Herds that
The Grass seems humble where he us'd to
But chiefly all his Friends with Anguish m
And have their Hearts withGrief andSorrow
All his acquaintance bathe his Urn with T
A sprightly Youth, in midst of blooming Y
A winning Aier, a manly Innocence,
A Conversation void of all Offence ;
Nay comely too, and decent in his Mein,
A thousand winning Graces in him seen.
Where are they now ? where is he gone ? ah
He feeds the Worms that can't be brib'd t

O ye his Brethren and Sister say,
How kind a Brother now is mov'd away,
Into the Grave, from whence he cannot Rise,
His Face shall bless no more your longing Eyes,
I fail LL fail ! or else I would relate,
The boundlefsGrief of the unfortunate)
Young *Marg'ret Fisher* his designed Mate.
In doleful Strains the mourning Damsel Crys,
But Death is deaf to all her Agonies ;
This Night he left me, but I little thought,
To see him die, I should so soon be brought ;
Oh ! cruel Death your conquer'd Victim spare,
And let him once but beat the yielding Air,
To speak one Word to me before he go,
And tell me something that I want to know.
But Oh farwel ! He's dying now ev'nd,
His Life and Breath is scatter'd in the Wind ;
Farewell my Friend, my kind Associate,
I thought that Heaven design'd you for my Mate,
My Heart is yours, only my backward Hand,
Was not stretch'd forth to tye the Nuptial Band.
You can't return, but I shall go to you,
Farewell sweet Soul, Adieu, Adieu, Adieu.
But cease to Mourn, your boundless Passions sway,
God says be mute, therefore you must obey ;
He governs all in Wisdom by his Power,
And orders out your Lot from Hour to Hour.
And though by you, his Ways ben't Understood,
They always end in the Eternal Good,
Of those that have an int'rest in his Love,
I wish you all this Blessing from above,
Dry up your Tears, and now like Christians say,
Blessed be God, who gives and takes away.

F I N I S.

AN ELEGY ON THE MUCH LAMENTED DEATH OF
NATHAN STARR, B.A., JUNE 9, 1752
[The Massachusetts Historical Society]

SIZE, 10½ by 16 inches. Probably a Connecticut imprint. If so, and if it were issued in 1752, it must have come from the press of Timothy Green of New London, since at that time he owned the only printing press in the colony.

Almost all the known facts concerning Nathan Starr, except the date of his birth, are recorded in the heading to this elegy. He was born September 6, 1732, in Danbury, where he died. He was a graduate of Yale College, of the class of 1750. His father, Comfort Starr, was one of the influential men of Danbury, and a notable benefactor in the town.

[S]miling he sees the God-Head Face to [Face,]
[T]ells in sweet Songs the Wonders of his [Grace,]
[A]nd in it shall the STAR for ever move,

This epitaph is cut on Nathan Starr's tombstone in Wooster Street Cemetery, in Danbury. For a photograph of his grave and his father's, see James Montgomery Bailey's *History of Danbury* (New York, 1896, opposite p. 506).

An Elegy

On the much Lamented Death of

Nathan Starr, B. A.

Who departed this Life, *June* 9th *Anno Domini*, 17 52. Aged *Nineteen Years, Nine Months & three Days*; having been a worthy Member of *Yale-College*, near *Six Years*.--- Not only the only Son, but the only Child of his Father, Mr. **Comfort Starr**, Merchant in *Danbury*, in *Connecticut*, and Grandson to the Reverend Mr. SETH SHOVE, late Pastor of the Church there.

AH! Blasted Hopes of Parents, withering Joys!
Built on meer Air, and centering in Toys.
A Friend, a Child, is but an empty Name,
A gliding Shadow, or a pleasing Dream.
Our Fancies rise upon a waxen Wing,
When we our Hopes build on some mortal Thing;
The young and sprightly, generous and brave,
Submit to Death, and lye down in the Grave.
Yet with their Offspring, Parents please their Eyes,
And let their tow'ring Hopes out-soar the Skies;
Their Children sicken, then yield up their Breath,
And unexpected fall a Prey to Death:
Down drop the Parents Hopes below Relief,
And plunge their sinking Hearts in hopeless Grief.---
Here's your own Case, dear Parents, now who mourn,
And with your Tears bedew your NATHAN's Urn.
How were your flatter'd Souls prepar'd to see
By this one Son, a num'rous Progeny:
Your new risen STAR fill'd all your Hearts with Joy,
Your Joys and Hopes grew up as grew the Boy.
In him you tho't to see your Hopes complete,
And in his Life find each desired Sweet;
Him to enjoy you hop'd while num'rous Years
Revolve their various Seasons round the Spheres,
That each new Year should still confirm his Strength,
And draw his Life to an uncommon Length.
But when your Hopes had labour'd up this Height,
The airy Basis cann't support the Weight:
The cruel Death clips off the vital Thread,
Shuts up the Scene, and your dear NATHAN's dead!
Your look'd-for Pleasures flee pursuing Sight,
Vail'd with Death's Shade, and wrap'd in sable Night.
'Tis pleasant now t'indulge your painful Grief,
Whilst Sympathy of Friends yields no Relief;
Could this but ease you, every gen'rous Heart,
Would share your Grief, nay bear a double Part.
Alas! a gen'ral Grief would all be Vain,
Encrease of Mourners, but encreases Pain:
I'd rather draw past Scenes of your Delight,
Bring up your late set STAR once more to Sight,
Invite your throbbing Souls just to reflect,
On his short Life, and only recollect,
His well-spent Morning, and the Path he trod,
Of early Piety towards his GOD.
To calm your surging Griefs, t'asswage your Pain,
In Knowledge view your Son's uncommon Gain:
While in the Sphere of *Yale* he shin'd, how bright,
How dazling, how refulgent was his Light?
Quick he imbib'd those Arts, which form the Mind,
To all that's useful, generous, good and kind;
And as he learn'd, he liv'd, to GOD and You,
A Life complete, altho' his Years were few.

Surely the Youth was some Ætherial Mind,
By Heaven decreed in Flesh to be confin'd:
From you to spring, and of you to be born,
Your House to grace, and Kindred to adorn.
His happy Soul was of angelic Frame,
It's Nature and it's Tendency the same.
Whilst here he liv'd he soar'd on flamy Wing,
His raptur'd Mind convers'd with heavenly Things.

Well, mournful Pair, drop all your doleful
Cast up your Eyes, assume your Joys again:
Your STAR's not set, but shines divinely bright,
In the bless'd Realms of Day, and Robes of Light,
Your only Son, now both a King and Priest,
Doth at JEHOVAH's Table richly Feast,
On Beauties all divine, with stedfast Eyes,
Whilst in his Breast new Joys do ever rise,
Full Joys, unknown beneath these circling Skies.
His Passions all express'd divinely Sweet,
His Love full-fed makes all his Bliss complete.
Your STAR still shines in the bright Realms of Day,
Your Son still lives, then put your Griefs away.
Leave his dear Soul to take it's perfect Rest,
Till you from Bands of Clay too be releas'd:
Wing swiftly upward thro' th' Ætherial Road,
With him your JESUS sing, with him enjoy your GOD.

An Acrostick.
. . . .

Near the bright Morning-Star our STAR doth shine,
And blaze in brightest Lustre all divine;
The fav'rite Youth has gain'd the Victory,
High now he reigns above our starry Sky,
Amongst whole crowned Nations of the Blest,
Now is he crown'd, and in full Glory dress'd.

Smiling he sees the God He Page to
Tells in sweet Songs the Wonders of his G
And joins in Chorus the angelic Throng,
Round Heav'n's high Arches sounds th' eternal Song.

EPITAPH.

THE Orb is set in Dust,
The STAR doth ever shine,
The Orb this Tomb shall burst,
In Beauty all divine.
And in it shall the STAR for ever move,
In one eternal Round of flaming Love.

No. 20
THE FOLLOWING LINES WERE OCCASIONED BY THE DEATH OF MISS MARY HEDGES, FEB. 17, 1768

[The New York Historical Society]

Size, 9¾ by 15 inches, with margins trimmed. This may be a New York imprint, as the verses record a tragedy of East Hampton, Long Island. To judge from the cut, it was a sea tragedy.

Mary Hedges, the victim, was presumably the daughter of Stephen Hedges of East Hampton, since he had a daughter Mary, whose baptism, recorded of 1749, would check with the age of the Mary in this poem. The title states that she was in her nineteenth year. The author's concern for wayward youth, and his ministerial admonitions, suggest that the elegy may possibly have been written by Samuel Buel, pastor of the East Hampton church at this time. There is no record, however, to support this conjecture, except the fact that in 1770 one named Samuel Buell wrote verses on four other victims of drowning, and in 1775 published a poem entitled "Youth's Triumph." Both of these issues were New London imprints. They are recorded in Oscar Wegelin's *Early American Poetry* ([New York, 1903], I, 14), and may, of course, refer to another Samuel Buell. Discrepancies in the spelling of proper names are so frequent as to be of little significance.

THE FOLLOWING LINES

Were occasioned by the Death of Miss MARY HEDGES,

who departed this Life February 1*th, 1768, in the 19th Year of her Age.*

AWAKE my muse, and strike the mournful lyre,
Virtue and grief demand poetick fire :
Justice and love forbid thee to refuse,
The humble tribute of the grateful muse.
A lovely spirit from our world is fled,
A charming youth is number'd with the dead:
Death flung his shaft before mid-noon,
For us, alas ! but not for her too soon.
Could fondest wishes kept her spirit here,
Parental love, or friendship firm and dear,
Fair piety, youth's rare, but high applause ;
Or true religion's vastly weighty cause :
She still had dwelt with us below the skies,
And sav'd from anxious griefs that now arise.
Nature averse to grief, would fain explore,
Why she so soon must quit the mortal shore.
Had she a longer date of life possess'd,
And we a longer space with her been bless'd,
An empty mansion in the heavenly sphere
Had been secure, had we enjoy'd her here.
But stop, advent'rous muse ! 'tis not for thee
To ken the wisdom of the DEITY.
The grace that did her youthful life adorn,
Form'd her for bliss above, in early morn,
Death flew, commission'd by eternal love,
To waft her soul from earth, to joys above.
Doom'd to an early, not untimely grave,
The fear of death, by faith she did out-brave.
Her soul, while here on earth, confin'd from home,
Panted in view of endless life to come.
" My father GOD, she cry'd, with weeping eyes,
" I thirst, I thirst for thee, in cloudless skies !
He heard, he spake, " Go Angels wing away,
" This child bring safe to realms of endless day."
There now in everlasting bloom of youth,
She knows each promise an eternal truth.
" That now no cloud shall veil, nor pow'r destroy,
" The soul's calm sun-shine, and the heart-felt joy."
Hark from on high, methinks she speaks, we hear,
" Drop not for me, my friends, the fun'ral tear.
" 'Twas right, 'twas kind, that thus the great decree
" Fix'd early death, and early bliss for me.
" True happness attends my Father's call :
" If happiness for one, why not for all ?
" If absolute perfection was amiss,
" Then the celestial realms were void of bliss.
" My bliss, the more than balance of your rod,
" Your own yet more, if you submit to GOD.
" Thus heaven's grand design will end in love
" To you below, to me, to all above."

No more my muse, paint her seraphick lays,
Immortaliz'd in love, in joy, and praise.
Turn, and address the pious young in years,
Who did lament her flight with flowing Tears.
And those with whom the marble heart is found,
Who in their vice and folly still abound.
Ye happy youth, who piety pursue,
Who have a Christ-like aim, and heaven in view ;
Mark well the bright example of your friend,
Her faith triumphant, and her peaceful end.
By pattern, and by precept, taught to tread
The pleasing path your happy friend has led.
Learn where your bliss and vast advantage lies ;
To know and serve the LORD, is to be wise.
Boldly pursue religion's glor'ous cause,
Believe each promise, and observe her laws.
In life, in death, joy in belief of this,
True virtue will be crown'd with endless bliss.
Ye wanton youth, bound for Eternity,
Unfit to live, and unprepar'd to die,
Warm in the chace of false felicities,
Bold to contemn the glories of the skies ;
Fond to embrace, and lusting to possess,
The hellish-painted shreds of happiness.
What leaden slumbers bind the captive soul ?
Or pow'rs Infernal act without control ?
That you can exile Death, and Judgment too,
Forget eternal weal, eternal woe ?
How can you meet those awful scenes before ?
When all your mirth and time shall be no more ?
Stung with remorse, rack'd by cold Death's embrace,
And the eternal vault now face to face ?
When heav'n's thunders rock the world below,
And flaming wrath descends on ev'ry foe ;
Where will you hide or screen the guilty soul,
From the dread Ire that flies from pole to pole ?
By life, by death, by all the force that springs,
From the full weight of everlasting things,
Resign the heart to CHRIST, who makes demand ;
Believe, obey, or be forever damn'd !
Now seek, now chuse the prize, and share a part
In bliss sublime, that fills the boundless heart :
Angels will join with you, in deep amaze,
And strike the lyre to everlasting praise !

The EPITAPH *upon her* GRAVE-STONE.
This happy youth resign'd her breath,
Prepar'd to live, and ripe for death.
Ye blooming youth, who see this stone,
Learn, early death may be your own.

East-Hampton, ex meo musæo, March 1st, 1768.

No. 21
A DIALOGUE BETWEEN FLESH AND SPIRIT: COMPOSED
UPON THE DECEASE OF MR. ABIJAH ABBOT, 1768
BY PETER ST. JOHN
[*The New York Public Library*]

SIZE, 7¾ by 10 inches. This American version of the Body and Soul Debate is interesting as an attempt on the part of the elegist to break away from the conventional tribute eulogizing the departed.

Further record of Abijah Abbot, whose death occasioned these reflections, appears to be lacking. He may, like his elegist, have belonged to Norwalk, where the Abbot family was numerous at this time.

Peter St. John, a native of Norwalk, was a schoolmaster. He was born January 11, 1726, and died January 4, 1811. He was a man of intelligence, and is said to have written many pieces. Among these is one of the best known of Revolutionary ballads, "American Taxation, Or the Spirit of Seventy-six exemplified in a song written in the golden days which tried men's souls." He is credited with various other pieces, several of which are extant.

A Dialogue between Flesh and Spirit: Composed upon the Decease of Mr. ABIJAH ABBOT, who was kill'd at the raising of a Building in New-York, in the Year ———; in the Name of the bereaved Widow.

FLESH.

WHAT dismal Scenes of unexampled Woe,
I'm doom'd by Providence to undergo!
Few Minutes past I thought my Mountain strong,
And fleeting Minutes smoothly past along.
No ill presaging Fears oppress'd my Mind,
But now, alas! what sorrows do I find.
I look'd around, and saw on every Side,
Both Peace and Plenty like a flowing Tide;
But now, alas! how awful is my Grief,
Too much to bear——admitting no Relief.
The doleful Object fills me with Surprise;
My Husband's Corpse lies pale before my Eyes!
How is mine Soul oppress'd with trembling Pain?
I seek Relief, but seek alas! in vain.
His awful Wound would not admit a Cure,
Nor can my Soul these sorrows long endure.
Why did the Lord in this amazing Day,
Take all my sublunary Joys away.
As in a Moment all my earthly Joys,
This fatal separating Stroke Destroys.

SPIRIT.

Cease thy Complaining, O, impatient Tongue!
It was the Lord, who cannot do thee Wrong;
Had perfect Judgment to the Line been laid,
And Righteousness been for the Plummet made,
Where, O, repining Flesh! where hadst thou been
Hadst thou the just Demerit of thy Sins;
Consider how innumerous Times,
Thou hast provok'd the Almighty by thy Crimes?
Does not indulgent Heaven always shine,
And shower down Blessings with a Hand divine?
Hast thou a Right, thy Maker to arraign;
Or of unerring Wisdom to complain?
The Time, the Means, and Manner of his Death,
Were ordered by the Author of his Breath.
Twas not a blind, fortuitous Event,
That came by Chance, without a wise Intent.
The great Eternal, who presides Above,
And to his Children manifests his Love.
Took but the Breath, which his own Spirit gave,
And hides the Casket in the silent Grave.
He saw 'twas best in this surprising Way,
To take the Spirit from this Lump of Clay.

FLESH.

But O this fatal, separating Stroke,
By which the matrimonial Tie is broke,
To take my Guide and Counsellor away;
My better Half, O, this amazing Day!
I look around, through Telescopes of Tears,
And every Thing a gloomy Aspect wears——
My Infant Train, while weeping round the Clay,
Augment the Sorrows of this bitter Day.
O, how they wring their little Hands and Cry,
Dear Mamma, must our loving Father die?
Alas, alas! pray whither shall we go?
You must be Father and be Mother too.
Affecting Truth! distressing Weight of Care!
Too much for my poor broken Heart to bear!
Ill boding Thoughts, oppress my tortur'd Mind;
On every Side, a Weight of Grief I find.
The Time as well as Manner of his Death,
That awful Hour when he resign'd his Breath,

Was circumstanc'd to aggravate my Smart,
And all conspire to break my wounded Heart.
His honoured Parents from their rural Seat,
We every Hour expecting were to meet
In a kind Visit; but alas! my Woe,
No Mortal knows what 'tis I undergo!
How chang'd my State, on this distressing Day,
I with my Spouse, give all my Joys away.

SPIRIT.

Cease O repining Flesh, forbear thy Tongue,
It was the Lord, who cannot do the wrong;
The Lord is won't his Children to chastise,
To wean them from these sublunary Joys.
This World by Providence was not design'd
To be our Home, but we should bear in Mind,
That we are mortal, and must shortly go,
To endless Joys, or everlasting Woe.
'Tis true, the Frown of Providence is great,
To be bereaved of so dear a Mate.
And many Circumstances seem to join,
To aggravate, and break this Heart of mine.
A Weight of Cares will consequently flow,
Being a Father and a Mother too.
But Thanks to Heaven, I am not bereft
Of every Thing but many Comforts left.
How many destitute of daily Bread,
At every Door, petition to be fed.
Whose Cloathing in no Measure would suffice,
To warm their Bodies, should a Tempest rise.
No House or Home, nor Habitation where,
They might be safe from the Inclement Air,
While gracious Heaven bounteously bestows,
My Table crowns, my Cup it overflows.
Sufficient Clothes to keep our Bodies warm,
An House to shelter from the raging Storm,
The sacred Pages ever at my Side,
I may peruse and take them for my Guide.
That sacred Fountain, unexhausted Treasure,
O, may I read with Profit and with Pleasure!
O, thou Eternal Conditer of Heaven!
Who hast this Rule of Faith and Practice given.
Teach me to read thy Word both Night and Day,
And grant thy Spirit to direct my Way.
Lord guard my Feet from every fatal Snare,
And may my House be thy peculiar Care.
Protect my Orphans in their Infant State,
And teach me Lord, my House to regulate.
May they be early taught in Wisdom's Way,
And be their Guide until their dying Day.
Lord thou hast promis'd in thy Word to be,
A God and Father to my Babes and me.
I plead thy Promise Lord, do not deny,
It is the Word of him who cannot lie.
That Promise which Eternal Goodness spoke,
Sure everlasting Truth will not revoke.
Thy awful Frown has brought me very low;
I'm scarcely able to endure the Blow;
Yet thy chastising Hand I would adore,
And humbly thy supporting Arm implore.
Shew Pity Lord, and lend a gracious Ear
To my Request, and my Petition hear.

By PETER ST. JOHN, of Norwalk.

No. 22
ON THE DEATH OF FIVE YOUNG MEN WHO WAS MURTHERED, MAR. 5, 1770

[*The Massachusetts Historical Society* (Photostat)]

SIZE, 5½ by 12½ inches. This broadside was reproduced in the "Massachusetts Historical Society Proceedings," LVI (1923), opposite p. 268. At the time of this reproduction, the original was owned by Mr. Frank E. Heald of Manchester, New Hampshire. The sheet was probably printed by Edes and Gill, publishers of the *Boston Gazette and Country Journal*. They had used four of the coffin cuts (said to have been made by Paul Revere) in the *Gazette* of March 12, and the fifth in the issue of March 19.

The elegy honors the five victims of the Boston Massacre of March 5, 1770, an event which aroused all America, and especially Boston. Their names, indicated by the initials on the five coffins, were Samuel Gray, Samuel Maverick, James Caldwell, Crispus Attucks, and Patrick Carr. The hourglass on the coffin of Samuel Maverick was intended as a reminder of his extreme youth. He was seventeen years old. Patrick Carr lived until March 14. This broadside was probably issued soon after his funeral, which took place on March 17. A detailed account of the funeral ceremonies for the first four victims is included in the *Gazette* account of March 12, which states:

It is supposed that there must have been a greater Number of People from Town and Country at the Funeral of those who were massacred by the Soldiers, than were ever together on this Continent on any Occasion.

John Rowe is more specific. He wrote in his *Diary*,

. . . Such a Concourse of People I never saw before—I believe Ten or Twelve thousand. One Corps with their Relations followed the other then the Select Men Inhabitants. . . . *Letters and Diary of John Rowe, Boston Merchant* (Boston, 1903), p. 199.

By the 29th Regiment
In command of Thomas Preston. He was judged "Not Guilty" at the conclusion of his trial in October of the same year. For a complete account of the proceedings, see *A Short Narrative of the Horrid Massacre in Boston*, published by the town, 1770. It is included in Frederic Kidder's *History of the Boston Massacre* (Albany, 1870).

King-street
Where the riot occurred. The funeral procession also started in King Street.

And let successive Years augment your PRAISE.
This Anniversary was kept annually until 1784, when it was supplanted by the Fourth of July celebration.

On the Death of Five young Men who was Murthered, *March* 5th 1770. By the 29th Regiment.

MOURN O my Friends, let solemn numbers flow,
From thy sad thoughts, fit for the scenes of Woe
For in *King-Street* their breathless Bodies lay ;
For Dead, ah ! Dead for ever Dead are they.

By cruel Soldiers, five Men were slain,
Their everlasting happiness to gain ;
And when fierce Troops urg'd thick on ev'ry Side,
They spurn'd their Fate, and spread Destruction wide.

Till in their Bodies log'd the fatal Lead,
Beat low the Force of Life, and left them dead ;
They have made their Dress with scarlet Flame :
Like the deep red which speaks a modest Shame.

My streaming Eyes gush plenteous o'er their hearse,
While thus I strove, the fading honours of my Verse ;
For who unmov'd can see their lovely Limbs,
Stretch'd on the Ground, and dy'd with purple Streams.

But now, O ! dreadful thoughts, eternal Night,
Has clos'd their Eyes, and veil'd them out of sight ;
Shall then the Murd'rers eternal live :
And all the waste of envious Time survive.

While their sad Fate employs a silent woe,
And Death shall seize their Name and Body too :
Now live dear Youth's, green with immortal Bays,
And let successive Years augment your PRAISE.

FINIS

A FEW THOUGHTS COMPOS'D ON THE SUDDEN & AWFUL DEATH OF MRS. FESSENDEN, MAY 30, 1770

[The Massachusetts Historical Society]

SIZE, 8 by 14 inches. The Milk Street address does not identify the printer with certainty, but the sheet may have been printed by Seth Adams and John Kneeland, who had a printing office in Milk Street about this time. The piece is of interest chiefly as a specimen of the funeral elegy turning into a ballad. It is less a tribute to Mrs. Fessenden than a tale of parted lovers for which her tragedy supplies details.

Mrs. Fessenden's death resulted from an accident, an account of which is given in the *Boston Gazette and Country Journal* of June 4, 1770. The elegist did not see fit to use all the details, which are as follows:

Boston, June 4. We hear from Cambridge, That last Wednesday Afternoon Mrs. Fessenden, Wife of Mr. Nathaniel Fessenden of that Town, was unhappily killed by the following Accident, viz. A Number of Persons had been shooting at Marks, and after they had done, went to the House of Mr. Philip Beamis, Father to the unfortunate deceas'd, and put their Guns against the House, when a Lad of about 13 Years old, took one of the Guns not knowing it to be loaded, and snap'd it at a Girl in order to frighten her, when the Gun went off; but it missing the Girl, the Ball went in Mrs. Fessenden's eye, lodg'd in her Head, and killed her instantly. Mrs. Fessenden had her Infant about Nine Months old in her Lap, which providentially was unhurt. She was the only Daughter of Mr. Beamis; and it is remarkable the Gun by which she was kill'd belong'd to her Husband. Mrs. Fessenden was a Woman of unblemish'd Virtue, and her chief Ornament was *Modesty*—Her untimely Death is lamented by all her Acquaintance, and her Husband in particular, *refuses to be comforted*.

Election Day

The day provided by the Royal Charter for the election of Counselors for the province. On this day the General Court administered oaths to the members of the House of Representatives. There was a procession to the meeting-house, and an election-day sermon.

He kissed her Clay Lips so sweet,

It is unusual to find traditional ballad conventions of this sort in American funeral elegies. But by 1770, the elegist no longer spoke the language of the pulpit.

A few Thoughts compos'd on the sudden & awful *Death* of Mrs. *Fessenden*, wife of Mr. *Nathanael* *Fessenden*, of *Cambridge*, who was shot May 30, 1770.

I.
I Pray all People lend an Ear,
To these few Lines which you may hear;
A stranger Thing you never knew,
Although it is most certain true.

II.
In Cambridge liv'd a loving Pair,
A tender Wife and Husband dear;
Whose kind Behaviour was so free,
That in all Things they did agree.

III.
They always bore a constant Mind,
A truer Love we ne'er can find;
When very young they did agree,
As by the Sequel you may see.

IV.
For when in Love they did engage,
She was but eleven Years of Age;
But yet she constant was and true,
This I affirm, for well I knew.

V.
A true Contraction there was made,
Betwixt this Gentleman and Maid;
And when to Age they did appear,
They married were, as we do hear.

VI.
They liv'd a very happy Life,
For this young Man ador'd his Wife;
And ev'ry one that lived by,
Did much admire her Modesty.

VII.
She was a hopeful modest Youth,
And in all things she lov'd the Truth;
A soberer one you'll seldom see,
But yet she was both kind and free.

VIII.
She lov'd her Husband tenderly,
And in her Heart he was quite nigh;
Their kind Affection was so sweet,
A happier Pair did never meet.

IX.
But cruel Death hath her beguil'd,
She's left her Husband and dear Child;
And ev'ry one that did her know,
For to lament her Overthrow.

X.
On Election Day we well do know,
She to her Father's House did go,
For to respect her Parents dear;
But Oh! how dreadful 'tis to hear.

XI.
That she away from home must go,
To meet this awful fatal Blow!
She had been there scarce half a Day,
Before that she was snatch'd away.

XII.
This harmless Creature there did sit,
Embracing of her Infant sweet,
When Death did send this fatal Ball,
Which prov'd her sad and dismal Fall.

XIII.
Oh! how distressing 'twas to see,
Her sent into Eternity!.
Without one Moment for to know,
Where then that she was bound to go.

XIV.
'Twas 'nough to make one's Heart to ake,
To see this awful turn of Fate;
And see her in her Blood to lie,
And in a Moment forc'd to die!

XV.
Her pretty Babe was in her Arms,
Not knowing or fearing any Harm!
And hanging on it's Mother's Breast,
When she was snatch'd away by Death.

XVI.
Oh! how affecting it must be,
Unto all them that did it see!
This harmless Babe lay in the Blood,
That ran from it's Mother like a Flood.

XVII.
How distressing it was to hear,
Her kind and tender Husband dear
A weeping over his sweet Wife,
The Joy and Comfort of his Life.

XVIII.
He kissed her Clay Lips so sweet,
When they were almost cold with Death!
Oh! this would melt a stony Heart,
That these two Lovers so must part.

XIX.
The tender Parents of the Dead,
Refused to be comforted!
And all the People every where,
In Floods of Tears they did appear.

XX.
And in the Year when she did die,
Was Seventeen Hundred and Seventy
She was not nineteen Years of Age,
When she did leave this earthly Stage.

XXI.
And now to you her Husband dear,
Be pleas'd with these few Lines to hear
Oh! now refrain your flowing Tears,
Your Wife is gone beyond your Cares.

XXII.
We trust that she in Heav'n is lodg'd,
With Christ th' eternal Son of God;
And in due Time I hope you'll be,
With her to all Eternity.

BOSTON: Printed and Sold in MILK-STREET, 1770.

No. 24

AN ELEGIAC POEM, ON THE DEATH OF THAT CELEBRATED DIVINE, AND EMINENT SERVANT OF JESUS CHRIST, THE LATE REVEREND, AND PIOUS GEORGE WHITEFIELD; SEPT. 30, 1770

BY PHILLIS

[*The Pennsylvania Historical Society*]

SIZE, 9½ by 15 inches. Advertised for sale, October 15, 1770, in the *Boston Gazette and Country Journal*, as "Sold by Ezekiel Russell in Queen-Street, and John Boyles, in Marlboro-Street." The advertisement was repeated in other newspapers of the same month. For other broadside imprints which survive, see Ford, 1546–1560, 3388.

George Whitefield was one of the sensations of his day, both in England and America. He was born December 16, 1714, in Gloucester, England, and educated at Pembroke College, Oxford. While there, he came under the influence of John Wesley, and although he subsequently took orders in the Church of England, his unorthodox views and methods closed many pulpits to him, and he became an itinerant preacher, speaking in the fields as often as in the churches. He first embarked for America in 1737 on a mission to Georgia, and subsequently spent much of his time in the colonies. He made in all seven visits, most of them of several years' duration. His name was widely known, and his revivals the occasion for much opposition and controversy, particularly in New England, where his preaching did much to break up the old order. He died September 30, 1770, at Newburyport, Massachusetts, and was buried before the pulpit of the Presbyterian Church, in which he was to have preached on the day of his death. He was the subject of numerous elegies and tributes.

Phillis, his present elegist, was a negro servant, belonging to Mr. John Wheatley of Boston. She attracted some attention for a time, because of a volume of poetry, attested to be hers, which was published in London in 1773. It was entitled *Poems on Various Subjects, Religious and Moral.* Phillis was taken to London in that year and introduced to various persons of prominence, but her vogue was short-lived, and had more to do with her race and condition than with the merit of her verse. She died in 1784.

the Countess of Huntington
> She was also the friend and benefactress of Phillis, whose volume was dedicated to her. She was chiefly known for her religious interests, having founded a sect of Calvinistic Methodists, popularly called "Lady Huntington's Connection."

the Orphan Children in Georgia
> The occasion of Whitefield's first visit to America had been the establishing of an "orphan-house" in Georgia. It was built in 1740, at Bethesda, and was thereafter one of his dearest concerns. At his death, the management was left to the Countess of Huntington.

An ELEGIAC
POEM,

On the DEATH of that celebrated Divine, and eminent Servant of JESUS CHRIST, the late Reverend, and pious

GEORGE WHITEFIELD,

Chaplain to the Right Honourable the Countess of Huntingdon, &c &c.

Who made his Exit from this transitory State, to dwell in the celestial Realms of

Bliss, on LORD's-Day, 30th of September, 1770, when he was seiz'd with a Fit of the Asthma, at Newbury-Port, near Boston, in New-England. In which is a Condolatory Address to His truly noble Benefactress the worthy and pious 'Lady Huntingdon,---and the Orphan-Children in Georgia; who, with many Thousands, are left, by the Death of this great Man, to lament the Loss of a Father, Friend, and Benefactor.

By Phillis, a Servant Girl of 17 Years of Age, belonging to Mr. J. Wheatley, of Boston :---And has been but 9 Years in this Country from Africa.

HAIL happy Saint on thy immortal throne !
  To thee complaints of grievance are unknown ;
We hear no more the music of thy tongue,
Thy wonted auditories cease to throng.
Thy lessons in unequal'd accents flow'd !
While emulation in each bosom glow'd ;
Thou didst, in strains of eloquence refin'd,
Inflame the soul, and captivate the mind.
Unhappy we, the setting Sun deplore !
Which once was splendid, but it shines no more ;
He leaves this earth for Heaven's unmeasur'd height :
And worlds unknown, receive him from our sight ;
There WHITEFIELD wings, with rapid course his way,
And sails to Zion, through vast seas of day.

When his AMERICANS were burden'd sore,
When streets were crimson'd with their guiltless gore !
Unrival'd friendship in his breast now strove :
The fruit thereof was charity and love
Towards *America*-----couldst thou do more
Than leave thy native home, the *British* shore,
To cross the great Atlantic's wat'ry road,
To see *America*'s distress'd abode ?
Thy prayers, great Saint, and thy incessant cries,
Have pierc'd the bosom of thy native skies !
Thou moon hast seen, and ye bright stars of light
Have witness been of his requests by night !
He pray'd that grace in every heart might dwell :
He long'd to see *America* excell ;
He charg'd its youth to let the grace divine
Arise, and in their future actions shine ;
He offer'd THAT he did himself receive,

A greater gift not GOD himself can give :
He urg'd the need of HIM to every one ;
It was no less than GOD's co-equal SON !
Take HIM ye wretched for your only good ;
Take HIM ye starving souls to be your food.
Ye thirsty, come to this life giving stream :
Ye Preachers, take him for your joyful theme :
Take HIM, "my dear AMERICANS," he said,
Be your complaints in his kind bosom laid :
Take HIM ye *Africans*, he longs for you ;
Impartial SAVIOUR, is his title due ;
If you will chuse to walk in grace's road,
You shall be sons, and kings, and priests to GOD.

Great COUNTESS ! we *Americans* revere
Thy name, and thus condole thy grief sincere :
We mourn with thee, that TOMB obscurely plac'd,
In which thy Chaplain undisturb'd doth rest.
New-England sure, doth feel the ORPHAN'S smart ;
Reveals the true sensations of his heart :
Since this fair Sun, withdraws his golden rays,
No more to brighten these distressful days !
His lonely *Tabernacle*, sees no more
A WHITEFIELD landing on the *British* shore :
Then let us view him in yon azure skies :
Let every mind with this lov'd object rise.
No more can he exert his lab'ring breath,
Seiz'd by the cruel messenger of death.
What can his dear AMERICA return ?
But drop a tear upon his happy urn,
Thou tomb, shalt safe retain thy sacred trust
Till life divine re-animate his dust.

We hear no more the music of thy tongue,

> The extraordinary voice of Whitefield is almost as frequently remarked as his doctrines. He is said to have been heard by 20,000 in his open-air sermons. Benjamin Franklin's oft-cited computation, based upon personal experiment, placed the figure at 30,000. *Autobiography,* "Works" (Smyth ed., 1905), I, 358.

Thy wonted auditories cease to throng.

> The crowds that flocked to hear him were undiminished to the end. For his six o'clock morning sermon, the congregation would often begin to assemble as early as three.

When streets were crimson'd with their guiltless gore!

> In the Boston Massacre of March 5, 1770. Whitefield had given evidence of his sympathy with America's resentment.

his lab'ring breath

> He had died of asthma. After speaking for years from forty to sixty hours a week, he had been obliged, toward the end of his life, to put himself "on short allowance," as he said. By this he meant, to preach once a day, and three times on Sunday.

No. 25

A HYMN, COMPOSED BY THE REVEREND MR. WHITEFIELD, TO BE SUNG OVER HIS OWN CORPS, MAY 1, 1764

[*The Pennsylvania Historical Society*]

SIZE, 8½ by 13⅞ inches. Three other issues of this hymn are extant. (Cf. Ford, 1555, 1556, 1560.) A fourth, which apparently has not survived, was advertised in the *Essex Gazette* of October 9, 1770, as printed by Samuel Hall, to be sold the following day. Verses on Whitefield were to be printed on the same sheet. The present issue is interesting as exhibiting neater workmanship on the part of the printer than was customary, even as late as 1770.

A HYMN,

Compoſed by the Reverend

Mr. Whitefield,

To be ſung over his own Corps.

Taken from the Original, May 1, 1764.

AH ! Lovely appearance of death,
 No ſight upon earth is ſo fair ;
Not all the gay pageants that breathe,
 Can with a dead body compare.
With ſolemn delight I ſurvey
 The corps when the ſpirit is fled ;
In love with the beautiful clay,
 And longing to lay in his ſtead.

How bleſt is our brother bereſt
 Of all that could burthen his mind ;
How eaſy the ſoul that has left
 This weariſome body behind.
Of evil incapable thou,
 Whoſe relicks with envy I ſee,
No longer in miſery now,
 No longer a ſinner like me.

This Earth is afflicted no more
 With ſickneſs—or ſhaken with pain ;
The war in the members is o'er,
 And never will vex him again.
No anger henceforward or ſhame,
 Shall redden his innocent clay ;
Extinct is the animal flame,
 And paſſion is vaniſh'd away.

This languiſhing head is at reſt,
 Its thinking and aching are o'er ;
This quiet immoveable breaſt,
 Is heav'd by affliction no more.
This heart is no longer the ſeat
 Of trouble and torturing pain ;
It ceaſes to flutter and beat,
 It never ſhall flutter again.

The lids he ſo ſeldom could cloſe,
 By ſorrow forbidden to ſleep,
Seal'd up in eternal repoſe,
 Have ſtrangely forgotten to weep.
The fountains can yield no ſupplies,
 Theſe hollows from waters are free ;
The tears are all wip'd from theſe eyes,
 And evil they never ſhall ſee.

To mourn and to ſuffer is mine,
 While bound in this priſon I breathe,
And ſtill for deliverance pine,
 And preſs to the iſſues of death.
Wh.t now with my tears I bedew,
 O might I this moment become ;
My ſpirit created anew,
 My fleſh be conſign'd to the tomb.

Mr. Whitefield,

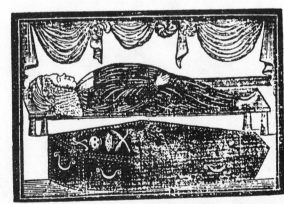

This FIGURE repreſents dreſs'd as he was laid out & buried.

No. 26

A FUNERAL ELEGY, OCCASIONED BY THE TRAGEDY, AT SALEM, JUNE 17, 1773

[*The Boston Public Library*]

Size, about 10 by 17½ inches, with edges trimmed. The torn lower left-hand margin may have contained a colophon. These verses show the funeral elegy turning into a versified news account in ballad stanza. For other imprints called forth by this tragedy, see Ford, 1679, 1681. The *Essex Gazette* for June 22, 1773, prints a detailed account of this shipwreck, which is described as "one of the most melancholy and distressing Events that ever happened in or near this Place."

Thursday Aft[ernoon]
[and Thr]ee Men
The dismal Boat and Relicts they
    Possibly *relicts* in the sense of *remains* of those deceased (a rare usage), or possibly in the sense of *survivors*.
Urns
    Coffins. The word is often used in this sense.
Corpse
    The next stanza suggests that the author is probably referring to the funeral procession.

A FUNERAL ELEGY, occasioned by the
TRAGEDY,

At SALEM, near BOSTON, on Thursday Aft — —the Seventeenth of JUNE, 1773, at which Time the 10 following Persons, Seven Women and Three Men were drowned, having been out on a Party of Pleasure : Their Names are,

Mrs. SARAH BECKET, Wife of Mr. John Becket, jun. Boatbuilder, and Daughter of Mr. William Brown, deceased.—Mr. NATHANIEL DIGGADON, Tidewaiter, and Mrs. DIGGADON, his Wife.—Mr. WILLIAM WARD, Boatman, and Mrs. MARY WARD, his Wife, Daughter of Mr. John Masary.—Miss ESTHER MASURY, Sister to Mrs. Ward.—Mrs. DESIRE HOLMAN, Wife of Mr. John Holman, Mariner, now at Sea.—Mr. PAUL KIMBALL, Cooper, and Mrs. LYDIA KIMBALL, his Wife, Daughter of Dr. Fairfield. Mrs. REBECCA GILES, Widow of the late Mr. Eleazer Giles, and Laughter of Capt. John White. Mr. Becket and a Lad were saved.

I.
AWAKE, my Muse, and tune the Song
To harp a doleful Sound,
Enough to melt the mournful Throng,
Which echoes o'er the Ground.

II.
What Heart but feels the heavy Stroke
Sent by GOD's awful Hand,
When Ten poor Souls were lately cast
Ashore upon the Sand.

III.
Think, O poor SALEM, think upon,
And hear this dreadful Thing,
e'er let it pass without Regret ;
But fear your heav'nly KING.

IV.
Yes, ten poor Souls I've heard them say
Went lately to the Bottom :
SALEM, O let it not be said
Their Names were e'er forgotten.

V.
May we not say Fifteen poor Souls
Were plunged in the Sea,
As Five th' unhappy Women were
Advanc'd in Pregnancy.

VI.
A shocking Sight must it not seem,
And dismal for to see
The loving Husband and the Wife
Who once did well agree ?

VII.
Now they embrace each other's Arms,
And take a watry Grave ;
All Nature sure it must alarm
To see that Men can't save.

VIII.
O who could bear to hear the Shrieks
And Cries none could prevent,

Among these wretched dismal Souls,
It makes my Heart relent.

IX.
The tender Hand of Help was near,
No Help it could afford,
Though Friends were nigh, behold and cry
They could not get aboard.

X.
May grateful Thanks be ever paid
To MARBLEHEAD's kind Town;
Whose Hearts relent,* their Strength they spent
And sav'd Two Souls not drown'd.

XI.
When Gentle, Simple, all agree
To lend an aiding Hand,
With Heart and Voice they now rejoice
To form a helping Band.

XII.
Their pitying Hand was kindly shewn,
May it remember'd be,
When Friends, Relatives, Neighbours were
So late drown'd in the Sea.

XIII.
The dismal Boat and Relicts they
With much Ado did save,
To SALEM Wharff they landed them,
For which kind Thanks they have.

XIV
Alass, who then but grieves and mourns,
With many a Sigh and Tear,
Beholding of their dismal Urns,
Their Corpse is drawing near.

XV.
Hark, hark ! we hear the passing Bell,
Along as they do go ;
Traveller, stop and shed a Tear,
This is a Scene of Woe.

---

* Surely no one can fully express the horror and anguish of mind these people's friends at Marblehead must suffer (who are remarkable for their hospitality even to distressed strangers : much more affecting then must it be for them to have such a loud call from their relatives and neighbours for relief, without a possibility of affording them the least help) on viewing them perishing, as it were, at their elbows, they being scarcely one hundred yards from the unhappy Sufferers, and not able to lend them assistance, by reason of the tempestuous weather at the time this fatal disaster happened. It must shock the imagination, and cause the most hard hearted person to relent with pity and compassion, who reflects on the calamitous situation of these distressed Objects in general, but of the women in particular, the circumstances of five of them being peculiarly critical, makes this mournful affair more affecting. O who could bear the excruciating pain of heart it must give the mourning Spectators on hearing the horrid screeches,

dismal lamentations and bitter groans of these poor souls on this solemn event, which seemed to rend the heavens, and to make all nature shudder ! What female hearts, especially of those who are mothers, but must feel and sympathize with the tenderest sensations of pity on this melancholy occasion ! What bowel of compassion but must yearn at this awful providence ! In short, such was the direful consequence resulting from this amazing catastrophe, and which must form such a shocking scene, that it can better be imagined than expressed : For even an attempt to describe the same would be as vain as it would be impossible. Suffice it to say, we believe such a tragical scene never before happened in NEW-ENGLAND or AMERICA since its first discovery, and GOD grant we may never hear of the like again. But may we all make a right improvement of such an awful warning as this from GOD, who is continually saying not only by this but by many other awakening dispensations and calls, BE YE ALSO READY.
A FRIEND TO THE DECEASED

(Price Coppers.)

No. 27
AN ELEGY, OCCASIONED BY THE MELANCHOLLY CATAS-
TROPHE, WHICH HAPPEN'D IN THE NIGHT
OF THE 10TH OF AUGUST, 1774

[The Pennsylvania Historical Society]

SIZE, 9 by 14⅛ inches. The Milk Street office was probably that of John Knee-land, who continued to print here after 1772, when his partnership with Seth Adams was dissolved.

Boston's early history contains the record of many tragic fires. Cf. pp. 71, 75, *infra*, for other verses, not in elegiac form, written on the fires of 1760 and 1787. This fire of 1774 is recorded in the "Diary of Mr. Thomas Newell of Boston" ("Massachusetts Historical Society Proceedings," XV [1877], p. 356), as follows:

Aug. 10, 1774.
This night, about 11 o'clock, a fire broke out in a large brick house in Fish Street. The fire had got to such height before the unhappy tenants were apprised of it, that the following unhappy persons perished in the flames: viz. Mrs. Ruth Murphy, far gone with child; Ruth and Catherine Murphy, her children; Mrs. Elly Flinn, and Mrs. Hannah Whittemore.

John Rowe, whose *Diary* of this period makes mention of many fires, does not speak of this one in Fish Street. Boston newspapers contain detailed accounts, which were widely copied.

Last Night! But Oh how dreadful to relate!
One of the numerous suggestions of immediacy in compositions of this sort.

An E L E G Y,

O C C A S I O N E D   B Y

The Melancholly Cataftrophe,

'Which happen'd in the Night of the 10th. of Auguft, 1774 :)

In which the following Perfons perifhed in the unrelenting Flames, which fpread with fuch Rapidity through every Part of their Habitation, that it was beyond the Power of their fympathizing Friends to afford them any Relief, viz. Mrs. *Murphy and her two fmall Children,* Mrs. *Fling* and Mrs. *Whitemore,* the Remains of whofe Bodies being by their Friends taken from the Rubbifh, afforded a Spectacle truly melancholly.

THERE's not a Day goes by, but we behold,
A Truth, that Men need often to be told :
That this vain World with all it's glitt'ring Toys,
Does but deceive the Mind with empty Joys.
This Truth, the melancholly Tale I fing
To ev'ry Mortal's Mind will fober bring.
Laft Night ! But Oh how dreadful to relate !
Five fuch as we were fummon'd hence by Fate !
When the bright Sun it's genial Rays withdrew,
And in it's Stead appear'd Night's fable Hue ;
When bufy Mortals quit the Scenes of Day,
Thefe, like all others, did to Reft away ;
To Reft indeed ! 'Till the Arch Angel's Sound
Shall rend the Graves and fhake the rugged Ground.
When Sleep it's kindly Influence beftow'd,
Hufband and Wife and Children too it fhow'd :
But when the Fire ! Oh moft unnat'ral Day !
Did from our Eye-Lids chafe fweet Sleep away,
Nought to our fympathizing View appears,
But a fond Hufband drown'd in Grief and Tears.
Say you who do poffefs this tender Name ;
You, who though two, are yet in Mind the fame :

Say you whom Heaven's moft indulgent King,
Has blefs'd with Children blooming as the Spring ;
What various Paffions would your Minds poffefs,
By Turns the Hufband, then the Sire exprefs.
The Wheels of Time in quick Rotation mov'd,
And you depriv'd of what you dearly lov'd.
What pleafing Schemes, and what fond Dreams of Joy,
Does fuch a Night as this intire deftroy !
Impartial Death, nor Old nor Young regards,
Though unknown Reafons oft the Stroke retards ;
Thefe unknown Reafons here were far remov'd,
And old and young alike his conquer'd prov'd :
The aged Matrons now their Courfe have run,
And pratling Infants rifing like the Sun.
What pleafing Scenes to Day may we behold !
And what dread Things To-morrow may unfold !
And what's more true than that which Ifrael's King,
Long fince declar'd of every earthly Thing !
They nought prefent, that Man can fatisfy,
But one by one is ftampt with Vanity.

A BLOODY BUTCHERY, BY THE BRITISH TROOPS: OR, THE RUNAWAY FIGHT OF THE REGULARS, APR. 19, 1775

[The Essex Institute]

SIZE, 15 by 19½ inches. Printed in Salem by Ezekiel Russell. This piece is more interesting as a contemporary news account of the battle of Lexington and Concord, than as a funeral elegy for the slain. The battle, characterized in the heading as an event "on which, perhaps, may depend the future FREEDOM, and GREATNESS of the COMMON-WEALTH of AMERICA," took place on April 19, and marked the outbreak of actual hostilities in the War of the Revolution. The news account here reprinted had appeared in Russell's *Salem Gazette* on April 21; the elegy, in the *Essex Journal and Merrimack Packet* on April 26. This broadside was probably issued soon after May 5, the date of the Salem item included. The conventionality of the elegy is easily explained. In the midst of stirring events, the author reverted to the traditional elegiac form, which long practice had made easy to write, and which would be understood by all. The torn portion of the news account reads as follows:

By an account of the loss of the enemy, said to have come from an officer of one of the men of war, it appears that sixty-three of the regulars, and forty-nine marines were killed, and one hundred and three of both wounded: In all two hundred and fifteen. Lieut. *Gould*, of the fourth regiment who is wounded, and Lieut. *Potter*, of the marines, and about twelve soldiers, are prisoners.

Mr. *James Howard* and one of the regulars discharged their pieces at the same instant, and each killed the other. The public most sincerely sympathize with the friends and relations of our deceased brethren, who gloriously sacrificed their lives in fighting for the liberties of their country. By their noble, intrepid conduct, in helping to defeat the forces of an ungrateful Tyrant, they have endeared their memories to the present generation, who will transmit their names to posterity with the highest honor.

The above account is the best we have been able to obtain. We can only add, that the town of *Boston* is now invested with a vast army of our brave Countrymen, who have flown to our assistance from all quarters. GOD grant them assistance in the extirpation of our cruel and unnatural enemies.

Salem, May 5.

On the nineteenth of April were killed, among others, by the *British* troops, at *Menotomy*, as he was courageously defending his country's rights, the good, the pious, and friendly Mr. Daniel Townsend, of *Lynn-End*.

Rob. Monroe, Jonas Parker, Samuel Hadley, J. Harrington, C. Harrington, Isaac Muzzy, John Brown, John Raymond, Nat. Wyman, Jed. Munroe, Jason Russell, Jabez Wyman, Jas. Winship, Deacon Haynes, — Reed, Capt. Miles, Capt. Wilson, Capt. Davis, — Horsmer, J. Howard.

Azael Porter, Dan. Thompson, Jam. Miller, W Barber's son, Isaac Gardner, John Hicks, Hen. Putnam, Ab. Ramsdell, D. Townsend, Will. Flint, Thomas Hadley, Henry Jacobs, Sam. Cook, Ebe. Goldthwait, Geo Southwick, Ben. Daland, Jot Webb, Per. Putnam, Benj. Pierce, — Kennison.

A BLOODY BUTCHERY, BY THE BRITISH TROOPS: OR, THE RUNAWAY FIGHT OF THE REGULARS.

Being the PARTICULARS of the VICTORIOUS BATTLE fought at and near CONCORD, situated Twenty Miles from BOSTON, in the Province of the MASSACHUSETTS-BAY, in NEW-ENGLAND, between Two Thousand REGULAR TROOPS, belonging to his BRITANNIC MAJESTY, and a few Hundred PROVINCIAL TROOPS, belonging to the Province of MASSACHUSETTS-BAY, which lasted from Sunrise to Sunset of the Nineteenth of APRIL, One Thousand Seven Hundred and Seventy-five, when it was decided greatly in favor of the latter. Part of which has never before been printed. These Particulars are now published in this cheap Form, at the Request of the Friends to the Deceased WORTHIES, who died gloriously fighting in the CAUSE OF LIBERTY and their COUNTRY; and it is their Desire that every Housholder in AMERICA, who are sincere Well-wishers to the AMERICAN COLONIES, may be possessed of the same, either to frame and glass, or otherwise to preserve in their Houses, not only as a Token of Gratitude to the Memory of the DECEASED FORTY PERSONS, but as a perpetual Memorial of that important event, on which, perhaps, may depend the future FREEDOM and GREATNESS of the COMMON-WEALTH of AMERICA. To which is annexed, A FUNERAL ELEGY on those who were slain in the Battle.

From E. RUSSELL's *Salem* Gazette, or *Newbury* and *Marblehead* Advertiser, published on Friday, April 21, 1775.

ON Tuesday evening the eighteenth instant, a body of soldiers under the command of Lieutenant-Colonel *Smith*, to the amount of about eight hundred men, embarked from *Barton*'s-Point, in *Boston*, about eleven o'clock, crossed *Charles*-River, landed at *Phips*'s-Farm, in *Cambridge*, and marched immediately up to *Lexington*, near twelve miles from *Boston*; at sunrise they observing between thirty and forty inhabitants exercising near the meeting-house, the Commanding-Officer ordered them to lay down their arms and disperse, which not being directly complied with, he "*damned them for a pack of rebels*," ordered his men to fire upon them, and killed eight men on the spot, besides wounding several more. The army then proceeded to *Concord*, drew up on the parade, near the meeting-house, during which time the inhabitants from the neighboring towns collected and took possession of the adjacent hills; about eleven o'clock the firing began on both sides, which lasted near an hour, when the regular troops began to retreat, the provincials closely pursuing them to a bridge at a small distance, which the regulars took up as they passed; they then renewed the fire, and some were slain on both sides; but the regulars still retreated, and the provincials pursued them down to *Lexington*, where the regulars, about three o'clock in the afternoon, met with a reinforcement of about twelve hundred men, commanded by Earl *Percy*, with two brass field pieces; they again renewed the attack upon the provincials, but soon thought proper further to retreat towards their head-quarters, the provincials pursued them into *Charlestown*, where they arrived about sunset; taking immediately an advantageous post on *Bunker*'s-Hill, about a mile from the ferry; the provincials now discontinued the contest. The loss on either side we have not yet been able to ascertain, but it is said about one hundred regulars were killed and fifty wounded, among which were several officers: Two officers and a number of soldiers were taken prisoners. On the part of the province, we hear that thirty-five were slain, and several wounded. The above is as particular an account of the engagement, as can at this time be collected, in the present confused state of the province.

We hear an officer and his servant, with two pair of pistols, were yesterday taken and secured by our people, at *Roxbury*, on their way to Castle-*William*.

SALEM, Apr. 25.

LAST Wednesday, the nineteenth of *April*, the troops of his *Britannic* Majesty commenced hostilities upon the people of this province, attended with circumstances of cruelty not less brutal than what our venerable Ancestors received from the vilest savages of the wilderness. The particulars relative to this interesting event, by which we are involved in all the horrors of a civil war, we have endeavored to collect as well as the present confused state of affairs will admit.

On Tuesday evening a detachment from the army, consisting, it is said, of eight or nine hundred men, commanded by Lieutenant-Colonel *Smith*, embarked at the bottom of the common in *Boston*, on board a number of boats, and landed at *Phips*'s farm, a little way up *Charles-River*, from whence they proceeded with silence and expedition, on their way to *Concord*, about eighteen miles from *Boston*. The people were soon alarmed, and began to assemble, in several towns, before day-light, in order to watch the motion of the troops. At *Lexington*, six miles below *Concord*, a company of militia, of about one hundred men, mustered near the meeting-house; the troops came in sight of them just before sun-rise; and running within a few rods of them, the Commanding-Officer accosted the militia in words to this effect:—"*Disperse you rebels—Damn you, throw down your arms and disperse:*" Upon which the troops huzza'd, and immediately one or two officers discharged their pistols, which were instantaneously followed by the firing of four or five of the soldiers, and then there seemed to be a general discharge from the whole body: Eight of our men were killed, and nine wounded. In a few minutes after this action the enemy renewed their march for *Concord*; at which place they destroyed several carriages, carriage-wheels, and about twenty barrels of flour, all belonging to the province. Here about one hundred men going towards a bridge, of which the enemy were in possession, the latter fired, and killed two of our men, who then returned the fire, and obliged the enemy to retreat back to *Lexington*, where they met Lord *Percy*, with a large reinforcement, with two pieces of cannon. The enemy now having a body of about eighteen hundred men made a halt, picked up many of their dead, and took care of their wounded. At *Menotomy*, a few of our men, belonging to the detachment from *Lynn-End*, attacked a party of twelve of the enemy, (carrying stores and provisions to the troops) killed two of them, wounded several, took six prisoners, shot five horses, and took possession of all their arms, stores, provisions, &c. without any loss on our side; among those who were killed was a Lieutenant, who went with the provisions for his recreation, and to view the country, the officer of the guard who generally attends on such occasions being only a serjeant.—The enemy having halted one or two hours at *Lexington*, found it necessary to make a second retreat, carrying with them many of their dead and wounded, who they put into chaises and on horses that they found standing in the road. They continued their retreat from *Lexington* to *Charlestown* with great precipitation; and notwithstanding their field pieces our people continued the pursuit, firing at them until they got to *Charlestown* neck, (which they reached a little after sunset) over which the enemy passed, proceeded up *Bunker*'s-Hill, and soon afterwards went into the town, under the protection of the *Somerset* man of war of seventy-four guns.

In *Lexington* the enemy set fire to Deacon *Joseph Loring*'s house and barn, Mrs. *Mulliken*'s house and shop, and Mr. *Joshua Bond*'s house and shop, which were all consumed. They also set fire to several other houses, but our people extinguished the flames. They pillaged almost every house they passed by, breaking and destroying doors, windows, glasses, &c. and carrying off cloathing and other valuable effects. It appeared to be their design to burn and destroy all before them; and nothing but our vigorous pursuit prevented their infernal purposes from being put in execution. But the savage barbarity exercised upon the bodies of our unfortunate brethren who fell, is almost incredible: Not content with shooting down the unarmed, aged, and infirm, they disregarded the cries of the wounded, killing them without mercy, and mangling their bodies in the most shocking manner

We have the pleasure to say, that notwithstanding the highest provocations given by the enemy, not one instance of cruelty, that we have heard of, was committed by our victorious militia; but, listening to the merciful dictates of the christian religion, they "breathed higher sentiments of humanity."

By an account of the loss of the enemy, said to have come from an officer of one of the men of war, it appears that sixty-three of the regulars, and forty-nine marines were killed, and one hundred and three of both wounded: In all two hundred and fifteen. Lieut. *Gould*, of the [illegible]th regiment, who is wounded, and Lieut. *Potter*, of the marines, and about tw[illegible] soldiers, are prisoners.

Mr. *James Howard* and one of the reg[illegible] discharged their pieces at the same instant, and each killed the other.

The public most sincerely sympathize w[illegible] [fri]ends and relations of our deceased brethren, who gloriously sacrificed th[illegible] fighting for the liberties of their country. By their noble, intrepid [illegible] g to defeat the forces of an ungrateful Tyrant, they have ende[illegible] to the present generation, who will transmit their names [illegible] test honor.

The above account is the bes[illegible] obtain. We can only add, that the town of *Boston* is now inve[sted] [illegible] of our brave Countrymen, who have flown to our assistance fro[m] [illegible] GOD grant them assistance in the extirpation of our cruel and un[illegible]

SALE[M], [M]ay 5.

ON the nineteenth of April were k[illed] [am]ong others, by the *British* troops, at *Menotomy*, as he was courageou[sly] [defend]ing his country's rights, the good, the pious, and friendly Mr. DANIEL TOWNSEND, of *Lynn-End*. He was a constant and ready friend to the poor and afflicted; a good adviser in case of difficulty, and an able, mild, and sincere reprover of those who were out of the way. In short, he was a friend to his country, a blessing to society, and an ornament to the church, of which he was a member. He has left an amiable consort, and five young children, to bewail the loss.

Lie, valiant *Townsend*, in the peaceful shades.—We trust
Immortal honors mingle with thy d[ust]
What! tho' thy body struggled in its gore;
So did thy Savior's body long before;
And as he rais'd his own, by power divine;
So the same power shall also quicken thine,
And in eternal glory, mayst thou shine.

On Thursday the twentieth past, the bodies of eleven of the unfortunate persons who fell in the battle, were collected together and buried at *Medford*.

And on Friday the bodies of Messieurs HENRY JACOBS, SAMUEL COOK, EBENEZER GOLDTHWAIT, GEORGE SOUTHWICK, BENJAMIN DALAND, jun. JOTHAM WEBB, and PERLEY PUTNAM, of *Danvers*, who were likewise slain fighting in the GLORIOUS CAUSE OF LIBERTY AND THEIR COUNTRY, on the nineteenth of April, were respectfully interred among their friends in the different parishes belonging to that town, their corpse being attended to the place of interment by two companies of minute-men from this place, and a large concourse of people from this and the neighboring towns; previous to their interment, an excellent and well-adapted prayer was delivered by the Reverend Mr. HOLT, of that place.

Same day the remains of Messieurs AZAEL PORTER and DANIEL THOMPSON, of *Woburn*, who also fell victims to tyranny, were decently interred at that place, attended to the grave by a multitude of persons who assembled on the occasion from that and the neighboring towns. Before they were interred, a very suitable sermon and prayer was delivered by the Reverend Mr. SHERMAN.

Captain *Thomas Knight*, of the fifth regiment died at *Boston* next day after the engagement, of his wounds he received in the same. He was greatly regretted, being esteemed one of the best officers among the King's troops.

Lieut. *Hull*, of the regulars, died of his wounds on Wednesday last at the provincial hospital: His remains were next day conveyed to *Charlestown*, attended by a company of provincials, and several officers of distinction, and there delivered to the order of General *Gage*. Twenty-three wounded soldiers lately died at the Castle.

Lieutenant *Hawkshaw* was wounded in the cheek, and it is tho't will not recover.

Lieutenant *Gore*, was wounded in the arm: About 12 other officers are wounded.

We can assure the public, from the best authority, that our brethren, of all the colonies which we can yet have heard from are firm and unshaken in their attachment to the common cause of *America*; and that they are now ready, with their lives and fortunes, to assist us in defeating the cruel designs of our implacable enemies.

We have received no particulars of the transactions between General *Gage* and the inhabitants of *Boston*. It is certain that the people have delivered up their arms; very few of them have, however, been permitted to leave the town, notwithstanding the promise of the General.

The following is a List of the Provincials who were KILLED and WOUNDED.

BELONGING TO *LEXINGTON*.

KILLED.

1 * Mr. ROBERT MONROE,
2 * Mr. JONAS PARKER,
3 * Mr. SAMUEL HADLEY,
4 * Mr. JONATHAN HARRINGTON,
5 * Mr. CALEB HARRINGTON,
6 * Mr. ISAAC MUZZY,
7 * Mr. JOHN BROWN,
8 Mr. JOHN RAYMOND,
9 Mr. NATHANIEL WYMAN,
10 JEDIDIAH MONROE.

WOUNDED.

1 Mr. JOHN ROBBINS,
2 Mr. JOHN TIDD,
3 Mr. SOLOMON PIERCE,
4 Mr. THOMAS WINSHIP,
5 Mr. NATHAN FARMER,
6 Mr. JOSEPH COMEE,
7 Mr. EBENEZER MUNROE,
8 Mr. FRANCIS BROWN,
9 PRINCE EASTERBROOKS, (a Negro Man)

MENOTOMY.

KILLED.

11 Mr. JASON RUSSELL,
12 Mr. JABEZ WYMAN,
13 JASON WINSHIP.

MISSING, (supposed to be on board one of the men of war.)

Mr. SAMUEL FROST, Mr. SETH RUSSELL,

SUDBURY.

KILLED.

14 DEACON HAYNES, 15 Mr. —— REED.

CONCORD.

KILLED.

16 Captain JAMES MILES.

BEDFORD.

KILLED.

17 Captain JONATHAN WILLSON.

ACTON.

KILLED.

18 Captain DAVIS,
19 Mr. —— HORSMER,
20 Mr. JAMES HOWARD.

WOBURN.

KILLED.

21 * Mr. AZAEL PORTER, 22 Mr. DANIEL THOMPSON.

WOUNDED

10 Mr. GEORGE REED, 11 Mr. JACOB BACON.

CHARLESTOWN

23 Mr. JAMES MILLER, 24 Capt. WILLIAM BARBER's Son, aged 14.

BROOKLINE.

KILLED.

25 ISAAC GARDINER, Esquire.

CAMBRIDGE.

KILLED.

26 Mr. JOHN HICKS.

MEDFORD.

KILLED.

27 Mr. HENRY PUTNAM.

WOUNDED.

12 Mr. WILLIAM POLLY.

LYNN.

KILLED.

28 Mr. ABEDNEGO RAMSDELL,
29 DANIEL TOWNSEND,
30 WILLIAM FLINT,
31 THOMAS HADLEY.

WOUNDED.

13 Mr. JOSHUA FELT, 14 Mr. TIMOTHY MUNROE.

DANVERS.

KILLED

32 Mr. HENRY JACOBS,
33 Mr. SAMUEL COOK,
34 Mr. EBENEZER GOLDTHWAIT,
35 Mr. GEORGE SOUTHWICK,
36 Mr. BENJAMIN DALAND, jun.
37 Mr. JOTHAM WEBB,
38 PERLEY PUTNAM.

WOUNDED.

15 Mr. NATHAN PUTNAM, 16 Mr. DENNIS WALLIS.

SALEM

KILLED.

39 Mr. BENJAMIN PIERCE.

BEVERLY.

KILLED.

40 —— KENNISON.

WOUNDED.

17 Mr. SAMUEL WOODBURY. 18 Mr. NATHANIEL CLEAVES.

FRAMINGHAM.

19 Mr. —— HEMMENWAX.

BEDFORD.

20 Mr. JOHN LAKE.

Those distinguished with this mark [*] were killed by the first fire of the enemy.

SALEM, *N. E.* Printed and Sold by E. RUSSELL, at his Printing-Office, removed next Door to JOHN TURNER, Esq; in the Main-street.

A FUNERAL

ELEGY,

TO T[HE] IMORTAL [ME]MORY

Of those WORT[HIES who we]re slain in the [Ba]ttle of [illegible] 9. 1775. [illegible] assist,

[illegible]

Americans, go drop a tear
Where your slain brethren lay!
O! mourn and sympathize for them!
O! weep this very day!
What shall we say to this loud call
From the Almighty sent;
It surely bids both great and small
Seek GOD's face and repent.
Words can't express the ghastly scene
That here presents to view,
When forty [illegible] Countrymen
[illegible] are bi[illegible] dieu.
thi[illegible] must seem,
[illegible]
[illegible] children
[illegible] was sent.

The tender babes, nay those unborn,
O! dismal cruel death!
To snatch their fondest parents dear,
And leave them thus bereft.
O! *Lexington*, your loss is great!
Alass! too great to tell,
But justice bids me to relate
What to you has befell.
Ten of your hardy, bravest sons,
Some in their prime did fall;
May we no more hear noise of guns
To terrify us all.
Let's not forget the *Danvers* race,
So late in battle slain,
Their courage and their valor shewn
Upon the crimson'd plain.

Sev'n of your youthful sprightly sons
In the fierce fight were slain,
O! may your loss be all made up,
And prove a lasting gain.
Cambridge and *Medford*'s loss is great,
Though not like *Acton*'s town,
Whose three fierce military sons
Met their untimely doom.
Menotomy and *Charlestown* met
A sore and heavy stroke,
In losing five your brave townsmen
Who fell by tyrant's yoke.
Unhappy *Lynn* and *Beverly*,
Your loss I do bemoan,
Five your brave sons in dust doth lye,
Who late were in their bloom.

Bedford, *Woburn*, *Sudbury*, etc.
Have suffer'd most severe,
You miss five of your choicest chore,
On them let's drop a tear.
Concord your Captain's fate rehearse,
His loss is felt severe,
Come, brethren, join with me in verse,
His mem'ry hence revere.
O 'Squire *Gardiner*'s death we feel,
And sympathizing mourn,
Let's drop a tear when it we tell,
And view his hapless urn.
We sore regret poor *Pierce*'s death,
A stroke to *Salem*'s town,
Where tears did flow from ev'ry brow,
When the sad tidings come.

The groans of wounded, dying men,
Would melt the stoutest soul,
O! how it strikes thro' ev'ry vein,
My flesh and blood runs cold.
May all prepare to meet their fate
At GOD's tribunal bar,
And may war's terrible alarm
For death us now prepare.
Your Country calls you far and near,
America's sons 'wake,
Your helmet, buckler, and your spear,
The LORD's own arm now take.
His shield will keep us from all harm,
Tho' thousands 'gainst us rise,
His buckler we must sure put on,
If we would win the prize.

THE COLUMBIAN TRAGEDY, . . . A FUNERAL ELEGY
ON THE OCCASION, NOV. 4, 1791
[The New York Historical Society]

SIZE, 16⅝ by 21¾ inches. This is one of the latest examples of the funeral elegy in broadside form. For other issues see Ford, 2613, 2614. The New York Public Library possesses another issue, not listed by Mr. Ford.

The disaster which these verses record resulted from a surprise attack by the Indians upon the unprotected half of General Saint Clair's army near Fort Washington in the Northwest Territory, November 4, 1791. All America was aroused, and General Saint Clair was for a time the target for indignant and bitter criticism. He was later vindicated from all personal blame by the Congressional committee of investigation.

6. *And fatal prov'd of old,*
   The British had been twice unsuccessful in this same region.
8. *Where Braddock fell*
   General Braddock was defeated July 9, 1755, in a forest battle near Fort Duquesne. His failure was in part attributed to his unwillingness to allow his men to fight from behind trees, Indian fashion, as Washington had counseled. As he died, he is reported to have said, "We shall better know how to deal with them another time." He was buried at Great Meadows, a mile from Fort Necessity.
9. *Our Washington with chosen Men,*
   Washington had been with Braddock at the time of his defeat, and had been the only mounted officer to survive the battle. This line, however, probably refers to his own repulse at Great Meadows, July 3, 1754.
41. *His buckler we must sure put on, . . .*
   The "Bloody Butchery" elegy closes with the same couplet. Cf. p. 57, *supra*.

Maj. Gen. RICHARD BUTLER, Slain in the Battle at Miami Village, Nov. 4.

BLOODY INDIAN BATTLE, Fought at MIAMI VILLAGE, Nov. 4, 1791.

THE COLUMBIAN TRAGEDY:

CONTAINING A PARTICULAR AND OFFICIAL

ACCOUNT

Of the BRAVE and UNFORTUNATE OFFICERS and SOLDIERS, who were
SLAIN and WOUNDED in the EVER-MEMORABLE and

BLOODY INDIAN BATTLE,

Perhaps the most shocking that has happened in AMERICA since its first Discovery; which continued Six Hours, with the most unremitted Fury and unparalleled Bravery on both sides, having lasted from day-break, until near ten o'clock on Friday Morning, Nov. 4, 1791; between Two Thousand AMERICANS, belonging to the UNITED ARMY, and near Five Thousand Wild Indian Savages, at Miami Village, near Fort-Washington, in the Ohio Country, in which terrible and desperate Battle a most shocking Slaughter was made of Thirty-nine gallant AMERICAN OFFICERS and upwards of Nine Hundred brave youthful SOLDIERS, who fell gloriously fighting for their COUNTRY.—These Particulars and Elegy are now published in this SHEET by the earnest Request of the Friends to the DECEASED WORTHIES, who died in Defence of their COUNTRY, not only as a Token of Gratitude to the DECEASED BRAVE, but as a PERPETUAL MEMORIAL of that important Event, which, perhaps may very essentially depend the future FREEDOM and GRANDEUR of Fifteen or Twenty States, that might, at some Period, be annexed to the AMERICAN UNION.

List of KILLED and Wounded OFFICERS.

KILLED; 1 Maj. Gen. RICHARD BUTLER.—2 Col. Oldham—Majors 3 Ferguson—4 Clark 5 Hart.—Captains 6 Bradford 7 Phelon 8 Kirkwood 9 Van Swearing—10 Tipton—11 Smith—12 Purdy—13 Prate—14 Guthrie—15 Cribbs—16 Newman—Lieuts. 17 Spear—18 Warren—19 Boyd 20 McMath—21 Burgess—22 Kelso—23 Read—24 Little—25 Hopper—26 Lickins.—Ensigns 27 Cobb—28 Balch—29 Chase—30 Turner—31 Wilson—32 Brooks—33 Beatty—34 Purdy.—Q. Mast. 35 Reynolds—36 Ward.—37 Adj. Anderson.—38 Dr. Grasson.

WOUNDED; 1 Adj. Gen. Sargent—2 L. Col. Gibson—3 Dark—4 Maj. Butler.—Capts. 5 Doyle—6 Trueman—7 Ford—8 Buchanan—9 Dark—10 Slough.—Lieuts. 11 Greaton 12 Davidson—13 DeButts—14 Price—15 Morgan—16 McCrea—17 Lysle—18 Thompson—19 Adj. Whistler—20 Crawford.—21 Ens. Bines.—Vir. Majestic, Volunteer, Aidecamp to Gen. ST. CLAIR.

A FUNERAL ELEGY on the Occasion.

2 SAMUEL, chap. i.

Ver. 19. The Beauty of Israel is slain upon thy high places: How are the Mighty fallen!—20. Tell it not in Gath, publish it not in the streets of Askelon: Lest the Daughters of the Philistines rejoice, lest the Daughters of the uncircumcised triumph.—21. Ye Mountains of Gilboa, let there be no dew, neither let there be rain upon you, nor fields of offerings; for there the shield of the Mighty is vilely cast away.

YE Friends to men attend the Tale,
Ye brave ones all give ear,
With solemn steps and slow,
And shed a Sorrow here.
2. Behold the various Evils!
This hour is mirth and glee,
The next we're free'd from care and strife,
And to eternity.
3. Joyful from Boston's happy Town,
These brave Men took their way,
Ah! soon were slain upon the ground,
To BLOODY BRUTES a prey.
4. Adieu to wanton songs and joys,
To idle tales that fill the ear,
A mournful theme my heart employs,
And hope the living will it hear.
5. A horrid Fight there hap'd of late,
The fourth day of November;
When a vast Number met their fate,
We all shall well remember.
6. 'Twas on renown'd Ohio's Land,
A land fatal prov'd of old,
Sad to relate our FEDERAL BAND,
Were slain by INDIANS bold!

7. Ah cursed Spot! Ah cruel Land!
New-England will rejoin,
Where thousands of our Countrymen
Their wasted bones inshrine.
8. By much too dear the Land was bo't,
It's stain'd with English gore,
Where BRADDOCK fell! O sad to tell!
Full thirty years before.
9. Our WASHINGTON with chosen Men,
All ruddy, youthful too,
There rally'd some of British Train,
Coop'd by internal Crew.
10. A horrid covert, where there lay
Whole legions of black Men,
But by the courage of that Youth,
They're hunted from their den.
11. A handful of Columbians too,
Their Standard fast from them,
Foul tatter'd when fam'd Berwick bled,
And Tallard felt its arm.
12. The flower of British pride was lost,
In one great day they fell;
BRADDOCK'S defeat, young SHIRLEY'S loss
Our Annals all can tell!
13. Such scenes apart! my Muse still hear
The groans of dying Friends;
The horrid shrieks do fill the air,
Of wounded, dying Men.
14. Will not Columbia's Youth now rouse,
And cheerful take the Field,
Columbia's Cause they will espouse,
Nor to those BLOOD HOUNDS yield.
15. My Muse must quit that mournful Tale,
A worse one to record,
Before we shall weep and sore bewail
The stroke sent by the LORD.
16. Our Countrymen of youthful bloom,
Most in their vig'rous prime,
Are summon'd hence to meet their GOD,
And snatched out of time.

17. Thus GENERAL BUTLER's Loss we feel,
And OLDHAM's Death bemoan,
Let's drop a tear when it we tell,
And view their naked —.
18. Young NEWMAN fell! and TURNER,
With PHELON at their Head, (brave
No friendly arm there was to save,
They're number'd with the dead.
19. The names of WARREN, BALCH and
Let's mourn now o'er their grave, (COBB,
Who late with courage spilt their blood,
And fell with many brave.
20. Ah! WARREN's valor full was shewn,
A Name we'll now renew,
Who fell too soon! ah! much too soon!
Tho' twelve fierce Brutes he flew.
21. Let's sing of BRADFORD and whole
Of OFFICERS so brave, (scores
They're call'd to the Elysian shores,
And mingled in one grave.
22. We must relate the Warrior's fate
Of GREATON, young and brave!
A cruel shot his body pierc'd,
But yet his life was sav'd.
23. Of Thirty brave Youth in his core,
But Three surviv'd the Brunt,
Was ever such a scene before?
Ah! fatal Indian Hunt!
24. Columba's Land a scene presents,
Of blood and slaughter too,
The Widows heart doth sore lament,
To bid their Friends adieu.
25. What shall we say when 'tis decreed,
By fate it must be so,
To see our dearest Brethren bleed,
And ev'ry vein to flow.
26. What heart that feels for others woe,
Can stop the gushing tear,
Or not the pangs of pity show,
When such events they hear.
27. But if such pity here imparts,
Think O! what griefs assail,
Their Widow's and their Children's hearts,
When they shall hear the tale!
28. The thought already fills each breast,
With kind condoling care,
And hope in Heav'n, they'll meet at rest,
Their Friends and Fathers there.
29. We feel and sympathize for them,
Who late in battle fell,
We mean those hardy, youthful men,
Their names to ages tell.

30. Though Powers Immortal are averse.
O LORD! the praise is thine!
The GOOD GOD of Grace reverse
And take us unto thine.
31. We fear all their Tribes they
Made INDIANS sue for peace;
Hunt in each Savage from his den,
When we shall win the chace.
32. If great JEHOVAH takes the shield,
And guards us round about,
No INDIAN will his Tomax wield,
Nor arrow dare to shoot.
33. My trembling hand can scarcely hold
My faint, devoted quill,
To write the actions of the Bold,
Their valor and their skill.
34. Let's not forget the SOLDIERS bra
Who fell with Indians ire,
Who scorn'd to flinch their lives to save,
Nor on them turn'd their backs.
35. NINE HUNDRED hardiest of our Sons.
Some in their early prime,
Have fell a victim to their rage,
And are cut off from time.
36. Great numbers met an awful death,
In Battle they were slain,
But we that live upon the earth,
their mem'ry will sustain.
37. If that the LORD is on our side,
We need not fear our foe,
And if that gracious Isr'el's GOD
Now with our armies go;
38. Our heads he'll cover when in fight!
From harm he will us keep,
If that we seek his face aright,
Nor let our feet to slip.
39. With conq'ring might he will us shield,
And INDIANS all destroy,
He'll help us thus to win the field,
And slay those that annoy.
40. Our Country calls us far and near,
Columba's Sons awake,
For helmet, buckler and our spear,
The LORD's own arm we'll take.
41. His shield will keep us from all harm,
Tho' thousands 'gainst us rise,
His buckler we must sure put on,
If we would win the prize.

AMERICA:
BOSTON; Printed by E. RUSSELL,
for THOMAS BASSETT, of Dunbarton (New-Hamp.)—[Pr. Six Pence.]
Of Sal Bassett sells Bickerstaff's Almanack for 1792, as CHEAP as at this Office.

No. 30
LADY WASHINGTON'S LAMENTATION FOR THE DEATH OF HER HUSBAND [1799]

[*The Essex Institute*]

SIZE, 8¾ by 10¾ inches. A broadside entitled "Lady Washington's Lamentation" was advertised for sale in 1799, among "Songs to be had at the Printing-Office, (head of the stairs,), No. 4, Middle-Street, Newburyport." (Cf. Ford, 2919.) This title may not have applied to the present verses, but it is probable that, like others of their sort, they were issued soon after Washington's death, which took place December 14, 1799. This specimen is typical of the scores of newspaper elegies and tributes which appeared during the weeks immediately succeeding. It is included in this collection for the contrast it presents to earlier examples in the same *genre*, for by the end of the century, the funeral elegy had gotten well away from its earlier traditions.

LADY
WASHINGTON'S
LAMENTATION FOR THE
DEATH OF HER HUSBAND.

WHEN Columbia's brave sons sought my hero to
    lead them,
To vanquish their foes and establish their freedom,
I rejoic'd at his honors, my fears I dissembled,
At the thought of his dangers my heart how it
    trembled,
    Oh, my Washington ! O my Washington !
    Oh, my washington ! all was hazardous.

The contest decided, with foes to the nation,
My hero return'd 'midst loud acclamation,
Of men without number and praise without measure,
And my own heart exulted in transports of pleasure,
    Oh my Washington. Oh, &c. all was hazardous.

Our freedom with order by faction rejected,
A new constitution our country elected,
My hero was rais'd to preside our the union,
And his cares interrupted our bliss and communion.
    Oh, my happiness ! &c. &c. how precarious.

Declining the trust of his dignified station,
With joy to the seat of his dear estimation,
Surrounded with honors he humbly retreated,
Sweet hope softly whisper'd my bliss was completed.
    Oh, my happiness ! &c. &c. how precarious.

When the pangs of disease, had, ah ! fatally seiz'd
    him,
My heart would have yielded its life to have eas'd
    him,
And I pray'd the Most High if for death he design'd
    him,
That he would not permit me to loiter behind him.
    Oh, my Washington ! &c. &c. all was dubious.

When my hopes had all fled, and I saw him resign-
    ing
His soul to his God without fear or repining,

What, my heart, were thy feelings ? lamenting, ad
    miring,
To behold him so calmly, so nobly expiring.
    Oh, my Washington ! &c. &c. has forsaken us.

When I follow'd his corpse with grief unconfined,
And saw to the tomb his dear relics consigned,
When I left him in darkness and silence surround-
    ed,
With what pangs of fresh anguish my bosom was
    wounded !
    Oh, my Washington ! &c. &c. has forsaken us.

An aspect so noble pale grave clothes disfigure,
His conquering arm is despoil'd of its vigour,
On those limbs which dropt wisdom is silence im-
    posed,
And those kind beaming eyes now forever are
    closed,
    Oh, my Washington ? &c. &c. has forsaken us.

When with tears of sweet musing I ponder the
    story,
Of his wars, of his labours, his virtues and glory,
I breathe out a pray'r with sad order of spirit,
Soon to join him in bliss and united inherit
    Endless Blessedness ! &c. &c. oh, how glorious.

But why with my own single grief so confounded,
When my country's sad millions in sorrows are
    drowned,
Let me mingle the current that flows from my bosom,
With my country' vast ocean of tears while they
    lose them,
    Tho' my Washington, &c. &c. has forsaken us.

PRINTED AND SOLD BY NATHANIEL COVERLY, JR
  CORNER THEATRE-ALLEY, *Milk-Street*—BOSTON.

MEDITATIONS UPON PORTENTOUS EVENTS

EARTHQUAKES, TOKENS OF GOD'S POWER AND WRATH, JUNE 3, 1744

[The New York Public Library]

SIZE, 9¼ by 15½ inches. The *Boston Weekly News-Letter* for June 14, 1744, has a notice of this imprint, the second edition of the verses. It was advertised as sold by Benjamin Gray, a book dealer in Milk Street. The cut alone would have sold out the first edition in a week.

The *News-Letter* for June 7 had printed the following account of the earthquake:

Last Lord's Day between 10 and 11 o'Clock in the Forenoon we were surprized with a violent Shock of an Earthquake attended with a loud rumbling Noise, whereby People were put into a very great Consternation, and many who were attending the Divine Worship ran out into the Streets fearing the Houses would fall upon them: A great many Bricks were shook off from several Chimneys in this and other Towns, and much of the Stone Fences in several Places in the Country was tumbled down by it: It was perceived to continue longer and be more severe in some Places than at others; and 'tis tho't by some to be felt near equal to that which we had in the year 1727. How extensive it was we cannot yet learn, but by Information at present we are assured it reach'd above 100 Miles. Another Shock was felt at *Salem*, and other adjacent Towns, about five o'Clock in the Afternoon of the same Day, which was considerable, and again surprized the People very much. Three or Four smaller Shakes were perceived in the Night and Morning succeeding. . . .

[The Earth did quake and shake likewise,]

In Heaven and Eart[h an]d the great Deeps,
 Vast Magazines o[f Powe]r,
[Which all] now wai[t to execute]

Fly for [Security.]

And like a Furnace [burn].

 The Vulcano's will ro[ar]
Amazingly the Earth [wi]ll quake,
 The World a flam[ing] be
an't

An illiterate contraction for is not. *Ain't* is a later form.
[The] Earth likewise before the L[ord]

 And gives you one Call more,
Accept the call, embrace his CHRIST,
 And you're for e'er secure.

Earthquakes.

Tokens of GOD's Power and Wrath. The Di[ssolution]
of the present World ; and the approaching C[onflagra]-
tion, when all Things shall be burnt up : Wit[h a]
Description of the drowning the old World, and *Christ*'s
coming to Judgment. Being a Warning to Sinners and
Comfort to the Children of GOD

Second Epistle of *Peter*, iii. Chap. 10, & 11, Verses. But the Day of the Lord will come as a Thief in the Night, in the which the heavens shall pass away
with a great Noise, and the Elements shall melt with fervent Heat, the Earth also and the Works that are therein shall be burnt up. Ver. 11. Seeing then that
these Things shall be dissolved, what Manner of Persons aught ye to be in all holy Conversation and Godliness.

THE SECOND EDITION.

INspired JOB speaking of GOD,
  The high and holy One,
Declares he's wise in Heart, in Strength
  He mighty is alone.
Who doth remove the Mountains great,
  Tho' stedfastly they stand,
And in his Anger overturns
  Them with his mighty Hand.
Who turns the Earth out of her Place,
  And makes the Pillars shake,
And all its strong Supporters too
  To tremble bow and quake.
The holy Psalmist, when employ'd
  In giving Thanks to GOD,
For great Salvations unto him
  He often did afford.
Proceeds to speak of his great Power,
  And what his GOD had done,
When he appear'd and wrought for him
  So great Salvation.
That then the Earth, the Earth did shake,
  Ye and did tremble too,
Foundations then of Heaven were mov'd,
  GOD was provoked so.
And when the Lord of Life did die
  Upon the cursed Tree,
The Rocks, tho' obdurate and hard
  Did break immediately.
The Earth did quake and shake like [...]
  A Token of GOD's Wrath,
When Jews the Blood of his dear Son
  Did cruelly shed forth.
Again the Lord did shake the Earth,
  When CHRIST was in the Tomb,
When from the glorious heavenly World
  A glorious Angel came.
Behold there was at that same Time
  An Earthquake strong and great,
Which made the Watchmen at the Tomb
  To tremble shake and quake.
Again when *Paul* and *Silas* was
  Once into Prison cast,
And cruelly the Keeper had
  In Stocks made their Feet fast.
Like the dear Children of the Lord,
  They to their Father sing,
They Praises sing unto the Lord
  Till all the Prison did ring.
When lo, immediately there was
  A terrible Earthquake,
Which made the whole Foundation of
  The Prison-House to shake.
The Doors fly open by its Power,
  And now wide open stand,
Till these dear Prisoners of the Lord,
  Are loosed from their Bands.
And thus we see in very Truth,
  This wondrous Work is done,
By none but the eternal GOD,
  And *Israel*'s holy One.
And that they're Tokens of his Wrath,
  O let not one gain-say,
For sure the Lord is much provok'd,
  When he speaks in this Way.
Be then excited, O dear Friends,
  With vigorous accord,
And all the Might and Strength you have,
  To turn unto the Lord.
For lo ! on the last Sabbath Day, *
  The Lord did plainly shew,
What in a single Moment's Time
  He might have done with you.
A solemn Warning let it be,
  To all with one accord,
For their Soul's precious Life to haste
  - Their turning unto GOD.

Remember what vast agonies,
  Your Souls were in that Day,
Expecting every Moment would
  Consume you quite away.
But to return,---the mighty GOD
  Hath wise and holy Ends,
When to a wicked secure World,
  Such shaking Calls he sends.
Hereby we're loudly call'd upon
  Aloud for to prepare,
To meet the glorious Lord and Judge.
  Who quickly will appear ;
With's glorious Angels and his Saints,
  Behold the Lord will come,
And give to every Soul on Earth,
  Their final lasting Doom.
Before him shall be gathered,
  All Nations far and near,
And by the Lord's most just command,
  Be forced to appear.
And then the Earth shall shake and quake,
  More than it e'er hath done,
When GOD the Lord shall judge the World,
  By CHRIST his chosen One.
For ever since the World began,
  GOD hath laid up in Store,
In Heaven and Earth and the great Deeps,
  Vast Magazines of [...]
[...] now [...]
  His holy blessed Will,
For Wind and Seas, and Earthquakes all,
  His just Decree fulfill.
When Man had sinn'd most heinously,
  Before the World was drown'd,
The Lord commands his Storehouses
  To open all around.
No sooner spake the almighty GOD,
  Unto the bounded deep,
But over every Hill it ran,
  And every Mountain leapt.
To drown a base unthankful World,
  Who Mercy had abus'd,
The Grace and Patience of their GOD,
  Most shamefully misus'd.
Oh how amazing was the Sight,
  On Mountains Tops to see,
So many poor distressed Souls,
  Fly for Security.
If by that Means they might escape,
  From GOD's almighty Hand ;
But lo the swelling foaming deep,
  Ascends o'er every Land.
And swept them all away at once,
  Who would no Warning take,
Tho' *Noah* in the Name of GOD,
  Had often to them spake.
Perhaps you'l think the Danger's past,
  That all is safe and sure,
Because the mighty GOD hath said,
  He'll drown the World no more,
But Oh consider, dearest Friends,
  How vast his Judgments are,
And if you are resolv'd to Sin,
  To meet your GOD prepare.
Who hath his Magazines of Fire,
  In Heav'n and Earth and Seas,
Which always wait on his Command,
  And run whene'er he please.
If GOD the awful Word but speak,
  And bid the Fire run, :
The Magazines together meet,
  And like a Furnace be.
Above our Head, below our Feet,
  GOD Treasures hath in Store,
And when he gives out his Command,
  The *Vulcano*'s will roar.
Amazingly the Earth will [...]
  The World a flame be,
When GOD, the great the mighty GOD,
  Gives forth his just Decree.

But Oh the Stupidness of Men !
  Who will no Counsel hear,
Tho' GOD repeats his Calls to them,
  By Earthquakes, Death, and War.
When *Noah* warn'd the ancient World
  Of the approaching Flood,
No doubt like harden'd Sinners they
  Despisingly then stood.
No doubt they tho't the ancient Saint
  Not worth their noticing,
'Till GOD in his just Judgment did
  The awful Judgment bring.
And an't it now the very Case
  Of Sinners at this Day,
Who will not hear the mighty GOD,
  Nor what his Preachers say.
Altho' the holy Lord hath said,
  He'd come in flaming Fire,
And punish a most sinful World,
  In his avenging Ire.
That all the Heav'ns shall be in flames,
  The Elements likewise
With fervent Heat shall melt away,
  To their awful Surprize.
What an amazing Sight it is,
  To see Men quite secure,
When in the Heav'ns sometimes we hear
  GOD's dreadful Thunders roar.
[...] before the L[...]
  Doth shake and tremble to[...]
And roar beneath the crying Si[...]
  Of such a wretched Crew.
That Men can't be prevail'd upon
  Tho' with our strong Desire,
To get prepar'd against that Day
  When all the World on Fire
Shall burn and blaze about their Heads,
  And they no Shelter have,
No Rock to hide their guilty Heads,
  Nor nor no wat'ry Grave.
For Rocks will melt like Wax away
  Before the dreadful Heat,
And Earth and Sea and all will flame
  In one consuming Heap.
The Earth beneath abounds with Stor[e]
  Of Oils and Sulphurs too,
And Turfs and Coal, which all will fl[ame]
  When GOD commands the Blow.
The flaming Lightning which we see,
  Around the Heavens run,
Do lively now represent
  The Conflagration.
Those flaming Magazines of GOD,
  Have Fire enough in Store,
And only wait their Lord's Command
  To let us feel their Power.
Which once receiv'd they then will run,
  They'l run from Pole to Pole,
And all the Strength of Earth and Hell,
  Cannot their Power controul.
Justly may we now stand amaz'd
  At GOD's abundant Grace,
To think so base and vile a World
  Is not all on a Blaze.
When far the greatest Part thereof
  Are poor vile Infidels,
Among the christian Part thereof,
  Are Sins as black as Hell.
Be then entreated, precious Souls,
  To join with one accord,
In praising of the holy Name
  Of the eternal GOD.
The [...] is waiting still on you,
  [...] you one Call more,
[...], embrace his CHRIST
  [...] for e'er secure.

* Lord's Day [...] 3. 1744. between 10 & 11
o'Clock, a [...] Shock of an Earthquake
which was felt far above an hundred Mil[es].

FINIS.

EARTHQUAKES IMPROVED: OR SOLEMN WARNING TO THE WORLD, NOV. 18, 1755

[The Boston Public Library]

SIZE, 10¾ by 15¾ inches. The J. Green of the imprint was probably John Green, who became partner of John Russell about this time. Early in the following year, the joint advertisement "Green & Russell" appeared frequently. Other verses on this earthquake, written by Jeremiah Newland, were also published in broadside. (Cf. Ford, 1042.)

This earthquake, which seems to have been unusually severe in New England, occasioned much comment, interest being heightened by reports of a more destructive earthquake in Lisbon on November 1. The range of current discussion is suggested by the lists of timely publications advertised for sale in the newspapers of the next few months. Scientific inquiry is seen to have existed side by side with such attempts at religious interpretation as the present verses and various contemporary sermons and treatises supply. The title of one of these, "An Improvement of the Doctrine of Earthquakes, being the Works of God, and Tokens of his just Displeasure," may have been the inspiration of the present verses, although the title had been used before. Thomas Prince of the Boston South Church was the author, and the "treatise," as it was labeled in the advertisement, was announced for sale in the *Boston Weekly News-Letter* of January 9, 1756. The author traced the history of earthquakes with emphasis upon the destruction they had caused, and the lessons to be drawn therefrom. Apparently the present author had some such historical sketch in mind.

News accounts were of course immediate. The *News-Letter* of November 20, two days after the earthquake, detailed the damage done in Boston, and concluded thus:

> By this astonishing Event, the Inhabitants of the Town were, in general, put into great Consternation, fearing, every Moment, least they should be buried under their Houses; but, thro' the Divine Favour, no Life was lost. . . .

Among diaristic accounts, that of John Adams is of particular interest, in that mention of this event is the first entry in his record. (*Works* [Boston, 1850], II, 3.)

> November 18. We had a very severe shock of an earthquake. It continued near four minutes. I then was at my father's in Braintree, and awoke out of my sleep in the midst of it. The house seemed to rock and reel and crack, as if it would fall in ruins about us. Chimneys were shattered by it within one mile of my father's house.

Where the new Fountain bubbles up,

> Samuel Deane's *History of Scituate* (1831), repeats this detail, asserting that "the spring thus opened continues to run to the present time."

Earthquakes Improved:

Or folemn Warning to the World ; by the tremendous EARTHQUAKE which appen'd on Tuefday Morning the 18th November 1755, between four and five o' Clock.

I.
WHileGod fends forth his thundring Voice,
And bids the Earth to quake ;
Let Men attend the Sovereign Sound,
And all the Nations wake.

II.
All calm the Air, all clear the Sky,
All bright the filver Moon ;
And twinkling Stars ferenely fair,
In beamy Glory fhone.

III.
In Depth of Sleep, or Scenes of Guilt,
Sinners fecurely lay ;
When fudden fhook the tott'ring Ground,
And threatned to give Way.

IV.
See ! how poor Wretches from their Beds
Affrightedly arife,
And to their clatt'ring Windows run,
With Horror in their Eyes !

V.
Around them crack their fhatter'd Walls,
The Beams and Timber creak ;
And the Inhabitants amaz'd
With difmal Out-crys fhreak.

VI.
Buildings leap up, the Joints give Way,
The crumbling Chimney groans ;
The loos'ned Bricks toft from on high
Come thund'ring on the Stones.

VII.
Say, Travellers through Scituate,
What Breaches fright your Eye !
Where the new Fountain bubbles up,
And Loads of Afhes lye !

VIII.
The Birds flew flutt'ring through the Air,
The Cows and Oxen low'd ;
And the Stone-Fence the Country round,
Lies fcatt'red o'er the Road.

IX.
Tall Mountains pil'd of horrid Rocks,
Shook o'er Infernal Caves ;
While the loud Ocean roar'd and quak'd,
Thro' all its dafhing Waves.

X.
Fifhes in Shoals expire, and float
O'er all the briny Lake ;
And ev'n the huge Leviathans
Rife to the Top and quake.

XI.
Ah ! Sinners, whither will you fly ?
Where fafely can you ftand ?
When the Sea boils, and God, incens'd,
Shakes all the folid Land !

XII.
The Day comes on, (and Earthquakes warn
That it approaches nigh)
When the laft Fire fhall wrap up all
The Earth, and Sea, and Sky.

XIII.
What Thunders roll ! what Lightnings flafh !
What Terrors ftalk around !
What Clouds of Smoke rufh driving by !
What Earthquakes rock the Ground !

XIV.
See the Rocks rend, the gaping Graves
Difclofe the fleeping Juft ;
The joyful Souls fly down ; the Good
From their dark Prifons burft.

XV.
See all the Sky with Glory blaze,
As Angels wave their Wings ;
While burning onwards down defcends
The Judge ; the King of Kings

XVI.
" Gather my Saints, my Angels fwift ! "
JESUS Triumphant fays ;
A thoufand fiery Carrs fly down
To wait the chofen Race.

XVII.
Each Saint fteps in, both quick and rais'd,
Rapt up each Chariot flies ;
So Enoch, and Elijah once,
Were ravifh'd to the Skies.

XVIII.
The Lots are gone, what now remains ?
Fire fhow'rs thro' all the Air !
Ye Wicked, howl !—no Man to make
One Heaven-accepted Prayer.

XIX.
How to efcape the Judge's Eyes,
The guilty Rebels fly !
Fall on us, Rocks and Mountains, faid,
In bitter Woe they cry.

XX.
Alas ! the Rocks in Splinters fly,
The Mountains melt away ;
To Fires eternal you muft be,
The everlafting Prey.

XXI.
The Saints on high in Triumph look
Serene in Glory down ;
While Heaven's eternal Juftice They
In Songs immortal own.

XXII.
How thankful fhould New-England be,
To God our high Support,
So many dreadful Earthquakes felt,
In Life and Limb unhurt !

XXIII.
Confider how in other Parts,
Sometimes the Earth has fplit,
And here and there a fingle Man,
Dropt down into the Pit.

XXIV.
Sometimes Men have been buried whole,
Sometimes been funk half Way,
Where they have been devour'd by Dogs,
And Birds and Beafts of Prey.

XXV.
Sometimes the Ground has gap'd fo wide,
Houfes have funk beneath,
Shatter'd to Bits, or keeping whole
The People ftarv'd to Death.

XXVI.
Sometimes whole Streets, with dreadful Noife,
At once have plung'd down-right,
Vaft Cities, with their People all,
Have vanifh'd from the Sight.

XXVII.
Rocks, Mountains, mighty Tracts of Land,
Gone down with thundrings dire,
To boyling Waves, and melted Ore,
And Furnaces of Fire.

XXVIII.
While o'er fuch Caverns horrible
We often fhook have been ;
Yet of God's Goodnefs, Monuments
We to this Day remain.

XXIX.
And now, bear Earthquakes call us loud,
" For the Great Day prepare !
" By Faith, Repentance, Holinefs,
" By Patience, and by Prayer.

XXX.
" Forfake your Sins for which you fhook ;
' " When Confcience loudly roar'd ;
' Kill your Corruptions, be your Luft
" More than Hell-Fire abhor'd.

XXXI.
" To juftify you in the Sight
" Of an offended God,
" Plead Jesus' active Righteoufnefs,
" And Merits of his Blood.

XXXII.
" From Love to him, obey his Law,
" Love God with Love fupreme ;
" And as you'd have your Neighbour do
" To you, do you to him.

XXXIII.
" Dare not to live a Day or Night
" Without your Clofet Prayer ;
" Would you hear God ? your Bible take,
" For lo your God fpeaks there.

XXXIV.
" How you'd reflect this very Night,
" Should Earthquakes fink you dead,
" I pray'd not in my Family,
" Before I went to Bed.

XXXV.
(" A Town in Switzerland funk down,
" While one Houfe ftood it's Ground,
" Where Praying with his Family,
" A holy Man was found.)

XXXVI.
" Dare not mif-ufe Chrift's Minifters,
" Who point the Heavenly Way,
" Becaufe the Judge will fure pronounce,
" Ye did it unto Me.

XXXVII.
" Love not this World where Nothing fixt,
" But all Things tott'ring are :
" You and your Idols fhall be burnt,
" In one devouring Fire.

XXXVIII.
" Give to your God, and to his Poor,
" His Part of what you have :
" And keep his Sabbath as you'd wifh
" Ever in Heav'n to live.

XXXIX.
" Not one known Duty dare delay,
" Watch with a hopeful Dread,
" And boaft not of another Day ;
" This Night thou may'ft be dead.

XL.
" Then Sing, tho' Thoufand Earthquakes fhake
" This Feeble Cottage down,
" I'll to my Saviou's Courts affend,
" And win an Heav'nly Crown.

Sold by J. Green, oppofite Mr. Church's Vendue Houfe.

No. 33
BLAZING-STARS MESSENGERS OF GOD'S WRATH: IN A FEW SERIOUS AND SOLEMN MEDITATIONS UPON THE WONDERFUL COMET, APRIL, 1759

[*The New York Historical Society*]

Size, 10⅛ by 16¼ inches. These verses were reissued in 1769, upon the appearance of another comet. (Cf. Ford, 1480.)

The comet of 1759 was Halley's comet. Upon its appearance in 1682, it had been generally interpreted as a sign of divine displeasure. It was the occasion for Increase Mather's "Discourse Concerning Comets" (1683), wherein he attempted to inquire into the nature of blazing stars, and to prove them portents of destruction. By 1759 this attitude was to some extent leavened by a scientific interest in such phenomena, and yet there is much evidence that the religious interpretation still represented the popular view. Ten years later a writer in the *Boston Gazette and Country Journal* of October 2, after a long explanation of the course of the 1769 comet, says:

I cannot conclude without expressing my concern at the panic into which great numbers of people have been thrown by an absurd and ridiculous article from Elizabeth-town in the Jerseys, published in the Papers. The Writer, however good his intentions might be, appears quite unacquainted with Astronomy. Nothing can be more idle & contemptible than the calculation he pretends to have made of the Comet; and the "alarming consequences which might follow, should the Comet come between us and the Sun," need not alarm any body, as that supposition cannot possibly take place in the present revolution.

Coun[sel]
That [dark] and awful Day,
'Gainst wicked Sisera.
> Captain of the host of Jabin, king of Canaan. The stars in their courses fought against him. Judg. 5.20.

Beho[ld v]ast Clouds of [Smo]ke ascend,
A[nd o'er] the C[ity sto]od,
In sixteen Hundred sixty five
> This comet is mentioned in John Hull's *Diary*, p. 215. "A comet with a blaze appeared about 8th of November, and did not wholly disappear till about February; as see Mr. Thomas Danforth's description in print." Hull was wrong about the name. It was Samuel Danforth of Roxbury who had written the treatise. He had attempted to show that the movement of comets is according to mathematical law, but he had also believed them to be portentous.

The Si[gns] of God's most dreadful Wrath
An[d great] Events declare.

Blazing=Stars
Messengers of GOD's Wrath:
In a few serious and solemn Meditations upon the wonderful

COMET:

Which now appears in our Horizon, *April,* 1759 : Together with a solemn
Gir to Sinners, and Coun to Saints ; how to behave themselves wh
GOD is in this wise speaking them from Heaven.

CANST thou by searching find out *God,*
  The high and Holy one,
Or th' almighty Majesty,
  Unto Perfection.
Where wast thou, faith th'eternal GOD,
  To *Job,* that holy Man,
When I the Earth's Foundations laid,
  Declare now if you can.
When th'Morning Stars together sang,
  With glorious Melody,
And all the Sons of GOD did shout
  With loud triumphant Joy ?
Where is the Place where Light doth dwell,
  And as for Darkness, where ?
If thou dost know its vast Recess,
  My Servant now declare.
The lovely Psalmist, when he'd spread
  The great JEHOVAH's Fame,
Declares,—He numbers all the Stars,
  And calls them all by Name.
That Fire, and Mist, and Hail, and Snow,
  Whirlwinds with one Accord,
Obey the holy just Command
  Of their most glorious Lord.
And in the Time of *Israel's* Straights,
  That
The Stars in martial Order fought,
  'Gainst wicked *Sisera.*
These are among the wond'rous Works
  Of the eternal ONE,
Who also chearfully obey,
  When he speaks, lo ! tis done,
He bids them stand o'er Kingdoms, Towns,
  All in a flaming Fire ;
And great Attention to his Voice,
  The Lord doth now require.
The ancient Fathers learn'd and wise,
  When they did see them burn,
Prognosticated evil Things,
  Soon on the World would come.
Heralds of GOD his Messengers,
  The World to preach unto,
And learn'd and wise and holy Men
  Fully agree thereto.
O what amazing Changes have
  A sinful World oft seen !
And Nations, Kingdoms, Cities too
  Where these great Sights have been.
Great Griefs and sore Calamities,
  Have oft succeeded them,
And sore Destruction overtook
  A World of sinful Men,
But to relate, one, two, or three,
  At this time may suffice,
Together with the one you see
  Now blazing in your Eyes.
When this our World was young in Years
  Not seventeen Hundred quite,
A large and blazing Comet was
  Presented in their Sight.
Soon after which *Methuselah*
  The oldest Man on Earth,
Surrendred up his Life into
  The Hands of potent Death.
And lo ! the Year, the very Year
  After that he was dead,
The old World all, except eight Souls,
  By Water perished.

An hundred Instances or more
  I might have added here,
But by two faithful Witnesses
  Great Truths establish'd are.
In sixteen hundred sixty four
  Behold in lofty Sky,
A flaming Comet did appear
  Large and conspicuously.
Soon after which most awful Sight
  A bloody War began
'Twixt *England* and the *Hollanders*
  Most violent did become.
An awful Plague in *England* too
  As ever had been known,
Near Seven Thousand in one Week,
  Unto the Pit went down.
That in the Space of but one Year,
  An hundred thousand fell,
Victims unto voracious Death,
  An awful Spectacle.
Soon after which, even the next Year,
  The *Papists* do conspire,
And by their Craft and Subtilty,
  LONDON they set on Fire.
  ast Clouds of S ke ascend,
  An the Ci on,
By means whereof Moon was dark
  And Sun became like Blood.
In sixteen Hundred sixty five
  In our Hemisphere,
A burning blazing Comet did
  For many Nights appear.
Which follow'd was with scorching Drought
  In *Britain,* and this Land,
And might have soon destroy'd us all,
  Hadn't GOD witheld his Hand.
Thus we were spar'd ; but O behold,
  What awful Trouble fell,
On many Places in the World
  No Tongue can fully tell.
To name but one or two dear Soul's
  Or more if you require,
In *Hungary* four hundred Towns
  Destroy'd by Sword and Fire.
Great Floods o'erflow'd the *Netherlands,*
  That in one fatal Night,
Thousands, ye *Thousands* there were drown'd
  Before the Morning Light.
But to return, wise holy Men
  They verily have Thought
That those great flaming Messengers,
  Were never sent for nought.
No, no, Dear Soul's they don't think so
  But rather that they are,
The Sig of GOD's most dreadful Wrath
  A Events declare.
As awful, dreadful, bloody Wars,
  Plagues, Pestilence and Storms,
'Mongst Nations great, and mighty they
  Portend awful Alarms.
That they are Messengers of Death,
  Sent by the mighty GOD,
And therefore he that sees and views,
  Should bow before the LORD.
Floods they may cause, and Droughts likewise
  And Earthquakes strong and great,
So that the Earth's Foundations,
  May tremble, shake, and quake,

A fam'd Philosopher of old,
  Conjectur'd that before
The mighty GOD to Judgment comes
  In his majestick Power ;
Comets and fearful Sights more brief
  Then ever yet have been,
More frequently and commonly
  Would in the World be seen,
And are not we now Witnesses,
  Let all our Fathers say,
Ever GOD before them past
  In such awful Way.

IMPROVEMENT.

AND now O Earth, O Earth attend
  The mighty Voice of GOD,
Who in his Wrath is coming down
  By Sickness ; Fire and Sword.
GOD calls aloud, awake, awake,
  And from your Slumber rise,
When in Heavens he sets such Sig
  Of Wonder and Surprize.
Adore mighty sovereign LORD
  And before him low,
Who sen timely Wa orth
  Before the
Prepare, O Land, prepare for what
  The LORD's about to do,
For what awful Events are nigh
  The LORD alone doth know.
Unto your Chambers enter strait
  GOD's Folk, and shut the Door,
Till all the Storms of his fierce Wrath
  Shall all be past and o'er.
And O you christless graceless Souls,
  Can you abide GOD's Power ?
When out of *Zion* he will shout
  And as a Lion roar.
When all his Wrath set in array
  Against your Souls will blaze,
O tell me Sinner, tell me where
  You'l find a secure Place.
If Death o'ertakes you in your Sins
  Then down to Hell you must,
And with the Prisoners there in Chains
  Eternally be curs'd.
And lo the Guilt of your Soul's Blood
  On your own Head will lie,
And so solorn and helpless be
  To all Eternity.
But O dear Sirs, there yet is Hope,
  Cry mightily to GOD,
To turn away his dreadful Wrath,
  And his devouring Sword.
Zion's Son's and Daughters now return
  Return unto the Lord,
Or else prepare to meet him soon
  With flaming Fire and Sword.
Cast off your foolish vain Attire,
  With Sackcloth now be clad,
Which at this Day becomes a Land
  Who have provok'd their GOD.
Awake ye Priests of GOD the LORD,
  'Twixt Porch and Altar cry,
Spare, spare thy People blessed GOD,
  Let not *New-England* die.
Add Prayer and Fasting hereunto,
  It may be GOD will hear,
And out of *Zion* send us Help
  And yet his People spare.

BOSTON: Printed and Sold by *R. Draper* in *Newbury-*Street ; and by
Fowle & *Draper* in *Marlborough-*Street. 1759.

No. 34

A POEM ON THE REBUKE OF GOD'S HAND IN THE AWFUL DESOLATION MADE BY FIRE IN THE TOWN OF BOSTON, MAR. 20, 1760

REPRODUCED from a facsimile included in *Boston Records*, City Document No. 100 (1900), Record Commissioners' Report, No. 29, "Miscellaneous Papers relating to the Great Fire," opposite p. 88. The original broadside, according to Mr. Edward W. McGlenen, the author of the preface, had belonged to his predecessor as Record Commissioner and City Registrar, Mr. William H. Whitmore, the compiler of the report. At Mr. Whitmore's death it was sold to a private collector, but record of the purchaser is not available. Measurements of the broadside are given by Mr. McGlenen as 12 by 15 inches, and the author as possibly Andrew Johonnot.

There is an account of this fire of 1760 in Thomas Hutchinson's *History of the Province of Massachusetts Bay* (London, 1828), III, 80–81.

A fire in Boston, the night after the 20th of March, exceeded the great fire, as it has always been styled, in 1711. It began in Cornhill, at a house known by the name of the Brazen Head, south of the town-house. Three or four houses were burnt, and the progress of it seemed to be stopped, when a violent wind at north-west came on suddenly, and it consumed, in that direction, between Cornhill and the harbour, one hundred and fifty houses great and small. The newspapers made the damage amount to three hundred thousand pounds sterling.

There appears to have been considerable dispute over the amount of the damage, and much delay in the adjustment of the losses. The *Diary* of Deacon Tudor, who states that he was one of the committee to sit with the selectmen in making the distribution of donated funds, supplies detail on this point, as follows:

Colections was made in England as well as in America on the acc^t I was one of the Overseers of the poor at this time & with the Selectmen Sat to examin the Acc^{ts} of the Sufferers & to distribute 1st to the Widows 2^{ly} to the Tradesmen 3^{dy} to the Midling people, the Rich had none of s^d Colection which came to about £55,000. Sterling there was many privat colections whereby many received in boath ways full as much as they lost & some of the poore more, as fully appear'd; this affair before it was all Settled in about 18 mon^s caus'd to the Selectmen & Overseers at least 100 Meetings, when the whole proceedings was laid before Governor Bernard & the Councle who appointed the Committee as aforesaid. *Deacon Tudor's Diary* (Boston, 1896), pp. 10–11.

Whitefield had been instrumental in securing the bulk of the donation from England.

A POEM

On the Rebuke of GOD's Hand

In the *awful Desolation* made by

FIRE

In the Town of

Boston,

On the 20th Day of *March*, 1760,

By which, in about 6 or 7 Hours, between *three* and *four hundred* *Buildings* were confumed :——To which is added, Some brief Hints on the *great Conflagration* ——*gation of all Things.*

---Shall there be Evil in a City *the* LORD *hath not done it ?*---

I Sing th' Almighty GOD, whofe awful Hand
Difperfes Judgments over Sea and Land :
He rules the World by his unerring Skill,
And governs us according to his Will.
His Providence, which he has often wrought,
Is far beyond the moft fagacious Thought.
His Ways feem dark to us, and quite unknown ;
Yet, fpotlefs *Juftice* dwells before his Throne :
To fhew his *Mercy* is his dear Delight ;
And, fince 'tis fo, he orders all Things right.---
His Judgments oftentimes he does retard,
While we run on in Sin and don't regard ;
And when he fends them then we think He's hard :
But pray examine, think on what's the Caufe,
Isn't it Contempt of his moft righteous Laws ?
Then can we clear ourfelves, a'n't we to blame
Who fin without Remorfe, and caft off Shame
And pay no Rev'rence to his holy Name ?---
This is the Caufe He fent *this* Judgment down,
This *awful Defolation* ! on the Town.
The *North-weft-wind,* and *Flame* he did employ,
Our ftately Habitations to deftroy,
What fpacious Structures ftood but th' other Day,
And now they all in Heaps of Afhes lay
I know not how to write, or to exprefs
The awful Time, or paint the fad Diftrefs
Of thofe our Friends who did to Bed retire
And wak'd furrounded by a Flame of Fire !---
The Sick and Dying forc'd to quit their Beds.
And then, perhaps, no where to lay their Heads.
O what Confufion ! what tremendous Grief !
While mercilefs Flames afforded no Relief !
Whole Streets of Houfes foon embrac'd the Ground,
Which left the Marks of fad Deftruction round !
And Goods, in vaft Repofitories ftor'd,
Were chief confum'd, in burning Walls immur'd !
We ftrove in vain, we could not ftop its Force
While GOD prevail'd, and did direct its Courfe.
O ! with what Grief did we lift up our Eyes,
To fee the Flames in rolling Volumns rife,
And Smoke from Buildings cloud the fparkling Skies!
An awful Emblem we did then behold
Of the *Great Day,* from ancient Date foretold ;---
When the bright *Sun,* that radiant fhining Car
Whofe lucid Splendor darkens ev'ry Star,
No more fhall roll his Courfe around the Globe,
But mourn our Fate wrap'd in a fable Robe.

The *Moon* will ceafe to give her fplendent Ray ;
(While Stars are darken'd thro' the milky Way)
The fhining Luftre fhe fo often fhed
Will then be cover'd in a crimfon Red,
While o'er her Face a fanguine Mantle's fpread.
Stars will forfake their Spheres and fall from Heav'n,
And thro' the Earth the fcatter'd Flames be driv'n.
The Elements fhall melt with fervent Heat,
While heavy Trains of awful Judgments meet
All Nature's final Ruin to compleat.--
The heavy Rocks into the Air are hurl'd,
And Horror feizes all the guilty World :--
Thoufands of *Seraphs* through the Æther fly,
Our JUDGE's Chariot then is haft'ning nigh
And with its Swiftnefs burns along the Sky.
Tremble, O Earth, Inhabitants admire
To fee your JUDGE defcend in flaming Fire !
And while you fhudder, O lift up your Eyes !
Sequious *Angels* guard him through the Skies :
A fparkling Azure cleaves to make Him Way,
And now comes on the great Tribunal Day :---
All Nature owns her Great Creator---now
The tow'ring Forefts and the Mountains bow,
The melting Hills diffolve in Flames of Fire
Blazing Comets ready to expire--
the ALMIGHTY's Vengeance now difplays,
He in his Wrath will kindle all his Rays
And fet the fpacious Univerfe on blaze ;--
'Till Nature fhall diffolve, and quite expire,
In one continual Made of flaming Fire .
O may we then be found at his Right-Hand,
And there rejoicing and triumphant ftand ;
While he fhall doom the Nations of the Land--
To endlefs Pain, or everlafting Reft !
Then may we hear thofe joyful Words exprefs'd,
Come my beloved, faithful, juft and true,
Poffefs the Realm which was prepar'd for you
Before the World her firft Foundation knew.
Free-Grace forever then we fhall adore,
Where earthly Troubles will moleft no more.

A. J.

BOSTON · Printed and Sold at Fowle & Draper's Printing Office, in Marlborough-ftreet. 1760.

A WARNING PIECE, A POETICAL THOUGHT, OR PARA-PHRASE, OCCASIONED BY THAT STUPENDOUS AND UNNATURAL DARKNESS, MAY 19, 1780

[The Boston Public Library]

PRINTED on the same sheet with "Bold Conscience and Old Self." The whole sheet measures 18½ by 21½ inches. Another issue of verses on this same eclipse, entitled, "A few Lines composed on the *Dark Day*, of May 19, 1780," is also extant. (Cf. Ford, 2268, and also 2269–2270.)

Such a phenomenon regularly provoked intelligent discussion as well as warning pieces. In October of this same year, 1780, although the country was still involved in war, the Commonwealth of Massachusetts thought scientific inquiry sufficiently important to be willing to fit out a vessel conveying a group of observers to Long Island in Penobscot Bay where, according to calculation, an eclipse was expected to be total. Application was made to the British garrison at Penobscot Bay for permission to take up a suitable location for the observations. The report of Professor Williams of Harvard, who headed the expedition, is printed in the *Memoirs of the American Academy of Arts and Sciences* (1785), I, 86–102.

There is mention of the May eclipse in *The Diary of William Pyncheon of Salem* (Boston, 1890), p. 63, as follows:

19. Friday. . . . A dark morning; about ten the darkness increased, and at eleven and twelve o'clock it was so great that people used candles to get dinner by and to read; the cocks began to crow, as in the night; people in the streets grew melancholy, and fear seized on all except sailors; they went hallooing and frolicking through the streets, and were reproved in vain; . . . they cried out to the ladies as they passed, "Now you may take off your rolls and high caps and be d——d." Dr. Whitaker's people met at the meeting house, and he preached from Amos VIII, 9: "I will darken the earth in the clear day," etc. He urged that it was owing to the immediate act of God for people's extortion and other sins, and enumerated them. At four P.M. it grew somewhat lighter; in the evening, although the moon was up and full, it was, until 12 o'clock darker than ever was seen by any.

old Lucifer
Satan, from the rebel archangel, whose fall was supposedly referred to in Isa. 14.12.
Salem's street
For Jerusalem. Cf. the Arnold verses, p. 15, *supra*.

A WARNING PIECE.

A POETICAL THOUGHT, or PARAPHRASE,

Occasioned by that stupendous and unnatural Darkness, or interposing Cloud, which obscured the
light of the Sun on the 19th day of May in the
present year 1780, which happened about
the same time of the year, and on the
self-same day of the week, as did the
supernatural Eclipse of the Sun,
at the Crucifixion of the Messiah :
A circumstance worthy of notice.

YE sons of light, who saw the night,
   Triumphing at high noon,
The nineteenth day of the month of May,
   Mark well the dismal gloom.

No orb above, in course could move,
   Thus to eclipse the sun ;
Then understand, it was the hand,
   Of the Eternal One,

Who drew the pale, and sable veil,
   Which interpos'd the light ;
And overhead a curtain spread,
   Converting day to night.

For every town all burning down,
   And forest in our land,
Would not create a gloom so great,
   'Twas God's immediate hand.

America observe that day,
   Call Egypt into mind,
Whom God did smite with three days night,
   And struck her people blind.

Which was a sign of wrath divine,
   And that internal night,
That did o'erwhelm the Egyptian realm,
   When void of Israel's light.

Do ye not know it will be so,
   When Jesus doth appear,
Darkness as great and consummate,
   Will seize the sinners here.

Therefore I say mark that black day,
   Doubtless to us a sign,
The internal Sun in every one,
   Will quickly cease to shine.

That radiant star, old Lucifer,
   Who shines in us so bright,
Whose orient ray is our soul's day,
   Of diabolic light,

From heaven will fall and from us all
   Withdraw his wonted light,
That sun-like star, eclips'd so far,
   Our souls will feel the night.

Reason's a sun to every one,
   A bright internal ray,
Which like a robe invests our globe
   With light of spiritual day.

Well if this day of reason's ray
   Be the internal kind,
Which Christ shall shroud in his dark cloud,
   Will not our souls be blind !

When he shall come and spread his gloom,
   O'er this internal sphere,
Will not our sun, our stars and moon,
   In sackcloth then appear !

Brimstone and fire of vengeful ire,
   From this dark cloud will fall,
And as the host of Sodom's coast,
   Soon overthrow us all.

For in the days of Sodom's blaze,
   All were destroy'd we see,
And 'tis the word of Christ the Lord,
   So shall my coming be.

As every frame of human Name,
   In Sodom felt her fire :
So every soul in flame must roll,
   When Jesus shews his ire.

When his dark Cloud shall thunder loud,
   And pour out gospel wrath,
That fiery gloom will soon consume
   The sinners from the earth.

As vengeance hurl'd the elder world,
   With clouds and dreadful storms,
From off the earth ; so gospel wrath,
   Will come in that sad form.

Messiah's car of Gospel war,
   Will fill our souls with dread ;
Clouds, fire and shield will mark the field,
   Where his Pavilion's spread.

Those orbs of light in reason's height,
   Which yield our souls their day
And shine so clear in Babel's sphere,
   Will then eclipsed lay.

Confounded and in darkness stand
   Ashamed in their sphere,
In sackcloth dress'd, with shades depress'd,
   Ingulph'd with opaque fear.

Like as that bright stupendous light,
   Which brings the natural day,
Was wrapt in shrouds of dismal clouds ;
   The nineteenth day of May.

Doubtless this sign bespeaks the time
   When Jesus is at hand,
Who from his cloud will sound aloud
   The fourth trump through our land.

Great darkness then will seize on men,
   The trumpet bid them hark,
Their stars and moon, their sun at noon,
   In reason's sphere grow dark.

Amazing shade will thus invade,
   In this fourth trumpet blast ;
Yet not so great and consummate,
   As comes in the three last.

When three trumps more are heard to roar,
   Great Babel's popular world,
Which rules the earth in blood and wrath,
   Will from the earth be hurl'd.

A world will then be rais'd again,
   (When Babel's disappears,)
Of righteous men with Christ to reign,
   On earth a thousand years.

This prince of peace will make war cease,
   This thousand years therefore,
Old Babel's sons with swords and guns,
   Shall then destroy no more.

No wars, no fears of shields or spears,
   Shall round the earth be hurl'd :
No heroes feet tread Salem's street :
   Nor harm this holy world.

Peace will abound the earth around,
   And Salem's subjects sing :
Her peaceful realms with grateful psalms,
   And Hallelujahs ring.

A POEM, DESCRIPTIVE OF THE TERRIBLE FIRE, WHICH MADE SUCH SHOCKING DEVASTATION IN BOSTON, APR. 21, 1787

[The Massachusetts Historical Society]

Size, 9⅝ by 14¾ inches. The "Office next Liberty-Pole" was that of Ezekiel Russell.

In Boston's long record of disasters by fire, this devastation of 1787, according to current newspaper accounts, "was never equalled in this place, excepting in the years 1711 and 1760, since its first settlement." Detailed accounts were included in all Boston papers of the time and these were widely copied. A circumstantial account is also to be found in a letter from Jeremy Belknap to Ebenezer Hazard dated April 23, 1787. The letter together with a pen sketch showing the burned area, is included in *The Belknap Papers*, "Massachusetts Historical Society Collections" (5th series), II, 470–471.

The identity of H. W., the author, is not known.

Gentle Clio calm my Passions,
> Such bookish affectations were the very stock in trade of newspaper poets of the seventies and eighties, and had quite displaced the ministerial phrases of earlier versifiers. Cf. other examples in these same verses: *fierce Aeolus, Aetna's bellowing Thunder,* etc.

Which will scarce admit Simile.
> One of the many examples of rhyming by desperation, if not by ignorance.

Close attack thy lofty Spire!
> The spire burned first and in falling carried the fire to other buildings.

Hundreds left without a Shelter!
All their Substance lost [in Flames,]

A POEM, descriptive of the terrible FIRE, which made such shocking Devastation in Boston, on the Evening of FRIDAY April 21, 1787, in which were consumed one House of Worship, of which the Rev. EBENEZER WIGHT was Pastor, and upwards of one Hundred Dwelling-Houses and other Buildings.—The Loss of Property by this sorrowful Disaster is computed at near £. 70,000.——Composed by H. W.

GENTLE Clio calm my Passions,
　Rest my panting Heart a while,
Let me paint this sad Disaster,
　Which will scarce admit Simile.

When refreshing feeble Nature,
　Friends were sitting round their Board,
Curling Smoke surrounds their Dwellings,
　With Commission from the LORD.

Fierce Æolus spreads his Pinions,
　Howls along with hideous Groan,
Flaming Arrows tare the Structures,
　All is in Confusion thrown.

Loud as Ætna's bellowing Thunder,
　Or Vulcano's horrid Glare,
Livid Terrors fill their Faces,
　Tumult darkens to Despair.

Clatt'ring Tiles and pointed Chrystal
　Rudely strews the parched Ground;
Children shrieking, Parents groaning,
　Flaming Torrents bursting round.

Hast'ning on like rav'nous Vultures,
　Spread their Trophies thro' each Street,
Clap their Wings and bid Defiance,
　When they Opposition meet.

Hark ! the murm'ring Eccho * ceases,
　Are the Flames extinct or not ?
Cast your swimming Eyes around you,
　Come behold the sacred Spot.

Ah ! delightful Seat of Worship,
　All inclos'd with Smoke and Fire,
Burning Shafts promiscuous flying,
　Close attack thy lofty Spire !

The Rope burnt and the Bell melted before the Sexton made his Escape.

Now my trembling Muse forsakes me,
　See the smiling Queen of Night
Throw aside her radiant Vesture,
　Cloath'd with Blood instead of Light.
Famous BOSTON ! Seat of Traffick !
　How thy Structures shone like Gold !
Now sits pensive as a Widow,
　An Amazement to behold !
Hundreds left without a Shelter !
　All their Substance lost in
Aged Widows, helpless Children,
　Now your tender Pity claims !
Rich and Poor salute each other,
　Hand in Hand they mourning go,
No Respect to Age or Station,
　Flames no Mercy on them show.
Once renown'd beloved City,
　How I deprecate thy Loss !
How thy Glory lies in Ashes,
　Soon thy Gold is turn'd to Dross !
Now secure a better Treasure,
　Seek an House not made with Hands,
When all Nature sinks in Ruin,
　Yet that Mansion safely stands.
While each virtuous Heart is bleeding,
　May their Hands bestow Relief,
Heaven an Hundred Fold repay them
　Who assuage another's Grief.
Open wide your Hearts and Houses,
　GOD the cheerful Giver loves,
Now's a Time to act that Temper,
　He rewards and well approves.
May you all with calm Submission,
　Pass the fiery Trial through,
And like Gold come forth more precious,
　Thus my FRIENDS I bid adieu.

Sold at the Office near Liberty-Pole.

No. 37
A TRUE AND PARTICULAR NARRATIVE OF THE LATE TREMENDOUS TORNADO, OR HURRICANE, AT PHILADELPHIA AND NEW-YORK, ON SABBATH-DAY, JULY 1, 1792

[The New York Historical Society]

SIZE, 15½ by 21¾ inches, with margins trimmed. Printed by Ezekiel Russell, and probably issued soon after the disaster it records.

The news account printed in the *New York Daily Advertiser*, July 3, 1792, is as matter of fact and as wholly devoid of preachment or interpretation as a news account would be at the present day. These verses, by contrast, perpetuate the attitude of an earlier day, and a more northern geography.

many serious Fr[iend]s
part of th[e U]nion
t[im]e set apart
they wisely enacted Laws

> In the Massachusetts laws for the Sabbath, "going on shipboard" was listed among desecrations of the day. For the first offense culprits were admonished; for the second, fined five shillings; for the third, ten shillings; and after that they were turned over to the General Court for a penalty to be assigned. Unwillingness to pay the fines meant whipping. Cf. the section "Sabbath" in *General Lawes of the Massachusetts Colony, Revised and Published by Order of the General Court in October, 1658* (Boston, 1889), pp. 189–190.

14. *Met Death; all of them [have]*

20. *Strephon with his Delia fair*

> Favorite names in newspaper balladry of the hour.

23. *Tho' glass was hurl'd with furious force,*

> Referring to the window in Christ Church, which blew down into the aisle during service, but harmed no one. Cf. the news account, included in the broadside.

35. *Bonarge*

> Boanerges. The surname of James and John, so called from their fiery zeal. Mark 3.17.

Stentor

> A Greek herald who, according to Homer, had a voice equal to those of fifty men together.

38. *Our Commerce shall increased be,*

> A post-Revolution touch. The prosperity of America was the theme of the hour.

41. *Tho' on our Cause he lately frown'd:*

> At the disastrous Indian battle of Fort Washington. Cf. the elegy included in this volume, p. 59, *supra*.

A True and Particular NARRATIVE of the late Tremendous TORNADO, or

HURRICANE,

At PHILADELPHIA and NEW-YORK, on SABBATH-DAY, July 1, 1792: When several PLEASURE-BOATS were loft in the Harbor of the *latter*, and THIRTY Men, Women and Children, (taking their Pleafure *on that* SACRED DAY) were unhappily drowned in NEPTUNE's raging and tempeftuous Element !!!!!!!!----Tell this *not in* MASSACHUSETTS ! Publifh it not in the Streets of CONNECTICUT ! lefs their sober-minded young Men and Maidens fhould bitterly reproach thee in the Day of thy Calamity, and triumph over thee when thy Defolation cometh; and afk of thee, Where art thy MAGI-STRATES ? Or do they bear the Sword of the LORD in vain ?----Where art thy WATCH-MEN ?----Have, they deferted their Watch-Tower ? Or have they fallen afleep ?

[This *Narrative* and *Poem* annexed are printed in this form by the requeft of many ferious Fry. It, with a view that it might be preferved in the hands of every well-difpofed Houfholder in America, as a *Memento* of the moft forrowful *Event* of the kind, that has happened in any part of the *Union* fince its difcovery !----In an efpecial manner it or to be noticed by every thinking Mind, as it happened on the *holy Sabbath*, a day that our *worthy* and *pious* FOREFATHERS revered as to e fet apart for religious worfhip, and (as appears by the *Hiftory* of this and feveral other States) they wifely enacted *Laws*, with fevere *Penalties* annexed, for the due obfervation of the fame; and appointed *Magiftrates* who feared God and dared to put their *Statutes* in execution.----To depicture this unhappy *Cataftrophe* in its true colors, would fhock the tendereft feelings of humanity, and fore to protract this *Narrative* to the fize of a volume inftead of a fheet.----Shocking indeed muft one imagine it for their Friends and Connexions on fhore in *New-York*, and at the fmall diftance of a few hundred yards of the unhappy fcene of death and deftruction, to behold their FATHERS, MOTHERS, BROTHERS, SISTERS or KINSMEN, juft launching into an awful and never-ending ETERNITY, and not able to afford them the leaft affiftance !----Surely the fhrieks and cries of the poor *drowning fouls*, which feemed to reach the Heavens, muft pierce the foul of the Spectator, and melt his heart even were it adamant !]

PHILADELPHIA, JULY 2, 1792.

Yefterday will be remarkable in the hiftory of the climate of *Pennfylvania*.----At 2 o'clock P. M. the mercury in the thermometer ftood at 91 d. in the fhade ; with a ftrong breeze from N. W. At 3 heavy clouds began to rife from N. N. W. and immediately commenced a moft terrible HURRICANE or TORNADO, which lafted 15 min. with aftonifhing violence.----One of the large windows of *Chrift-Church* was blown into the ifle, which, though in divine fervice, did no injury to any of the congregation.----Several houfes were unroofed, and many ftacks of chimnies blown down.----The river exhibited a moft awful fcene ; the veffels in the harbor were toffed to and fro in every direction, and many were overfet.----A brig was driven on the bar and remains there aground ; and a fine fhip lying near vine-ftreet was forced from her moorings and overfet ; fortunately, having no ballaft, fhe drifted on her beam-ends with the tide, about a mile down the river, and then got aground : It is hoped fhe will be brought off, without any material injury.----Throughout the whole of this furious TEMPEST, no lives are loft except a Boy who was drowned by overfetting a which was near vine-ftreet, an overfet within up roof of Cooper's wharf.

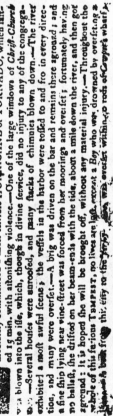

there were in the boat Cap. SCOTT,* Mr. *Blake*, his wife and 4 fmall children, a young woman, and Mr. *Berti*, in all nine perfons, none of whom could fwim but Capt. *Scott*.----The Capt. by the moft aftonifhing and praife-worthy exertions, was able, providentially, to fave them all ; He fwam afhore with one child hanging round his neck, and one to each arm ; and returned to the boat amidft the boifterous waves raging in a furious and frightful manner, and brought the others, who had with much difficulty held by the boat, fafe to land.

The intrepid Hero is Capt. WILLIAM SCOTT, of Groton, in this Commonwealth ; an invalid Officer of the United States...

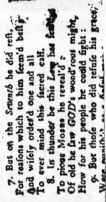

NEW-YORK, JULY 4.

T 4 clock P. M. laft SABBATH, this city and vicinity were exceedingly alarmed by a tremendous TORNADO, which continued 20 minutes, twifting off limbs of trees, unroofing houfes, and tumbling down chimnies in various parts of the city.----Unmindful to fuch unruly gufts, the citizens, particularly the *Fair*, were thrown into a momentary confternation.----Terrible was the havoc on the water.----In vain did the SABBATH-BREAKERS cry for mercy !----In a moment ! in the twinkling of an eye, were they hurled to the bottom, and melancholy was the fcene !----It is faid, *Thirty* perfons loft their lives in this neighborhood, but cannot afcertain who they were for certainty. Report fays, that a Mr. *Wade*, his wife and 2 of their children, his brother, and a young man, were all, except the laft mentioned, drowned from one boat near *Yellow-Hook*, a few miles from the city.----It is alfo faid *fhoop overfet*, with 16 perfons, and all but one drowned.

---

7. But on the *Seventh* he did reft,
   For reafons which to him feem'd beft,
   And wifely order'd one and all
   To ever mind this facred call.

8. In thunder be this *Long* has fpoken
   To pious Mofes he reveal'd ;
   Of old he faw GOD's wond'rous might,
   How for his people he could fight :

9. But thofe who did refufe his grace,
   Were punifh'd as a faithlefs...

20. Ah! thoufelf *Strephon* with his *Delia* fair,
    On *Sabbath* took delight in rural air !
    But once too oft the *youthful Fair One* went,
    Perhap too much on worldly pleafures bent !

21. They little tho't when *Sol* had ftreak'd
    the fky,
    Before the eve' they'd reach eternity ;
    We fee that *Sports* on facred Days
    May end in grief e'er ev'ning ray.----

33. O! may this folemn SCENE and SONG,
    Awake the tho'tlefs *youthful Throng*,
    Who headlong plunge themfelves in grief,
    Alaf! paft hope ! and paft grief !

34. O had I but a pen of brafs,
    I'd wear it out to warn each *Lafs*,
    And *Lad* gainft finful pleafures vain,
    By which they do GO D's Day profane.

35. Had I *Bomere* or *Sterne's*...

PHILADELPHIA, July 8, 1792.

Yesterday will be remarkable in the history of the climate of Pennsylvania.—At 5 o'clock P. M. the mercury in the thermometer stood at 91 d. in the shade; with a strong breeze from N. W. At 3 heavy clouds began to rise from N. N. W. and immediately commenced a most terrible HURRICANE or TORNADO, which lasted 15 min. with astonishing violence.—One of the large windows of Christ-Church was blown into the isle, which, though in divine service, did no injury to any of the congregation.—Several houses were unroofed, and many stacks of chimnies blown down.—The river exhibited a most awful scene; the vessels in the harbor were tossed to and fro in every direction, and many were overset.—A brig was driven on the bar and remains there aground; and a fire ship lying near nine-street was forced from her moorings and overset; fortunately having no ballast, she drifted on her beam-ends with the tide, about a mile down the river, and then got aground: it is hoped she will be brought off, without any material injury.—Throughout the whole of this furious Tempest, no lives are lost, except a Boy who was drowned by overfetting a small boat from this city to the Jersey...

...Monday, TORNADO, which continued 20 minutes, blew down trees, unroofed houses, and rumbling down chimnies in various parts of that city.—It even threw the citizens, particularly the Fair, into... Unjumped to feel unruly gusts...

...into a momentary consternation.—Terrible was the havoc on the... vain did the SABBATH-BREAKERS cry for mercy!—In a moment in the scene.—It is said, Thirty persons were they buried to the bottom, but cannot ascertain who they were for certainty: Re...loss their lives in this neighborhood... his brother, and a young man... port say, that a Mr. Wade, his wife and 2 of their children, drowned from one boat near Fellow-Neck; few were all, except the last mentioned, with 16 persons, with 18 persons, with 26 persons, and all but two drowned from the city.—It is also said a sloop overset, with...

THE NEW-YORK TRAGEDY.

Being a Relation of the drowning of Thirty
Men, Women and Children, at the late
shocking and tremendous TEMPEST,
in that City on LORD's-DAY, July 1,
1792, when taking their Pleasure on the
Water!—O Tempora! O Mores!!

[The serious Reader may, perhaps, do himself a favor by turning to Exod. chap. xx.
v. 1, 2, 8, 9, 10, 11, 18, 19. Deut. v. 15.]

YE giddy YOUTH, attend the call,
Which from the LORD is ...
A shocking Scene within our sight,
Which make me tremble as I write,

2. Behold how tho'tless mortals wage (write,
A war with GOD, his Laws engage;
But he hath said once and again,
His Spirit will not strive with men.

3. A solemn warning all may take,
And fear his sacred Laws to break:
Which shews he is a sov'reign GOD,
Who makes us feel his heavy rod.

4. You that do trample on his Laws,
Shall find he will espouse his Cause;
He lays the proud and haughty down,
And gives the meek a glorious crown.

5. In midst of light'nings' blaze and smoke,
GOD by his faithful Servant spoke;
On lofty Sinai, he was there,
And bid good Moses to declare.

6. The Sabbath sure shall hallow'd be
By all who faithfully obey:
Six days GOD did himself allow
To form all things that are below;

7. But on the Seventh he did rest,
For reasons which to him seem'd best;
And wisely order'd one and all
To ever mind this sacred call.

8. In thunder be this Law has been
To pious Moses he reveal'd;
Of old he saw GOD's wond'rous might,
How for his people he could fight:

9. But those who did refuse his grace,
Were punish'd as a sinful race:
Tho' many felt his awful rod.

10. When light'nings flash, with thunder loud,
Vile finners felt his dreadful ire;
See livid streaks confusion hurl'd

11. It GOD's fierce wrath begins to rise,
We fall at once beneath the stroke:
His awful judgments let us fear,
And at our minds a Talk to hear.

12. Tempestuous clouds infests the sky,
While roofs and chimnies round them fly
In vain the Fair Ones hug their Spouse,
Or Lovers doat on slighted vows:

13. Thirty poor souls have felt his rod,
And took their flight to meet their GOD,
Unhappy were the loss of Wade,
With Wife and Children, who 'tis said,

14. Met Death—all of them
Beset plunged in a wat'ry grave!
His Brother too met the same fate!

15. A warning great and solemn talk
To keep GOD's Sabbaths one and all;
As on that sacred Day they fell,
And did ascend to Heaven or Hell.

16. Nor scarce had time one word to say,
Or to their GOD for mercy pray
O! in a moment they were tost'd,
And in the dreadful Ocean lost.

17. Methinks I hear their Kindred cry,
With bitter groans they rend the sky;
In sable clad bemoan and wail,
For their dear Friends lost in the gale.

18. The Mother rends her hair anon,
She's lost her Spouse and loving Son!
A tender Father's griev'd with care,
Perhaps he's lost an only Heir!

19. The Brother weeps, and sighs and groans,
His Brother's gone! he's left alone;
Friends weep, bow'd down with sorrows
For some who slighted were in Hymen's bands

20. Ah! tho'tless Strephon with his Delia fair,
On Sabbaths took delight in rural air!
But once too oft the youthful Fair One went,
Perhaps too much on worldly pleasures bent!

21. They little tho's when Sol had streak'd
the sky,
Before the eve' they'd reach eternity.
We see their Sports on sacred Days
May end in grief e'er ev'ning ray.—

22. Contrast the Scene and view with awe,
The fate of those who broke his Law;
While those who met to worship GOD
Escap'd the anger of his rod.

23. Tho' glass was hurl'd with furious force,
No one met with the smallest loss:
While some engaged were in pray'r,
Numbers were caught in Satan's snare.

24. The good preserv'd were we see,
The wicked perish'd in the sea:
By this we view his mercy free,
To those his Saints who humble be.

25. Protecting them that fear his Law,
But Sinner's ways he doth abhor.
GOD grant that they may mercy find,
Tho' harden'd in their sin and blind!

26. See how the sable Picture mourn!
View Plaisterer-Boors to Coffin turn!
New Ships lie torn away how'd,
While the stout elms around are sway'd!

27. Whoe tow'ring tops ascend on high,
As tho' they would the Fates defy:
Hear hasty chimnies' horrid clash,
Whilst light'ning's blaze, flash after flash!

28. The roofs to pieces split and tare,
While peals of thunder rend the air:
Affrighted Villagers amazed fly,
While Wives and Children round them cry.

29. To see their flocks and herds struck dead,
Their fields strip'd bare, their prospect fled:
In vain the Husbandman may toil,
In vain he plants the fertile foil.

30. Unless the LORD his labor bless,
And give the grain its due increase:
Paul and Apollos plow and plant,
But GOD must sure the harvest grant.

31. His eye pervades the spacious earth,
Who can give plenty or cause dearth:
The Wind commands and bids it read
A guilty world who him offend.

32. Unless the LORD the Watchman eye each ward,
In vain perfume our Fort to shade.
Unless the LORD our icons do brave,

33. O! may this solemn Scene and Song
Awake the tho'tless youthful Throng;
Who headlong plunge themselves in grief,
Alas! past hope! and past relief!

34. O had I but a pen of brass,
I'd wear it out to warn each Lass,
And Lad 'gainst sinful pleasures vain,
By which they do GOD's Day profane.

35. Had I Boanerges or Stentor's lungs,
I'd cry aloud until my tongue
Was fairly worn, to warn each Youth,
To turn from folly to the Truth.

36. To aged too I'd caution give,
If peaceful in the land they'd live.
May all a resolution take,
With good Joshua our choice to make;

37. Who, with his house, said they'd obey,
And serve the LORD of earth and sea,
Then will our flocks increase—and grain,
Nor shall we call on GOD in vain.

38. He'll shower down blessings from above
On those who do him fear and love:
He'll prosper those who skim the sea:
Our Commerce shall increase be.

39. And bring our ships with wealth from far,
Because our GOD is always near:
Our Arts will thrive, there, our domains,
Nor Science rear her help in vain.

40. Our Arms shall strench all around,
When Swords, Pens nor Hands surrounded
GOD will our hands prepare for war,
And girt our fingers with the sheir.

41. Then will our Foes be trodden down,
Tho' on our Coast he lately frown'd:
Which made our Foes triumphant fly,
Where is your GOD in Battle-day?

42. But should we yet repent and turn,
His anger won't forever burn;
He'll cause the jarring nations all
To hear his voice, and mind his call.

43. He'll bless mankind with ease and peace,
When they do cause their Sins to cease:
He'll spread good-will from pole to pole,
'Till mighty oceans cease to roll.

44. Till Sun and Moon shall cease to shine,
O LORD! the glory all is Thine!!!
Then while we Hallelujahs raise,
We'll chose Amen! and sing his praise!

BOSTON: Printed and Sold by E. Russell, next the corner of Lib.-Tree. [Pr. Six Pence.] Where may be had, Mary and Martha, &c.

DYING CONFESSIONS AND WARNINGS AGAINST CRIME

THE WAGES OF SIN; OR, ROBBERY JUSTLY REWARDED: A POEM: OCCASIONED BY THE UNTIMELY DEATH OF RICHARD WILSON, OCT. 19, 1732

[The Library of Congress]

SIZE, 7¾ by 12 inches. The Heart and Crown address identifies this as an imprint of Thomas Fleet of Boston.

According to the early colonial laws of Massachusetts, burglary was punishable by death after the second offense. This provision, as stated in the *General Lawes of the Massachusetts Colony*, p. 127, was as follows:

Forasmuch as many persons of late yeares, have been & are apt to be injurious to the goods and lives of others, notwithstanding all care and means to punish the same:

It is therefore Ordered by this Court and Authority thereof, that if any Person shall commit Burglary: by breaking up any dwelling house, or shall rob any person in the field or highwayes, such person so offending, shall for the first offence, be branded on the forehead, with the letter (B), and if he shal offend in the same kind, the second time, he shall be branded as before, & also be severely whipped; and if he shall fall into the like offence, the third time, he shall be put to death, as being incorrigible. And if any person shal commit such burglary or rob in the fields or houses on the Lord's day; besides the former punishment of Branding, he shal for the first offence, have one of his eares cut off; and for the second offence in the same kind, he shal lose the other eare in the same manner. And for the third offence he shal be put to death.

(1642. 47.)

The *Boston Weekly News-Letter* for October 27, 1732, records Wilson's execution in the following item:

On Thursday the 19th Instant *Richard Wilson* was executed here for Burglary, pursuant to a Sentence of the Superiour Court held here in August last.

Earlier notices concerning his crime, his sentence, his three weeks' reprieve, and the final date of his execution, had also appeared.

The Wages of Sin;

OR,

Robbery juſtly Rewarded:

A

POEM:

Occaſioned by the untimely Death of

Richard Wilſon,

Who was Executed on ——— Neck, for Burglary,

On *Thurſday* the 19th of *October*, 1732.

THis Day from Goal muſt *Wilſon* be
conveyed in a Cart,
By Guards unto the Gallows-Tree,
to die as his Deſert.

For being wicked overmuch,
there for a wicked Crime,
Muſt take his fatal Lot with ſuch
as die before their Time.

No human Pardon he can get;
by Interceſſion made;
But flee he muſt unto the Pit,
and by no Man be ſtay'd.

The fatal ſad and woful Caſe,
this awful Sight reveals,
Of one whom Vengeance in his Chaſe
hath taken by the Heels.

Here is a Caution in the Sight,
to wicked Thieves, and they
Who break and rob the Houſe by Night,
which they have mark'd by Day.

We ſee the Fall of one that caſt
his Lot in by Decree,
With thoſe that wait the Twilight paſt,
that ſo no Eye may ſee.

That wicked Action which he thought
by Night would be conceal'd,
By Providence is ſtrangely brought
thus far to be reveal'd.

By which we ſee apparantly,
there is no Places ſure,
Where Workers of Iniquity
can hide themſelves ſecure.

There is no Man by human Wit,
can keep his Sin conceal'd
When he that made him thinks it fit
the ſame ſhould be reveal'd.

He that gets Wealth in wicked Ways,
and ſlights the Righteous Rule,
Doth leave them here amidſt his Days,
and dies at laſt a Fool.

Here we may ſee what Men for Stealth
and Robbing muſt endure;
And what the Gain of ill got Wealth
will in the End procure.

Here is a Caution high and low;
for Warning here you have,
From one whoſe Feet are now brought to
the Borders of the Grave.

He does bewail his miſſpent Life,
and for his Sins doth grieve,
Which is an hopeful Sign that he
a Pardon will receive.

He ſays, ſince he forſook his God,
God has forſaken him,
And left him to this wicked Crime
that has his Ruine been.

He calls his Drunkenneſs a Sin,
with his neglect of Prayer,
The leading Crimes have brought him in
to this untimely Snare.

All you that practice curſed Theft,
take Warning great and ſmall,
Leſt you go on, and ſo are left
to ſuch untimely fall.

Repent of all your Errors paſt,
and eye the Stroke of Fate,
Leſt you thus come to Shame at laſt,
and mourn when 'tis too late.

Remember what the Scripture ſaith,
a little honeſt Wealth,
Is better far than mighty Store
of Riches got by Stealth.

This Warning ſoundeth in our Ear,
this Sentence loud and Shrill,
*O Congregation, hear and fear,
and do no more ſo ill.*

F I N I S.

BOSTON: Printed and Sold at the Heart and Crown in Cornhill.

No. 39

ADVICE FROM THE DEAD TO THE LIVING: OR, A SOLEMN WARNING TO THE WORLD, OCCASIONED BY THE UNTIMELY DEATH OF POOR JULIAN,

MAR. 22, 1733

[The Boston Public Library]

SIZE, 8⅛ by 13¼ inches. Printed by Thomas Fleet, who also issued Julian's "Last Speech and dying Advice." (Cf. Ford, 628.) The cut adorning this second sheet is a queer jumble and was probably executed by the same unskilled hand that made the illustration for the present verses. In the Boston Public Library copy the verses and the prose speech are printed on the same sheet, which measures 13¼ by 17 inches.

Julian, as the artist crudely attempted to show, was an Indian. He had run away from his master and was advertised for, with an offer of reward for his capture. Mr. John Rogers of Pembrook, seeing one of the advertisements, instituted search. He caught the Indian, recaptured him after he had escaped once, and was on his way home when Julian escaped a second time. Rogers pursued him into a cornfield near Braintree, where the Indian murdered him with a jackknife. The two other figures in the cut are probably intended for those of Scot the tavern keeper, and of the negro who ran to the assistance of Rogers. A detailed account of this murder was printed in the *Boston Weekly News-Letter* for September 14, 1732, two days after the crime, and various items relative to Julian's trial and impending punishment were published during the spring of 1733. The issue of April 12 concludes his story with this gruesome finale:

Boston, March 30.
The Body of *Julian* the Indian Man, who was Executed here last Week, having been granted to several young Students in Physick, Surgery &c. at their Request; The same has for several Days past been dissecting in their presence, in a most accurate manner; and 'tis hoped their critical Inspection, will prove of singular Advantage. The Bones are preserv'd, in order to be fram'd into a Skeleton.

There are similar items as to the disposition of the bodies of other criminals.

His pious Master
According to the *News-Letter* account, Julian, at the time of his escape, belonged to Mr. Howard of Bridgewater. He had previously belonged to Major Quincy of Braintree.

Advice from the Dead to the Living;
O R, A
Solemn Warning to the World.

Occasioned by the untimely Death of

poor Julian,

Who was Executed on *Boston* Neck, on *Thursday*
the 22d. of *March*, 1733. for the Murder of Mr.
John Rogers of *Pembroke*, the 12th of *September*,
1732.

Very proper to be Read by all Persons, but especially young People, and Servants of all Sorts.

THIS Day take warning young and old,
By a sad Sight we here behold,
Of one whom Vengeance in his Chase
Hath taken in his sinful Race.

Here we behold amidst the Throng,
Condemned *Julian* guarded strong,
To Gallows bound with heavy Heart,
To suffer as his just Desert.

Where we for Warning may observe
What cruel Murder doth deserve,
Also the sad procuring Cause
Why Sinners die amidst their Days.

Here now we have a lively View,
Of *Cain*'s vile Action fresh and new,
That old Revenge is by Permit
Prevailing in our Natures yet.

Revenge is sweet, we often hear,
How bitter now doth it appear?
It leads to Ruine, Death and Fate,
And bitter Mourning when too late.

We often hear Men to complain,
Their Punishment like guilty *Cain*,
Which justly falleth to their Share,
Is great, and more than they can bear.

The Prisoner owns the bloody Act,
And saith the Sentence on his Fact,
Was pass'd on him impartially,
And therefore doth deserve to die.

By his Account he first was sold,
When he was not quite three Years old,
And by his Master in his Youth,
Instructed in the Ways of Truth.

Was also taught to Write and Read,
And learn'd his Catechise and Creed,
And what was proper (as he saith)
Relating to the Christian Faith.

His pious Master did with care,
By Counsels warn him to beware
Of wicked Courses, that would tend
To his Destruction in the End.

When Twenty Years were gone and past,
By his Account he took at last

To Drinking and ill Company,
Which prov'd his fatal Destany.

No timely Warnings would he hear,
From kind Reproofs he turn'd his Ear,
Provoked God for to depart,
And leave him to an harden'd Heart.

Since he despis'd the Ways of Truth,
And good Instruction in his Youth,
God then withdrew restraining Grace,
And let him run his wicked Race.

From Sin to Sin advancing thus,
By sad Degrees from bad to worse,
He did at length commit the Crime,
For which he dies before his Time.

He prays his sad untimely Fall,
May be a Warning unto all,
That they no such like Steps do tread,
Nor lead such Life as he has led.

That Children and all Servants they
Would in their Stations all obey,
Parents and Masters every one,
And not to do as he has done.

Obey them with a willing Mind,
Be always honest, just and kind,
And pray to God to give them Grace,
To do their Duty in their Place.

He thanks good Preachers heartily,
For all their Helps of Piety,
Which to his Soul they did extend,
To fit him for his latter End.

So here we leave his pitious Case,
In tender Arms of sov'reign Grace,
Altho' his Crimes are great and sore,
Grace can abound and pardon more.

Now may the Congregation hear,
This awful Voice, and stand in fear,
And being timely warn'd thereby,
may do no more so wickedly.

F I N I S.

BOSTON: Printed and Sold at the *Heart* and *Crown* in *Cornhill*.

Note, There being a foolish Paper printed, called *Julian's Advice to Children and Servants*, said to be published at his Desire;
this may certify that the said Paper is false and spurious, and disowned by the said *Julian* in the Presence of three Persons.

No. 40
A MOURNFUL POEM ON THE DEATH OF JOHN ORMSBY AND MATTHEW CUSHING, WHO WERE APPOINTED TO BE EXECUTED ON BOSTON NECK, OCT. 17, 1734

[The Boston Public Library]

SIZE, 8¾ by 13¾ inches. Printed by Thomas Fleet. Two other Ormsby imprints have survived: "The Last Speech and Dying Words of John Ormsby," and "A few Lines Upon the awful Execution of John Ormesby & Matth. Cushing, October 17ᵗʰ 1734." (Cf. Ford, 651, 652.)

An account of Ormsby's crime was printed in the *Boston News-Letter* for December 27, 1733. His name was mistakenly given as Amesby, and he was described as "A Man tho't to be disordered in his Senses." He had been put in jail the preceding week for wounding a man in the street with a fork. Matthew Cushing's crime was burglary, committed the preceding October, in the house of Joseph Cook. Both criminals were appointed to die on September 26, but were reprieved until October 17. Their execution appears to have attracted considerable attention, possibly only because there were two victims instead of one.

And we the Pleasure have to see

There was great concern over the repentance of criminals. The *News-Letter*, recording this execution in the issue of October 24, remarked, "Great Pains were taken to prepare them for their awful Change, which it's hoped were not in vain." This involved usually the preaching of a sermon in the hearing of the condemned, either on the preceding Sabbath, or at the place of execution. The same issue of the *News-Letter* has an advertisement of "A Sermon preach'd in the hearing of John Ormesby and Matthew Cushing, Two condemned Malefactors, on the Day of their Execution." To make the sermon more salable, the printer added an Appendix giving a faithful account of the behavior of Cushing prior to his repentance. His unbecoming levity at his own trial had previously been noted in the press.

Yet by the Law 'tis Death for those

Cf. the law concerning *burglary* as quoted, p. 80, *supra*.

To buy the Verse as well as Speech

Thomas Fleet had printed both.

A Mournful POEM on the Death of *John Ormsby* and *Matthew Cushing*,

Who were appointed to be executed on *Boston Neck*, the 17th of *October*, 1734.

YOU Sinners all, both young and old
   attend to what I write,
And lay to Heart while you have Time,
   this sad and doleful Sight.
Behold, I say, two Sinful Men,
   who for their wicked Crimes,
Are haft'ning to the Gallows Tree
   to Die before their Times.
Who being wicked overmuch,
   can't live out half their Days,
This is the Portion of all such
   as follow sinful Ways.
Behold poor *Ormsby* now in Chains,
   with sad, and heavy Heart,
Approaching to the Place where he
   will have his just Desert.
No hope of Favour can he have,
   from any human Hand,
The Blood which he has spilt must be
   purged from off the Land.
Yet if he in Sincerity
   to God his Pray'r does make,
He may find Mercy at his Hand,
   for *Jesus Christ* his sake.
And we the Pleasure have to see
   him mourning for his Sin,
Lamenting all the crooked Ways
   that he has walked in.
He does lament his Drunkenness,
   and every other Sin ;
And keeping evil Company,
   which has his ruin been.
His hasty Temper he bewails,
   and cruel Passion,
In which he did the Fact that prove
   his own Destruction.
Behold poor *Cushing* coming next,
   just in his youthful Prime,
Whose Life is forfeited also,
   by his most heinous Crime.
And tho' his Crime is short of that
   for which *Ormsby* must die,
Yet by the Law 'tis Death for those
   guilty of Burglary.
Oh ! that all Thieves would Warning take,
   by his most tragick End,
And would now without more Delay,
   their Lives and Actions mend.
For what great Profit does he gain
   who Robs without Controul,
And wallows for a while in Wealth,
   yet loses his own Soul ?

He thought (no doubt) the darksom Night
   would have conceal'd his Crime,
But it was brought to open Light
   within a little Time.
By which we all may plainly see
   there is no Place upon
This spacious Earth where Sinners may
   hide their Transgression.
Oh ! may the Fate of this young Man
   scarce turn'd of Twenty Three,
A Warning prove to all our Youth,
   of high and low Degree.
And let this Warning loud and shrill
   be heard by ev'ry one,
O do no more such Wickedness
   as has of late been done.
Lament and wail his woful Case,
   and by him Warning take ;
A Sight I think enough to make
   a Heart of Stone to ake.

EPITAPH upon *John Ormsby*.

HERE lies (hard by an ignominious Tree)
   The Body of unhappy *John Ormsby* ;
Who dy'd for murd'ring of poor *Thomas Bell*,
A Pris'ner with him in the common Goal.
Some sudden Frenzy surely seiz'd thy Brain,
Or this poor harmless Man had ne're been slain.
Madness indeed, thus to assault a Friend,
Who ne're in all his Life did thee offend ;
And leave him helpless welt'ring in his Gore,
Almost depriv'd of Life upon the Floor :
And not content with this most horrid Deed,
Thou didst assault another Man with Speed,
And hadst most surely kill'd him on the Spot,
With that uncommon Weapon, a *Quart Pot*,
(Which had dispatch'd poor *Bell* but just before,
Who then lay bleeding on the Prison Floor)
Had not the Keeper come i'th' Nick of Time,
And sav'd thee from a second bloody Crime.

On *Matthew Cushing*.

HERE lies the Body of young *Matthew Cushing*,
   Whose Crimes cannot be mention'd without blushing ;
He by the Province Law was doom'd to die,
For the detested Crime of *Burglary*.
He broke open the House of *Joseph Cook*,
A Shoe-maker in Town, and from him took
Some wearing Cloaths, and two Gowns from his Wife,
For which alas ! he pays them with his Life.
Oh ! may their Deaths a Warning be to all,
Inclin'd to *Theft* or *Murder*, great and small.

Good People all I you beseech
To buy the Verse as well as SPEECH.

Sold at the Heart and Crown in Boston.

A FEW LINES ON OCCASION OF THE UNTIMELY END OF MARK AND PHILLIS, WHO WERE EXECUTED AT CAMBRIDGE, SEPT. 18 [1755]

[The New York Historical Society]

SIZE, 8½ by 12½ inches. This cut had already appeared on "A few Lines Upon the awful Execution of John Ormesby & Matth. Cushing, October 17ᵗʰ 1734." (Cf. Ford, 652.) In the present imprint, one victim has been subtracted, as also in "A Warning to Young & Old: In the Execution of William Wieer," 1754. (Cf. Ford, 1003.) A cut which could be so easily duplicated as this one, hardly serves as identification for the printer. Thomas Fleet had issued the verses on which it appeared in 1734, and he may have printed this sheet also.

In the criminal annals of Massachusetts, the case of Mark and Phillis is of interest as a unique example of petit treason. The crime was poisoning. Three negroes, Mark, Phillis, and Phoebe, house servants of John Codman of Charlestown, resenting the strictness of their master's discipline, conspired to poison him. Their plot was successful and Codman died July 1, 1755. Phoebe was acquitted but Mark was hanged and Phillis burned at the place of execution in Cambridge, September 18, 1755. The body of Mark was afterward gibbeted in chains on Charlestown common, where it is said to have remained until shortly before the Revolution. An account of the execution appeared in the *Boston Evening Post*, September 22, and in the *Boston Weekly News-Letter*, September 25, 1755. As might have been expected, considering the interest in the case, the execution "was attended by the greatest Number of Spectators ever known on such an Occasion."

Lucius R. Paige's *History of Cambridge* (Boston, 1877, p. 217) quotes from an interleaved almanac belonging to Professor Winthrop under date of September 18, 1755, the day of the execution, as follows:

A terrible spectacle in Cambridge: two negroes belonging to Capt. Codman of Charlestown, executed for petit treason, for murdering their said master by poison. They were drawn upon a sled to the place of execution; and Mark, a fellow about 30, was hanged; and Phillis, an old creature, was *burnt to death.*

For a detailed account of the whole case, including the legal record, see a paper by Mr. Abner C. Goodell, "Massachusetts Historical Society Proceedings," XX (1882), 122–157.

but one by Law is clear'd;
Phoebe. She was supposedly sent to the West Indies.

A few Lines

On Occasion of the untimely End of

Mark and *Phillis*,

Who were Executed at *Cambridge*, September 18th for Poysoning their Master, Capt. *John Codman* of *Charlestown*.

I

WHAT sad and awful Scenes are these
  presented to your View
Let every one Example take,
  and Virtue's Ways pursue.

II.

For here you see what Vice has done,
  in all it's sinful Ways ;
By *Mark* and *Phillis* who are left,
  to finish now their Days.

III.

The Sight is shocking to behold,
  and dismal to our Eyes ;
And if our Hearts are not o'er hard,
  will fill us with Surprize.

IV.

God's Vengeance cries aloud indeed,
  and now his Voice they hear,
And in an Hour or two they must
  before his Face appear.

V.

To answer for their Master's Blood,
  which they've unjustly spilt ;
And if not Pardon'd, sure they must,
  Remain with all their Guilt.

VI.

Their Crimes appear as black as Hell,
  and justly so indeed ;
And for a greater, I am sure,
  there's none can this exceed.

VII.

Three were concerned in this Crime,
  but one by Law is clear'd ;
The other two must suffer Death,
  and 'tis but just indeed.

VIII.

Their Master's Life they took away,
  and that they thought with Ease ;
By poys'ning him from Time to Time,
  which kill'd him by Degrees.

IX.

Their Cursed and their Hellish Plot,
  which was their sole intent,
To kill the Root, and slay the Branch :
  But God did that prevent.

X.

God grant that Servants black and white,
  may in their Saviour trust ;
And may these poor unhappy Souls,
  this Day be with the Just.

XI.

Let Servants all in their own Place,
  their Masters serve with Fear ;
Lest God should leave them to themselves
  As these poor Creatures were.

XII.

May every Soul who views the Sight,
  be careful how they View ;
Lest while they do remain in Sin
  Eternal Death pursue.

XIII.

God grant, that all, this Day may strive
  for to make sure their Peace ;
That so his Blessings they may have
  by Riches of his Grace.

XIV.

And with swift Wings of Love and Grace,
  be ready all to fly,
To live with *Jesus* when he calls,
  to all Eternity.

F I N I S.

THE AGONIES OF A SOUL DEPARTING OUT OF TIME INTO ETERNITY; A FEW LINES OCCASIONED BY THE UNTIMELY END OF JOHN HARRINGTON, MAR. 17, 1757

[The Massachusetts Historical Society]

SIZE, 8¼ by 12¾ inches. John Harrington's "Last Words and Dying Speech" is also extant. (Cf. Ford, 1077.)

The crime of John Harrington, which appears to have attracted very little interest, if press notices are an indication, was recorded in the *Boston Weekly News-Letter* of September 2, 1756, as follows:

Boston, Sept. 2.

Last Evening a sorrowful Affair happened at Watertown, one John Herrington and Paul Learned, scuffling together, the former stuck a long Knife in the other's Back, which gave him a mortal Wound, and died within two Hours after. Herrington we hear surrendered himself up to Justice.

And Groan for every G[ro]an.

The Agonies of a Soul departing out of Time into Eternity.

A few Lines occasioned by the untimely End of *John Harrington*, Who is to be Executed at *Cambridge* this Day, being the 17th of *March*, 1757, for the Murder of *Paul Learnard*, the 1st of *September* last.

1.
AND is my Life already past?
  Too early fled away;
And will these Moments be my last?
  And must I die to day?

2.
Death! nameless Horrors, swell the sound;
  And o'er my Conscience roll:
I feel his Stings, O how they wound!
  And terrify my Soul.

3.
Will no kind Being interpose,
  And mitigate the Smart;
No friendly Hand allay the Woes,
  That terrify my Heart.

4.
See! all astonish'd at my Crime
  My hated Presence fly;
Nor would one Hour of Life redeem,
  Or pity, though I die.

5.
Justice arrouz'd; puts on her Frown,
  In me her Terrors meet:
Her killing Accents melt me down;
  I shudder at her Feet.

6.
Go Murd'rous Wretch, deep-drench'd in Gore;
  With human Blood prophan'd;
Thy Life we must admit no more,
  A Burthen to the Land.

7.
Thy harden'd Soul to Mercy steel'd,
  Unpitying dealt the Blow:
Thy Rage Remorseless, plain reveal'd,
  The unrelenting Foe.

8.
Go Wretch, devoted to the Grave,
  Let Death for Death atone;
Go learn what Agonies you gave,
  And Groan for every Groan.

9.
Thus from the Earth indignant hurl'd,
  Ah! whither shall I roam;
What other distant unknown World
  Shall be my future Home?

10.
Shall I with all my horrid Guilt
  To God exalt my Prayer?
Will he forgive the Blood I've spilt,
  And shroud a Murd'rer there.

11.
O save me gracious King of Heaven;
  Enthron'd in State above;
Be all my mighty Sins forgiv'n,
  Redeem me by thy Love.

12.
For ev'ry Stain, I'll drop a Tear;
  And at thy Feet I'll fall;
Kind Mercy, smile away my Fear,
  And Pardon me for all.

13.
Tho' I have multiply'd my Crimes;
  So numerous and so great,
And sinn'd ten thousand thousand times;
  And dar'd Almighty hate.

14.
With thy Benevolence divine;
  A prostrate Wretch survey;
And be the glorious Blessing thine,
  To open glorious Day.

15.
Dispell the Mists that cloud my Mind,
  And all my Pangs abate;
Give this Example to Mankind,
  Of Love and Grace compleat.

16.
Submissive to thy gracious Will,
  I'll then resign my Breath;
Earth's just Demands, I'll glad fulfill,
  And even smile in Death.

17.
Thy blissful Presence be my Joy,
  And all my Gloom dispell:
This shall the Sting of Death destroy,
  And sooth the Pangs of Hell.

18.
Then shall this Truth be ever known,
  While God sustains this Frame;
In me his boundless Mercy shone,
  And Goodness is his Name.

INHUMAN CRUELTY OR VILLANY DETECTED [OCT. 4, 1764]

[*The Pennsylvania Historical Society*]

Size, 9⅛ by 14½ inches. This cut had been used as early as 1734 on the Ormsby and Cushing verses, printed by Thomas Fleet. (Cf. p. 85, *supra.*) It also appeared later on "A Solemn Farewell to Levi Ames" in 1773 (Ford, 1646), and on "A Dialogue between Elizabeth Smith, and John Sennet" (Ford, 1692), in the same year—two issues from the Draper press. For the present punishment the cut is misapplied, since the culprits were not executed. The date of their public humiliation, possibly also the date of this sheet, is established by an entry in John Rowe's *Diary*, p. 65:

Oct. 4, 1764.

Went after dinner upon Boston Neck & saw John & Anne Richardson set on the Gallows for Cruelly & Willfully endeavouring to starve their Child. the man behaved in the most audacious manner so that the mob pelted him which was what he deserved. . . .

Had the child died, the penalty would have been death. The law providing for this penalty was chiefly directed against women, and numerous executions are recorded in pursuance of it. The case of Rebecca Chamblit, executed in Boston, September 27, 1733, was particularly notorious. Her "Declaration, Dying Warning and Advice" is extant. (Cf. Ford, 623.)

Inhuman Cruelty

Or Villany Detected.

Being a true Relation of the most unheard-of, cruel and barbarous Intended Murder of a Bastard Child belonging to JOHN and ANN RICHARDSON, of *Boston*, who confined it in a small Room, with scarce any Victuals, or Cloathing to cover it from the cold or rain, which beat into it, for which Crime they were both of them Sentenc'd to set on the Gallows, with a rope round their Necks, &c.

ADIEU to wanton jests, both false and vain,
　To foolish sland'ring tales, and songs profane ;
A mournful theme my heart and tongue employs,
Afflicts my mind and flattens all my joys.

I sing the cruel, miserable pair,
Th' unhappy Man, and the accursed *Fair*,
Whose base and horrid fact torments my ears,
Distracts my soul, and drowns my eyes in tears.

Then on my muse, let all the vulgar know
The barb'rous cause from whence my sorrows flow
Proclaim the Wretch and his infernal Wife,
Whose restless malice sought her Infant's life.

Who in a wet, a cold and loathsome room
Confin'd her Babe, the off-spring of her womb :
'Twas there she made the half-starv'd Infant lay,
To sob alone and waste its flesh away.

Nor did the base and cruel Mother feel,
The least remorse --- her breast was harden'd steel :
With looks serene, the Tigress could behold
Her panting Infant naked, wet and cold.

Thus she the helpless, tender Infant us'd,
She vex'd its spirits, and its body bruis'd ;
And thus you see how *John* and bloody *Ann*,
The cruel Mother and unnatural Man.

Invented means to stop this Infants breath,
And sought to kill it by a ling'ring death ;
But thanks to GOD, who fits inthron'd on high,
Supream o'er all, dread Sov'reign of the sky,

Who did his rich and wond'rous grace extend,
To save the Child from that untimely end ;
How freely does his tender mercies flow,
To rescue Mortals from the depths of woe.

When sore distress'd he mitigates our pain,
Regards our tears, nor lets us cry in vain :
He hears our pray'rs, when we implore his grace,
And loves and pities, while he hides his face.

But as for those whom goodness can't reclaim,
Who scorn his mercies, and blaspheme his name :

Those rebels soon shall feel his heavy rod,
And know the justice of an angry GOD.

So shall these Felons whose detected crime,
Has mark'd them out the scandal of our time :
This day the Man and his accomplish'd Dame
Are both expos'd to everlasting shame.

Behold him, Sirs, with his inviting *Fair*,
High on the gallows, see him seated there :
Behold how well the pliant halter suits
These harden'd monsters, and unnatural brutes.

Behold, I pray, this Female's brasen face,
Which gives the gallows that becoming grace ;
See how she sets without concern or dread,
Bites in her lip, and rears her guilty head.

Behold, ye Swains, how great their guilt has been ;
Then stand in awe, and be afraid to sin :---
Ye virgin Nymphs---ye few and virtuous Fair,
The earth's great joy, and Heav'ns peculiar care.

Be constant now, while in your youthful prime ;
Abhor this Harlot, and avoid her crime :
Detest this Man, and ev'ry villains face,
Who dare be cruel, impudent or base.

And now that we may have our sins forgiven,
May live at ease, and die in peace with Heav'n ;
Let us attend to wisdom's sacred call,
Who thus concludes with an address to all.

Ye simple mortals, harken to my voice,
And take me now for your eternal choice ;
Now let my sayings in your hearts descend,
Receive my law, and to my words attend.

Keep far from passion, cruelty and strife,
And I'll conduct thee in the paths of life :
Exalt me now and I'll prolong thy days,
I'll save thy soul and prosper all thy ways,

Tho' all forsake thee, I'll be with thee still,
I'll be thy guide and keep thee free from ill,
I'll lead thee here and be thy kind convoy
Safe to the Haven of eternal joy.

A FEW LINES ON MAGNUS MODE, RICHARD HODGES & J. NEWINGTON CLARK, . . . SENTENC'D TO STAND IN THE PILLORY AT CHARLESTOWN [APR. 30, 1767]

[The Pennsylvania Historical Society]

SIZE, 7¾ by 9⅞ inches. The same cut was used on "Cooke's Speech from The Pillory" (Ford, 1514), and "Cot-er's Speech from the Pillory" (Ford, 1515), both undated. "Cooke's Speech" was printed by Zechariah Fowle, who was probably also the printer of the present broadside. The date of the punishment herein described is established by an item in the *Massachusetts Gazette and Boston News-Letter* for May 7, 1767. The item is as follows:

Last Thursday, Magnus Mode, Richard Hodges, and John Newingham Clark, pursuant to their Sentence at the Superior Court at Charlestown, stood one Hour in the Pillory there, and had one of their Ears cut off, and were afterwards publickly whipped 20 Stripes, for Forging and making of Pewter and other mixed Metals, sundry Pieces of false and counterfeit Money to the likeness of Spanish Milled Dollars — — They were all committed to the House of Correction, there to remain for the space of one Year, at hard Labour, and then to pay all Costs, &c.

Other news items of various dates indicate that the penalty for forgery was sometimes more severe. The *Essex Gazette* for September 7, 1773, mentions four counterfeiters in New Jersey who received sentence of death. To judge from the number of such items, counterfeiting was one of the most frequent offenses with which the law had to deal.

A few LINES on

Magnus Mode, Richard Hodges & J. Newington Clark.

Who are Sentenc'd to stand one Hour in the

Pillory at Charlestown;

To have one of their EARS cut off, and to be Whipped 20 Stripes at the public Whipping-Post, for making and paffing Counterfeit DOLLARS, &c.

BEHOLD the villains rais'd on high !
(The Poſt they've got attracts the eye :)
Both Jews and Gentiles all appear
To ſee them ſtand exalted here ;
Both rich and poor, both young and old,
The dirty ſlut, the common ſcold :
What multitudes do them ſurround,
Many as bad as can be found.
And to encreaſe their ſad diſgrace,
Throw rotten eggs into their face,
And pelt them ſore with dirt and ſtones,
Nay, if they could would break their bones.
Their malice to ſuch height ariſe,
Who knows but they'll put out their eyes :
But pray conſider what you do
While thus expos'd to public view.
Juſtice has often done its part,
And made the guilty rebels ſmart ;
But they went on did ſtill rebel,
And ſeem'd to ſtorm the gates of hell.
To no good counſel would they hear ;
But now each one muſt looſe an EAR,

And they although againſt their will
Are forc'd to chew this bitter pill ;
And this day brings the villains hence
To ſuffer for their late offence ;
They on th' Pillory ſtand in view :
A warning ſirs to me and you !
The drunkards ſong, the harlots ſcorn,
Reproach of ſome as yet unborn.
But now the Poſt they're forc'd to hug,
But loath to take that nauſeous drug
Which brings the blood from out their veins,
And marks their back with purple ſtains.
    From their diſgrace, now warning take,
And never do your ruin make
By ſtealing, or unlawful ways ;
(If you would live out all your days)
But keep ſecure from Theft and Pride ;
Strive to have virtue on your ſide.
Deſpiſe the harlot's flattering airs,
And hate her ways, avoid her ſnares ;
Keep clear from Sin of every kind,
And then you'll have true peace of Mind.

No. 45
THE LIFE, AND HUMBLE CONFESSION, OF RICHARDSON, THE INFORMER [1770]

[The Pennsylvania Historical Society]

SIZE, 8 by 13¼ inches. The date of composition for these verses cannot be definitely fixed even by such lines as

> On Tuesday next I must appear,
> And there my dismal sentence hear;

since Richardson's case was subject to numerous delays. It is probable, however, that the sheet was issued during the intense excitement incident to his trial, which took place April 20, 1770. The cut is interesting as showing the shop of Theophilus Lillie, in front of which the riot had begun.

Ebenezer Richardson was one of the most notorious criminals of Revolutionary times for the reason that his crime was very closely bound up with the events of the Boston Massacre of March 5, 1770. As an inferior officer in the Boston Custom House during the non-importation excitement of the late sixties, he had acquired the odious title of Informer, and was accordingly an object of suspicion and hatred. This became open antagonism on February 22, 1770, when he attempted to remove a wooden image which some citizens had erected in front of the shop of Theophilus Lillie, listed as an importer. In the confusion which followed, Richardson fired a random shot which fatally wounded Christopher Sneider, a boy of eleven. The excitement aroused by this episode was intense. The boy was given an impressive funeral, marked by much patriotic demonstration. Richardson and George Wilmot, found in Richardson's house at the time of the arrest, were tried April 20, 1770. Wilmot was acquitted, but Richardson was found guilty of murder. Governor Hutchinson, thinking the crime to be properly manslaughter instead of murder, refused to sign the writ of execution. A king's pardon was eventually secured for Richardson, but there was much judicial parley, and, as a result, he was confined in the Boston jail for two years. For a detailed account of the original episode, see the *Boston Gazette* "Supplement" for February 26, 1770, and immediately succeeding issues.

To think the Parson
> A reference to the false charge which in 1752 had been placed against the Rev. Edward Jackson, pastor of the Woburn church. His name was cleared by court decision in 1754, but he died later in the same year. An account of this case is included in Samuel Sewall's *History of Woburn* (Boston, 1868), pp. 319–327. Richardson's alleged connection with the affair is a fabrication of the balladist.

notimy
> For "notamy," a variant of anatomy. Cf. the news item as to the disposition of Julian's body, p. 82, *supra*.

THE
LIFE,
AND
HUMBLE CONFESSION,
OF
RICHARDSON,
The INFORMER.

I.
INjured BOSTON now awake,
While I a true CONFESSION make,
Of my notorious fins and guilt,
As well the harmlefs blood I've fpilt.

II.
WOOBURN, my native place can tell,
My crimes are blacker far than Hell,
What great difturbance there I made,
Againft the people and their Head.

III.
A wretch of wretches prov'd with child,
By me I know, at which I fmil'd,
To think the PARSON he muft bare
The guilt of me, and I go clear.

IV.
And thus the worthy man of GOD
Unjuftly felt the fcourging rod,
Which broke his heart, it prov'd his end,
And for whofe blood I guilty ftand.

V.
The halter now is juftly due,
For now I've kill'd no lefs than two,
Their blood for vengeance loud doth cry,
It reach'd the ears of Heaven on high.

VI.
But yet ftill wicked, yet ftill vile,
I've liv'd on honeft Merchant's fpoil,
For this I juftly got the name,
The INFORMER, though with little gain.

VII.
Little indeed when I compare,
The ftings of confcience which I bare,
And now I frankly own to thee,
I'm the INFORMER, I am he.

VIII.
By my account poor BOSTON's loft,
By me in only three years paft,
Full fixty thoufand pounds---yea more
May ftill be added to the fcore.

IX.
But what's all that to this laft crime,
In fending SEIDER out of time !
This cuts my heart, this frights me moft ;
O help me, LORD, I fee his ghoft,

X.
There,--there's a life, you now behold,
So vile I've been,--alafs fo bold ;
There'd fcarce a Lawyer undertake
To plead my cafe, or for me fpeak.

XI.
On Tuefday next I muft appear,
And there my difmal fentence bear ;
But O !----my confcience, guilty cries,
For confcience never can tell lyes.

XII.
And now alafs, my injur'd friends,
Since I can make you no amends,
Here is my body you may take,
And fell, a notiny to make.

A MONUMENTAL INSCRIPTION ON THE FIFTH OF MARCH. TOGETHER WITH A FEW LINES ON THE ENLARGEMENT OF EBENEZER RICHARDSON, MAR. 5, 1772

[The Massachusetts Historical Society]

SIZE, 11 by 18 inches, with margins considerably trimmed. The date of printing is announced in the first column as March 5, 1772. The sheet was obviously issued as a contribution to the excitement this anniversary of the Boston Massacre would cause. The cut was made from an engraving by Paul Revere which had been published two years before, immediately after the event which it depicts. It was printed at that time by Edes and Gill, publishers of the *Boston Gazette*, and probably also the printers of this broadside. Some details of the original engraving are lacking in this cut, as, for example, the label "Butchers Hall" over the Custom House on the right. For a reproduction of the original engraving see "The Original Narrative of the Boston Massacre," frontispiece in Frederic Kidder's *History of the Boston Massacre* (1870). The New York Historical Society possesses an original.

Enlargement
Release from confinement or bondage.

Seider's corps
The boy's name was *Sneider*. The son of an obscure German, he became a hero in his death, and was mourned as the "first martyr to the noble cause." An account of his funeral appeared in the *Boston Gazette* for March 5, 1770. It read in part as follows:

". . . The little Corpse was set down under the Tree of Liberty, from whence the Procession began. About Five Hundred School Boys preceded; and a very numerous Train of Citizens followed, in the estimation of good Judges at least Two Thousand of all Ranks, amidst a Crowd of Spectators; who discover'd in their Countenances and Deportment the evident Marks of true Sorrow. . . ."

A PARDON may arrive
Richardson had been pardoned, but Governor Hutchinson demanded documentary evidence of this fact.

by reason of old Lines
The crime was technically manslaughter, but the enraged populace had demanded the penalty for murder. After two years' delay, the feeling was still so strong that even after Richardson's release, he was in constant jeopardy. Two years later still, John Rowe's *Diary* contained the following entry (p. 261):

Jan. 26, 1774.

A Great Concourse of People were in Quest of the Infamous Richardson this night. They could not find him; very lucky for him.

Cushing
Judge Thomas Cushing, Speaker of the House of Representatives.

A MONUMENTAL INSCRIPTION

ON THE

Fifth of March.

Together with a few LINES

On the Enlargement of

EBENEZER RICHARDSON,

Convicted of MURDER.

AMERICANS!
BEAR IN REMEMBRANCE
The HORRID MASSACRE!
Perpetrated in King-street, BOSTON,
New-England,
On the Evening of March the Fifth, 1770.
When FIVE of your fellow countrymen,
GRAY, MAVERICK, CALDWELL, ATTUCKS,
and CARR,
Lay wallowing in their Gore!
Being *basely*, and most *inhumanly*
MURDERED!
And SIX others badly WOUNDED!
By a Party of the XXIXth Regiment,
Under the command of Capt. Tho. Preston.
REMEMBER!
That Two of the MURDERERS
Were convicted of MANSLAUGHTER!
By a Jury, of whom I shall say
NOTHING,
Branded in the hand!
And *dismissed,*
The others were ACQUITTED,
And their Captain PENSIONED!
Also,
BEAR IN REMEMBRANCE
That on the 22d Day of February, 1770.
The infamous
EBENEZER RICHARDSON, Informer,
And tool to Ministerial hirelings,
Most *barbarously*
MURDERED
CHRISTOPHER SEIDER,
An innocent youth!
Of which crime he was found guilty
By his Country
On Friday April 20th, 1770;
But remained *Unsentenced*
On Saturday the 22d Day of February, 1772.
When the GRAND INQUEST
For Suffolk county,
Were informed, at request,
By the Judges of the Superior Court,
That EBENEZER RICHARDSON's *Case*
Then lay before his MAJESTY.
Therefore said *Richardson*
This day, MARCH FIFTH! 1772,
Remains UNHANGED!!!
Let THESE things be told to Posterity!
And handed down
From Generation to Generation,
'Till Time shall be no more!
Forever may AMERICA be preserved,
From weak and wicked monarchs,
Tyrannical Ministers,
Abandoned Governors,
Their Underlings and Hirelings!
And may the
Machinations of artful, *designing* wretches,
Who would ENSLAVE THIS People,
Come to an end,
Let their NAMES and MEMORIES
Be buried in eternal oblivion,
And the PRESS,
For a *SCOURGE* to Tyrannical Rulers,
Remain FREE.

AWAKE my drowsy Thoughts! Awake my muse!
   Awake O earth, and tremble at the news!
   In grand defiance to the laws of God,
The Guilty, Guilty murd'rer walks abroad.
That city mourns, (the cry comes from the ground,)
Where law and justice never can be found:
Oh! sword of vengeance, fall thou on the race
Of those who hinder justice from its place.
O MURD'RER! RICHARDSON! with their latest breath
Millions will curse you when you sleep in death!
Infernal horrors sure will shake your soul
When o'er your head the awful thunders roll.
Earth cannot hide you, always will the cry
Of Murder! Murder! haunt you 'till you die!
To yonder grave! with trembling joints repair,
Remember, SEIDER's corps lies mould'ring there;
There drop a tear, and think what you have done!
Then judge how you can live beneath the Sun.
A PARDON may arrive! You laws defy,
But Heaven's laws will stand when KINGS shall die.
Oh! Wretched man! the monster of the times,
You were not hung " by reason of *old* Lines,"
Old Lines thrown by, 'twas then we were in hopes,
That you would soon be hung with *new made* Ropes;
But neither *Ropes nor Lines,* will satisfy
For SEIDER's blood! But GOD is ever nigh,
And guilty souls will not unpunish'd go
Tho' they're excus'd by judges here below!
You are enlarg'd but cursed is your fate
Tho' *Cushing's* eas'd you from the prison gate
The —*Bridge* of *Tories,* *it* has borne you o'er
Yet you e'er long may meet with HELL's dark shore.

MR. OCCOM'S ADDRESS TO HIS INDIAN BRETHREN ON THE DAY THAT MOSES PAUL, AN INDIAN, WAS EXECUTED AT NEW-HAVEN, SEPT. 2, 1772

[*The New York Public Library* (Photograph)]

SIZE, 8¼ by 12 inches. Printed by Thomas Fleet. The sermon preached at the execution was afterwards printed. It was advertised for sale in the *Connecticut Journal & New Haven Post-Boy*, November 6, 1772. The versified account, which was probably later, may have been first printed in Connecticut. There was also a Salem issue of the sermon, containing a letter from another Indian. A few copies of this were advertised for sale in the October issues of the *Essex Gazette*, 1773, but there was no mention of a poetized version.

Samson Occom was an Indian preacher of the Mohegan tribe. He was born in 1723 and resided near New London, Connecticut. He had first become zealous for the christianizing of his brethren through the preaching of Eleazer Wheelock of Lebanon, Connecticut. In 1765 he went to England to collect funds for an Indian school which had been founded by Wheelock. While there he aroused much attention. He was introduced to persons of eminence, and preached to English congregations, being the first American Indian to do so. On his return to America in 1768 he settled among the Oneida Indians in New York and preached there until his death in 1792. The following advertisement inserted in the *Boston Gazette and Country Journal*, March 13, 1769, testifies to the interest aroused in England over his arrival there.

Printed & Sold by Henry Parker, Print-Seller, No. 82, Cornhill, near the Royal Exchange. *London*, A beautiful Metzzotinto Print, Of the Reverend Mr. Samson Occum, The first INDIAN MINISTER ever seen in Europe.

A news account, supplying detail as to the execution of Moses Paul, was printed in the *Connecticut Journal & New Haven Post-Boy*, September 4, 1772, as follows:

Last Wednesday, Moses Paul was executed agreeable to his Sentence, about a Mile from this Town. The Rev. Mr. Occom, preached a Sermon, previous to the Execution, in the Brick-Meeting house, (from Rom. VI. 23) and attended the Criminal to the Place of Execution, where, he made a short, but well adapted Prayer to the Occasion. The Criminal behaved with Decency and Steadiness, and appeared to be in the Exercise of fervent secret Prayer all the Way from the Gaol to the Gallows. A little while before he was turn'd off, he took a most affectionate Leave of his Countrymen the Indians, (many of whom were present) and exhorted them to shun those Vices to which they are so much addicted, viz. Drunkenness, Revenge, &c. He acknowledg'd that he kill'd Mr. Cook, though not with a Flat-Iron, as was supposed, but with a Club.

Notwithstanding the Day was very stormy, there was a very great Concourse of People, whose Curiosity was as much excited to hear Mr. Occom preach, as to see the Execution, altho' there has not been one in this Town, since the Year 1749.

Mr. Occom's Addreſs,

TO HIS

Indian Brethren,

On the Day that *Moſes Paul*, an Indian, was executed at *New-Haven*, on the 2d of *Septembr* 1772, for the Murder of *Moſes Cook*.

Put in Metre.

MY Kindred Indians pray attend and hear,
With great Attention and with Godly Feai'
This Day I warn you of that curſed Sin,
That poor deſpiſed Indians wallow in.

II.
'Tis Drunkenneſs, this is the Sin you know,
Has been and is poor Indians overthrow;
'Twas Drunkenneſs that was the leading Cauſe,
That made poor *Moſes* break God's righteous Law.

III.
When Drunk he other evil Courſes took,
Thus hurried on, he murder'd *Moſes Cook*,
Poor *Moſes Paul* muſt now be hang'd this Day,
For willful Murder in a drunken Fray.

IV.
A dreadful Wo pronounc'd by God on high,
To all that in this Sin do lie;
O Deviliſh beaſtly Luſt, accurſed Sin,
Has almoſt ſtript us all of every Thing.

V.
We've nothing valuable or to our Praiſe,
And well may other Nations on us gaze;
We have no Money, Credit or a Name,
But what this Sin does turn to our great Shame.

VI.
Mean are our Houſes, and we are kept low,
And almoſt naked, ſhivering we go;
Pinch'd for Food and almoſt ſtarv'd we are,
And many times put up with ſtinking Fare.

VII
Our little Children hovering roun' us weep,
Moſt ſtarv'd to Death we've nought for them to
All this Diſtreſs is juſtly on us come,
For the accurſed uſe we make of Rum.

VIII.
A ſhocking dreadful Sight we often ſee,
Our Children young and tender, Drunkards be;
More ſhocking yet and awful to behold,
Our Women will get Drunk both young and old.

IX.
Behold a Drunkard in a Drunken Fit,
Incapable to go, ſtand, ſpeak, or ſit;
Deform'd in Soul and every other Part,
Affecting Sight! enough to melt one's Heart.

X
Sometimes he Laughs, and then a hideous Yell,
That almoſt equals the poor damn'd in Hell;
When drown'd in drink we know not what we do,
We are deſpis'd and ſcorn'd and cheated too.

XI
On level with the Beaſts, and far below
Are we when with ſtrong Drink we reeling go;
Below the Devils when in this Sin we run,
A drunken Devil I never heard of one.

XII
My kindred Indians, I intreat you all,
In this vile Sin never again to fall;
Fly to the Blood of CHRIST, for that alone
Can this Sin and all your Sins atone.

XIII
Tho' *Moſes Paul* is here alive and well,
This Night his Soul muſt be in Heaven or Hell;
O! do take Warning by this awful Sight,
And to a JESUS make a ſpeedy Flight!

XIV
You have no Leaſe of your ſhort Time you know,
To Hell this Night you may be forc'd to go;
Oh! do embrace an offer'd CHRIST to Day,
And get a ſealed Pardon while you may.

XV.
Behold a loving JESUS, ſee him Cry,
With earneſtneſs of Soul, *Why will ye die!*
My kindred Indians come juſt as you be,
Then Chriſt and his Salvation you ſhall ſee.

XVI.
If you go on and ſtill reject Chriſt's Call,
'Twill be too late his Curſe will on you fall;
The Judge will doom you to that dreadful Place,
In Hell, where you ſhall never ſee his Face.

Sold at the Heart and Crown in Boſton; and by Bulkeley Emerſon at Newbury-Port.

No. 48

THE DYING GROANS OF LEVI AMES, WHO WAS EXECUTED AT BOSTON, THE 21ST OF OCTOBER, 1773, FOR BURGLARY

[The Pennsylvania Historical Society]

SIZE, 8½ by 13¾ inches. This is the same cut as that used on John Harrington's verses. (Cf. p. 89, *supra*.) For some reason, not apparent in the news records, the case of Levi Ames appears to have aroused much interest and sympathy. Two other sets of verses called forth by his execution are included in this volume. (Cf. pp. 103, 105, *infra*.) For other broadside issues which survive, see Ford, 1640, 1643–1646, 1648.

His crime was burglary, committed in the house of Martin Bicker, a Boston merchant. The others involved in the robbery escaped death, a fact which may have increased the popular sympathy for Ames. The speediness with which he was punished also helped to keep him in the public eye. During the two months between his crime and his execution the Boston papers contained many items relative to his case. After his sentence he was, according to custom, carried on Sunday mornings to the several meeting-houses, and made the particular target of the sermon. Thomas Newell's *Diary* records one such occasion. "Massachusetts Historical Society Proceedings," XV (1877), p. 343.

Oct. 17, 1773.

Sunday, fine; pleasant day. Went to Dr. Eliot's meeting; he preached to Levi Ames; very fine sermon.

Newell also records the execution.

Oct. 21, 1773.

Thursday, fine; clear day. This day was executed at Boston Levi Ames, for burglary, aged twenty-one years, who was born in Groton, in New England, of a credible Family.

The Dying Groans of

LEVI AMES,

Who was Executed at Boston, the 21st of *October*, 1773, for BURGLARY.

I.

YE youth! who throng this fatal plain,
  And croud th' accursed Tree :
O! shun the paths that lead to shame,
  Nor fall like wretched me.

II.

On the dark confines of the Grave,
  With trembling haste I tread ;
No Eye to chear, no Hand to save,
  I'm hurri'd to the dead.

III.

Justice forbids a longer Day,
  My dying Hour is come,
When my poor Soul must haste away,
  To her Eternal home.

IV.

Methinks I see your pitying Tears,
  You mourn my wretched State ;
To shun my Crimes, avoid the Snares,
  If you would shun my Fate.

V.

Tho' young in Years, I'm old in Crimes,
  To lawless Rapine bred ;
The Scourge and Scandal of these Crimes,
  When living and when dead.

VI.

Is there a Man thro'out this Throng,
  To sinful Robbery prone ?
Forbear to do thy Neighbour wrong,
  And mourn the Crimes You've done.

VII.

See angry Justice shakes her rod,
  And points to Guilt's black scroll ;
The terrors of a frowning God,
  Distract my sinking Soul.

VIII.

Unless kind Mercy interpose,
  And deep Repentance rain,
To change these momentary Throws,
  For Hell's Eternal pain.

IX.

O! for a beam of Love divine,
  To chear this gloomy Day ;
To make me chearfully resign,
  To give my Life away.

X.

Thou who did'st suffer Death and Shame,
  Such Rebels to restore :
O! for thy great and glorious Name,
  Accept one Rebel more.

XI.

Inspir'd by thee, I fix my Trust,
  On thine atoning Blood,
To join th'Assembly of the Just,
  And praise my Saviour GOD.

XII.

Farewell to Earth, farewell to Sin,
  One Pang will set me free ;
Support me, O! thou Rock divine,
  And snatch my Soul to Thee.

AN EXHORTATION TO YOUNG AND OLD TO BE CAUTIOUS OF SMALL CRIMES, . . . OCCASIONED BY THE UNHAPPY CASE OF LEVI AMES, EXECUTED ON BOSTON-NECK, OCTOBER 21ST, 1773, FOR THE CRIME OF BURGLARY

[The Pennsylvania Historical Society]

SIZE, 7⅝ by 12¼ inches. This cut illustrates one of the customary penalties for a second burglary offense. The culprit was made to sit for an hour on the gallows with one end of the rope around his neck, by way of ominous hint as to what awaited him if he sinned again in similar wise. Women suffered the same punishment as men. Broadside verses survive for Elizabeth Smith, who in 1773 received twenty stripes upon her naked back for thievery and sat for one hour in the gallows with John Sennet, who for another crime had received thirty-nine stripes. These verses take the ingenious form of a dialogue between the two offenders who perforce spend the hour together. (Cf. Ford, 1692.) Culprits who sat in the gallows were also placarded with large signs announcing their offenses. These naturally invited added indignities from the spectators.

Rigs
    Frolics or pranks. To run rigs is to play pranks or run riot.

An Exhortation to young and old to be cautious of small Crimes, left they become habitual, and lead them before they are aware into those of the most heinous Nature. Occasioned by the unhappy Case of *Levi Ames*, Executed on *Boston*-Neck, *October* 21st, 1773, for the Crime of Burglary.

I.

BEWARE young People, look at me,
   Before it be too late,
And see Sin's End is Misery:
   Oh! shun poor *Ames's* Fate.

II.

I warn you all (beware betimes)
   With my now dying Breath,
To shun Theft, Burglaries, heinous Crimes;
   They bring untimely Death.

III.

Shun vain and idle Company;
   They'll lead you soon astray;
From ill-fam'd Houses ever flee,
   And keep yourselves away.

IV.

With honest Labor earn your Bread,
   While in your youthful Prime;
Nor come you near the Harlot's Bed,
   Nor idly waste your Time.

V.

Nor meddle with another's Wealth,
   In a defrauding Way:
A Curse is with what's got by stealth,
   Which makes your Life a Prey.

VI.

Shun Things that seem but little Sins,
   For they lead on to great;
From Sporting many Times begins
   Ill Blood, and poisonous Hate.

VII.

The Sabbath-Day do not prophane,
   By wickedness and Plays;
By needless Walking Streets or Lanes
   Upon such Holy days.

VIII.

To you that have the care of Youth,
   Parents and Masters too,
Teach them betimes to know the Truth,
   And Righteousness to do.

IX.

The dreadful Deed for which I die,
   Arose from small Beginning;
My Idleness brought poverty,
   And so I took to Stealing.

X.

Thus I went on in sinning fast,
   And tho' I'm young 'tis true,
I'm old in Sin, but catcht at last,
   And here receive my due.

XI.

Alas for my unhappy Fall,
   The Rigs that I have run!
Justice aloud for vengeance calls,
   Hang him for what he's done.

XII.

O may it have some good Effect,
   And warn each wicked one,
That they God's righteous Laws respect,
   And Sinful Courses Shun.

THE SPEECH OF DEATH TO LEVI AMES, WHO WAS EXECUTED ON BOSTON-NECK, OCTOBER 21, 1773, FOR THE CRIME OF BURGLARY

[The Pennsylvania Historical Society]

SIZE, 7½ by 12¼ inches. This cut does not appear again on any imprint that has survived.

The verses may have been inspired by one of the sermons which Ames was made to hear in chains after his sentence had been pronounced. This practice suggests the ancient custom of St. Sepulchre's Church whereby the parson, on the night preceding an execution, rang the bell in solemn reminder, and on the following day uttered a prayer at the window of the prison and also as the dead cart passed the church. This service was in later times performed by the bellman. (*The Complete Newgate Calendar*, ed. G. T. Crook [1926], II, 325.)

The SPEECH of DEATH

TO

LEVI AMES.

Who was Executed on *Boston*-Neck, *October* 21, 1773, for the Crime of Burglary.

I DEATH, Poor *Ames*, pronounce your Fate,
Thus grining grimly through your Grate.
Remember all the Crimes you've done,
And think how early you begun.
Loft in the grand Apoftacy,
You were at firft condemn'd to die ;
In adding Guilt you ftill went on :
I doubly claim you for my own.
How often you the Sabbath broke !
GOD's Name in vain how often took !
A filthy Drunkard you have been,
And led your Life with the Unclean :
No Thoughts of GOD you ever chofe,
But chas'd them from you when they rofe :
In Idlenefs you did proceed,
And took fmall pains to learn to read :
With vile Companions, your Delight,
You often fpent the guilty Night :
Your Lips fcarce ever breath'd a Prayer,
You gave your Tongue to curfe and fwear :
You've been to all your Friends a Grief,
And from your Infancy a Thief ;
You know the Truth of what I tell,
No Goods were fafe that you could fteal ;
How many Doors you've open broke !
And windows fcal'd, and Money took :
Round Houfes you all Day have been,
To fpy a Place to enter in ;
Thence in the Night, all dark and late,
You've ftole their Goods and Gold and Plate.
Imprifon'd, whip'd, yet you proceed,
The Life you led you ftill would lead.
Your Confcience cry'd, " you'll be undone."—
You ftifl'd Confcience and went on.
And now, behold ! my poifon'd Dart,
I point directly at your Heart.

The Halter and the Gallows view,
Death and Damnation is your due.
Darknefs, and Horror, Fire, and Chains,
Almighty Wrath, and endlefs Pains.
—But lo ! I fee the Preacher come,
Salvation fpeaks——I muft be dumb.

The Preacher fpeaks—Behold I come,
A voice from Heaven to call you home.
Though you the chief of Sinners were,
I bring the Gofpel ; don't Defpair.
Nor death, nor Hell, fhall do you hurt,
Be JESUS only your Support.
To you he holds His Righteoufnefs,
He bled and dy'd to buy your Peace.
Pardon and Life are His to give,
'Tis thine, Poor Sinner, to believe.
Let Death in all it's Dread appear,
Though public Execution's near,
Of Wrath Divine He bore the Weight,
He fuffer'd too without the Gate,
He betwixt Heaven and Earth was hung,
He conquer'd Hell, and death unftung.

Now let the Guilty fee and hear,
And all the Congregation fear ;
This Spectacle your Hearts imprefs,
And do no more fuch Wickednefs ;
Hear fuch important Truths as thefe,
Ruin advances by Degrees :
The youth with leffer Crimes begins,
And then proceeds to groffer Sins,
From Step to Step he travels on,
And fees himfelf at once undone :
Surpriz'd ! unthought on ! finds his Fate,
His Ruin final, and compleat.

No. 51
A POEM OCCASIONED BY THE MOST SHOCKING AND CRUEL MURDER THAT EVER WAS REPRESENTED ON THE STAGE, . . . DEC. 17, 1782

[*The William Clements Library*]

SIZE, 13¾ by 16¾ inches, with margins trimmed. The Liberty Stump address was that of Ezekiel Russell, enterprising printer of timely utterances of all sorts. The present lurid tale, coming from a neighboring town, would have considerable news value if printed at once, and to judge from the colophon with its promise concerning the publication of the sermon "as soon as it comes to Hand," one may imagine that similar enterprise had inspired the issuance of this sheet. The news account below the verse is copied from the *Connecticut Courant* of December 17, 1782, six days after the murder had been committed. The last paragraph, which was comment rather than news, is omitted from the broadside sheet, probably because of lack of space.

A POEM,

Occasioned by the most shocking and

CRUEL MURDER

That ever was represented on the Stage; or the most deliberate MURDER that ever was perpetrated in human Life.—"He violated Nature's great original Law, defy'd eternal Justice, and seal'd his own Perdition."

I.

A BLOODY scene I'll now relate,
Which lately happen'd in a neighb'ring state,
A murder of the deepest dye, I say,
O be amaz'd! for surely well you may.

II.

A man, (unworthy of the name) who slew
Himself, his consort, and his offspring too;
An amiable wife, with four children dear,
Into one grave was put---Oh drop a tear!

III.

Soon in the morning on that fatal day,
Beadle, the murd'rer, sent his maid away,
To tell the awful deed he had 'in view;
To their assistance the kind neighbors flew.

IV.

It truly gives me pain for to pen down,
A deed so black, and yet his mind was found.
Says he, "I mean to close six persons eyes,
"Thro' perfect fondness, and the tend'rest ties."

V.

Detest the errors, to this deed him drew,
And mourn the helpless victims whom he slew;
And pray to GOD that Satan may be bound,
Since to deceive so many he is found.

VI.

Come pure religion, of heav'nly birth,
Dispel these glooms, and brighten all the earth;
Drive these destructive errors from the land,
And grant that truth as a sure guard may stand.

VII.

Hasten, our GOD, the glorious times,
When thou thyself shall reign;
And virtue and peace thro' all our climes,
Their triumph shall maintain.

VIII.

Fly swiftly round ye circling years,
Hail the auspicious day!
When love shall dwell in every heart---
Nor men their offspring slay!

HARTFORD, December 17, 1782.

ON the morning of the 11th instant, about sun-rise, at Wethersfield, a deed was perpetrated, of the most extraordinary and astonishing nature:—WILLIAM BEADLE, a native of South Britain, who has resided in that town nearly ten, and in America, about twenty years, who became acquainted with, and married (at Fairfield, in this State, about 14 years since) an amiable woman, of a reputable family, by whom he had four lovely and promising children, one son and three daughters, whose education he superintended with great care and seeming solicitude, and was apparently an affectionate husband.—His business, which was that of a trader, declining some years since, he betook himself more to books than usual, and was unhappily fond of those esteemed Deistical; of late he rejected all Revelation as imposition, and (as he expresses himself) "renouncing all the popular religions of the world, intended to die a proper Deist." Having discarded all ideas of moral good and evil, he considered himself, and all the human race, as mere machines; and that he had a right to dispose of his own and the lives of his family. In letters and papers he left, addressed to sundry persons of his acquaintance, wrote a short time before his death, he declares he has had in contemplation for three years past the awful tragedy he now proceeds to act, with all imaginable deliberation and composure of mind.

About sun-rise he sent his servant-maid (the only person of the family who survived) with a letter to a friend in the neighbourhood, therein announcing his dreadful purpose, and declaring that before his friend should read the letter he and his family should enter into a happier state, and desiring him to call two persons and come to his house, gently to alarm the neighbors, and advise them to be as collected in their minds and reason as he then was. Upon receipt of this line the house was instantly opened; but too late! All was over—He had made ready the knife, the ax and pistols, as weapons of death; the latter he made use of upon himself, the two former upon his family; these instruments he had carried with him to his bed-chamber for some weeks under pretence of defending himself against thieves.—With the utmost secrecy, unperceived by any, he destroyed a worthy and beautiful wife, in the midst of life, and four pleasant children, sleeping in their beds, the eldest about 12 years of age, who the evening preceding were like olive branches around his table—He closed the awful scene by destroying himself. Some circumstances render it probable that he had given an opiate to the family before they retired to rest.

Speaking of this catastrophe in one of his letters, he says, "I mean to close the eyes of six "persons, through perfect humanity and the "most endearing fondness and friendship; for "never mortal father felt more of these tender "ties than myself." Having become reduced in some degree in his circumstances, he rejected his former ideas of divine Revelation and belief of a future state of misery: He adopted this new theoritic system which he now put in practice.

The Jury of inquest were of opinion, that he was of sound mind, and returned their verdict accordingly. It is difficult to determine where distraction begins. It is very evident he was rational on every other subject; on this no one conversed with him.

The corpse of the murderer was laid on two barrels and exposed to shame, with the bloody knife fastened on his breast, after which it was placed on a horse sled, dragged to an obscure place and buried with every mark of infamy.

On Friday the unfortunate woman, with her children by her side were interred in one grave, with every mark of respect: When a sermon was preached suitable to the occasion, to a large concourse of people, and grief mingled with pity, displayed itself in every countenance, on the unusual and melancholy occasion.

Sold near LIBERTY-STUMP and next the SWAN-TAVERN, South-End. (Price 6 Coppers single.)——The Sermon refer'd to above will be immediately printed as soon as it comes to Hand.

A BRIEF ACCOUNT OF THE EXECUTION OF ELISHA THOMAS, JUNE 5, 1788

[The Pennsylvania Historical Society]

SIZE, 10 by 15¼ inches. Daniel Fowle, the first printer in New Hampshire, had died in the preceding year, 1787. This sheet, which was probably issued at the time of the Thomas execution, may have been printed at the office of the *New Hampshire Gazette* in Market Square, Portsmouth.

Executions were not frequent in Dover, and the death of Elisha Thomas accordingly made neighborhood history. Swazy Hill, on which the execution took place, was known as Gallows Hill thereafter. The spectators had assembled on this hill, and had looked down upon the gallows which stood at the foot. (Mary P. Thompson, *Landmarks in Ancient Dover* [Durham, N. H., 1892], pp. 81–82.)

[Behold the lamb, the great I AM,]
    [The] hapless sinner's friend,
[Was made] a curse, and dy'd for us,

Reach[es thy gaol, and] to thy soul
    [It offers mercy free.]

[Christ's merits plead:] if you will speed,
    [There may be grace] in store.

A brief account of the Execution of ELISHA THOMAS.

MR. THOMAS, was executed on Tuesday last at one o'clock, P. M. atttended by a very numerous concourse of spectators, report says, about 6000—He appeared to be much affected with his situation, and employed the few moments then allotted him, in pious exercises, but never addressed the spectators. Indeed the melancholly situation in which his rash conduct had placed him, operated so upon his mind, that it was with difficulty he could support himself from sinking under it. The High Sheriff, with a humanity, which did him much honour, treated the unhappy criminal with the greatest tenderness ; nor did he hurry him out of the world, but let him live till the last moment, which having arrived, THOMAS shook hands with the Sheriff, and was launched into eternity ! May his fate be a solemn warning to all, especially to such as suffer their passions to rage uncontrouled ; for in a moment, when they are not aware, they may fall into the snare.——Therefore, "*Let him that thinks he standeth, take heed lest he fall.*"

The Rev. M. GRAY, previous to the execution, addressed the Throne of Grace in a truly pathetic prayer.

A troop of Col. COOSWELL's corps of Light-Horse, attended as a support to the Sheriff, in the execution of his Office.

June 5th, 1788.

The following Verses were presented to ELISHA THOMAS, a few days previous to his being executed, for the inhuman murder of Captain PETER DROWNE.

UNHAPPY man ! I understand,
  You are condemn'd to die :
In a few days you must away,
  To vast eternity !
To be no more upon the shore
  Of this unstable world ;
In heav'n or hell your soul must dwell
  As you have oft been told.
O then despair of any share,
  Where saints in glory reigns ;
That kingdom we can never see,
  Unless we're born again.
Your state is sad, yet not so bad,
  But mercy you may have,
Speedily, to him you fly,
  No sinners came to save,

.... the ....
... topical sinner's friend,
...... a curse, and dy'd for us,
  That we might not be damn'd.
But sav'd from sin, and vengeance, in
  A way of truth and grace ;
O blessed way ; O beauty display
  Of righteousness and peace !
And tho' *Drowne's* blood doth unto GOD,
  Aloud for vengeance cry,
The saviour's veins hath louder strains,
  And sweeter melody.

O joyful found ! it echoes round
  The spacious earth and sea,
Reach ...... and to thy soul
  ....
Your time is short ; pray don't forget,
  That you must soon appear
Before the bar of GOD, and there
  Your final sentence hear.
O for God's sake, yourself betake
  Unto the slaughter'd lamb ;
Fly, Thomas ! fly, while Christ is nigh,
  Or else you must be damn'd.
Your sands do fall ; For mercy call ;
  O knock at Heaven's door ;
Christ's merits ...... if you will speed,
  There may be ... in store.
Who knows but such a sinful wretch,
  Who doth his state bewail
May pardon have this side the grave,
  And, from the gallows, sail
Above the pole where thunders roll,
  Into the state of those
Who walk in white, who dwell in light,
  And undisturb'd repose.
But if you will continue still
  The Saviour to reject,
I tremble to pronounce the woe
  That you cannot escape.

The sound, *depart !* will pierce your heart,
  Though harder than the steel ;
The sentence past——you must be cast
  Into a dismal hell.
There you must make the burning lake,
  Your everlasting gaol ;
Your company eternally,
  Devils and damned souls.
You must endure forevermore,
  The never dying worm,
Where gulphs of fire unlock'd do pour
  Forth their devouring flame.
O that you might escape that night,
  Where day can never dawn ;
Regions of woe, where God doth show
  And make his vengeance known.
O that you may for mercy pray,
  Till mercy you do find ;
Where sins abound poor souls have found,
  God merciful and kind.
The dying thief o'erwhelm'd with grief,
  A dying Lord implor'd ;
And on the cross, of Paradise
  The suiter was insur'd.
But to conclude—O may that God,
  Who gave his only Son,
Give you his grace, in Heaven a place,
  For Jesus' sake——Amen.

Printed and sold at the Printing-Office in Market-Street, Portsmouth.

WAR-TIME BALLADS AND MARCHING SONGS

SOME MEDITATIONS CONCERNING OUR HONOURABLE GENTLEMEN AND FELLOW-SOULDIERS, IN PURSUIT OF THOSE BARBAROUS NATIVES IN THE NARRAGANSIT-COUNTRY, DEC. 28, 1675

BY W. W. [WAIT WINTHROP]

[*The Massachusetts Historical Society*]

SIZE, 7⅞ by 12⅝ inches. If these verses were first issued on the date they bear, they were probably printed by Samuel Green of Cambridge. No copy of this 1675 imprint has yet come to light. The New London issue of 1721 is easily explained by the fact that the Indian problem had again become serious. The first issue of the *New-England Courant*, August 7, 1721, records the sailing of a government expedition from Nantasket to quell the disturbance along the coast. Subsequent issues report the continued depredations of the Indians and the success of the expedition against them.

The battle detailed in these verses is usually referred to as the Swamp Fight, one of the decisive engagements in King Philip's War. Representing the combined force of Massachusetts, New Plymouth, and Connecticut, against the Narragansetts, it was fought December 19, 1675, in a pine and cedar swamp, near what is now South Kingston, Rhode Island, and was a complete victory for the colonists. With the killing of King Philip in the following year, the power of the Narragansetts was effectually crushed. Philip had been present at the Swamp Fight but had escaped.

The initials W. W. are thought to be those of Wait Winthrop, son of Governor Winthrop of Connecticut. His full name was Wait Still Winthrop. He was born February 27, 1641/42, and lived the life of a soldier and jurist. Earlier in this same year he had been one of the Committee of the United Colonies to draw up a plan of campaign, and he was also present at the battle, in command of the Connecticut troops. Whether the verses are rightly credited to him or not, they have the interest of being the first American news ballad to survive in a broadside sheet.

The Indians then, [w]ere as strong men,
Six Score and Ten of Valiant Men,
　　The figures usually given are 86 killed and 150 wounded.
And then at night, they left the Fight,
　　They preferred to risk a fifteen-mile march at night, in a blizzard, carrying their wounded, to the possibility of facing a return attack by the Indians in the morning. The frozen surface of the swamp had made access to the fort possible, and the same advantage might turn in favor of the Indians on another day. The fort had, of course, been destroyed by the victors.

Some Meditations

Concerning our HONOURABLE

Gentlemen and Fellow=Souldiers,

In Purfuit of thofe

Barbarous NATIVES in the NARRAGANSIT-Country;

and Their Service there.

Committed into Plain Verfe for the Benefit of thofe that Read it.   By an Unfeigned Friend.

[1]
Thefe *Indians ftrong* have *waited long*
but now intend to fee,
If that they can fo play the man,
that they themfelves may free.

[2]
When I do Mufe, I cannot Chufe
but mind Gods hand therein,
How he at firft, *Indians* difperft,
that *Englifh* might begin,

[3]
The Ground to Till, the Land to Fill,
with Men and eke with Beafts.
This fifty year, fome have been here,
And have Enjoyed Peace.

[4]
The *Indians* then, were as ftrong men,
as now they feem to be,
And yet *two men* wou'd chace *twice ten*
and make them for to flee.

[5]
They ftood in dread and were afraid,
the *Englifh* to offend,
When they did meet 'em in the Street
their word was *VVhat Cheer Friend.*

[6]
It did appear that when they were
in Number many more
Than now they are, both near and far,
abroad, and at our door.

[7]
Then *Englifh* men, there was not Ten,
where Thoufands now appear,
And yet alas, it comes to pafs,
of them we ftand in fear.

[8]
Our Captains ftout, they have gone out,
to fight them in the Field :
But in the Wood they were *withftood,*
thefe Indians will not yield·

[9]
They had a Fight, in Heavens fight,
kept up as in a Pound,
Men ftrong & tall, were forc'd to fall,
and left upon the Ground.

[10]
Six Score and Ten of Valiant Men,
was wounded in that Fight,
And Fifty more, if not Three Score,
was flain thereby out-right.

[11]
And then at night, they left the Fight,
in Snow up to the knees,
And to their Tent, away they went,
almoft ready to freeze.

[12]
And as fome fay, they loft their way,
and Twenty Miles to go,
Marching all Night, till clear *Day light,*
up to the knees in Snow.

[13]
Some froze to Death, have loft their Breath
with fiercenefs of the Cold,
Some Froze their Feet, they being wet
'twas fad for to behold.

[14]
It grieves my heart, & makes it fmart
I cannot chufe but weep,
To think on thofe, who on the Snows
are forc'd to take their Sleep,

[15]
In Wildernefs, in great Diftrefs,
in Winters fierceft Cold,
'Tis grief to me to hear or fee,
'tis fad for to behold.

[16]
Brave Gentlemen, the which have been
brought up moft tenderly,
Are now come out, Ranging about,
and on the Ground do ly.

[17]
Open your Eyes, and Sympathize,
with thofe brave Gentlemen,
A heart of Flint, it would Relent,
to think how it hath been·

[18]
All who are wife, will Sympathize,
with this our Englifh Nation,
And forely grieve, and help relieve
them there in this fad ftation·

(19)
O Lord, arife, open the Eyes,
of this our Englifh Nation,
And let them fee, and alfo be,
faved with thy Salvation·

(20)
Caft thou a dread, and make afraid
thefe Indians ftrong and ftout,
And make 'em feel the Sword of Steel,
that fo they may give out.

(21)
Left they do boaft of their great Hoft,
and praife their god the Devil,
From whom indeed, this doth proceed
the Author of all Evil.

(22)
O *New-England,* I underftand,
with thee God is offended :
And therefore He doth humble thee,
till thou thy ways haft mended.

(23)
Repent therefore, and do no more,
advance thy felf fo High,
But humbled be, and thou fhalt fee
thefe Indians foon will dy·

(24)
A Swarm of Flies, they may arife,
a Nation to Annoy,
Yea Rats and Mice, or Swarms of Lice
a Nation may deftroy.

(25)
Do thou not boaft, it is God's Hoft,
and He before doth go,
To humble thee and make thee fee,
that He His Works will fhow.

(26)
And now I fhall my Neighbours all
give one word of Advice,
In Love and Care do you prepare
for War, if you be wife.

(27)
Get Ammunition with Expedition
your Selves for to defend,
And Pray to God that He His Rod
will pleafe for to fufpend.

(28)
And who can tell ! but that He will,
be Gracious to us here ?
Thofe that him ferve He will preferve
they need it not to fear.

(29)
Though here they dy immediately,
yet they fhall go to Reft,
And at that day the Lord will fay,
happy art thou, and bleft.

(30)
But unto thofe, that be His Foes,
the Lord to them will fay,
Depart from Me, even all ye
that would not Me Obey.

(31)
My Friends I pray, mark what I fay,
and to it give good heed,
And to the SON, fee that you Run,
and Him Embrace with fpeed.

(32)
And now my Friend, here I will End,
no more here fhall I write,
Or left I fhall fome Tears let fall,
and fpoil my Writing quite.

December 28,
1675.   WM. WM.

Re-printed at *N·London, April* 4. 1725

No. 54

A BRIEF NARRATIVE, OR POEM, GIVING AN ACCOUNT OF THE HOSTILE ACTIONS OF SOME PAGAN INDIANS TOWARDS LIEUTENANT JACOB TILTON, AND HIS BROTHER DANIEL TILTON, 1722

BY W. G.

[*The New York Historical Society*]

SIZE, 12½ by 16 inches. The date of the original imprint is not known. The date of the Newburyport reprint can be fixed within a year, as the partnership of Tinges and Thomas was formed in 1773, and continued for one year only. The verses have been reprinted several times: in *The New England Historical and Genealogical Register* (1848), II, 271–274; in *The Ipswich Antiquarian Papers*, May, 1880, and also in Thomas F. Waters, *Ipswich in the Massachusetts Bay Colony* (1917), II, 44–49. In these two last entries the title is given as "The Tragick Scene."

Seventeen hundred and twenty-two was a year of Indian depredations, particularly along the eastern coast. The incident recorded in these verses was only one of many such attacks suffered by Ipswich fishermen during this time. In fact their situation became so dangerous that during the following summer they were guarded by a government sloop which patrolled the coast of Massachusetts. The Tilton adventure is recorded (without names) in the *New-England Courant*, June 25, 1722. The record is as follows:

Boston, June 25. We have advice from the Eastward, that the Indians there are again in Arms, and have burnt several Houses, kill'd a considerable Number of Cattle, and taken five Men Prisoners, and one or two Sloops bound to this Place, from Annapolis Royal. Six Indians came arm'd on board a Scooner, which lay at Anchor, and bound two of the Men, (there being but one more on board who made no Resistance) but while they were plundering the Vessel, the Men found means to free themselves, and after a short Skirmish threw 4 of the Indians overboard, who ('tis said) are all drown'd: The other two made their Escape, and 'tis said the two Men are, pretty much wounded by the Indians.

Samuel Penhallow mentions the affair briefly as follows (*The History of the Wars of New-England with the Eastern Indians* [Boston, 1726], reprinted in "Collections of the New Hampshire Historical Society" [Concord, 1824], I, 91–92):

About the same time, [1722] Capt. Samuel with five others boarded Lieut. Tilton, as he lay at anchor a fishing, near Damaris Cove. They pinioned him and his brother, and beat them very sorely: but at last, one got clear and released the other, who then fell with great fury upon the Indians, threw one overboard, and mortally wounded two more.

The identity of the author, W. G., has not been established.

Your Boston Governor
Governor Samuel Shute, of Massachusetts.

[114]

A BRIEF
NARRATIVE, or POEM,

Giving an Account of the Hostile Actions of some Pagan Indians towards Lieutenant Jacob T
brother Daniel Tilton, both of the town of Ipswich, as they were on board of a small vesse'
ward ; which happened in the summer-time, in the year 1722. With an Account of th
Exploits of the said Tiltons, and their victorious Conquest over their insulting ener

DOWN at an eastward harbour call'd Fox Bay,
They in a Schooner at an anchor lay,
It was upon the fourteenth day of June,
Six stout great Indians in the afternoon
In two *Canoes* on board said Schooner came,
With painted Faces in a churlish frame ;
One of them call'd *Penobscot* Governor,
The other Captain *Sam* a surly cur,
The other four *great* Indians strong and stout,
Which for their ill design they had pick'd out.
Said Governor and *Sam* with one more went
Down the forecastle, bold and insolent ;
Unto Lieutenant *Tilton* they apply'd,
Themselves, and down they sat one at each side ;
The other plac'd himself behind his back,
Waiting the other's motion when to act.
INDIAN.
*What's matter Governor my men detain,
And no send hostage home to me again ?
What's matter he no good, but all one Devil ?
What ! no love Indian ! Governor no civil.
Penobscot Indian Governor great Man,
All one Governor* Shute, says Captain *Sam.*
TILTON.
Great while since we from Boston hither came,
We poor fishermen, are not to blame.
INDIAN.
Your Boston Governor *no good me see ;
Our Governor much better man than he.*
These Cannibals thus in their Indian pride,
The best of *Governor's* scorn and deride.
But they at length to hasten their design,
From underneath their Blanket pull'd a line, (round,
With which his Arms they would have compass'd
But he so strong and nimble, was not bound,
Till he got out the Cuddy door at last,
Before they had obtain'd to bind him fast.
These Cannibals being both strong and bold,
And upon him kept fast their Indian hold :
They got him down with their much struggling
And bound his arms behind him with their string.
The other three which kept above the deck,
Also had their design brought to effect.
Looking about him, presently he found
They had his brother *Daniel* also bound ;
For they with him had acted even so,
One at each side and one behind did go,
And down they sat, he not aware of harm,
The rogue behind him fasten'd on each arm,
And twitch'd them back ; the other two with line
Him pinioned : so thus were they confin'd.
They ty'd said *Daniel's* legs he could not stand,
Nor help himself neither with foot nor hand,
They struck them many blows on face and head ;
And their long Indian knives they flourished :
Triumphing over them, and saying, *Why
You so stout man that you no Quarter cry ?*
TILTON.
What Indian mean to act so in this thing.
Now Peace between the English and French king ?
INDIAN.
*Hah ? no : me war, your Governor no good,
He no love Indians* me understood.
TILTON.
What ails you now, you sturdy Captain *Sam,*
Do Indian now intend to kill and cram ?
INDIAN.
We Governor SHUTE's *men kill and take,
Penobscot (all one) Boston Prison make.*

*You English men our In.'an land enjoy,
They no surrender, then we them destroy.
Indian bimeby take Captain* Westbrook's *fort,
Some kill, some captive take ; that matchet sport.*

On board them a young lad and not confin'd,
They made him hoist the ancient to their mind !
Then Admiral of this same harbor rid,
In mighty triumph none could them forbid.
So two of these black rogues in their canoes,
On shore they go to carry back the news :
So was but four of them on board remain'd,
Of whom this favour *Daniel* then obtain'd,
For to unty his legs and ease his hand,
That he might have them something at command.
After which thing he presently contrives
What method then to take, to save their lives.
While they were plunder...g so busily,
He saw a splitting knife that was near by,
To which he goes and turns his back about,
Eyeing them well, lest they should find him out ;
And so he works said knife into his hand,
With which he cuts his line, but still doth stand,
Although two of said Indians him ey'd,
They did not know, but he remain'd fast ty'd.
Two of said Indians were plundering,
Down the Forecastle while he did this thing,
The other two so watchful and so shy,
And on him kept a constant Indian eye,
That he stands still waiting till he could find
A time when they did him not so much mind ;
But when for plunder they to searching goes
Then his contrivance presently he shows :
He to his Brother *Jacob* runs with speed,
And cuts his line : now both of them are freed.
The Indians now alarmed hereby,
In Indian language made a hideous cry :
Crying *Chau hau, chau hau :* for they espy'd,
That both these Englishman were got unty'd ;
Like roaring Lyons with an ax and knives
Made violent assaults to take their lives ;
But God who had determined to save,
Undaunted courage unto them he gave ;
That they with such a manly confidence,
Altho' unarm'd stood in their own defence ;
And tho' they had from these blood-thirsty hounds
Received many dismal stabs and wounds,
While in their skirmish blood was up and hot,
No more than Flea bites them they minded not.
Said *Daniel* still retain'd his splitting knife,
Who nimbly ply'd the same and fit for life ;
With one hand fended off the Indian blows,
And with the other cross the face and nose
Of Captain *Sam,* until his pagan head,
Was chop'd and gash'd, and so much mangled ;
Bits of his Indian scalp hung down in strings,
And blood run pouring thence as out of springs.
Jacob said Governor so managed,
He was so maul'd and beat, that he so bled,
His Indian head and face with blood was dy'd,
(*See what comes of his swelling Indian pride,*)
Of him he catch'd fast hold, and up him brings
Unto the side, and overboard him flings.
Then *Daniel* presently took Captain *Sam,*
And brought his Hand about his Indian ham,
And to the vessel side he nimble goes,
And his *black carcass* in the water throws.
Now by this time, behold *Jacob* his brother,
Of these black rogues had catch'd up another,
And overboard his *Indian carcass* sent

To scramble in the water as   , went,
And then said *Daniel* run the *fourth* to catch,
At which the rogue a nimble jump   fetch,
And overboard he goes, and swims to shore ;
This only rogue escaped out of four.
One of the other three he swim'd part way,
At length sinks down, and there was forc'd to stay.
Two of the other rogues with much ado
Got out of water into a canoe,
Which to the Vessel side was fastened,
Themselves awhile in it they sheltered,
Said Indians on board had left a gun,
Unto the same said *Jacob Tilton* run.
Catching it up to shoot them, it mist fire,
Which disappointed him of his desire.
He catching up a stout great *setting Pole,*
With all his might he struck them on the *Jole,*
Giving them many blows upon the head ;
Over they turns, and sunk like any leed.
*We think our Country now at Peace might rest,
If all our Indian foes were thus supprest.
Let God the glory of such conquest have,
Who can by few as well as many save.*
They having thus dispach'd this Indian crew,
Then presently consulted what to do :
Three more Canoes laden to the brim
With Indians as deep as they could swim,
Come padling down with all their might and mein
Hoping the valient *Tilton's* to retain.
Daniel, which was both nimble, stout and spry,
He fetch'd an ax, and running presently,
He cuts the cable ; then they hoist their sail,
Leaving their Neighbours, that they might bewail
Over their Governor who in dispute,
Had term'd himself *as great and good as* Shute.
Before that they had sailed many miles,
Their wounds began to be as sore as boils,
From whence the blood run streaming thro' the cloaths,
Quite from their shoulders down unto their toes,
There they sat down in woful misery,
Expecting every moment when to die ;
Not having any thing to chear their heart,
Nor dress their wounds to ease them of their smart,
And verily we think had perished,
Had not the lad (which has been mentioned)
Been very helpful in this sore distress.
*What reason then have they of thankfulness
That God hath spared him from this Indian crew,
For to help them when they could nothing do.*
After they had from foes escaped thus,
They sail'd and came into *Mintinnicus,*
Nigh twenty-four hours if not more,
They were a-coming from the former shore :
Here they among the English find relief,
Who dress their wounds which ease them of their grief,
Their course for *Ipswich* town they next contrive,
Where in few days their Vessel did arrive :
Through so much danger, misery and pain,
They are returned to their friends again.
Thus I have summed up this tragick scene,
As from their mouths it told to me has been ;
No alteration but in some expressions ;
Us'd other words ; then pardon such digressions,
Since I us'd such only for sake of verse,
Which might not less nor more than truth rehearse,
*Your candid servant in this poetrie,
Describ'd in letters two*-----

W. G.

Newburyport—from a Re-print by I. Thomas and H. W. Tinges—
Printed by W. & J. Gilman, No. 9, State-Street. June, 1834.

SOME EXCELLENT VERSES ON ADMIRAL VERNON'S TAKING THE FORTS AND CASTLES OF CARTHAGENA, IN THE MONTH OF MARCH LAST [1741]

[*The New York Public Library*]

SIZE, 8½ by 12 inches. Printed by Thomas Fleet. These verses appear to have been composed after the first news of the siege of Carthagena had been received. The last stanza with its promise of a second part, "When we have took the city," proves that the writer did not yet know the unsuccessful outcome of the expedition. Comparison of these verses with published news accounts serves to fix the date of composition approximately. The *Boston News-Letter* of May 14, 1741, gave a column and a half of its first page to news of Admiral Vernon's initial success at Carthagena, brought by Captain Rivers from Jamaica, and also by two letters from soldiers in the expedition. Various details emphasized in these accounts are used by the present balladist. Items in subsequent issues of the *News-Letter* continue to be encouraging until June 11, when there is news of a retreat and of sickness among the soldiers. On July 2 encouraging reports are denied and letters are published detailing Admiral Vernon's defeat and the depletion of his army by disease. The present ballad quite certainly was written at some time between May 14 and July 2, 1741. It was probably also printed during that time.

The siege of Carthagena was a major effort of the British to crush the power of Spain by attacking the most strongly fortified harbor in Spanish America. Admiral Vernon, a popular hero of the hour, was in command of a fleet of some 115 ships, and an army of 25,000 soldiers and sailors. The outcome of this venture was of much interest to America since a large proportion of the soldiers had been furnished by the New England colonies. Although announcement was made that Carthagena had fallen, the outcome of the expedition was disastrous in the extreme. Admiral Vernon was forced to withdraw on April 24, 1741, because of lack of provisions and the raging of a fever among his soldiers. Of the thousands of men who had enlisted from New England, only a bare handful returned.

St. Philip gone, and Terra-Bomba,
> Two of the smaller forts.

Boco-Chico
> Boca Chica, the name of the narrow entrance to the harbor.

Castle Legrand
> Carthagena was defended by several forts, the strongest of which was known as the Castle.

Don Blas
> In command of the Spanish forces.

Wentworth commands
> General Wentworth, in command of the English land forces.

Ad. *Vernon*   Ad. *Ogle,* Com. *Lestock.*   *Carthagena.*

Some Excellent VERSES

On Admiral VERNON's taking the Forts and Castles of *Carthagena,*
In the Month of *March* last.

(1.)
ATTEND all Nations round about,
 Who dwell on ev'ry Shore;
Where e'er old *Neptune's* Waves can float,
 Or *Britain's* Cannons roar.

(2.)
I found great VERNON's spreading Fame,
 Round Heav'n's expanded Arch;
Who thund'ring on the *Spaniards* came
 On the last Ninth of *March.*

(3.)
Four Ships against two Forts sail'd on,
 And took them as they stood;
Tho' both the Forts were built of Stone,
 And th' Ships were made of Wood.

(4.)
St. *Philip* gone, and *Terra-Bomba,*
 (Was ever seen the like—O!)
Resolv'd to cut the *Spaniards* Comb—a,
 They fir'd at *Boco-Chico.*

(5.)
The *Spaniards* star'd at the loud Ring,
 As at a Rod stares Dunce;
Like frighted Pidgeons they took Wing,
 And vanish'd all at once.

(6.)
Castle *Legrand* to guard the Boom,
 Stood threat'ning far and wide;
Two Men of War did boldly come
 And pour'd a whole Broad-side.

(7.)
But, gen'rous, give the Foes their due,
 There was no Sign of Fear;
VERNON *fire on, a Fig for you!*
 For not a Man was there.

(8.)
This Castle was their greatest Strain,
 Don *Blass* concluded right;
He ran away with all his Men,
 And left the Fort to fight.

(9.)
Into his Ship the Hero got,
 Then sail'd away to Town,
Then bid them fire, then bid them not,
 Then run, then stop'd, then run.

(10.)
So a young Lady in new Stays
 Tail-nestling keeps a Rout;
And so a Maggot in a Cheese
 Rolls wriggling round about.

(11.)
You said, Don *Blass,* you'd drink a Glass
 With VERNON, could you catch him;
He's coming on, why do you run?
 Pray can't you stay to pledge him?

(12.)
Fastned in *Carthagena* close,
 No further can he fly;
Armies by Land, or Fleets let loose
 Will catch him by and by.

(13.)
How dolefully with eighty Guns,
 Don *Blass's* Ship was seen!
Taken from Seventy *Spanish* Dons,
 By Five and Twenty Men.

(14.)
In haste they sunk Three Men of War,
 To stop the Channel up;
The rest amaz'd they set on Fire,
 Each Ship, and Snow, and Sloop.

(15.)
Don *Blass* beheld, he sobb'd and whin'd,
 His huge black Whiskers tore;
And had he not fear'd to be sin'd,
 He would have curs'd and swore.

(16.)
While these brave Things were done at Sea,
 Our Soldiers work'd for Blood,
Built on the Land a Battery,
 Behind a hideous Wood.

(17.)
Wentworth commands, down go the Trees,
 With horrible Report;
Agast, the trembling *Spaniard* sees
 The Negroes and the Fort.

(18.)
Our Picture shows all this with Art,
 (Was ever Work so pretty!)
And soon you'l see the second Part,
 When we have took the City.

Sold at the *Heart and Crown* in Cornhill.

No. 56

[A BRIEF] JOURNAL OF THE TAKING OF CAPE-BRETON, 1745
BY L. G.

[The New York Historical Society]

SIZE, 8¼ by 10¾ inches. The margins have been trimmed. This is probably a New London imprint, issued soon after the return of the Connecticut soldiers. It is the earliest of the news ballads which survive from the French and Indian Wars.

Fort Louisburg, on the eastern coast of Cape Breton, was a strategic point in that it protected the entrance to Canada. Plans for its capture were formulated by Governor Shirley of Massachusetts. At Canseau, William Pepperell, chosen to lead the colonial army, joined forces with the British commanded by Commodore Warren, and the combined armies forced the surrender of the fort on June 17, 1745.

The identity of L. G. is not known. No officer in the Connecticut regiment had these initials.

The Regiment from Connecticut
> This regiment consisted of 500 men for the land force, and 100 men for sea service.

Of the Transports that did ly Anchor'd there in the Ro[de]
> Joshua Hempstead's *Diary* has an entry concerning the departure of the troops. "Collections of the New London County Historical Society" (1901), I, 440.

Apr. 13, 1745.

> . . . the Souldiers of the 8 Companys are getting on Bord the Transports. I was up in the Evening to take Leave of Several &c. the wind SE some days. Sund 14 fair. mr adams pr all Day. the Fleet Sayled for Cape Briton about [ ] & one, wind SW fresh gale. . . our Country Sloop Semd to out Sayle all [ ]. (Subsequent entries record the arrival of news from the expedition.)

[The Major-General had come on Board and Officers all round,]
> Roger Wolcott, Deputy Governor at the time, accompanied the expedition to Louisburg in the capacity of major general. The narrative details of this ballad may be checked by the record of events in his journal, kept during this period. "Collections of the Connecticut Historical Society" (Hartford, 1860), I, 131–161.

Ensign Leeds
> Sergeant Leeds, with a few Indians, entered the Royal Battery, May 1, and with 16 men drove back 80.

At the Lighthouse we did erect a Fascine Battery,
> This was built by Colonel Gorham's regiment, and was accomplished with great difficulty.

[118]

THE JOURNAL

Of the Taking of

CAPE-BRETON,

Put in Metre, by *L. G.* one of the Soldiers in the Expedition.

[I.]

THE Regiment 'from *Connecticut* at *New-London* came down
And a Battalion drew up in the middle of the Town,
And Articles they were read off at the Head of all the men,
Which were well pleasing unto us all when we came to hear them.

[II.]

Our Regiment it was all Ordered directly on Board
Of the Transports that did ly Anchor'd there in the Road,
And was to be Convoy'd by the *Tartar* and *Defence*,
And all the Charges of the same at the *Governments* Expence.

[III.]

It was the Fourteenth day of *April* † our Fleet it did set Sail,
And bore away to the Eastward with a fair pleasant Gale.
The Generals Word came on Board and Officers all round,
And the very next day the Fleet arriv'd in *Martins Vineyard Sound*.

[IV.]

From thence we stood for *Canso* & we join'd the *Boston* Fleet,
And Anchor'd in the *Harbour* there, they much rejoic'd to see it.
Our Forces being all well agreed resolved to make no Stay,
We soon all became under Sail & stood for *Chipperague-Bay*

[V.]

It was the last of *April* that we did Arrive in the Bay,
With abundance of Prosperity, the whole Army will say,
Our Enemies they march'd down, being in a most dismal heat,
We soon landed part of our men which caus'd them to retreat.

[VI.]

St. *Georges* Colours we did hoist upon the Land so high,
Which caused the *French* Foes to look upon us very Shy,
They being so much in Surprize & in such a dismal Fright,
That they never dar'd to sally out to give us a Field Fight.

[VII.]

Soon after that then Ensign *Leeds* was sent with *Eighteen Men*,
And espied the Grand-Battery and boldly March'd in:
(He being the first of our Army that ever marched therein)
And we hold it to this very day for the Honour of George our King.

[VIII.]

So then the *Bombs* & *Cannon* shot flew from all parts of the Town,
They fir'd briskly upon us, brave Boys, but did us but little wrong,
Then our Batteries we did Erect and we drew up our Guns,
And so we paid them the old debt, we sent them two for one.

[IX]

Our Battery's we did advance under their Walls so nigh,
And batter'd down part of their Walls which they built so high:
Their *Flagstaff* we cut down three times, which caus'd them to fear
For to Fight us any longer it would prove never the near.

[X.]

At the Lighthouse we did Erect a Fascine Battery,
And fired briskly with our Guns right into the City:
We hove our Bombs & our Cannon shot right into the *Island Fort*,
And made the *Frenchmen quit the spot*, for we shew'd 'em fine sport.

[XI.]

Within the Fort it was so hot they were all obliged to Flee,
There was no place of shelter there, they betook them selves to the Sea,
They run up into the water to their Arm-pits so high:
For they had not courage to stand where the Cannon-balls did fly.

[XII.]

So then they saw they were all surrounded both by Land & Sea,
And had no long time of abiding there, nor no where to Flee:
Oh! they were a People sore distrest, encompas'd round with grief,
And none was able to come in to give them any Relief.

[XIII.]

Then a *Flag of truce* came out whilst we were incam'p at the Bay
And desir'd a cessation of Arms until the very next Day:
To which our *Generals* did consent & return'd the *Flag* again,
And demanded of them an Answer by the next day at Noon.

[XIV.]

Accordingly the Flag returned by the prefixed Time,
With these Proposals they bro't out, 'the City they would Resign
' If they might have the Plunder all, & be sent home to France;
' Then the City Gates they'd open to us & our Regiments might advance.

[XV.]

To which our Generals did confent without the least delay,
And so drew off part of their Troops & bravely march'd away;
With beat of Drum & Colours flying they bravely marched in,
And so the day was ended in drinking Healths to George our King.

[XVI]

But now let us ascribe the Praise to whom it doth belong,
Knowing the Race is not to the swift, nor the Battle to be strong;
But it was the Lord that fought for us, the world may see therefore,
And so let us ascribe the Praise to Him for ever more.

Anno Domini, 1745.

F I N I S.

And demanded of them an Answer by the next day at Noon.

In addition to not being a rhyme, *noon* is inaccurate. According to Wolcott's journal, it was eight o'clock in the morning.

But it was the Lord

Wolcott's entry concerning the victory is of interest in view of the parallel to it in this closing stanza. He wrote, "But why do I speak of men, 'tis God has done it and the praise belongs to him alone."

No. 57
A BALLAD CONCERNING THE FIGHT BETWEEN THE ENGLISH AND FRENCH, AT LAKE-GEORGE
[SEPT. 8, 1755]

[*The Library Company of Philadelphia* (Ridgway Branch)]

SIZE, 7⅞ by 10 inches. From the note, this is a second impression. The verses were obviously written by one of the soldiers in the expedition, and were probably issued in Boston soon after the return of the Massachusetts troops. A rare imprint entitled "A Prospective Plan of the Battle fought near Lake George on the 8th of September 1755," is of interest in connection with this verse account. This "Plan" together with a pamphlet in explanation was made by a Boston shopkeeper, Samuel Blodget, "Occasionally at the Camp, when the battle was fought." It was reproduced by Mr. Samuel Abbott Green in his *Ten Fac-simile Reproductions*, pp. 35 ff.

As the only success in a disastrous year of fighting, this British victory occasioned much enthusiasm in England and America. On September 8, 1755, William Johnson, in command of some three thousand colonists and Indians, defeated a slightly smaller army of French regulars, on the shores of the Lake of the Holy Sacrament. The lake was forthwith renamed Lake George in honor of the King.

A [fa]tal Scheme our Foes had laid, . . .
W[e']d not a Thought so soon to meet . . .

A BALLAD concerning the Fight between the English and French, at Lake-George.

OH! Bless the God that gives Success unto our *English* Nation,
Who granted us a Victory beyond our Expectation.
Our Enemies encounter'd us with such undaunted Courage,
And fired so fierce on us at first, that they our Hearts discourag'd.
A fatal Scheme our Foes had laid, and cunningly devised,
Of which, if we had known in Time, we had not been surprized.
A Thousand then of chosen Men, were sent from our Encampment,
And when we on three Miles had gone, we had our hot Engagement.
They'd Notice of our coming out, and placed themselves in Order,
And not a Thought so soon to meet such Knaves within our Border.
In Ambush they were laid so Close, and by the Path so near,
Their reg'lar Troops in Order stood, all placed in their Rear.
Their Orders were to let us march, till all them surrounded,
Then we should be their easy Prey, all taken kill'd or wounded.
But Providence our Fate prevents, and frustrates their Design,
Too soon their Signal it was given, Thanks to the Power Divine.
Brave *Williams*, stood in Front while Guns, loud roar'd, and Balls
(were flying,

And there he for his Country died, and purchas'd Fame by dying.
Judicious *Whiting*, took his Place, and led us back retreating;
In spite of our more numerous Foes, all their Designs defeating.
An Hundred Men we lost before, we to our Camp arrived
And there our Friends they look'd so bold, that they our Hearts
(revived.

Our Enemies they pushed so close, and followed us so near,
We thought they were our own Men, a bringing up the Rear.
Brave *Johnson*, then directs the Fight, as bold as *Alexander*,
Resolv'd to do his Country Right, as being chief Commander:
He in the Battle risk'd his Life, when Bullets they were flying,
Too warmly bent on Victory, to have a Thought of dying,
Brave *Lyman* now, well skill'd in Law, a new Cause had undertaken,
Not such as those he used to plead, and seldom be mistaken;
Most Hero-like he did appear, and fought with Zeal unfeigned,
And never did he give it o'er, until the Cause he gained.

Our Colonels all, with Sword and Spear, appear'd in Pomp and
(Splendor,
They bid Defiance to the *French*, and *Jemmy* the Pretender.
Our Engineer despis'd all Fear, his Courage I must mention,
Which never can disputed be, what e'er was his Intention,
The Cannons with continual Noise, roar'd like to Claps of Thunder;
They kill'd 'tis true, not many Men, which need not be a Wonder:
But still the threatning Sounds they spoke, made all the *Indians* scatter;
(Stunn'd with the Noise, and Fire and Smoke) *Canadians* they fled after.
And now my Friends I will relate, while Cannons loud did rattle,
How our brave Soldiers did behave, amidst the flaming Battle.
Like Lions, they disdain'd to fear, in fighting for our Nation;
Our King, our Properties and Laws, against a *French* Invasion.
'Twas in the Morn at eight o'Clock, the Engagement first begun.
'Twas fix o'Clock in the Afternoon, before the Fight was done.
About that Time, our wearied Foes march'd heavily retreating;
And e'er they had got far from us, received another beating.
Our *Hampshire* Friends from *Edward Fort*, came out to our Assistance,
They risk'd their Lives to help their Friends, nor fear'd their Foes
(Resistance.

The *French* were like the wearied Sheep, just fitted for devouring,
They scatter'd them on every Part, this was their final scouring.
Their shatter'd Forces now dispers'd, in Woods by Streams and
(Mountains.
Like Sheep who from the Shepherd stray, and wander o'er the
(Fountains;
One Thousand and eight Hundred Men, of which their Force
(consisted,
Are sunk to Nought tho' once they thought, they could not be
(resisted.
They thought they should our Country drive, but found themselves
(mistaken,
Some few by Flight escap'd the Fight, but most were kill'd or
(taken.
Their Chief we have a Prisoner made, and Major General killed,
The Aid Decamp resign'd himself, with Grief their Hearts were
(filled.

Then let our Hearts encourag'd be, and let us not surrender,
Our Rights, Religion, Liberty, unto a false Pretender.
And since the Victory we've won, and brought the *Monsieurs* under;
We gladly would be marching back, to carry home the Plunder.

* This was call'd *Fort Frederick* by mistake in the former Impression.

ON THE VALIANT NEW-ENGLAND GENERAL, APR. 5, 1756
BY ABIEZER PECK

[*The John Carter Brown Library*]

SIZE, 8⅛ by 13 inches. The printer is unknown.

The General was John Winslow (1702–1774), who with a small army took Fort Gaspereau and Fort Beau Séjour in June, 1756. The forced emigration of the Acadians began in September of the same year.

Little is known of Abiezer Peck, except that he was a resident of Rehoboth, Massachusetts, and the son of Samuel Peck, a zealous Baptist minister of that town. He lived until 1800.

Brave W——w's hast'ning on his Race,
> General Winslow had embarked with the Massachusetts troops, May 20, 1756.

Maz'roth
> Mazzaroth, the twelve constellations of the zodiac. Job 38.32.

Barack
> Barak, a Naphtalite, who, with Deborah, defeated Sisera, leader of the Canaanites. Judg. 4.6–16.

Jaban
> Jabin, king of Canaan, and oppressor of Israel. Judg. 4.2. Sisera was captain of his army.

Deb'rah
> Deborah, prophetess and judge of Israel. Her song is given in Judg. 5.1–31.

Sisera flee alone
> He fled to the tent of Jael, and was killed by her. Judg. 4.21.

in Carthagenia Port
> General Winslow had had a command under Admiral Vernon at the siege of Carthagena in Spanish America during the spring of 1741.

Three Hundred dreadful Teeth of Brass,
> Boca Chica, the narrow entrance to the port of Carthagena, was strongly defended by several forts.

Son of Rapha's Head
> Rapha was reputed to be a great giant among the Philistines. His four sons were slain by David and his servants. II Sam. 21.15–22.

On the VALIANT
NEW-ENGLAND
GENERAL.

I.
PRAY why such Transports in each Breast,
  and Smiles in ev'ry Face?
Is all our Coasts in Health and Rest,
  and Plenty crown each Place?

II.
Brave *W———w*'s hast'ning on his Race,
  to lead *New-England* Bands;
That causeth Joy in every Place,
  and Gladness through our Lands.

III.
From East to West his Chariots run,
  to give the Nations Play;
The Circu't that the rad'ent Sun
  performs from Day to Day.

IV.
The Range the Moon and Stars compleats,
  in their unwearied Round;
The Course that Pleiades respects,
  and Path that Maz'roth found:

V.
'Twas this same Course they roll'd along,
  when glor'ous *Barack* led:
When *Isra'l* pray'd, and *Deb'rah* sung,
  proud *Jaban*'s Army fled.

VI.
Megiddo Streams, and *Kisbon* Flood,
  join'd the ætherial Throne;
To fight against old *Can'an*'s Brood,
  while *Sisera* flee alone.

VII.
O *W———w*, may thy Conquest gain,
  to Places yet unheard;
While our French Foes are cloath'd with Shame,
  and ev'ry Native scar'd.

VIII.
To this Intent may Saints arise,
  to plead the righteous Case;
And scale the Walls above the Skies,
  with Pray'rs of holy Dress.

IX.
O thou, thrice blest, who reins above,
  and rules th' Affairs of Man;
May *W———w* feel the quickning Love,
  of thine eternal Lamb.

X.
LORD, set him stedfast as a Seal,
  on thy dear Heart and Breast;
And grant his Soul may ever feel
  thou art his King and Priest.

XI.
Renew that Mark of Love divine,
  and seal him on thine Arm;
Ensure him, LORD, that he is thine;
  and lead him safe from Harm.

XII.
And when he heads our Army out,
  do thou thy Banner spread,
And cast thy Shield all round about,
  to screen and guard his Head.

XIII.
Direct his Mind in each Attempt,
  to trust in thy dear Name;
And purge the Things from ev'ry Camp,
  that's cursed or prophane.

XIV.
Come *W———w*, take the solemn Charge,
  to lead our warlike Bands:
Go drive the Foes of sov'reign GEORGE,
  to skulk in foreign Lands.

XV.
Remember how fierce the Lion was,
  in *Carthagenia* Port;
Three Hundred dreadful Teeth of Brass,
  in *Boco Checo* Fort.

XVI.
Think how you seiz'd his trembling Bones,
  and rent his Jaws to Racks;
Th' expiring Breath and dying Groans,
  resembling Thunder-Cracks.

XVII.
Again remind the surly Bear,
  At *Chequenecto* slain;
Go forwards now, O *W———w*, dear;
  thy Keeper's still the same.

XVIII.
Whene'er the Sling of Faith is took,
  with the smooth promise Stones,
Pick'd out of Humiliations Brook,
  'twill wreck *Goliah*'s Bones.

XIX.
I trust at your Return to sing,
  as th' Hebrew Females did;
When *David* brought to *Isr'el*'s King,
  the Son of *Rapha*'s Head.

Rehoboth, April 5, 1756.

ABIEZER PECK.

No. 59
AN ENDEAVOUR TO ANIMATE AND INCOURAGE OUR SOL-
DIERS, FOR THE PRESENT EXPEDITION [1758]
BY M. B.

[The Pennsylvania Historical Society]

SIZE, 7½ by 12¼ inches. Green and Russell moved to Queen Street in 1758. The sheet was probably issued in that year.

The identity of M. B. has not been established.

The "Present Expedition" had for its object the capture of Louisburg. An earlier attempt had been planned in 1757 under the leadership of Lord Loudon, but he had become alarmed at the reported strength of the French garrison and had turned back, after proceeding as far as Halifax. The enthusiasm of New England in raising an army for the second expedition was intense. The crusading spirit which had animated the soldiers of the 1745 expedition was revived, and hatred of popery again became a motive for enlistment, along with loyalty to King George.

Cape-Breton
The earlier siege. Cf. the ballad on p. 119, *supra*.
Accada
Acadia. The emigration had begun in September, 1756.
Lake-George
The battle had taken place September 8, 1755. Cf. the ballad, p. 121, *supra*.
To Papists utter Ruin.
The preaching of Whitefield had had much to do with the arousing of antipapist sentiment in the earlier campaign. Some attempt was made in 1758 to revive this antagonism.

An Endeavour to animate and incourage our Soldiers, for the prefent Expedition.

Made, and Fitted to the *Tune* of GEORGE's CORONATION.

THE Trumpet, and the warlike Drum,
Calls once again, brave Gallants come,
To Arms, to Arms Boys all as one,
And with true *Englifh* Valour :
In hafte advance for *Canada*,
And fet the Battle in Array,
There ftrike their Hearts with fore Difmay.
　　　　And win immortal Honour.

Nor, let it e'er Proclaimed be,
That we fhould turn the Back, and Flee,
From fuch as vilely bow the Knee,
　　　　To *Romifh* Superftition :
But let our Bold Heroick Train,
The BRITISH Spirit ftill Retain,
To form their Manners once again,
　　　　'Tis laudible Ambition.

Once *France* was our's, but did Rebel,
And now we muft their Force Repel,
And fend old *Lewis* to his Cell,
　　　　Or elfe to Purgatory ;
There let him lie, and loud Complain,
To *Popes* and *Fryars*, all in Vain,
The Virgin *Mary* will not dain,
　　　　To hear his Mournful Story.

Think how our Brave Renowned *Drake*,
The *Spanifh* Armado did Break,
And round the World rich Prizes take,
　　　　There-with to Blefs the Nation ;
As if the Seas were all his own,
Did rival *Neptune* on his Throne,
Difcovering Coafts, before unknown,
　　　　Worthy of Imitation.

Of late our Young, our Princely *Duke*,
Gave the *Pretender* a Rebuke,
While vengeful Juftice overtook
　　　　Them in the laft Confufion ;
With great Precipitance they Fled,
But left near half their Armies Dead,
And foon the bloody Plots they laid,
　　　　Were brought to a Conclufion.

Once more they mufter all their Pow'r,
America for to Devour,
With mighty Fleets our Seas they Scour ;
　　　　Our Hopes almoft Expire :
But Heaven with a Stormy Blaft,
And Peftilence did lay them Wafte ;
Some Slew themfelves, the reft in hafte
　　　　Were forced to Retire.

Brave Hearts of Gold, lofe not your Fame,
Which at *Cape-Breton* you did gain,
And *George*'s Rights did well Maintain,
　　　　And gain'd his Royal Favour :
Yea *Accada* we did Reclaim,
And at *Lake-George* the Vict'ry gain,
And fent the *Gallics* off with Shame,
　　　　To teach them good Behaviour.

Once more we never may forget,
The Planters of *New-England*'s Seat,
Our bold Advent'rors fet their Feet,
　　　　In a new World of Dangers ;
Where Numberlefs, and Mighty Foes,
On either Side did them Enclofe,
Our Infant Bands in Armour rofe,
　　　　And crufh'd thefe warlike Rangers.

And may thefe Motives all Excite,
Their true Heroick Sons to Fight,
Since ev'ry Blefling will Requite,
　　　　Through ev'ry Age Enfuing ;
And may fome kind propitious Stars,
Affift you in the Field of Mars,
And Heaven Crown our righteous Wars,
　　　　To *Papifts* utter Ruin.

　　　　　　　　　　M. B.

F I N I S.

BOSTON : Printed and Sold by GREEN and RUSSELL, in Queen-ftreet.

No. 60
ON THE LANDING OF THE TROOPS IN BOSTON,
SEPT. 13, 1758

[*The American Antiquarian Society*]

SIZE, 9½ by 14½ inches. The Newbury Street address probably identifies this as an imprint of John Draper, who was printing there in 1758.

These were the troops from Louisburg, commanded by Major General Amherst, who had led the successful expedition against Cape Breton. The *Boston Weekly News-Letter* for September 15, 1758, had a statement of their arrival and entertainment in Boston.

. . . He [General Amherst] was received and congratulated upon his Arrival, with the Respect and Esteem due to so brave a Commander.—On this Occasion, the Guns at Castle-William, those of the Batteries in the Town and at Charlestown, &c. were discharged, and the Bells of the Town were rung. . . .

Thence took a View of Ships and Town,

There were between thirty and forty transports in the fleet.

The Tents around, most beautiful,

The soldiers were encamped on the Common.

But now, the Day, the Day is come,

They left on Saturday, the 17th.

Relate, how FRONTENAC we took,

The reduction of Frontenac was accomplished under the leadership of Colonel Bradstreet, who, with an army of three thousand men, arrived August 17, forced a surrender of the garrison on August 25, destroyed the fort and all but two of the French ships, and returned to Albany in triumph. His achievement was important in that it put Lake Ontario entirely under British control.

The Women out with Tongs did run,

According to Colonel Bradstreet's report of the taking of Frontenac, there were in the Fort at the time of its capture, "110 Men, some Women, Children, and Indians. . . ." This report as contained in the Canadian Archives, is included in *The Journal of John Knox*, "Publications of the Champlain Society" (Toronto, 1914, 1916), I, 265–266.

Relate, how Dawn with Army great,

An allusion to contemporary events in Germany. Count Daun was commander of the Austrian forces in opposition to Frederick during the Seven Years' War. This is probably an allusion to the battle of Kolin, June 18, 1757, unless the ballad was written late enough for the author to be thinking of the more important battle of Hochkirk, October 14, 1758. His reference is not clear.

On the Landing of the Troops in *Boston*, 1758,

September 18th. Their March out *Sept.* 16th. And the Reduction of FRONTENAC, *August* 28, To which is added, The present State of EUROPE.

---

1. WHAT Sounds are thefe of gen'ral Joy,
   That on my Ear-Drums beat ?
   Each Face proclaims a merry Heart,
   And Frolicks fill the Street.

2. The Troops are come, Huzza ! Huzza's
   Is eccho'd thro' the Croud ;
   Guns from the Caftle flafh and roar,
   The Bells all ring aloud.

3. Then to the lofty 'fpiring Top,
   of Beacon-Hill we went ;
   Thence took a View of Ships and Town,
   a Show magnificent !

4. Some with Laughing fplit their Sides,
   others with Singing roar ; ,
   While fome 'tis fear'd in Taverns drink
   'Till they can drink no more.

5. 'Tis hop'd none ftagger round the Street,
   Nor dance nor caper high ;
   In Frolicks drink whole Bottles up,
   Then tofs them to the Sky.

6. And thus with jolly Mirth they fpend,
   The twice, thrice welcome Day ;
   The Night in Town-Houfe-Street fome ftand,
   To fee the Fire-works play.

7. The next Day, was a Day of Joy,
   It was a Thankfgiving :
   The Forces land, and add new Caufe,
   For us aloud to Sing.

8. The Tents around, moft beautiful,
   Form a delightfome Scene ;
   And thus they lye, all free from Care,
   Quite placid and ferene.

9. The next Day, Sports of various Kind,
   and Bufinefs fill'd their Hand :
   And while on the Green Grafs they lay,
   Them *Zephyrs* gently fan'd,

10. Some viewing were a Monkey Play,
    and others a Baboon ;
    Such antic Poftures pleas'd them fo,
    They mifs'd to dine at Noon.

11. Here fome that left their Sweet-Hearts dear,
    In doleful Dumps cry'd, "Oh!
    " Pray little Cupid how could you,
    " Pierce my poor, fond Heart fo ! "

12. The Women mind their proper Work,
    Tho' there were none a Spinning :
    Yet they were looking up their Meat,
    Or wafhing out their Linning.

13. No Brauls or Fighting was there feen,
    None wifh'd his Brother ill :
    Their Swords were made the *French* to cut,
    And not each other Kill.

14. Some liftning were to Mufick'sCharm,
    Which foftly mov'd along ;
    It Breath'd infpiring o'er the Plain,
    And pleas'd th' attentive Throng.

15. But now, the Day, the Day is come,
    That They muft take their March :
    The Sun glows bright, and pours its Beams,
    Thro' all the Heav'ns wide Arch.

16. Bufy as Bees, down go their Tents,
    The Carts receive their Store ;
    To leave the Town themfelves prepare,
    To Victory to foar.

17. Nor loitering in their Work are they ;
    But at the Hour of Six,
    They all are ready for their March,
    Not one Thing need they Fix.

18. The Drum now beats, " *Prepare to Arms !*
    They joyful at the Sound ;
    " *We go to Victory,*", (they cry)
    " *And make our Name renown'd.* "

19. " *Lo CANADA fhall foon be our's,* "
    (They to each other fay ;)
    Encouraging themfelves in this,
    They chearful go away.

20. The Streets all full to view the Sight,
    Each Window crouded is ;
    While They majeftic onward march,
    Their Hearts are big with Blifs.

21. See, all the Guns, they gliften bright,
    At Diftance feem to blaze ;
    While the fofe Mufick's gentle Sound,
    In charming Concert plays.

22. Behold them while they march along,
    In dazzling Armour dreft ;
    True Courage fhines in every Face,
    Undaunted is each Breaft.

23. But now they're gone ; O may Succefs,
    On all their Ways attend !
    May their bright Arms victorious prove,
    And Conquefts crown their End !

24. With Pleafure they will hear the News
    of Conquefts we have won ;
    And with true Emulation fir'd,
    Will fcorn to be out-done.

25. Relate, how FRONTENAC we took,
    Down fell the high thick Walls ;
    Th' Inhabitants all Wild with Fear,
    Are fcatter'd by our Balls.

26. The Women out with Tongs did run,
    The Cookmaids with their Spits ;
    Then from our Guns a Bullet flies
    Which fcares them into Fits.

27. The Men are frightn'd and difmay'd,
    Some down the Cellars fled ;
    And there, for fear they fhould be fcalpt,
    Do feign themfelves as dead.

28. Some leave their Cannon, Fort and all,
    And plunge into the Sea ;
    While others roar and cry aloud,
    " *What will become of We !* "

29. Such difmal Terrors were they in,
    When march'd our gallant Men ;
    They took their Fort and Plunder too,
    And nothing let remain.

30. Relate, how *Daun* with Army great,
    Refifted PRUSSIA's KING :
    HE took their Army, with Count *Daun*,
    Who look'd like any Thing.

31. O, may our Forces all do thus,
    Return with warlike Spoils,
    And thus with glorious Fame we will
    Reward them for their Toils.

No. 61
THE DEATH OF GEN. WOLFE [1759]
[The Massachusetts Historical Society]

SIZE, 8¾ by 10½ inches. There is no clue to the printer or the date of printing. Several issues of the same verses are extant. (Cf. Ford, 1156–1160.)

General Wolfe was killed at the battle of the Plains of Abraham, an engagement which brought Quebec into the hands of the English, and marked the end of the French power in Canada. The English army entered Quebec September 18, having laid siege to the city under Wolfe's leadership for over two months. James Wolfe was born January 2, 1727, and had been a soldier from boyhood, his military career having begun in his father's regiment. He had been commissioned second lieutenant at the age of fourteen, and was a major general at the time of his death. His exploits continued to be sung in America until the heroes of the Revolution displaced him in the popular thought.

I went to see my love only to woo her,
> After Wolfe's return to England, following the siege of Louisburg, he had become engaged to Katherine Lowther, afterward the Duchess of Bolton.

Love, here's a diamond ring
> The present writer probably did not know that in the first sentence of his will, Wolfe directed that Miss Lowther's miniature be returned to her, set in jewels to the amount of five hundred guineas. He would also have been pleased to know that, according to tradition, the Duchess always wore a jewel (possibly this one), in memory of her lover. See Beckles Willson, *The Life and Letters of James Wolfe*, London, 1909, pp. 503–505.

When shot from off his horse, fell this brave hero,
> The wound that proved fatal was the third Wolfe had received that day.

He lifted up his head while guns did rattle,
> Many claimants are on record for the honor of supporting Wolfe as he lay dying, and many versions of his last words have been reported. Although the quoted words differ slightly, all accounts agree in this, that when his own sight failed, Wolfe asked a question as to the progress of the battle, and being assured that the French were giving way, expressed himself content to die. An entire chapter is given to this subject in A. Doughty and G. W. Parmlee's *The Siege of Quebec* (1901), III, 201–237. The chapter is entitled "Wolfe's Dying Moments."

The second poem was written by Thomas Paine, supposedly in 1759, the year of Wolfe's death. The elaborate conceit around which it is built, the bookish vocabulary, and the artifice of the whole, make it seem out of place on a broadside sheet, adorned with so crude a cut, but the piece was very popular and was printed many times. During the Revolution it was modified to fit Generals Warren and Montgomery and was again popular.

The Death of
GEN. WOLFE.

CHEER up your hearts young men let nothing fright
  Be of a gallant mind, let that delight you ; (you,
Let not your courage fail 'till after trial,
Nor let your fancy move at the first denial.

I went to see my love only to woo her,
I went to gain her love, not to undo her ;
Whene'er I spake a word my tongue did quiver,
I could not speak my mind while I was with her.

Love, here's a diamond ring long time I've kept it,
'Tis for your sake alone, if you'll accept it,
When you the posy read, think on the giver,
Madam, remember me, or I'm undone forever.

Brave Wolfe then took his leave of his dear jewel,
Most sorely did she grieve, saying don't be cruel ;
Said he 'tis for a space that I must leave you,
Yet love, where'er I go, I'll not forget you.

So then this gallant youth did cross the ocean,
To free America from her invasion,
He landed at Quebec, with all his party,
The city to attack, both brave and hearty.

Brave Wolfe drew up his men in form most pretty,
On the plains of Abraham, before the city ;
There just before the town the French did meet them,
With double numbers they resolv'd to beat them.

When drawn up in a line, for death prepared,
While in each other's face their armies stared ;
So pleasantly brave Wolfe and Montcalm talked,
So martially between their armies walked.

Each man then took his post at their retire,
So then these numerous hosts began to fire ;
The cannon on each side did roar like thunder,
And youths in all their pride were torn assunder.

The drums did loudly beat, colours were flying,
The purple gore did stream and men lay dying—
When shot from off his horse, fell this brave hero,
And we lament his loss in weeds of sorrow.

The French began to break their ranks and flying,
Brave Wolfe then seem'd to wake as he lay dying,
He lifted up his head while guns did rattle,
And to his army said, how goes the battle !

His aid-de-camp reply'd, 'tis in our favor,
Quebec with all her pride, we soon shall have her ;
She'll fall into our hands, with all her treasure,
O then reply'd brave Wolfe, I die with pleasure.

Death of Gen. WOLFE.

IN a sad mould'ring cave where the wretched retreat,
  Britannia sat wasted with care,
She mourn'd for her Wolfe and exclaim'd against fate,
  And gave herself up to despair.
The walls of her cells she had sculptur'd around
  With deeds of her favorite son ;
And even the dust as it lay on the ground,
  Was engrav'd with some deeds he had done.

The fire of the gods from his christaline throne,
  Beheld the disconsolate dame,
And mov'd with her tears he sent Mercury down,
  And these were the tidings that came,
Britannia, forbear ! not a sigh nor a tear,
  For thy Wolfe so deservedly lov'd ;
Your tears shall be chang'd into triumphs of joy,
  For thy Wolfe is not dead but remov'd.

The sons of the east, the proud giants of old,
  Have crept from their darksome abodes,
And this is the news as in heav'n we're told,
  They were marching to war with the gods.
A counsel was held in the chamber of Jove,
  And this was the final decree,
That Wolfe should be call'd to the armies above,
  And the charge was entrusted to me.

To the plains of Quebec, with the orders I flew,
  Where Wolfe with his army then lay ;
He cry'd, O forbear ! let me victory view,
  And then thy commands I'll obey.
With a darkening film I encompas'd his eyes,
  And bore him away in an urn,
Lest the fondness he bore for his own native shore,
  Should tempt him again to return.

LIBERTY, PROPERTY, AND NO EXCISE, AUG. 14, 1765

[The Boston Public Library]

SIZE, 14 by 18½ inches. For obvious reasons, the printer omitted his name. These verses were reprinted in *The Magazine of History*, Extra No. 83, Vol. XXI (1922), No. 3, pp. 41–47.

The sight referred to was the effigy of Andrew Oliver, Stamp Distributor for Boston, together with a boot (for the Earl of Bute), found hanging on the Great Tree opposite Boylston Market in Boston on the morning of August 14, 1765. The effigies remained throughout the day, and at nightfall were taken down by the Sons of Liberty, who had placed them there, and solemnly carried through the streets at the head of a long procession. The citizens engaging in this pageant marched through the State House, shouting, "Liberty, Property, and No Stamps," and thence proceeded to demolish the frame of a building in Kilby Street, intended by Oliver for a stamp office. With the wood from this structure, they built a funeral pyre and burned the effigies in front of Oliver's house on Fort Hill. This demonstration was the beginning of America's organized defiance. Henceforth, the Great Tree was known as the Liberty Tree, and was the rallying place for patriotic celebrations throughout the war.

The Stamp Act was passed by Parliament March 22, 1765, to take effect November 1, following. It was repealed March 18, 1766, to take effect May 1, following.

[In] spite of knaves
LIBERTY and PITT
> William Pitt, the Elder, popularly known as The Great Commoner. "Pitt and Liberty forever" was the popular cry in England at the time of these verses.

'till thousands fill'd the place,
> The *Boston Weekly News-Letter*, in detailing the day's events, mentioned the "great concourse of people, some of the highest reputation."

Behold the man, whose heart was set on gain,
> George Grenville. Back of his policy of taxation was the necessity to retrieve England's losses in the Seven Years' War. He appears to have thought chiefly in terms of revenue.

Curst be the man that leaves the bodies here
> The morning placard had read, "Whoever takes this down is an enemy to his country."

In solemn order
> Contemporary accounts indicate that except for the assault on Oliver's house, the demonstration was carried through in an orderly manner.

Down to the court
> The Boston State House.

the appointed hill
> Fort Hill.

Liberty, Property, and No *Excise.*

A Poem,

Compos'd on occasion of the SIGHT seen on the GREAT TREES, (so called) in
BOSTON, NEW-ENGLAND, on the 14th of AUGUST, 1765.

LET *Albion's* sons in praise their tongues employ:
New-England smile, and *Boston* shout for joy:
Dispite of knaves, their politics and wit,
She still enjoys her *LIBERTY* and *PITT*.
She rests secure from ev'ry foreign foe,
Derides their plots, and sees their overthrow;
And soon shall see the wretch completely curs'd
Who strove to *STAMP* her glory in the dust.
" Freedom, (she cries) I cannot cringe to knaves,
" My sons are free, and never will be slaves:"
Let tyrants rule with arbitrary sway,
Villains command, and whining fools obey:
Let dastards live in infamy and shame,
While *Britons* fight for liberty and fame:
Let all her foes like bees prepare to swarm;
Old *Pluto* rage, and *Purgatory* storm:
Let *Charon* raise his oars and long-boat take,
And force with fury down the torrid lake.
Speak *Proserpine,* thy will shall be obey'd,
Bid ev'ry fiend forsake the gloomy shade:
Give these commands to each infernal ghost,
" Go spit your venom on the *British* coast;
" Haste there and spread contention wide and far,
" Perplex her isle, and set her sons at war:
" Then to *America* with vengeance go,
" Let them in slavery own the powers below."
Suppose this done, and all the winged bands
At this new world with thunder in their hands:
Our hardy youth would still their force repel,
Defeat their wiles and drive them back to hell;
These sons of *Mars* their courage would confound,
A conquest gain and still maintain their ground.
If men would e'en devils be compell'd to own,
Our sovereign lives and God supports his throne:
Thus blast his foes in ev'ry base design
All-gracious heaven, and bless the royal line.
O give us favor in our monarch's eyes,
Defend our rights, remove the late *EXCISE:*
Let truth prevail and fierce oppression cease,
And bid our Prophet speak the words of peace.
Lo! here he comes, softly he seems to tread,
Now rolls his eyes, now bows his rev'rend head:
He like a God appears in form divine,
Whose very aspect speaks some deep design;
Hither he comes, on purpose to relate
Each sacred truth, and tell some hidden fate,
" *Boston,* (he cries) your woes are at an end,
" Your foe shall fall and times shall quickly mend;
" With shame o'erwhelm'd he soon shall hide his face,
" Then hark while I predict the time and place.
" The day now dawns, the gloomy night is spent,
" And soon your eyes shall see the grand event.
" See fair *Aurora* from her couch arise,
" Whose chearful blushes paints the morning skies:
" The shades are chac'd, the ling'ring stars are fled,
" And yonder *Phæbus* lifts his golden head:
" (Then cries the Prophet) I must haste away,
" The Gods command and mortals must obey."
No more I heard from out his sacred mouth,
He took his leave and went towards the *South:*
Then I beheld amazing wonders there,
Saw human shapes and monsters in the air.
A stately elm appear'd before my eyes,
Whose lofty branches seem'd to touch the skies;
It's limbs were bent with more than common fruit,
It bore the Devil, O——r, and B--te.
Well then, said I, my doubts are wholly fled,
I find the truth of what the father said:
But while I stood to gaze upon the tree,
Another and another came to see;
Each moment I beheld a diff'rent face,
For on they prest 'till thousands fill'd the place,
Here stands a child and looks with wond'ring eyes,
And there a champion of gigantic size;
Yonder a maid at humbler distance stands,
And here a jilt with lifted eyes and hands.

This pleasing prospect entertains the throng,
All join as one, and thus begin their song,
" With grateful joy, O *Boston,* now behold
" These truths fulfill'd, which lately were foretold.
" With thankful hearts now see the villains swing,
" Who hate their country, and would sell their king:
" Behold the man, *whose heart was set on gain,*
" And view the wretch, who wish'd some tyrant's reign."
Thus having observ'd they entertain'd the day,
In songs and chat they past the hours away,
Now *Sol* retires, and journies down the West,
And weary nature seems in sable dreft.
And now a hero lifts his voice aloud,
Stretches his hand, and speaks to all the crowd.
" Hear me, (he cries) and be not too severe,
" Curst be the man that leaves the bodies here
" Expos'd to all the dangers of the night,
" Then bear them hence with every fun'ral right."
Thus having spoke, they all with willing hands
Began to execute their chief's commands:
With rapid haste some to the tree repair,
And on their shoulders bear a ladder there.
One draws his knife, and running to their aid,
Ascends the limbs, that bear each lifeless shade,
Then cuts the ropes in presence of them all,
And as he cuts the ghastly *objects* fall.
Down on the earth in horrid form they lie;
A frightful sight to each beholding eye:
What now, (said I) is all compassion fled?
Can none be found, that will relieve the dead?
Their chief reply'd, " Go place them on the bier,
" Prepare yourselves and quickly bring them here."
This done, he cries, " Let ev'ry man resort
" In solemn order with the corps to court.
" March then, (said he) in one united throng,
" And as you march, be this the fun'ral song.
" Great haughty trees, and go these mortals must;
" 'Tis fit we stamp, and *STAMP* 'em in the dust."
Then as they move, the words are sung by all,
Down in the court and thro' the pompous hall:
Soon as this arose a grand debate,
(Such as attend the fun'rals of the great)
And wild disorder seizes all the band;
Forth some advance, while others make a stand.
One bids them halt, another " still march forth
" And visit all the region of the *North.*"
A third proclaims, " Let these be first convey'd
" In peaceful silence to the dreary shade."
Then spake their head, (the regent of the night)
" Alas! our host is in a shameful plight:
" Is this the way to get a hero's name?
" The road to honor and immortal fame?
" Cease wrangling then, let each in order stand,
" Join arm to arm, like one external band,
" Then here (he cries) be all contention fled,
" Come follow on, your chief at the head."
Thus having spake, all hear the wond'rous man,
And forth they move; (the champion leads the van)
All seem impatient to obey his will,
And bend their course for the appointed *hill,*
Whose lofty summit once contain'd a *fort,*
To this they haste and quickly leave the *court.*
Freedom and friendship centers in each soul,
They shout and sing without the least controul:
Here then we find no obstacles arose,
Noise could offend, and nothing dare oppose,
(Nothing) except a stately *EDIFICE*,
This stops their course, but soon they down with this,
Low in the dust they made the structure lie,
Then *STAMPT* the bricks, and bore the wood away,
Now from the ruins ev'ry one retire,
Up to the *mount* and raise the fun'ral fire.

* Supposed to be built for a *STAMP-OFFICE.*

ON THE DEPARTURE OF AN INFAMOUS B - R - - - T [1769]

[The American Antiquarian Society]

SIZE, 9¾ by 14½ inches. Probably issued soon after Governor Bernard's departure. The printer is not known.

Francis Bernard, Governor of Massachusetts since 1760, had made himself disliked in America by his policy of coercion and antagonism. Opposition had increased when he asked that troops be quartered in Boston, and had urged the forfeiture of the charter. When the opposition to him became more insistent, he was recalled to England. Though continued as nominal Governor of Massachusetts for a time, he never returned to America. His departure, July 25, 1769, was the occasion for a noisy demonstration in Boston. Bells were rung, cannon fired, the Liberty Tree decked out with flags, and a great bonfire built on Fort Hill. Various abusive verses were published, and, for a time, the word "baronet" became a term of ridicule and opprobrium. Bernard had received the title in April, 1769.

Tom-cod
A young cod. Applied to human beings as a term of ridicule.
Could those brave heroes . . .
A very frequent subject of eloquence in patriotic verses and speeches of the day.
And be a Tyrant, Verres, . . .
Verres was a Roman official, who as Governor of Sicily in 72–71 B.C. plundered the island of art treasures, was prosecuted by Cicero, went into exile, and was finally put to death by Antony, 43 B.C.
Tyburn
Until 1783 the place of public execution in London.
Ketch
A common appellation for a hangman. From Jack Ketch, a notoriously cruel hangman of a century earlier.

ON

The DEPARTURE

of an

infamous B-R---T.

Gov.r Bernard [handwritten annotation]

GO B------d, thou minion !--- to thy country go,
For BOSTON, loud proclaims you, Freedom's foe ;
Why will you stay, where mankind scorns your name
Where ev'ry year adds blackness to your fame,
Where if you die, few friends your deeds will bawl,
In British cries, or ditties of Fingall ?
Haste, haste O B------d, and betake your way,
Where snows eternal chill the face of Day :
Where torped rocks and mountains threat' the skies,
And hills o're hills in barren pomp arise ;
Where poverty supreme for ever reigns,
Nor envy'd wealth, disturb the peasants brains.
E'en croaking ravens, will rejoice your flight,
And join in chorus with the birds of night :
The rav'nous tyger, with the hind will play,
And glad with joy, th' unfeeling ass will bray.
If thus all nature for your absence long,
What wonder then, if I should join the throng :
When yet of evils, I more feel can name,
Enough to blast you to the latest fame :
Of ills ! that half the northern world annoys,
That mars their trade, their liberty destroys,
That makes them slaves, or meer mechanick tools,
To work for nought, as fools do work for fools.
Go on ye Pilferer, with all the rage
That half-starv'd spani'ls for a bone engage,
Be like your brothers here, a tyrant crew,
Do all that fell rapacious souls can do ;
Make right and wrong an equal ballance hold,
And prove or disapprove, as weighs the gold.
Like these, in all the majesty of desk,
Look big, command, and flout, and jeer the best.
As you have done, the last passing year,
Made the new world in anger shed the tear ;
Unmindful, of their native once lov'd isle,
They'll bid All-g--nce cease her peaceful smile,
While from their arms, they tear Oppression's chain,
And make lost LIBERTY once more to reign.
Could those brave heroes, who now sleep in rest,
But know how much their children are opprest'd,
Methinks they'd rise and murmur from their graves,
" Were we not wretched ! must our sons be slaves !
" Are there no stores of vengeance for that race ?
" That long have dar'd th' Almighty to his face,
" Who to half earth have prov'd so fell a pest,
" That living, dying, and the dead can't rest ;"
And as they vanish'd, pray ; " Hear, oh my God !
" Preserve this country from a TYRANT's rod."
Shall such low vagrants, whom some L--D has rais'd

For such harsh conduct be esteem'd or prais'd ?
Are they more faithful to the S-te or C-- n,
Than those whose honesty, with friendship join ?
No ! I proclaim that man at once a knave,
Who scorns those virtues which adorn the brave :
Honour can't bind him, that no friendship knows,
He's sure a villain, that delights in woes,
And proves or disapproves as profit flows.
Must it not fill all men of sense with scorn,
To see a muckworm of the earth, low born,
The chance production of some am'rous spark,
In ignorance supreme, profoundly dark ?
To see him seat his mighty self in state,
With arms a-kimbo, deal to each its fate.
Fly cringing minion ! from all converse fly,
Den with the wolves, and learn the wolv'rins cry,
Go join in concert with the croaking frogs,
Or howl in chorus with a pack of dogs ;
With monkeys go, and chatter on a stage,
Or turn a mastiff, and each curr engage.
Better do worse ! turn pandor, pimp or slave,
Turn highway-man, turn murderer, or knave ;
All do, that thy fell soul can think as evil,
And be a Tyrant, Verres, or a Devil.
What are such crimes ? when ballanc'd with the woes,
That from the vagrant ! to thy country flows ;
Meer nought and trifling, light as empty air,
They harm but few, but these whole countries share ;
On one on all, th' oppressive evil lights,
And like a tyrant robs them of their rights.
Can jealousy extend its horrid sway
To harm the tender offspring of a day,
To hurt a country, but in opening bud,
A people link'd by strongest ties of blood ?
It can, it does, all kindred ties begone ?
Nought here but riches please the rav'nous throng ;
A golden fury, rages in each breast,
Let sink who will, or swim, they will be blest.
Like fools they've plan'd, it is to keep you down,
To make you love them, and to fear their frown.
Were I a K***! I'd think it noble sport,
To kick such mongril tyrants from my C****.
No knavish soul, that's aggrandiz'd by wealth,
Obtain'd by force, or got by meanest stealth ;
Should tread the threshold of the R---l dome,
But like a robber, be exil'd from home ;
Or share; what best becomes a thievish wretch,
A Tyburn salutation from a Ketch.

No. 64
DESCRIPTION OF THE POPE, 1769

[The New York Historical Society]

SIZE, 5½ by 11 inches. The margins have been considerably trimmed. The same cut had appeared before, also on Pope-Night verses. (Cf. Ford, 1467.)

This anniversary of the Gunpowder Plot had been annually celebrated in America for many years. It was the occasion for pageantry and the exhibiting of effigies denoting hatred of popery. With the approach of the Revolution, resentment of the Stamp Act and other measures combined with this abhorrence of popery to make these demonstrations even more spirited. Obnoxious political characters were added to the familiar figures of the devil, the pope, and the Pretender, and carried through the streets in a procession. Prior to 1765, Boston had had two celebrations, one for the North End, and one for the South, but in 1765 the two parties formed a union, and celebrated jointly thereafter. The 1769 celebration very naturally reflected the antagonism of Massachusetts toward Governor Bernard, who had been recalled several months before. Apparently the authorities, realizing the state of unrest, had issued a proclamation threatening punishment in case of a Pope-Night riot, for the *Boston Gazette* of November 13 noted with satisfaction that no such disturbance had arisen: ". . . for the Pageantry was carried on with Decorum, as has been usual for a Number of Years past."

John Mein

A Boston printer and book dealer, who because of his importation of British books during the non-importation excitement of 1768 and 1769, became the object of hatred and calumny. His name was printed week after week in the *Boston Gazette* and other patriotic sheets in "A List of the Names of *those* who AUDACIOUSLY continue to counteract the UNITED SENTIMENTS of the Body of Merchants thro'out NORTH AMERICA; by importing British Goods contrary to the Agreement." In the *Boston Chronicle*, of which he was one of the publishers, Mein recorded his defense from August to October, 1769, but this in turn became the target for indignant and abusive comment. His name appears scores of times and was a synonym for disloyalty. Shortly after this Pope-Night celebration, he was forced into hiding until he could take secret passage back to Europe.

Wilkes and Liberty, No. 45.

This was the slogan with which doors and shutters had been chalked at the time of the expulsion of Wilkes from the House of Commons in 1764. *No. 45* was the issue of the *North Briton* in which he had censured the King's speech at the opening of Parliament, an offense for which he had been sent to the Tower. His attack on the ministry of Lord Bute had gained him much sympathy in America, and various details of the Wilkes's demonstrations in England were borrowed by his American admirers. The exhibiting of a jackboot, in punning derision of Lord Bute, was one of these.

Informer

No term was applied with more contempt and hatred at this time. Cf. "The Life and Humble Confession of Richardson," p. 95, *supra*.

Defcription of the POPE, 1769

Toafts on the Front of the large Lanthorn.
Love and Unity.---The American Whig.---Confufion to the
Torries, and a total Barnifhment to Bribery and Corruption.
On the Right Side of the fame.---An Acroftick,
J nfulting Wretch, we'll him expofe,
O 'er the whole World his Deeds difclofe,
H ell now gaups wide to take him in,
N ow he is ripe, Oh Lump of Sin.
M ean is the Man, M--n is his Name,
E nough he's fpread his hellifh Fame,
L nfernal Furies hurl his Soul,
N ine Million Times from Pole to Pole.
Labels of the Left Side.

Now fhake, ye Torries I fee the Rogue behind,
Hung up a Scarecrow, to correct Mankind.
Oh had the Villain but receiv'd his Due,
Himfelf in Perfon would here fwing in View :
But let the Traitor mend within the Year,
Or by the next he fhall be hanging here.
Ye Slaves ! ye Torries who infeft the Land,
And fcatter num'rous Plagues on ev'ry Hand,
Now we'll be free, or bathe in honeft Blood ;
We'll nobly perifh for our Country's Good,
We'll purge the Land of the infernal Crew,
And at one Stroke we'll give the Devil his Due.
Labels on each Side the fmall Lanthorn.
WILKES and LIBERTY, No. 45.
See the Informer how he ftands, If any one now takes his Part,
An Enemy to all the Land He'll go to Hell without a Cart
May Difcord ceafe, in Hell be jam'd,
And factious fellows all be dam'd.

From B-----, the verieft monfter on earth,
The fell production of fome baneful birth,
Thefe ills proceed,---from him they took their birth,
The Source fupreme, and Center of all Hate.
If I forgive him, then forget me Heaven,
Or like a WILKES may I from Right be driven.
Here ftands the Devil for a Show,
With the I--p--rs in a row,
All bound to Hell, and that we know.
Go M--n lade deep with Curfes on thy head,
To fome dark Corner of the World repair,
Where the bright Sun no pleafant Beams can fhed,
And fpend thy Life in Horror and Defpair.
Effigies,---M--n, his Servant, &c.---A Bunch of TOM-CODS.

No. 65
A NEW SONG, CALLED THE GASPEE [1773]
[The Rhode Island Historical Society]

SIZE, 9⅜ by 14 inches. The date is conjectural. The line in Stanza 2, "In seventeen hundred and seventy-two," might suggest that 1772 was past. But the line in Stanza 6, "Here on the tenth day of last June," would imply that the succeeding June had not yet come. If the sheet were printed in 1773, it would have issued from the press of John Carter, the only printer in Providence at that time. It is so assigned in *Rhode Island Imprints* (Providence, 1914).

The burning of the *Gaspée* took place June 8, 1772, and resulted from the resentment aroused in Rhode Island over the British attempt to enforce the revenue laws, so distasteful to the colonists. The immediate occasion was the pursuit of the American schooner *Hannah* by the *Gaspée*. The *Hannah*, in command of Captain Lindsey, having reported her cargo at Newport, was proceeding up the river to Providence, when the *Gaspée* gave chase. The *Hannah* succeeded in crossing the shallow water at Namquit Point, but the *Gaspée* ran aground in attempting to follow. On the evening of the same day, citizens of Providence, having learned of the *Gaspée's* plight from Captain Lindsey, set out in boats for Namquit Point, six miles away. They boarded the *Gaspée* by night, removed the crew and set fire to the vessel. Upon their approach, William Duddingston, in command of the *Gaspée*, fired shots, and was wounded by a return shot. These shots are said to be the first to be fired in the Revolution. Governor Wanton issued a proclamation offering reward for the discovery of the citizens involved; the British Government subsequently offered larger rewards; a court of inquiry was appointed, but in accordance with the prophecy of the concluding stanza of this ballad, the identity of the participants was never revealed. A complete account of this whole affair is included in *Records of the Colony of Rhode Island* (Providence, 1862), VII, 55–192. These verses, which are printed at the end of the record, have been attributed to Captain Swan of Bristol, one of the alleged participants in the affair. The ballad is also reprinted in Wilfred H. Munro's *The History of Bristol* (Providence, 1880), pp. 172–174.

[That play'd the parts of pirates there;]
Belial
> Strictly, a worthless person, but in the New Testament and in later usage, the term is treated as a proper name for the personification of evil or Satan. In Milton, the name of one of the fallen angels.

insert
> Apparently for assert, as indicated in the marginal correction.

Some Narragansett Indianmen,
> The citizens participating in the Boston Tea Party were also disguised as Indians.

if I remember
> Annotated by the note at the bottom of the sheet.

N W
S O N G,
CALLED THE
G A S P E E.

'TWAS in the reign of George the third,
Our public peace was much difturb'd
By fhips of war, that came and laid
Within our ports, to ftop the trade.

2.
In feventeen hundred and feventy-two,
In Newport harbour lay a crew,
~~Their purpofe ~~~~was of pirates there~~
The fons of freedom could not bear,

3
Sometimes they'd weigh and give them chace,
Such actions fure was very bafe;
No honeft coafters cou'd pafs by,
But what they would let fome fhot fly;

4
And did provoke to high degree,
Thofe true born fons of liberty;
So that they cou'd no longer bear
Thofe fons of Belial ftaying there,

5
But 'twas not long 'fore it fell out,
That William Duddingfton, fo ftout,
Commander of the Gafpee tender,
Which he has reafon to remember;

6
Becaufe as people do infert,
(He almoft had his juft defert
Here on the tenth day of laft June,
Betwixt the hours of twelve and one,

7
Did chace the floop call'd the Hannah,
Of whom one Linfey was commander;
They dog'd her up Providence found,
And there the rafcal g t a ground.

8
The news of it flew that very day
That they on Namquit point did lay:

That night about half after ten,
Some Narraganfett Indianmen,

9
Being fixty-four if I remember,
Which made this ftout coxcomb furrender;
And what was beft of all their tricks,
They in his britch a ball did fix,

10
Then fet the men upon the land,
And burnt her up we underftand;
Which thing provokes the King fo high,
He faid thofe men fhall furely die.

11
So if he could but find them out,
The hangman he'll employ no doubt;
For he's declared in his paffion,
He'll have them tri'd, a new fathion.

12
Now for to find thefe people out,
King George has offer'd very ftout;
One thoufand pounds to find out one
That wounded William Duddingfton.

13
One thoufand more he fays he'll fpare
For thofe who fay they fheriffs were:
One thoufand more there doth remain,
For to find out the leaders name.

14
Likewife five hundred pound per man
Of any one of all the clan,
But let him try his utmoft fkill,
I'm apt to think he never will
Find out any of thofe hearts of gold,
Though he fhould offer fifty fold.

F I N I S.

Providence : Printed for the Purchafers.

TEA, DESTROYED BY INDIANS [After 1773]

[The Massachusetts Historical Society]

SIZE, 8⅛ by 12¾ inches. Printer and date of printing are unknown.

The Boston Tea Party took place December 16, 1773. The details of this episode are well known. Under cover of night some fifty residents of Boston, disguised as Indians, emptied the entire cargo of three tea ships into Boston Harbor, thereby ending a long controversy as to the enforcement of the tea tax, so obnoxious to the colonists. This tax, imposed by Townshend six years before, had not been repealed April 2, 1770, when the duty on certain other articles was withdrawn. This occurrence, which was the subject of much comment in the press and in other contemporary annals, was also frequently memorialized in verse, most of which was printed in the newspapers during the early months of 1774, rather than in broadside.

T E A,

DESTROYED BY INDIANS.

YE GLORIOUS SONS OF FREEDOM, brave and bold,
That has ftood forth----fair LIBERTY to hold ;
Though you were INDIANS, come from diftant fhores,
Like MEN you acted-----not like favage Moors.

CHORUS.

Boftonian's SONS keep up your Courage good,
Or Dye, like Martyrs, in fair Free-born Blood.

Our LIBERTY, and LIFE is now invaded,
And FREEDOM's brighteft Charms are darkly fhaded !
But, we will STAND---and think it noble mirth,
To DART the man that dare opprefs the Earth.

Boftonian's SONS keep up your Courage good,
Or Dye, like Martyrs, in fair Free-born Blood.

How grand the Scene !----(No Tyrant fhall oppofe)
The T E A is funk in fpite of all our foes.
A NOBLE SIGHT---to fee th' accurfed T E A
Mingled with MUD----and ever for to be ;
For KING and PRINCE fhall know that we are FREE.

Boftonian's SONS keep up your Courage good,
Or Dye, like Martyrs, in fair Free-born Blood,

Muft we be ftill--- and live on Blood-bought Ground,
And not oppofe the Tyrants curfed found ?
We Scorn the thought- ---our views are well refin'd
We Scorn thofe flavifh fhackles of the Mind,
"We've Souls that were not made to be confin'd."

Boftonian's SONS keep up your Courage good,
Or Dye, like Martyrs, in fair Free-born Blood.

Could our Fore-fathers rife from their cold Graves,
And view their Land, with all their Children SLAVES ;
What would they fay ! how would their Spirits rend,
And, Thunder-ftrucken, to their Graves defcend.

Boftonian's SONS keep up your Courage good,
Or Dye, like Martyrs, in fair Free-born Blood.

Let us with hearts of fteel now ftand the taft,
Throw off all darkfome ways, nor wear a Mask.
Oh ! may our noble Zeal fupport our frame,
And brand all Tyrants with eternal SHAME.

Boftonian's SONS keep up your Courage good,
And fink all Tyrants in their GUILTY BLOOD.

No. 67
THE FARMER AND HIS SON'S RETURN FROM A VISIT
TO THE CAMP [1775]

Reproduced through the kind permission of Dr. A. S. W. Rosenbach

SIZE, 11⅛ by 6⅞ inches. The printer is unknown. These same stanzas are also extant under other titles. Another issue, entitled "The Yankey's Return from Camp," has the same cuts as the present imprint. There are slight differences in spelling and printing. A third issue is entitled "A Yankee Song." It is probable that this version, printed under these several titles, represents the earliest form in which the verses appeared in print. For a list of the issues which survive, see Ford, 1940–1941 and 3417–3420. The present broadside was reproduced in *The Saturday Evening Post* of June 15, 1929.

Commentary on this song and speculation as to its origin have filled many pages. The earliest version is thought to have emanated from the British camp during the French and Indian Wars, and to have been inspired by the ludicrous appearance of the colonials in their assorted garbs. If so, no one of the original stanzas survives in the present version, which was clearly born of Revolutionary times. Their author was said by Edward Everett Hale, in his *New England History in Ballads* (Boston, 1904), to have been Edward Bangs, a member of the class of 1777 of Harvard College. No contemporary support of this attribution appears to have come to light. But whoever the author, the verses contain what would seem to be unmistakable evidence of an origin at the provincial camp early in the Revolution, possibly in 1775. The most complete and authoritative treatment of this much-discussed song is contained in Oscar George Theodore Sonneck's *Report on "The Star-Spangled Banner," "Hail Columbia," "America," "Yankee Doodle,"* published by the Library of Congress, 1909.

The Farmer and his Son's return from a visit to the CAMP.

FATHER and I went down to camp,
　Along with Captain Gooding,
And there we see the men and boys
　As thick as hasty pudding.
Yankey doodle keep it up, yankey doodle
　dandy,
　Mind the music and the step,
　And with the girls be handy.

And there we see a thousand men,
　As rich as 'squire David,
And what they wasted every day,
　I wish it had been saved.
　　Yankey doodle, &c.

The 'lasses they eat every day,
　Would keep an house a winter;
They have as much that I'll be bound,
　They eat it when they're mind to.
　　Yankey doodle, &c.

And there we see a swamping gun,
　Large as a log of maple,
Upon a ducid little cart,
　A load for father's cattle.
　　Yankey doodle, &c.

And every time they shoot it off,
　It takes a horn of powder,
And makes a noise like father's gun,
　Only a nation louder.
　　Yankey doodle, &c.

I went as nigh to one myself,
　As 'Siah's underpinning;
And father went as nigh again,
　I thought the duce was in him.
　　Yankey doodle, &c.

Cousin Simon grew so bold,
　I thought he would have cock'd it;
It scar'd me so I shriek'd it off,
　And hung by father's pocket.
　　Yankey doodle, &c.

And captain Davis had a gun,
　He kind of clapt his hand on't,

And stuck a crooked stabbing iron
　Upon the little end on't.
　　Yankey doodle, &c.

And there I see a pumpkin shell,
　As big as mother's bason,
And every time they touch'd it off,
　They scamper'd like the nation.
　　Yankey doodle, &c.

I see a little barrel too,
　The heads were made of leather,
They knock'd upon 'ith little clubs,
　And call'd the folks together.
　　Yankey doodle, &c.

And there was captain Washington,
　And gentlefolks about him,
They say he's grown so tarnal proud,
　He will not ride without them.
　　Yankey doodle, &c.

He got him on his meeting clothes,
　Upon a flapping stallion,
He set the world along in rows,
　In hundreds and in millions.
　　Yankey doodle, &c.

The flaming ribbons in his hat,
　They look'd so taring fine ah,
I wanted pockily to get,
　To give to my Jemimah.
　　Yankey doodle, &c.

I see another snarl of men,
　A digging graves they told me,
So tarnal long, so tarnal deep,
　They tended they should hold me,
　　Yankey doodle, &c.

It scar'd me so I hook'd it off,
　Nor stopt as I remember,
Nor turn'd about 'till I got home,
　Lock'd up in mother's chamber.
　　Yankey doodle, &c.

No. 68
A SONG, COMPOSED BY THE BRITISH BUTCHERS,
AFTER THE FIGHT AT BUNKER-HILL ON
THE 17TH OF JUNE, 1775

[*The New York Historical Society*]

SIZE, 7½ by 11½ inches. The margins have been trimmed. The address in the colophon was the printing office of the sons of Thomas Fleet. Their sign had been changed about this time from the Heart and Crown to the Bible and Heart. These verses were printed numerous times, and in their several versions show both Tory and colonial sympathies. The word *butchers* in the title of this version is an example of such variants. It is written *soldiers* in other issues. With the minimum of change, the story was told from the point of view of either side. For other issues, see Ford, 1931–1934.

The Battle of Bunker Hill, fought June 17, 1775, was a costly British victory. The British were commanded by General Gage, and the Americans by Colonel Prescott. The British took the offensive. On the third assault, the Americans were forced to withdraw, because their ammunition was exhausted.

With their strong works they [had] thrown up, . . .
Like rebels stout they stood it [out] and thought . . .
With expedition we embark'd, [our] ships kept cannonading.
Where showers of balls like [hail did] fly, . . .
Brave William Howe on our [right wing], . . .
You soon will see the rebels fle[e], . . .
To our grape shot and musquet [hot,] . . .
For making hay with musquet [pil]ls, . . .
He allows us half a pint a day, [to] rum we are not strangers;

A Song.

Compoſed by the Britiſh Butchers, after the Fight
at Bunker-Hill on the 17th of June 1775.

IT was on the ſeventeenth by break of Day, the Yankees did ſurprize us,
With their ſtrong works they had thrown up, to burn the town and drive us;
But ſoon we had an order came, an order to defeat them,
Like rebels ſtout they ſtood it out and thought we ne'er could beat them.

About the hour of twelve that day an order came for marching,
With three good flints and ſixty rounds, each man hop'd to diſcharge them;
We marched down to the long wharf, where boats were ready waiting;
With expedition we embark'd, our ſhips kept cannonading.

And when our boats all filled were with officers and ſoldiers,
With as good troops as England had, to oppoſe who dare controul us;
And when our boats all filled were, we row'd in line of battle,
Where ſhowers of balls like hail did fly, our cannon loud did rattle.

There was Cops-hill battery near Charleſtown, our twenty-fours they play'd;
And the three frigates in the ſtream, that very well behav'd;
The Glaſgow frigate clear'd the ſhore, all at the time of landing,
With her grape ſhot and cannon balls, no Yankees ne'er could ſtand them.

And when we landed on the ſhore, we draw'd up all together,
The Yankees they all mann'd their works, and thought we'd ne'er come thither;
But ſoon they did perceive brave Howe, brave Howe, our bold commander;
With grenadiers and infantry, we made them to ſurrender.

Brave William Howe on our right wing, cry'd boys fight on like thunder,
You ſoon will ſee the rebels fly, with great amaze and wonder;
Now ſome lay bleeding on the ground, and ſome full faſt a running,
O'er hills and dales and mountains high, crying zounds brave Howe's a coming.

They began to play on our left wing, where Pigot he commanded,
But we return'd it back again, with courage moſt undaunted;
To our grape ſhot and muſquet balls, to which they were but ſtrangers,
They thought to come with ſword in hand, but ſoon they found their danger.

And when the works we got into, and put them to the flight, ſir,
Some of them did hide themſelves, and others died with fright, ſir;
And when their works we got into, without great fear or danger,
Their works we made ſo firm and ſtrong, the Yankees are great ſtrangers.

But as for our artillery, they all behaved dinty,
For while their ammunition held, we gave it to them plenty;
But our conductor he got broke, for his miſconduct ſure ſir,
The ſhot he ſent for twelve pound guns, was made for twenty-four ſir.

There is ſome in Boſton pleaſe to ſay, as we the field were taking,
We went to kill their countrymen, while they their hay were making.
But ſuch ſtout whigs I never ſaw, to hang them all I'd rather,
That marching by with muſket balls, and buck ſhot mix'd together.

Brave Howe is ſo conſiderate, as to prevent all danger,
He allows us half a pint a day, to rum we are not ſtrangers;
Long may he live by land and ſea, for he's belov'd by many,
The name of Howe the Yankees dread, we ſee it very plainly.

And now my ſong is at an end, and to conclude my ditty;
It is the poor and ignorant, and only them I pity;
And as for their king that John Hancock, and Adams if they're taken,
Their heads for ſigns ſhall hang up high upon that hill call'd Bacon.

Sold at the Bible and Heart in Cornhill, Boſton.

No. 69
POETICAL REMARKS UPON THE FIGHT AT THE BOSTON LIGHT-HOUSE, 1775

BY E. R. [ELISHA RICH]

[The Boston Public Library]

SIZE, 9½ by 15½ inches, with margins trimmed. The same cut was used by Nathaniel Coverly, the printer, on another set of verses signed E. R., issued in the following year. These were entitled "A Poem On the late distress of the Town of Boston." (Cf. Ford, 2037.)

The initials E. R., following the note of explanation beneath the heading of this sheet, appear to be those of Elisha Rich, "Minister of the Gospel," as he signed himself on the "Poem On the Bloody engagement that was Fought on Bunker's Hill," also an imprint of Nathaniel Coverly. (Cf. Ford, 1922.) In the "Poem On the late distress of the Town of Boston," his initials are included in the last line of the last stanza.

This "fight," occurring on July 31, 1775, was one of several skirmishes which had for their purpose the cutting off of supplies to the British, encamped in Boston. The lighthouse was destroyed. When an attempt was made by Tory carpenters and a guard of marines to rebuild it, American volunteers, commanded by Major Tupper, killed or captured all of the workmen. General Washington praised the volunteers for their valor.

Tho' many of your Sons this year are slain,
    This was the year of the battles of Lexington and Concord, and Bunker Hill.
[And may with ease tread down their enemies.]
For which if you give God his proper [praise,]
The BOSTON Light-House that did help our foe,
    The lighthouse on Thatcher Island, commonly called Cape Ann Light, and the lighthouse at the entrance of Boston Harbor, were both destroyed.
[W]ho were defeated i[n their wi]cked plot,
Fetter'd in Chains it's [hop'd will be] their Lot.

Upon the Thirty-[first of last July,]
Brave Tupper [and his Troops with] speed did fly,
And drawing near [the Light-House where] they found
Our Bloody foe who [fain would kept] their ground,

[They can't escape a common despot's] lot,
[Since they their] country's wealth and Blood have sought.

Their Freedom now cannot be bought with B[ail,]
But must be kept [confin'd] in closer goal,

Some of the [Regulars] that taken were
With chearful [countenances] did appear,
While Torr[ies bore a mal]efactor's face,
They feared [Death deserv'd,] and sad disgrace.

[144]

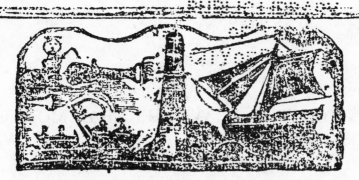

POETICAL

REMARKS upon the Fight at the BOSTON

LIGHTHOUSE

Which happen'd between a Party of ***** belonging to the UNITED COLONIES, Commanded by Major TUPPER, and a Number of Regulars.

¶ Having wrote some POEMS on the Military operations in AMERICA this Year, I was requested among the rest to write one on the taking and demolishing the Light-House; it by this means the good Hand of Providence towards the American Forces may be more particularly noticed and kept in Memory, perhaps it may apologize for my attempt. So I rest a Friend, E. R.

BRAVE Valiant Soldiers of AMERICA,
Whose eyes behold the troubles of the Day,
While Tyrants frown and spread their terrors wide,
You keep your ground, and do not fear their pride.

Tho' many of your Sons this year are slain,
Yet still undaunted courage you retain,
While Liberty your generous hearts admire
You fight to quench oppression's raging fire.

Americans attend and pray now view,
The mighty arm that hath appear'd for you,
Who by degrees doth give thee victories,
****** ***** **** ** *** * enemies.

Amidst the loss you this year sustain,
Yet thro' God's blessing victory you gain,
For which if you give GOD his proper,
Your Land above oppressive pow'r may raise,

The BOSTON Light-House that did help our foe,
By God's assistance thou did'st overthrow,
By means of which in danger they must be,
Should other Ships of War come against thee,

But when thy foe this Building would repair
That they may pass the Channel without fear,
They met with fore repulse to their surprise,
Their works were all destroy'd before their eyes.

Americans behold with joyful eyes,
The lofty LIGHT-House now in ruin lies,
It gives no light to Bloody TYRANTS here,
And tho' they fight this should not move thy fear,

This narrative I will in brief relate,
And shew some of the TORRIES shameful fate,
Who were defeated in their wicked plot,
Fetter'd in Chains it's ***** their Lot,

Upon the Thirty-*****
Brave TUPPER and ***** did fly,
And drawing near the ***** they found
Our Bloody foe who ***** their ground,

When TUPPER and his men had landed there
Their enemies to fight them did prepair,
But all in vain they could not them withstand
But fell as victims to our valiant band.

Three TORRIES there, they killed on the spot,
And five MARINES were wounded by our shot,
Who fighting for a cruel TYRANT KING,
Our LAND in SLAVERY they fain would bring.

A Lieutenant of the MARINES there dy'd,
Two private Soldiers fell down at his side,
Who wallow'd in their bloody crimson gore,
And dyed fighting for TYRANICK power.

All those who were not kill'd and wounded there,
Were taken captive by our men we hear,
Tho' numbers came to set the captives free,
They kill'd but one we hear, and wounded three.

Their sad example well may others dread,
Who heard the fate of them that were shot dead,
And warning take least they at last should share,
The fate of those who foul oppressors were.

Among the PRISONERS that they brought here,
Eleven TORRIES, then, there did appear,
With guilt & shame they through our Towns were led,
Their visage told all men their fear and dread,

By guards they were convey'd to Worcester town,
Where Sons of Liberty did on them frown,
** **** *** *** ** *** for,
**** **** their country's wealth and Blood have fought,

Their FREEDOM now cannot be bought with Bribe,
But must be kept confin'd in closer goal,
There to reflect their bloody treachery,
Without respect from Friends to LIBERTY,

Some of the R**** that taken were
With changing ***** did appear,
While TORRI** ***** benefactor's face,
They feared ***** ** and sad disgrace.

One Captain White of Marshfield we hear say,
A noted foe of North-America,
Among the rest was there a PRISONER made,
Whose fate may make such as himself afraid,

A noted TORRY from New-York we hear,
A master Carpenter that worked there,
Was forc'd to lay his Ax and Hammer by,
And like a murderer bound in chains must lie,

Mere nature must reel to see their tears
Filled with shame and rackt with panic fears,
Yea tender hearts concerning them agree
That their deserts for future warnings be,

Should future ages hear how they did fall,
And their unhuman deeds to memory call,
May serve to crop such treachery in the bud
Before oppression rolls her swelling flood.

Before this narrative I had not pend,
Had I not hop'd 'tmight answer some good end,
Should it cause us to fear a tyrants path,
It might secure us from impending wrath.

Give GOD the glory of what thou dost gain,
And he thy glorious leader will remain,
Who like a friend shall head your Martial bands,
And give thy tyrant foes into thy hands.

If thou on GOD doth truly rest thy cause,
Thou need not dread thy Foes oppressing laws,
Give GOD the glory that his work do claim,
And thou thine enemies shall put to shame,

So shall the vile oppressors hide their head,
Nor rob the innocent shall be afraid,
While those who love true Peace & Liberty,
With honor shall be crown'd and seated high.

CHELMSFORD: Printed and Sold by Nathaniel Coverly, where may be had Verses by the Gross ***** or Single.

MDCCLXXV

TWO SONGS ON THE BRAVE GENERAL MONTGOMERY, AND OTHERS, WHO FELL WITHIN THE WALLS OF QUEBEC, DEC. 31, 1775

[*The Essex Institute*]

SIZE, 8 by 13¾ inches, with margins trimmed. Probably an imprint of Ezekiel Russell, who was printing in Danvers at this time in a house known as The Bell Tavern. It is of course possible that another printer had a printing office "Next the Bell-Tavern," as the advertisement states. Both of these cuts were frequently used.

Richard Montgomery, in command of the northern division of the colonial army, was killed in an unsuccessful attack upon Quebec, December 31, 1775. Although not yet forty years old, he was an experienced soldier, and had already distinguished himself by his exploits. During the French and Indian Wars he had fought at Louisburg and Montreal. In 1772 he sold his commission and became a resident of America. Because of the illness of General Schuyler, his superior, he became commander in chief of the northern army, and had already been victorious in several engagements. He was greatly beloved and his death caused widespread sorrow in America and England. Though a "rebel," he was eulogized in Parliament by Burke, Chatham, and others.

Domestic happiness resign'd,
> He had married, and purchased a large property on the Hudson shortly before he assumed active command of the colonial troops.

Carlton
> The British general, who permitted Montgomery to be buried with military honors.

Warren
> Joseph Warren, a physician, and one of the most able leaders of the colonial forces in the early days of the Revolution. He was killed at Bunker Hill.

Putnam
> Israel Putnam, a veteran of the French and Indian Wars, made a major general in the colonial army for distinguished service at Lexington and Concord and at Bunker Hill.

Lee
> Charles Lee, second major general under Washington. His later career was hardly such as to number him among ballad heroes. He was court-martialed in 1778.

Two SONGS on the Brave General

MONTGOMERY,

and others, who fell within the Walls of QUEBEC, Dec. 31, 1775, in attempting to Storm that City.

COME Soldiers all in chorus join,
To pay the tribute at the shrine
Of brave MONTGOMERY, &c.
Which to the memory is due,
Of him who fought and dy'd for you,
Might live and yet be free, &c.

With chearful and undaunted mind,
Domestic happiness resign'd,
He with a chosen band, &c.
Through desarts wild, with fixt intent,
Canada for to conquer went,
Or perish sword in hand, &c.

Six weeks before St. John's they lay,
While cannon on them constant play,
On cold and marshy ground, &c.
When Prescott forc'd at length to yield,
Aloud proclaim'd it in the field,
Virtue a friend had found, &c.

To Montreal he wing'd his way,
Which seem'd impatient to obey,
And open'd wide its gates, &c.
Convinc'd no force could e'er repell
Troops who had just behav'd so well,
Under so hard a fate, &c.

With scarce one third part of his force,
Then to Quebec he bent his course,
That grave of Hero slain, &c.
The pride of France the great Montcalm,
And Wolfe the strength of Britain's arm,
Both fell on Abraham's plain, &c.
Having no less of fame requir'd,
There too Montgomery expir'd,
With Cheeseman by his side, &c.
Carlton 'tis said, his corps convey'd
To earth, in all the grand parade
Of military pride, &c.

HARK! Hark! the joyful news is come,
Sound sound the trumpet, beat the drum,
Let manly mirth abound, &c.
Where Freedom's sacred ensigns wave,
Supported by the virtuous brave,
There Victory is found, &c.

From east to west, from south to north,
American's brave sons step forth,
All terrible in arms, &c.
Their Rights and Freedom to maintain,
They dauntless tread the bloody plain,
And laugh at war's alarms, &c.

Montgomery gains our applause,
He to assist fair Freedom's cause,
Domestic peace forsakes, &c.
The sword he grasps goes boldly on,
Nor quits 'till life is fairly done,
The war he undertakes, &c.

Kind providence the troops inspire,
With more than Greek or Roman fire,
Therefore our cause prevails, &c.
Favor'd by Heaven the virtuous few,
Tyrannish legions shall subdue,
For justice seldom fail, &c.

Let joyful temperate bowls flow round,
With songs to their just fames resound,
Who have their bravery shewn, &c.
To Warren and Montgomery,
To Putnam and the gallant Lee,
To glorious Washington, &c.

Printed and Sold next the Bell-Tavern, in
Danvers: Where Travelling-Traders, &c.
may be supplied with sundry Pieces on the
Times.—Cash paid for Linnen Rags.

ON THE EVACUATION OF BOSTON BY THE BRITISH TROOPS, MARCH 17, 1776

[*The Bostonian Society*]

SIZE, 7¾ by 13⅞ inches. This same cut had been used by Thomas Fleet on "New England Bravery" in 1745. (Cf. Ford, 833.) There is another imprint, measuring 9 by 16 inches, with the same cut, and almost the same text. It is entitled "Two favorite Songs made on the Evacuation of the Town of Boston." The differences between the two imprints are very slight, involving chiefly changes in spelling and in type, but these show that either the sheet was issued from another press or that the verses were reset. The Essex Institute possesses an original of the second imprint. (Cf. Ford, 2040, 2041.) There is still another issue of the same verses, printed by Thomas Fleet and entitled "Two new Songs: On the disgraceful Flight of the Ministerial Fleet & Army From Boston and Bunker-Hill on March 17, 1776." The sheet has no cut. The William Clements Library possesses an original of this imprint.

The evacuation of Boston by the British troops on March 17, 1776, was the first decisive victory of the war for the colonists, and was accordingly the occasion for enthusiastic demonstration. It was the result of one of General Washington's most brilliant maneuvers and was accomplished almost without loss of life on either side. With amazing speed Washington threw up fortifications on Dorchester Neck during the night, thereby putting the British ships in peril, and making the position of Howe's army untenable. He had begun to lay siege to the city on March 5, the anniversary of the Boston Massacre.

Pilgarlic
A bald head, ludicrously likened to a peeled head of garlic. Applied to Howe in this instance.

In burning the Castle as they pass'd along,
The British in making their escape, burned the blockhouse on Castle Island and blew up the fortifications.

ON THE EVACUATION OF BOSTON
by the *British Troops,* March 17th, 1776.

IN seventeen hundred and seventy six,
On March the eleventh, the time was prefix'd,
Our forces march'd on upon Dorchester neck,
Made fortifications against an attack.

The morning next following, as Howe did espy,
The banks we cast up were so copious and high,
Said he in three months, all my men with their might,
Cou'd not make two such forts as they've made in a night.

Now we hear that their Admiral was very wroth,
And drawing his sword, he bids Howe to go forth,
And drive off the Yankees from Dorchester hill,
Or he'd leave the harbor and him to their will.

Howe rallies his forces upon the next day,
One party embark'd for the castle they say,
But the wind and the weather against them did fight,
On Governor's Island it drove them that night.

Then being discourag'd they soon did agree,
From Bunker and Boston, on board ship to flee :
Great Howe lost his senses, they say for a week,
For fear our next fort should be rais'd in King-street,
But yet notwithstanding the finger of God,
In the wind and the weather that often occurr'd ;
Still Howe, Pharaoh like, did harden his heart,
Being thirsty for victory to maintain his part.

He gives out fresh orders on Thurday it's said,
Forms his men in three branches upon the parade ;
Acknowledging it was a desperate case,
In their situation the Yankees to face :
Yet nevertheless being haughty of heart,
On Friday one branch of his men did embark :
A second stood ready down by the sea side :
His Dragoons were mounted all ready to ride.

Great Howe he now utters a desperate oration,
Saying fight my brave boys for the crown of our nation;
Take me for your pattern, and fight ye as I,
Let it be till we conquer, or else till we die.

But all of a sudden with an eagle ey'd glance,
They espied a fire being kindled by chance,
In a barrack at Cambridge, as many do know,
And then in confusion they ran to and fro.

Moreover as Providence order'd the thing,
Our drums beat alarm, our bell it did ring,
Which made them cry out, O the Yankees will come !
O horror they'll have us ! so let us be gone.

Then hilter skilter they ran in the street,
Sometimes on their heads, and sometimes on their feet,
Leaving cannon and mortars, packsaddles and wheat,
Being glad to escape with the skin of their teeth.

Now off goes Pilgarlic with his men in a fright,
And altho' they show cowards, yet still they show spite,
In burning the Castle as they pass'd along,
And now by Nantasket they lie in a throng.

Let e'm go, let e'm go, for what they will fetch,
I think their great Howe is a miserable wretch ;
And as for his men they are fools for their pains,
So let them return to Old England again.

IT was'nt our will that Bunker Hill,
From us should ne'er be taken,
We thought 'twould never be retook,
But we find we are mistaken.

The soldiers bid the hill farewel,
Two images left sentries,
This they had done all out of fun
To the American Yankies.

A flag of truce was sent thereon,
To see the hill was clear,
No living soul was found thereon,
But these images stood there.

Their hats they wave, come if you please,
There's none here to molest us,
These wooden men that here do stand,
Are only to defy us.

These images they soon threw down,
Not one man's life was lost then,
No sooner they were on the hill,
But some landed into Boston.

The women come and children run,
To brave PUTNAM rejoicing,
Saying now is the time to man your lines,
For the soldiers have left Boston.

The troops you've fairly scar'd away,
On board the ships they're quarter'd,
The children laugh'd, saying over the wharf,
They threw their best bomb-mortar.

With the blazing of your guns that night,
And roaring of your mortars,
The soldiers cry'd the Yankees come
To tear us all in quarters.

The barracks being set on fire,
Which made the soldiers quiver,
They soon embark on board their ships,
May they stay there forever.

Soon after this the fleet fell down,
It's what we long desir'd,
We think their Gen'rals were afraid,
That they'd be set on fire.

The shipping now have all set sail,
No cause have we to mourn,
But seem afraid because 'tis said
That they will soon return.

Some say they're sail'd for Halifax,
And others for New York ;
Howe let none know where he was bound,
When the soldiers did embark.

Where they are bound there's none can tell,
But the great GOD on high,
May all our heads be cover'd well,
When cannon balls do fly.

No. 72
SONG MADE ON THE TAKING OF GENERAL
BURGOYNE [1777]

[The Boston Public Library]

SIZE, 9¼ by 12¼ inches. There is no clue to the printer or the date of printing, but this version of the song would appear to be earlier than others which survive. The author was apparently a soldier in the campaign. There is another broadside issue of these verses, owned by the Boston Athenaeum, which has cuts of four mounted soldiers in the act of charging. Half of the sheet is torn away, leaving only the four soldiers and eleven stanzas in the first column of the song. The verses are nearly identical with those of the present imprint. The half sheet measures 5½ by 17¼ inches.

Burgoyne's expedition had for its purpose the weakening of Washington's position on the Hudson by an attack from the north. After an indecisive skirmish at Bemis Heights, and a defeat at Stillwater, he attempted a retreat, but was surrounded and decisively defeated at Saratoga by General Gates, to whom he surrendered his six thousand men on October 17, 1777. This victory was particularly important to the Americans at this time in that it encouraged the French to lend assistance.

Come all you gallant heroes, of courage stout and bold,
When General St Clair
    Then in command of Ticonderoga.
Hubbard Town
    Hubbardton.
[Our rear guards he defeated, which he thought great renown.]
[And that we had retreated] near Albany to rest;
[With] Hessians [and] Canadians . . .
[With] Savages [and] Tories . . .
Commanded [by a] Tory . . .

We took all their artillery
    In an engagement at Hoosick, New York, August 16.
The fifteenth [of Septem]ber, . . .
Brave Gates he [said unto his men], . . .
Burgoyne he [now advances and]
But to main[tain our country's] right, . . .

The news [was quickly brought] us, . . .
And our [brave boys did m]eet them, . . .
    At Stillwater. Burgoyne was defeated here October 10.
To send out General Arnold
    Benedict Arnold, to whose daring offensive the American victory was largely due.
[Which he at last completed and set our country free.]

SONG
made on the taking of
General Burgoyne.

COME all you gallant ..ces, of courage flout and bold,
Who fcorn as long as life does laft ever to be controul'd
Give ear unto my ditty, for I the truth will tell,
Concerning many a foldier that for his country fell.

Brave General Burgoyne from Canada fet fail,
With eight thoufand brave Regulars, he thought would never fail,
With Indians and Canadias, and Tories as we hear,
Befides a fleet of fhipping o er lake Champlain did fteer.

Before Ticonderoga, the firft day of July,
Their fleet and and army did appear and foon we did them fpy :
Their motions we obferved full well both night and day,
And our brave boys prepared all for a bloody fray.

Our garrifons they viewed and ftraight their troops did land,
When General St. Clair he came to underftand,
That the great Mount Defiance they then would fortify,
He found we muft furrender or every man muft die.

It was on July fifth that we had orders to retreat,
And the next morning left our forts, Burgoyne he thought us beat,
And clofely did purfue us it was near to Hubbard Town,
Ou... ...guard li... ...whit...l... ....

When our Congrefs came to hear that we our forts had left,
...that we had retreated near Albany to reft ;
...General Gates they fent us our country to retrieve,
...th... fhouts and acclamations, with joy we him receive.

Burgoyne fent out a party of fifteen hundred men,
With Heffians   Canadians came near to Bennington,
With Savages   Tories our cattle for to fteal,
Commanded.   Tory, they call'd him Colonel Skeen.

Brave Gates our bold commander, hearing of Skeen's conduct,
He fent out a fmall party his march for to obftruct ;
We took all their artillery, and Skeen his fate may mourn,
For of fifteen hundred men, fcarce five hundred did return.

Burgoyne then finding out that his fchemes would not fucceed,
He then with his artillery and army did proceed,
Thinking for to frighten us and make us for to fly,
Soon he found out his miftake, he found we would fooner die.

The fifteenth   ...ber, the morning fair and clear,
Brave Gates he   ...n, my boys be of good cheer,
Burgoyne he r   we will never fly,
But to mair   right, we'll fight until we die.

The news w   ...ugh.. us, their ... ny it was near,
and our brave b   ...eet them, all without dread or fear.
It was about *Stillwa...*, we met about noon day,
And quickly you fhall hear my boys, began a bloody fray.

We fought them full fix hours like valiant hearts of gold,
Each party fcorn'd for to give way, we fought like Britons bold
Until the leaves with blood were ftain'd, our General then did cry,
It is diamond cut diamond, fight on until we die.

The night being coming on, to our lines we did retreat,
Which made the Britons for to think our army it was beat,
But early the next morning they beheld before their eyes,
We were ready to engage again, which did them much furprife:

Then fighting they feem'd tired of, therefore to work they go
To bury all their dead, and intrenchments up they throw,
Thinking thereby with fhot and fhells our army to deftroy,
But Gates he kept fuch orders that we did them defy.

They began a cannonading from every mountain hill,
And our brave boys return'd the fame, and with a right good will ;
And then they threw both fhot and fhells enough to tertify,
Our hearts ... ... been Cæfars, yet neither part would fly.

Then the Almighty God he infpired great Gates's mind,
To fend our General Arnold to fee if he could find,
A paffage through the enemy, and make them for to flee
... ...and fet our country free.

They burned all their baggage they fled with hafte and fear,
And up to Saratoga, Burgoyne with his troops did fteer,
Brave Gates our bold commander foon after him did hie,
Refolving for to take them or every man to die.

Then foon we overtook them, it was near to Saratogue,
Which they had burnt, as they had done all houfes in their road ;
The fixteenth of October was forc'd to capitulate,
Burgoyne and all his army they were our prifoners made

As for the Britifh foldiers, they fought like hearts of gold,
And fcorn'd as long as life does laft ever to be controul'd ;
But as for the poor Heffians they prov'd cowardly of late,
Or they refus'd to fight us, which caufed their defeat.

Here's a health unto our army, and our commander Gates,
To Washington and Lincoln, but all the tories hate ;
Likewife unto the Congress, God fend them long to reign,
To do our country juftice, our rights for to maintain.

So to conclude my ditty, my fong is at an end,
I hope no bold American will flight what I have penn'd,
Our caufe is juft, in God we truft, therefore my boys ne'er fear,
Brave Gates will clear America before another year.

No. 73
BATTLE OF THE KEGS [1778]
BY FRANCIS HOPKINSON
[The Boston Public Library]

SIZE, 8¼ by 11 inches. The margins have been trimmed. These verses were first printed in the *Pennsylvania Packet*, March 4, 1778, and they may also have appeared in broadside at that time. If so, no imprint is known to have survived. The present issue is undated, and may be later than 1800, although the verses were advertised as printed in broadside in 1799. (Cf. Ford, 2919.)

The occasion for this ballad was the consternation caused among the British soldiers by a number of kegs set afloat in the Delaware River by the Americans during the British occupation of Philadelphia in 1778. Rumor had it that these were filled with powder and fitted with springs so that they would explode upon striking obstacles. Alarmed at the peril to their ships, the British manned the wharfs and fired at the kegs.

Francis Hopkinson, the author, was a resident of Philadelphia and an accomplished gentleman who occasionally turned his versatile pen to the writing of satires and burlesques in the cause of Independence. He was born September 21, 1737, was a graduate of Princeton, a member of Congress, a judge, a Signer of the Declaration of Independence, and a lifelong patron of the arts, especially music and painting. He composed airs for some of his own songs, and is said not to have greatly enjoyed the reputation the present ballad, sung to the tune of "Yankee Doodle," brought him.

BATTLE OF THE KEGS.

GALLANTS attend, and hear a friend,
    Trill forth harmonious ditty :
Strange things I'll tell, which late befel
    In Philadelphia city.
'Twas early day, as poets say,
    Just when the sun was rising,
A soldier stood, on log of wood,
    And saw a sight surprising.
As in a maze, he stood to gaze,
    The truth can't be deny'd, sir,
He spy'd a score —of kegs, or more,
    Come floating down the tide, sir.
A sailor too, in jerkin blue,
    The strange appearance viewing,
First damn'd his eyes, in great surprise,
    Then said some mischief's brewing.
These kegs now hold the rebels bold,
    Pack'd up like pickled herring :
And they're come down t'attack the town,
    In this new way of ferrying.
The soldier flew, the sailor too,
    And, scar'd almost to death, sir,
Wore out their shoes, to spread the news,
    And ran till out of breath, sir.
Now up and down, throughout the town,
    Most frantic scenes were acted :
And some ran here, and some ran there
    Like men almost distracted.
Some fire cry'd, which some deny'd,
    But said the earth had quaked :
And girls and boys, with hideous noise,
    Ran through the town half naked.
Sir William he, snug as a flea,
    Lay all this time a snoring,
Nor dreamt of harm, as he lay warm
    In bed with Mrs. L——y.
Now in affright, he starts upright,
    Awak'd by such a clatter ;
He rubs both eyes, and boldly cries,
    "For God's sake what's the matter ?"
At his bed side, he then espy'd
    Sir Erskine at command, sir,

Upon one foot he had one boot,
    And t'other in his hand, sir.
Arise ! arise ! Sir Erskine cries ;
    The rebels—more's the pity—
Without a boat, are all on float,
    And rang'd before the city.
The motly crew, in vessels new,
    With satan for their guide, sir,
Pack'd up in bags, or wooden kegs,
    Come driving down the tide sir.
Therefore prepare for bloody war ;
    These kegs must all be rou'ed ;
Or surely we despis'd shall be,
    And British courage doubted.
The royal band now ready stand,
    All rang'd in dread array, sir,
With stomach stout, to see it out,
    And make a bloody day, sir.
The cannons roar, from shore to shore ;
    The small arms make a rattle :
Since wars began, I'm sure no man
    E'er saw so strange a battle.
The fish below swam to and fro,
    Attack'd from ev'ry quarter ;
Why sure, thought they, the devil's to pay,
    'Mongst folks above the water.
These kegs, 'tis said, tho' strongly made,
    Of rebel staves and hoops, sir,
Could not oppose their pow'rful foes,
    The conq'ring British troops, sir.
From morn to night, these men of might
    Display'd amazing courage ;
And when the sun was fairly down,
    Retir'd to sup their porridge:
An hundred men with each a pen,
    Or more upon my word, sir,
It is most true, would be too few,
    Their valour to record, sir.
Such feats did they perform that day
    Upon these wicked kegs, sir,
That years to come, if they get home,
    They'll make their boasts and brags, sir.

No. 74
CAPT. PAUL JONES'S VICTORY [After 1779]
[The Boston Public Library]

SIZE, 8⅜ by 10½ inches. The imprint is undated, but is probably much later than the date of the event. For another issue, cf. Ford, 3004.

This ballad concerns a desperate battle fought by night in the North Sea, on September 23, 1779. The combatants were the *Serapis*, a British ship commanded by Captain Pearson, and the *Bon Homme Richard*, commanded by John Paul Jones. The battle became a hand to hand conflict, as the two vessels were so close to each other that the muzzles of their guns touched, and their spars and rigging became entangled. Under such conditions, the fight went on for over three hours, Captain Pearson surrendering only when his main mast was cut in two. When the ships were disentangled, the *Bon Homme Richard* sank. For this victory Congress gave John Paul Jones a medal and named him commander of the *America*, a ship which was later given to France. Still later, Captain Paul Jones entered the service of Russia. He died July 18, 1792. America paid him further honor by interring his body in the crypt of the chapel at the Naval Academy, Annapolis, Maryland.

the Poor Richard
An example of ballad carelessness with reference to facts.
Percy came along side,
Another such example. The captain's name was Pearson.
We fought them eight glasses,
In nautical usage, a *glass* is a half hour.

Capt. PAUL JONES'S VICTORY:

Capt. Paul Jones of the ship called
the Poor Richard, of 40 guns,
took an English ship called the
Serapis of 44 & a 20 gun ship
called the Lion, at one engagement.

AN American frigate, a frigate of fame,
With guns mounted forty, call'd the Rich-
ard by name,
For to cruise in the channel of old England,
And a valiant commander, Paul Jones is the man.

We had not sail'd long before we did espy,
A large forty four and a twenty so nigh,
Well mann'd with bold seamen, & plenty of store,
They quickly pursu'd us from old England's shore.

About twelve at noon, Percy came along side,
With a long trumpet whence came you? he cry'd,
Give me an answer, for I hail'd you before,
Or this moment a broadside into you I'll pour.

Then Paul Jones he smil'd, and bid every one,
To keep up his courage, and stand to his gun.
A broadside it came from the bold English man,
Then the sons of America return'd it again.

The contest was bloody, both decks ran with gore,
The sea seem'd to blaze when the cannon did roar;
Fight on my brave boys, then Paul Jones he cry'd,
We soon will humble this bold Englishman's pride.

Stand firm to your quarters, your duty don't shun,
The first man that quits them, thro' his body I'll run,
Tho' their force is superior, yet they shall know,
What true brave American seamen can do.

We fought them eight glasses, eight glasses so hot,
Till seventy bold seamen lay dead on the spot,
And ninety bold seamen lay bleeding in their gore,
While the pieces of cannon like thunder did roar.

Our gunner in a fright, to Paul Jones he came,
We make water quite fast, and our side's in a flame,

Then Paul Jones he said in the height of his pride,
If we can't do no better boys sink along side.

Then Paul Jones he smil'd and says to his men,
Let every brave seamen stand fast to his gun.
The Lion bore down while the Richard did rake,
Which caused the heart of poor Percy to ake.

To us they did strike, their colours pull'd down;
The fame of Paul Jones will be heard with renown,
His name will be rank'd among heroes that's brave,
Who fought like a freeman our county to save.

Now all you brave seamen whoever you be,
Who hear of this battle that's fought on the sea,
Like them may you do, when call'd to the same,
And your names be enroll'd on the pages of fame.

Your country will boast of sons that's so brave,
And to you she will look her rights for to save,
She'll call you dear sons, your names they will shine,
And about your brave brows bright laurels entwine.

So now my brave boys, we have taken a prize,
A large forty four, and a twenty likewise.
Then God bless the mother that cause has to weep
For the loss of her son in the ocean so deep.

Here's a health to the girls that cause has to mourn,
For the loss of their lovers that's overboard thrown.
With a health to Paul Jones and all his brave crew,
And give them great praise, for it's truly their due.

No. 75
DEATH OF MAJOR ANDRE [After 1780]

SIZE, 9¼ by 10¼ inches. This is a late imprint of verses written soon after the death of Major André in 1780. Copied from a ballad sheet of 1783, the present version was included in Frank Moore's *Songs and Ballads of the American Revolution* (New York, 1856), pp. 316–321. The ballad was entitled "Brave Paulding and the Spy." The present issue may have come from the press of Henry Trumbull, a Providence printer, who, according to a directory of 1828, was doing business at 25 High Street at that time.

Major John André, a British officer belonging to the staff of Sir Henry Clinton, was captured by the Americans near Tarrytown, New York, as he was returning from an interview with Benedict Arnold concerning the betrayal of his country. André was tried as a spy and convicted. His execution took place October 2, 1780. John Paulding was one of his three captors.

O then up steps John Spalding
    The name was John Paulding.
They wished that Andre was set free . . .
    Regret at André's fate was general in America.

Death of Major Andre.

COME all you brave Americans I pray you lend an ear,
I will sing you a short ditty your spirits for to cheer,
Concerning a young gentleman whose age was twenty-two,
He is fit for North America, with a heart that's just and true.

The British took him from his lodging and did him close confine
They in strong prison bound him & kept him there sometime,
But he being something valient resolv'd there not to stay,
He got himself at liberty and from them come away.

And when that he had returned home to his own country,
There was many a plan contriving to undo America;
Plotted by General Arnold, and his bold british crew,
They tho't to shed our innocent blood and America to undue.

It was of a scouting party that sail'd from Tarrytown,
They met a British officer of fame and high renown ;
And sail to this young gentleman you are of the british core,
And I trust that you can tell me if the dangers are all o'er.

O then up steps John Spalding saying you must dismount,
And where you are agoing you must give a strict account ;
I am a British flag sir, I've a pass to go this way,
Upon an expedition in North America.

O then up steps John Spalding saying you must dismount,
And where you are agoing give me a more strict account ;
For I will have you searched before that you pass by—
On a strict exammation he was found to be a British Spy!

" There take my gold and silver and all I have in store,
And when down to New York I come will send you thousands
 more !
I scorn your gold and silver, I've enough of it in store,
And when my money it is gone I will bodily fight for more.

O then he found that all his plans were like to be bro't to light,
He call'd for pen and paper and begged leave to write
A line to General Arnold to let him know his fate,
He begged of him assistance but alas, it was too late !

When Arnold he this letter read it made his heart relent,
He called for his barge, down to New York quickly went ;
There he is amongst the Britons a fighting for his king
He has left poor Major Andre on the gallows for to swing !

If you are a man from Britain with courage stout and bold,
I'le fear no man of valour tho' he be cloth'd in gold ;
This place it is improper our valour for to try,
And if we take the sword in hand one of the two must die !

When he was executed he being both meek and mild,
Around on the spectators most pleasantly did smile,
I fill'd each one with terror and caus'd their hearts to bleed,
They wished that Andre was set free and Arnold in his stead.

Success unto John Spalding, let his health be drank around,
Likewise to those brave heroes who fought against the crown
Here is a health to every Soldier who fought for liberty,
And to the brave and gallant Washington of North America.

Printed and Sold at No, 25, High Street, PROVIDENCE, where may be obtained 100 other kinds.

COMMENTS ON LOCAL INCIDENT

UPON THE DRYING UP THAT ANCIENT RIVER, THE RIVER MERRYMAK, JANUARY 15, 1719/20

S. S. [SAMUEL SEWALL]

[The Massachusetts Historical Society]

SIZE, 7¾ by 12 inches. Sewall's own record makes possible the dating of this imprint. He does not record the fact of the Merrimac's drying up, only the writing and printing of his verses on this subject. The entries are as follows (*Diary*, III, 240, 279, 283–284):

[Jan. 16, 1719/20.]
16.7. Writ to Mr. Williams of Derefield, inclosed Dr. C. Mather's Sermon of the 5th of Novr., and my Verses on Merrimak River finish'd yesterday. By a Wonderfull Thaw the Ferry Boat goes again.
Febr. 8 [1720/21.] Merrymak is printed off, about 300. I give Sam. Mather two of them.
March 7.3. I go to the funeral of Mary Pratt . . . Mr. Prince and I go next the Relations. I gave him Merrimack; he desired me to give him copies of all my performances. . . .

Sewall's *Letter Book* includes a letter to Timothy Woodbridge of Hartford, under date of February 1, 1719/20, in which he says,

. . . Inclosed *Merrimak* dry'd up, with the occasion of it. The remembrance of your going into the Waters of Merrimack near Pike's pond, will render them not ingratefull to you. "Massachusetts Historical Society Collections" (6th series), II, 104.

The companion piece, "Connecticut's Flood, on Merrymak's Ebb," is printed on the other side of this same sheet. It was probably written by one of Sewall's friends to whom he sent his own verses. When both poems were printed in the *New-England Weekly Journal*, June 23, 1735, this second piece was signed J. W.

Samuel Sewall, best remembered for that chapter in his career which he most bitterly repented, his part in the Salem witch trials, was active in American public life for nearly sixty years. He was born in England, March 28, 1652, and came to America as a child, first living with his parents at Newbury, Massachusetts. He took a degree from Harvard in 1671, entered the ministry, and preached until 1677. He began his public career as printer of the colony currency, and was successively a member of the Board of Assistants for the colony, Judge of the Superior Court, Member of the Executive Council, Judge of the Probate Court, and Chief Justice. For his part in the Salem witch trials, he made public confession of error, and asked pardon. Among his numerous writings, his *Diary*, which was never intended for publication, is, from the point of view of a later day, his most valuable contribution to American writings. It covers the years 1674–1729, and is a record of colonial life both public and private during that time.

Upon the drying up that Ancient River,
THE RIVER
MERRYMAK.

LONG did *Euphrates* make us glad,
Such pleasant, steady Course he had :
Fight *White*, fight *Chesnut* ; all was one,
In Peace profound our River Run
From his remote, and lofty Head,
Until he with the Ocean Wed.
Thousands of Years ran parallel,
View'd it throughout, and lik'd it well.
Herbs, Trees, Fowls, Fishes, Beasts, and Men,
Refresh'd were by this goodly Stream.
Dutiful *Salmon*, once a Year,
Still visited their Parent dear :
And royal *Sturgeon* saw it good
To Sport in the renowned Flood.
All sorts of *Geese*, and *Ducks*, and *Teal*,
In their Allotments fared well.
Many a *Moose*, and Thirsty *Dear*,
Drank to full Satisfaction here.
The *Fox*, the *Wolf*, the angry *Bear*,
Of Drink were not deny'd their share.
The Strangers, late Arrived here,
Were Entertain'd with Welcom chear ;
The *Horse*, and *Ox*, at their own will,
Might taste, and drink, and drink their fill.
Thus *Merrymak* kept House secure,
And hop'd for Ages to endure ;
Living in Love, and Union,
With every Tributary Son.
At length, an Ambushment was laid
Near *Powwow* Hill, when none afraid ;
And unawares, at one Huge Sup,
Hydropick *Hampshire* Drunk it Up !
Look to thy self ! *Wadchuset* Hill ;
And Bold *Menadnuck*, Fear some Ill !
Envy'd *Earth* knows no certain Bound ;
In HEAV'N alone, CONTENT is found.

January 15,
1719, 20.

S. S.

CONNECTICUT's Flood,
ON
MERRYMAK's Ebb.

AND is old *Merrymak* come to an End ?
CONNECTICUT remains yet to befriend ;
Ancient as *Tiber*, *Sein*, or *Thames* ;
Fertile as *Ganges*, *Nile* or *Volga's* Streams.
All Sorts of Creatures Range these Woods,
And Dainty Fish Dive in these Floods ;
Beside the *Salmon*, *Sturgeon*, and *Tawtauge*.
Vast Shoales of *Azures* Swim the *Quinebauge*.
The Stately *Elke*, and Panting *Hart*,
Drink at a *Sunkepauge* before they part.
The Lowing *Bull* and Generous *Horse*,
Up to the Eyes, Eat Clover Grass ;
On these Green Banks, Flowers all Winter do appear.
Rivers Glide on to *Neptune* with the Circling Year.
Here's Aged *Oakes* and *Cedars* Tall,
Which Zealous Axmen for the Temple Fall.
Among the Fether'd Tribe we've also *Teal*,
An Ample CRANE too, to Steer the Common Weal.
This Happyness to Future Ages may Endure,
Till the *Chiliad* the Saints Secure.
Store of *Foxes*, *Wolves*, and Hungry *Bear*,
That of the *Massachusett* Herd do Tear,
Pequott has *Beavers*, Otter, and the wary *Hare*,
With *Noahs Dove* ! and *Turtles* many a Pair.
When first our Fathers in the Desert, Travel'd here,
Samp with Rich *Shell Fish* was their Daily Chear.
With Thanks they Supt the Treasures in the Sard
Prais'd *Sions* GOD, for *Canaans* Fruitful Land.
Thus in Great Love they Merry made,
No Heathen Powwows made them sore Afraid,
Their Faith was Stay'd on CHRIST our Rock,
And therefore Fear'd no Tribulations Shock.
O're Mountains, Valleys, Waters, Peace !
Content don't Envy the Gay Pride of Grece.
Famous *Euphrates* ! shall Dry up,
And Martyrs, will Receive the Confolation Cup.
But now I'm on *Wachusetts* Lofty Top.
I'l pass *Monadnuck* and in HEAVEN Stop.

Extempore, March 10.
1720, 21.

Anthropos.

N. B. *Quinebauge* the Name of *New-London*, River.
Tawtauge an Excellent Fish amongst the Americans.
Sunkepauge the Natives call a Cold Spring.
Pequoit the Indian Name for the Town of *New-London*, &c.

No. 77
FATHER ABBEY'S WILL, DECEMBER, 1731
[*The Pennsylvania Historical Society*]

SIZE, 8½ by 13⅜ inches. Ten other issues of this burlesque legacy survive, in eloquent testimony to the hunger of the 1730's for a comic sheet. (Cf. Ford, 608–618.)

The supposed author of this doggerel was John Seccomb, a graduate of Harvard in the class of 1728, and a minister in Cambridge after 1733. Evidence for this attribution was supplied by Mr. J. Langdon Sibley in connection with his reprinting of the verses in the *Cambridge Chronicle*, November 18, 1854. The New Haven letter, apparently written soon after its prototype, has been attributed to Col. John Hubbard of New Haven. "Father Abbey's Will" was printed without explanation in *The Gentleman's Magazine* for May, 1732, and the New Haven letter one month later. Both sets of verses later appeared in *The London Magazine*. It may well be imagined that the comment they caused was unfavorable to the American genius. No wonder the American bard had a reputation to live down as well as one to achieve.

Father Abbey, in real life Matthew Abdy, was a sweeper and bedmaker at Harvard College for many years. At the time of his death he must have been a very old man. He is supposed to have been born about 1650.

Calabash
    A gourd used as a household utensil.
Burrage
    An obsolete form of *borage*, a plant formerly much esteemed as a cordial.

Father Abbey's Will.

To which is added, A Letter of Courtship to his virtuous & amiable Widow.

CAMBRIDGE, *December.* 1731.

Some Time since died here Mr. MATTHEW ABBEY, in a very advanced Age: He had for a great Number of Years served the College in Quality of Bedmaker and Sweeper: Having no Child, his Wife inherits his whole Estate, which he bequeath'd to her by his last Will and Testament, as follows, viz.

TO my dear Wife,
my Joy and Life,
I freely now do give her,
My whole Estate,
With all my Plate,
Being just about to leave her.

My Tub of Soap,
A long Cart Rope,
A Frying Pan and Kettle,
An Ashen Pail,
A threshing Flail,
An Iron Wedge and Beetle.

Two painted Chairs,
Nine Warden Pears,
A large old dripping Platter,
This Bed of Hay
On which I lay,
An old Sause-Pan for Butter.

A little Mug,
A Two Quart Jug,
A Bottle full of Brandy,
A Looking Glass,
To see your Face,
You'll find it very handy.

A Musket true,
As ever flew,
A Pound of Shot and Wallet,
A Leather Sash,
My Calabash,
My Powder-Horn and Bullet.

An old Sword Blade,
A Garden Spade,
A Hoe, a Rake, a Ladder,
A wooden Can,
A Close-Stool Pan,
A Clyster-Pipe and Bladder.

A greasy Hat,
My old Ram Cat,
A Yard and half of Linen,
A Pot of Grease,
A Woollen Fleece,
In Order for your Spinning.

A small Tooth Comb,
An ashen Broom,
A Candlestick and Hatchet,
A Coverlet
Strip'd down with Red,
A Bag of Rags to patch it.

A ragged Mat,
A Tub of Fat,
A Book put out by Bunyan,
Another Book
By Robin Rook,
A Skain or two of Spunyarn.

An old Black Muff,
Some Garden Stuff,
A Quantity of Burrage,
Some Devil's Weed
And Burdock Seed,
To season well your Porridge.

A chafing Dish,
With one Salt Fish,
If I am not mistaken,
A Leg of Pork,
A broken Fork,
And half a Flitch of Bacon.

A Spinning Wheel,
One Peck of Meal,
A Knife without a Handle,
A rusty Lamp,
Two Quarts of Samp,
And half a Tallow Candle.

My Pouch and Pipes,
Two Oxen Tripes,
An Oaken Dish well carved,
My little Dog,
And spotted Hog,
With two young Pigs just starved.

This is my Store,
I have no more,
I heartily do give it,
My Years are spun,
My Days are done,
And so I think to leave it.

****

New-Haven, January 1731 2.

Our Sweeper having lately buried his Spouse, and accidentally hearing of the Death and Will of his deceas'd *Cambridge* Brother, has conceiv'd a violent Passion for the Relict. As Love softens the Mind and disposes to Poetry, he has eas'd himself in the following Strains, which he transmits to the charming Widow, as the first Essay of his Love and Courtship.

MISTRESS Abbey,
To you I fly,
You only can relieve me,
To you I turn,
For you I burn,
If you will but believe me.

Then gentle Dame,
Admit my Flame,
And grant me my Petition,
If you deny,
Alas! I die
In pitiful Condition.

Before the News
Of your dear Spouse
Had reach'd us at New-Haven,
My dear Wife dy'd,
Who was my Bride
In Anno Eighty seven.

Thus being free,
Let's both agree
To join our Hands, for I do
Boldly aver
A Widower
Is fittest for a Widow.

You may be sure
'Tis not your Dow'r
I make this flowing Verse on;
In these smooth Lays
I only praise
The Beauties of your Person.

For the whole that
Was left by *Mat*,
Fortune to me has granted,
In equal Store,
I've one thing more
Which *Matthew* long had wanted.

No Teeth, 'tis true,
You have to shew,
The Young think Teeth inviting,
But silly Youths!
I love those Mouths
Where there's no fear of biting.

A leaky Eye,
That's never dry,
These woful Times is fitting,
A wrinkled Face
Adds solemn Grace
To Folks devout at Meeting.

Thus to go on
I would pen down
Your Charms from Head to Foot,
Set all your Glory
In Verse before ye,
But I've no mind to do't.

Then haste away,
And make no stay;
For soon as you come hither,
We'll eat and sleep,
Make Beds and sweep,
And talk and smoke together.

But if, my dear,
I must move there,
Tow'rds *Cambridge* strait I'll set me,
To towze the Hay
On which you lay,
If Aox and You will let me.

Thus Father Abbey left his Spouse,
As rich as Church or College Mouse, } {
Which is sufficient Invitation,
To serve the College in his Station.

No. 78

A JOURNAL OF THE SURVEY OF THE NARRAGANSETT BAY, AND PARTS ADJACENT, TAKEN IN THE MONTHS OF MAY AND JUNE, A.D. 1741

BY W. C. [WILLIAM CHANDLER]

[*The Massachusetts Historical Society*]

Size, 12¼ by 15⅛ inches. Printed at Newport, Rhode Island. At this date, the press of Anne Franklin, widow of James Franklin and his successor as colony printer, was the only printing press in Rhode Island.

The survey which these verses record had been authorized by the crown in connection with the settlement of a dispute between Rhode Island and Massachusetts, as to the eastern boundary of Rhode Island. The Royal Commission is printed in the *Records of the Colony of Rhode Island, 1707–1740* (Providence, 1859), IV, 587–590. The official report of the survey is included in the *Report of the Joint Committee upon the Boundary Line between the States of Rhode Island and Massachusetts* (Providence, 1849), pp. 24–25. The course of the survey as described in the present verses, can be very easily traced on a colonial map of Rhode Island.

The lines were written by Captain William Chandler, son of John Chandler of Woodstock, Connecticut. He was born November 3, 1698, in New London. His father, who was Woodstock's most distinguished citizen, and his grandfather before him, had also been surveyors. William owned a farm consisting of a thousand acres on the line of what is now Thompson, Connecticut, and was justice of the peace as well as farmer and surveyor. He died June 20, 1754. This *Journal*, which seems to be his only extant attempt in verse, was printed in *The Narragansett Historical Register*, July, 1885, and in Gertrude S. Kimball's *Pictures of Rhode Island in the Past* (Providence, 1900), pp. 41–46.

Crossing a Harbour, we came to the Town
> A reference to the town of Warwick, whose particularly mixed religious history dates from the time of Samuel Gorton, who had bought the site from the Indians in 1643. The town had been founded out of hostility to Puritanism.

Next we ascended Philip's Royal Seat,
> King Philip was driven into a swamp near Mount Hope and shot through the heart by a treacherous Indian. His head was sent to Plymouth where it remained, set up on a pole, for twenty years. One hand was sent to Boston as a trophy, and the other given to Alderman, the Indian slayer. The body was quartered and hung upon four trees at the spot where Philip died.

A JOURNAL

OF THE

Survey of the NARRAGANSETT BAY, and Parts adjacent, Taken in the Months of May and June, A. D. 1741.

By Order of the Honourable Court of

COMMISSIONERS Appointed by his Majesty KING GEORGE the Second.

Poetically Described by one of the Surveyors.

These Lines below, describe a just Survey
the Coasts, along the 'Gansett Bay:
fore attend, and quickly you shall know
e it begins, and how far it doth go.

Rom Pawcatuck we steer'd our Course away
And to Watch Hill we went without delay;
ch gave a Prospect of the Neighbouring Shore
distant Isles, where foaming Billows roar.
Fishers Isle appears, and looks just by,
Montauk Point we plainly cou'd descry;
Island also near us did appear,
ook their Course, and how each Place did bear.
hence our Course did lead us on the Sands,
rth[...] Bounds the Billows here Commands,
e raging Waves caress the Beach and Shore
endless Motion, and a murmuring Roar:
passing o'er the Breaches in our way
by the Surges of the raging Sea.
e in the Land Calm Ponds we here espy'd
ch rise and fall exactly with the Tide.
In these Ponds are Fish of Various Kind,
ch much delight and please both Taste and Mind,
many Fowls the Industrious Archer gains,
ch amply doth Reward his Time and Pains,
re in a Pond, our Caution to oppose
rse did launch and wet his Owners Cloaths,
frighted Jade soon tack'd himself about
ch made us laugh as soon as he came out.)
round Point Judith which was in our way
Courses there, and Length we did Survey,
Boston Neck along that pleasant Shore
ext survey'd, and found how each part bore;
nanicutt we also view'd full well,
other Parts too tedious here to tell.)
on this shore, round points of Lands and Coves
various Fields and most delightful Groves,
hence along unto North Kings-town shore
ing the Meads, which Verdant Greens now wore.
then for Greenwich next, we shap'd our way,
ing more Islands which lie in the Bay,
pe and Prudence that most pleasant Isle,
atience also, a most fruitful Soil)
ing a Harbour, we came to the Town
ch seems to be a Place of great Renown,
iberty of Conscience they here take
's Church and Baptist, also those that Quake,
om hence we went along with our Survey
rious Turns and came to Warwick Bay
n that Town did of their Dainties eat
in soft Slumbers pass'd the Night with Sleep.
neighbouring Orchards in their verdant Blooms
gentle Air sweetens with their Perfumes;
h pleasing Prospect did attract our sight
charm'd our Sense of smelling with Delight.
om hence we went on our Survey again
rtile Meads which join the wat'ry Main,
ing more Points, and p ssing on our way
e to a Place on which a Dead Man lay,
adful sight it was, our Blood ran chill
mp't our Joys and made our Spirits thrill,
what is Man? when he by Natures Laws
I'n a Prey, to Death's relentless Paws

But Vanity? His mortal Part I mean
But stop my Muse, and quit this mournful Theme.
From hence by Fields, and now and then a Ridge
We came at length unto Potuxett Bridge,
The Southern Bounds which Providence does claim
And does divide fine Warwick from the same.
Passing along still by the flowing Tide
The Famous Town of Providence we spy'd,
To which we came, viewing how Nature made
(with Art allied) this for a Place of Trade.
This Pleasant Town does border on the Flood
Here's neighbouring Orchards, & more back the Wood,
Here's full supply to chear our hungry Souls
Sr. Richard (strong) as well as Wine in Bowls.
Here Men may soon any Religion find
Which quickly brought brave Holland to my Mind.
For here like them, one with the greatest Ease
May suit him self, or quit all if He please.
Our haste in Business call'd us from this Town,
By Seaconk shore, away to Barrington
Passing that Ferry, something did accrue
Which the next Lines shall give unto your view,
Here jumping out our Horses from the Boat
One blundering sprang which rais'd up each Man's note
And tumbling o'er the Horse fell on his Back
Into the Deep and wet his Masters Pack.
For Bristol Town we shap'd our Course away,
And Poppossquash we quickly did survey,
But on this shore we turn'd a while to rove,
And went to Vials and walk'd thro' his Grove.
This charming Place was neat and clean, a Breeze
Attend the shade made by black Cherry Trees,
On either side a Row of large extent
And nicely shading every step We went:
Methinks young Lovers here with open Arms
Need no young Cupids to inspire their Charms,
For what can raise the Nymphs or Swains to love
In sweet Caresses, sooner than this Grove.
From hence (with Air) we past thro' Bristol streets,
Where Generous Hearts did give their liberal Treats,
Yet soon we found one of another Mould
For here a Crabbed Jade at us did Scold.
Her gravel'd Notes yet made some of us smile
whose impious Talk was near to Prattle Isle,
Which Place we nam'd to memor ze this Scold
And for her sake this story I have told.
Now next we took our Course to Cast's Isle
And pass'd away soon from this pleasant Soil
Finding ex ctly low Hog-stand b re
With Course and D stance to aquetnett shore,
Mount-Hope from hence we plainly now espy'd
Which was hard by, or near the flowing Tide,
To which we came taking the Courses here
To neighbouring sh res, and Islands that are near.
Turning aside we saw the Royal Spring
Which once belong'd unto an Indian King,
To chear our Hearts we drank the cooling stream,
In memory of Philip and his Queen.
Next we ascended Philip's Royal Seat,
Where he was slain, and all his Armies beat
We saw the Place where quartered he did hang,
Where joyful notes of Praise those Victors sang.

Upon this Mount the wand'ring Eye may gaze
On distant Floods, as well as neighbouring Bays
Where with one Glance appears Ten Thousand Charms
With fruitful Islands, and most fertile Farms.
Now from this Mount we went (like Men well skill'd)
By Flocks and Herds which verdant Pastures fill'd,
Unto Assonet took the Distance here
And turn'd about new Courses now to steer.
From hence we went by various Towns in haste,
And by Rhode-Island shore we also past
Where every Turn and Cove We noted down
Shaping our Course unto Seconet Town.
When we came near that pleasant place and soil
I heard a story which will make you smile.
A worthy Friend who lately had great Losses
Amongst his Stock, but chiefly in his Horses,
By evil Men, who haunts his Fields by night
When he's from home and kills them out of spight,
This Friend relates [whose Daughter was before me]
With chearful Air the following Famous Story:
" One Evening clear (said he) she took up Arms
" Laying aside a while her Virgin Charms,
" And walk'd abroad some of my Fields to view
" The Flocks and Herds to see what would ensue
" Then instantly with Courage being inspir'd
" She at an Armed Rogue her Pistol fir'd
" Crying aloud you Wretch begone from hence
" Or stand and fight me in your own Defence.
" But guilty Creature, he took to his Heels
" And left this Maiden in the Conquer'd Fields
" Who joy'd a while for this brave Action done,
" And then return'd unto her Peaceful Home.
From hence we pass'd along Seconet shore,
Unto its Point where Dreadful Billows roar,
Whose rolling Waves come tumbling from the main
And kiss the Shore, and then retire again.
Here may the Eye survey the tossing Sea
And sport the sight with Ships that sailing be.
Upon this Coast, which come from distant Lands;
And then may turn and view the Beach and Sands,
True Gratitude forbids I should be mute,
Where Generous Souls, our Spirits do Recruit.
Now sure this Town deserves our best of Praise,
Since none more striv'd our Spirits soon to raise.
But stop my muse, let's haste to our Survey
And stretch our Course along the Eastward Bay.
So then from hence we measur'd by the Sands
An Eastward Course along those pleasant Lands,
And came to Dartmouth a most liberal Town
Whose liquid Treats their generous Actions crown.
Here is the place where we did end our Work
Here we left off, (and did it with a Jirk)
And then retired, our Field Book for to scan,
And of this large Survey to make a Plan.

By Capt. Wm. Chandler of   W. C.

Thompson in Connecticut.
FINIS.
Printed at Rhode Island

A MOURNFUL LAMENTATION FOR THE SAD AND DEPLORABLE DEATH OF MR. OLD TENOR, A NATIVE OF NEW-ENGLAND, WHO . . . EXPIRED ON THE 31ST DAY OF MARCH, 1750

[*The Essex Institute*]

SIZE, 7½ by 13¼ inches, with margins trimmed. Advertised for sale in the *Boston Evening Post*, April 2, 1750, as published that day. The printer was Thomas Fleet. In 1751 a broadside having almost the same title, "A sad and deplorable Lamentation, &c. . . .," was the occasion for a Royal Proclamation offering a reward for apprehending Robert Howland of Duxbury, and Fobes Little of Little-Compton, the suspected printers and authors thereof, because their verse contained "sundry expressions tending to bring into Contempt and Subvert the Constitution of the Government." (Cf. Ford, 938.) For various documents involved in this procedure, see the "Massachusetts Historical Society Proceedings" (1910), XLIII, 255–260. The present broadside is reproduced in connection with the discussion. The verses were also reprinted in *The Magazine of History*, Extra No. 90, Vol. 23 (1923), No. 2, pp. 35–40. Another set of verses entitled "The Dying Speech of Old Tenor" had been issued in 1750. (Cf. Ford, 912.) This broadside is reproduced on page 128 of Mr. Ford's volume. (Cf. also 913.)

These mock-serious compositions had been occasioned by the withdrawal from circulation of certain issues of paper currency issued by the province of Massachusetts. The bills, which had been authorized in order to pay the soldiers who had served in the Canadian campaign, had depreciated in value to such an extent that recall was necessary. In the following year, Parliament put an end to further issues of such currency in the colonies.

The present verses have been attributed to Joseph Green (1706–1780), a noted wit, and the author of various satires and lampoons greatly admired in his day.

A
Mournful Lamentation

— the sad and deplorable Death of

Mr. Old Tenor,

A Native of *New-England*, who, after a long Confinement, by a deep and mortal Wound which he received above Twelve Months before, expired on the 31st Day of *March*, 1750.

He lived beloved, and died lamented.

To the mournful Tune of, *Chevy-Chace.*

A Doleful tale prepare to hear,
  As ever yet was told:
The like, perhaps, ne'er reach'd the ear
  Of either young or old.
'Tis of the sad and woful death
  Of one of mighty fame,
Who lately hath resign'd his breath;
  OLD TENOR was his Name.

In vain ten thousands intercede,
  To keep him from the grave;
In vain his many good works plead;
  Alas! they cannot save.
The powers decree, and die he must,
  It is the common lot,
But his good deeds, when he's in dust,
  Shall never be forgot

He made our wives and daughters fine,
  And pleased every body;
He gave the rich their costly wine,
  The poor their flip and toddy.
The labourer he set to work;
  In ease maintain'd the great:
He found us mutton, beef and pork,
  And every thing we eat.

To fruitful fields, by swift degrees,
  He turn'd our desart land:
Where once nought stood but rocks and trees,
  Now spacious cities stand.
He built us houses strong and high,
  Of wood, and brick and stone;
The furniture he did supply;
  But now, alas! he's gone.

The merchants too, those topping folks,
  To him owe all their riches;
Their ruffles, lace and scarlet cloaks,
  And eke their velvet breeches.
He launch'd their ships into the main,
  To visit distant shores;
And brought them back, full fraught with gain,
  Which much increas'd their stores.

Led on by him, our Soldiers bold,
  Against the foe advance;
And took, in spite of wet and cold,
  Strong CAPE BRETON from *France.*
Who from that *Fort* the *French* did drive,
  Shall he so soon be slain?
While they alas! remain alive,
  Who gave it back again.

From house to house, and place to place,
  In *paper doublet* clad,
He pass'd, and where he shew'd his face,
  He made the heart full glad.

But cruel death, that spareth none,
  Hath rob'd us of him too;
Who thro' the land so long hath gone,
  No longer now must go.

In *Senate* he, like *Cæsar*, fell,
  Pierc'd thro' with many a wound,
He sunk, ah doleful tale to tell!
  The *members* sitting round.
And ever since that fatal day,
  Oh! had it never been,
Closely confin'd at home he lay,
  And scarce was ever seen.

Until the last of *March*, when he
  Submitted unto fate;
In anno Regis twenty three,
  Ætatis forty eight. *
Forever gloomy be that day,
  When he gave up the ghost:
For by his death, oh! who can say
  What hath *New-England* lost?

Then good OLD TENOR, fare thee well,
  Since thou art dead and gone;
We mourn thy fate, e'en while we tell
  The good things thou hast done.
Since the bright beams of yonder sun,
  Did on *New-England* shine,
In all the land, there ne'er was known
  A death so mourn'd as thine.

Of every rank are many seen,
  Thy downfal to deplore;
For 'tis well known that thou hast been
  A friend to rich and poor.
We'll o'er thee raise a SILVER tomb,
  Long may that tomb remain,
To bless our eyes for years to come,
  But wishes ah! are vain.

And so God bless our noble state,
  And save us all from harm,
And grant us food enough to eat,
  And cloaths to keep us warm.
Send us a lasting peace, and keep
  The times from growing worse,
And let us all in safety sleep,
  With SILVER in our purse.

---

* Mr. OLD TENOR was born in the Year 1702.

F I N I S.

No. 80
A NEW AND TRUE RELATION, OF A LITTLE GIRL IN THE COUNTY OF HARTFORD, . . . WHO ACTED IN A STRANGE MANNER, SUPPOSED TO BE BEWITCH'D, MARCH, 1763

[*The Pennsylvania Historical Society*]

SIZE, 8¼ by 13⅞ inches. In 1766 the Milk Street address would probably mean the printing office of Seth Adams and John Kneeland, who printed there 1765–1772.

Exactly a hundred years earlier, in the spring of 1662/3, the accusations of a child, the daughter of John Kelley, had precipitated a witchcraft excitement in Hartford, which had in the end led to three executions. This was forty years before the Salem witch trials. Since 1692, with the retracting of many of the Salem confessions and the public admission of error on the part of several of those responsible for the trials, active persecution of supposed witches had largely ceased, but it was many years before the "delusion" was entirely a matter of the past. Strange behavior, such as that detailed in these verses, continued to arouse the suspicions of the credulous far into the eighteenth century.

A New and
TRUE RELATION,

Of a little Girl in the County of *Hartford*, at *Salmon-Brook* in *Simsbury* who acted in a *Strange* Manner, suppofed to be be-witch'd, in *March* 1763.

HARK ! hark ! come liften to my theme,
'Tis really true, it is no dream ;
In *simfbury* famous town doth dwell,
A gentleman who's known full well.

To tell his name I fhall forbear,
In writ from me you fhall not hear ;
This man he hath a little daughter,
As by my Song you'll know hereafter.

Alas ! alas ! we well may fear,
To write the news of her we hear ;
She to her parents is moft dear,
No doubt of her they take good care.

'Twas in the year feventeen hundred fixty three,
As you may know if you'll b'lieve me ;
And in the boift'rous month of March,
When cold Boreas doth all nature fearch.

O then, alas ! this pretty child fo dear,
Was feiz'd with frantic fits we hear ;
Which did her parents doubtlefs grieve,
While nothing could her pain relieve.

Some neighbours they are apt to fay,
This child's bewich'd both night and day ;
Sometimes fhe'll roar and fcream amain,
And then lie down to reft again.

Sometimes fhe'll jump and dance the room about,
And like one craz'd fhe'll make a fearful rout ;
Sometimes fhe'll jump and climb the chair,
And there fhe'll be, tho' no one's near.

Sometimes fhe fees black cats and crows that fly,
And other frightful fights juft by ;
Sometimes fhe's bit & fcratch'd by hands unknown,
Which makes this child to figh and groan.

But alas ! alas ! to tell you all,
That doth unto this child befall,
Would take more lines than two or three,
Therefore I pray you to quit me.

Some neighbours they are fond to cry,
'Tis vapours is the reafon why
This child is fill'd with frenzy fits,
But vapours 'tis which ill begets.

O then, alas ! where is the caufe,
We will inquire of nature's laws ;
O let us call the fyftem near,
And fee of them what we fhall hear.

Come thou prolific fun and fay,
Haft thou fuch poifon in thy ray ?
No, no, he makes us this reply,
Both man and beaft I fatisfy.

Come Mars and Jupiter and Venus too,
Tell what of all this rout you know ;
They cry alas ! and make their voices ring,
We like great heroes, ferve our king.

And if we name them all around,
Among them all there can't be found,
No fuch matters as we fee,
For it with nature can't agree.

Alas ! where fhall we find the caufe,
Since it's not writ in nature's laws ;
Nor founded in the deep below ?
Alas ! who does the caufe well know ?

Some neighbours they alas ! do cry,
She is bewich'd, alas ! fhe'll die ;
They pity do this child moft dear,
And fay it is fome neighbour near.

Some others they are bold to fay,
And tell it round from day to day ;
By which it may fpread thro' the nation,
Before it is fome near relation.

But who it is I cannot tell,
And you don't know I b'lieve full well ;
Therefore forbear to tell the name,
And you'll be clear from any blame.

And now to you her parents dear,
Pray, unto God, now lend an ear ;
And do not think to eafe the fmart,
By conjure or by foolifh art.

But unto God, fend up your cry,
For he's a God whofe mercy's nigh ;
And if in faith you do implore,
Behold, his mercy at the door !

For if to you the truth to tell,
I do believe fhe'll ne'er be well ;
'Till God by his almighty power,
Send fome relief in the fad hour.

Let chriftians all, in faith fo ftrong,
For unto them it doth belong,
To fend their cries unto the Lord,
That he his Mercy may afford

May God preferve our Britifh land,
From witchcraft, witches, and their band ;
And fend to us his gracious care,
And fave us from the Devil's fnare.

So then in glory we fhall fing,
And unto him great praifes bring,
Who lives forever and for aye,
Amen, amen, the Angels fay.

Bofton, Printed and Sold at the Head of Milk-ftreet. 1766.

No. 81
A POEM, OCCASIONED BY HEARING THE LATE REVEREND GEORGE WHITEFIELD PREACH [1771]

[The Boston Public Library]

SIZE, 8½ by 13¾ inches. The Queen Street address was that of Green and Russell, who had a printing office and auction room there until 1775. The date of this sheet is conjectural, but it was probably issued early in 1771. Whitefield had died September 30, 1770. Mr. Ford points out that this cut had appeared on the *Poems* of Jane Dunlap, which were printed "next to the Writing School in Queen-Street in 1771." This was Green and Russell's printing office. The same cut was later used to honor other clergymen. It appears on a Connecticut broadside of about 1778, entitled "A Short Discourse Delivered by Mr. Abraham Camp, at the Funeral of Amasa Tinkham, A.B." (Library of Congress), and on "A Baptism Hymn" of 1791, printed by Ezekiel Russell. (Cf. Ford, 2607.)

pronogated
> There is no such word. The author may mean *prorogated* in the sense of prolonged. There is also a rare use of the participle meaning *called* or *summoned*.

inades
> There is no such word. *Invades* would hardly make sense.

A
POEM,
OCCASIONED

By hearing the late Reverend GEORGE WHITEFIELD preach.

THERE does the human seraph preaching stand,
  Whose very looks th' attentive crowd command;
Divine perswasion, with a shining grace,
Sits on his lips and pity in his face ;
No Preacher's eyes did e'er before reveal
Such tender love mix'd with such ardent zeal :
That orator must certain be obey'd,
Whose mein is eloquent, whose hands perswade ;
See, now he speaks, spectators do not fear,
For if you cannot, sure his people hear,
Else how could every face such passions wear ;
With how much eagerness the list'ning throng
Gaze on his eyes, and hang upon his tongue.
On them his words like heavenly lightning dart,
They leave the body sound, but melt the heart,
And to their minds the seeds of truth convey,
Which glow in them, and kindle into day.
Celestial meekness with such ardour join'd,
Mild gravity, with so much fire comb'n'd ;
The most reluctant passions must controul
Pierce through the heart, and touch the inmost soul.
The Preacher with resistless eloquence
Does as the Sun from his bright orb dispence,
O'erflowing streams of pure æthérial light,
That chases far away the shades of night.
He shews such great concern such sacred awe,
As if the heavenly majesty he saw,
By whose supreme commission he was sent
To treat with rebel man, and bring him to repent :
Only that Preacher can the affections touch,
Who's so in earnest, and whose labours such.
Plain WHITEFIELD now his hearers do inspire,
With his own passions pronogated fire.
And while the Speaker with seraphic art
Divine enchantments sends to every heart,
He, by his own, close their devotion raise,
And to their breast his very soul conveys :
Then while with sacred flames their bosom glow,
And stony hearts begin to melt and flow,

He to compleat his masterly design,
On them imprints fair images divine.
See how he triumphs with resistless skill !
How he instructs the mind, commands the will !
His breath, like winds, that on the ocean blow,
Moves all the waving multitudes below,
And drives the tide of passion to and fro.
This mighty power his creditors confess,
Who such emotion in their looks express.
Was more sincere devotion ever known ?
Did e'er the soul such panted passions own ?
Were e'er her various shapes to such advantage shown ?
The Preacher's words divine desires produce,
And holy ferments through their breasts diffuse ;
From man to man the blest contagion flies,
They catch it at their ears, and drink it at their eyes.
The harden'd wretch with thunder he inades,
And with the terrors of the LORD persuades :
And as the hardy king his threats affright,
So his mild arts ingenious minds invite.
When they're enlighten'd and convinc'd of sin,
Shew in their eyes what pangs they feel within,
Their conscience binds them on their dreadful back,
And stretches all their heart-strings till they crack.
By the disturbance in his face appears
What pains he suffers, and what wrath he fears.
He's so undone so perfectly distress'd,
As melts with pity each spectators breast ;
That figur'd mind, how much it does relent :
With sadder looks can any face repent ?
How just a trouble, what a pious grief,
Temper'd with hope of mercy and relief,
His melting eyes, that swim in tears declare
How deep his wounds, how sharp his sufferings are.
View the next face, spectator, thou wilt say,
Confusion there does all its pomp display.
Did ever man so much his guilt deplore,
Detest and hate himself so much before ?
How that unfeign'd inimitable shame,
And oratorial grace advance his name.

ADMONITIONS AND TIMELY PREACHMENTS

A LITTLE BEFORE BREAK-A-DAY, JAN. 1, 1701
BY SAMUEL SEWALL
[The Boston Public Library]

SIZE, 6⅜ by 8⅛ inches. There is some doubt as to whether this sheet is properly included among broadside imprints, but the following entry from Sewall's *Diary* would imply that the 1701 version of this poem was printed separately at that time. The entry is as follows (II, 27) :

Jan. 2, 1700/1701.

. . . Just about Break-a-day Jacob Amsden and 3 other Trumpeters gave a Blast with the Trumpets on the comon near Mr. Alford's [In Margin—Entrance of the 18th Century]. Then went to the Green Chamber, and sounded there till about sunrise. Bell-man said these verses, a little before Break-a-day, which I printed and gave them. [In Margin—My Verses upon New Century.]

The three quoted stanzas which follow this entry differ slightly from the corresponding stanzas of the present version, which appears at the end of *Proposals touching the accomplishment of Prophesies humbly offered by Samuel Sewall, M.A., and sometime Fellow of Harvard College, in New England* . . . (Boston: Bartholomew Green, 1713). It is possible that these six stanzas were also issued separately, and that Bartholomew Green was the printer. The Boston Public Library copy, here reproduced, was bound at the end of Sewall's *Phaenomena quaedam Apocalyptica Ad Aspectum Novi Orbis configurata* (1727). This volume also was printed by Bartholomew Green.

WEDNESDAY, *January* 1. 1701.

A little before Break-a-Day, at *Boston* of the *Massachusets*.

ONCE more ! Our G O D, vouchsafe to Shine :
Tame Thou the Rigour of our Clime,
Make haste with thy Impartial Light,
And terminate this long dark Night.

Let the transplanted E N G L I S H Vine
Spread further still :   still Call it Thine:
Prune it with Skill : for yield it can
More Fruit to Thee the Husbandman.

Give the poor I N D I A N S Eyes to see
The Light of Life :   and set them free ;
That they Religion may profess,
Denying all Ungodliness.

From hard'ned J E W S the Vail remove,
Let them their Martyr'd J E S U S love ;
And Homage unto Him afford,
Because He is their Rightful L O R D.

So false Religions shall decay,
And Darkness fly before bright Day :
So Men shall G O D in C H R I S T adore ;
And worship Idols vain, no more.

So A S I A, and A F R I C A,
E U R O P A, with A M E R I C A ;
All Four, in Consort join'd, shall Sing
New Songs of Praise to C H R I S T our K I N G.

No. 83

A LAMENTATION OCCASION'D BY THE GREAT SICKNESS & LAMENTED DEATHS OF DIVERS EMINENT PERSONS IN SPRINGFIELD, APRIL, 1712

BY JONATHAN BURT

[The Massachusetts Historical Society]

SIZE, 7½ by 11⅛ inches. This may be a Connecticut imprint. Timothy Green was printing in New London in 1720, when the verses were issued.

Jonathan Burt, "Deacon Jonathan," as he was called, was one of the pioneer citizens of Springfield. He was born in 1632, probably in England, and came to Springfield as a child, before there was a town government or a church. Subsequently he had a large share in both. He was early made a deacon, and was one of the selectmen of the town for many years. He died October 15, 1715. A brief sketch of his life is included in *The Life and Times of Henry Burt of Springfield* (Springfield, 1893), pp. 115–160.

The sickness to which he refers is frequently mentioned in other records of that year. Apparently it was confined to Connecticut. The *Boston Weekly News-Letter* for January 21, 1711/12, has this item:

We are inform'd that the Sickness in Connecticut Colony is so Mortal, that since the Last Session of their General Court, which was but some few Month's Past, Twenty four Members of the said Court are dead.

The issue of March 31 corrects an exaggerated report of the mortality as follows:

By Misinformation we were lately told, that the Distemper in Connecticut had carried off 700 Persons; but last Post from a good hand we are well assured through Gods Goodness, that Distemper carried not off above 250, besides some that Dyed of other Distempers.

Cotton Mather, always timely in his utterances, published a sermon on the subject entitled, *"Some Seasonable Thoughts upon Mortality;* In a Sermon Occasioned by the Raging of a Mortal Sickness, in the Colony of *Connecticut;* and the many Deaths of our Brethren there."* It was advertised for sale in the *News-Letter* of February 25, 1712. As late as November of the same year, there were allusions to the sickness, which seems also to have recurred in milder form for several winters following. Possibly the 1720 printing of Jonathan Burt's verses was occasioned by another outbreak of the disease.

Nominate
   Call by name.
John Holyock
   Another pioneer resident of Springfield. He died February 6, 1712.
John Hichcock
   A selectman of the town. He died February 9, 1712.
Japhet Chapin
   He had been selectman eight times. He died February 20, 1712.

A LAMENTATION

Occasion'd by the

Great Sickneſs & Lamented DEATHS of divers Eminent Perſons in Springfield.
Compoſed by Mr. *Jonathan Burt*, (an Old Diſciple,) in his Fourſcore & Fifth Year.
(Since Deceaſed,) Left as a Dying Legacy to his Children, and Surviving Friends.

FRiends, I am now about to write,
  a Mournful Elegy ;
And therefore I all you Invite
  therewith for to comply.
We need for Mourning Women call,
  alſo that they make haſte ;
And teach their Daughters to Mourn
  for we do greatly waſte.   (all ;
Is there no Balm in *Gilead* ?
  nor no Phyſician there ?
No Medicine for to be had
  our Health for to repair ?
Many a Friend GOD taken hath
  away from us of late ;
Lord, grant that it be not in wrath :
  I ſhall ſome Nominate,
That godly Man *John Holyock*,
  we are bereft of thee,
Alſo good Deacon *John Hickcock*,
  Japhet Chapin, all three :
Gone off the Stage, ended their life,
  unto their reſt we truſt ;
It ſeem'd as if they were at ſtrife,
  which ſhould injoy it firſt.
The Lord on us hath greatly frown'd
  removing theſe by Death ;
The Church it did moſt ſorely wound
  it pants, it gaſps for breath.
Three Couples in this Town did die,
  the Husband and the Wife,
Follow each other ſpeedily
  ending their Mortal Life.
Some Young Men dyed in their prime
  and flower of their Age,
Others that liv'd ſome longer time
  ended their Pilgrimage.
Two Brethren dyed in one day
  few Hours was between ;
For Seventy Years the like, I ſay
  in this Town was not ſeen.
It is too hard for me to make
  a Record of them all,
For it doth make my heart to ake
  when I theſe things recall.

My Soul keep ſilence and be mute
  tho' of the Rod partaker,
Its not for Mortals to diſpute
  nor Potſhreads with their Maker.
CHRIST can turn Water into Wine,
  make all things turn to good ;
Let God's dealings with me & mine
  be rightly underſtood.
If that with our dear Ones we part
  let's not Mourn to exceſs,
But let the Lord have all our heart
  and give the Creature leſs.
But hath the Phyſick kindly wrought
  doth it purge out our droſs?
Nearer to GOD hath it us brought
  in HIM made up our loſs?
Methinks my Friends I ſee a Cloud
  greater than a Mans hand,
GOD by His Rod doth ſpeak aloud
  to us in *New-England*.
What GOD will do I do not know,
  to His diſpoſe let's yield ;
Good Lord do thou thy Mercy ſhow
  to this poor Town *Springfield*.
What do theſe Providences ſpeak ?
  will GOD leave *Shilo's* Tent ?
The Staves of bands & beauty brake !
  good Lord do it prevent.
O Friends its no time for to Sleep;
  no not to take a Nap ;
But on our guard a Watch to keep
  and ſtand up in the Gap.
To my dear Children that ſurvive
  I leave this Legacy ;
I am now Fourſcore Years and Five,
  therefore my Time draws nigh.
Avoid all Jarrs, and live in Love ;
  be Moderate in your Diet ;
And be you like unto the Dove,
  and ſtudy to be quiet.
And do not build upon the Sand
  or any ſuch foundation ;
For then your building will not ſtand
  in an Hour of temptation ;

But do you build upon the ROCK,
  Chriſt Jeſus, He did dye
That ſo He might remove that block
  that in our way did lye.
And unto *Chriſt* give all your Heart,
  not only give your Name ;
And with all other things to part
  if He call for the ſame.
O take heed of bad Company
  into it do not run :
Leſt you at laſt be forc'd to cry
  alas ! I am undone.
Of Worldly things have low eſteem ;
  it is a World of Sorrow :
Your preſent Time do you Redeem,
  you can't promiſe a Morrow.
Your great Concern be ſure to Mind,
  in that work make diſpatch ;
An Intereſt in CHRIST to find,
  and ſtand upon your watch.
But be not you like unto ſome
  that chuſe things of this Life ;
Nor unto him that could not come
  who had Married a Wife.
But, Oh ! do you take that adviſe
  that GOD gives in His Word ;
Do you be careful in your choice
  to Marry in the Lord.
Let not things of this preſent world
  up in your heart be ſet ;
Neither in it be you ſo hurld
  GOD & your Souls forget.
The Lord is pleaſed with the Rod
  to viſit me when Old,
But yet the Arms of *Jacobs* GOD
  under me do uphold.
It is from One in his Old Age,
  that willeth you no hurt ;
GOD take you for His Heritage,
  your Father *Jonathan Burt*.

Writ, April, 1712.

Printed in the Year, 1720.

Potshreads

   Potsherds, fragments of earthenware vessels.

I see a Cloud . . .

   A sign given to Elijah when he prayed on Mount Carmel. I Kings 18.44.

Shilo's Tent

   Shiloh, a city in Ephraim, was, until the time of Samuel, the seat of the Tabernacle.

To my dear Children that survive

   Of Jonathan Burt's seven children, only two survived him. His son John died January 29, 1712, possibly of this same pestilence.

No. 84
THE MERCIES OF THE YEAR, COMMEMORATED: A SONG FOR LITTLE CHILDREN IN NEW-ENGLAND,
DEC. 13, 1720

[*The John Carter Brown Library*]

SIZE, 7¼ by 12 inches, with edges trimmed. The first of these two poems was reprinted in 1910, by Mr. George Parker Winship, and both poems were reproduced in 1911 for the Club of Colonial Reprints, Providence, Rhode Island.

   The printing of this sheet must have pleased Cotton Mather, to judge from an entry in his *Diary*, September 27, 1713, as follows:

   I am informed, that the Minds and Manners of many People about the Countrey are much corrupted, by foolish Songs and Ballads, which the Hawkers and Pedlars Carry into all parts of the Countrey. By way of Antidote, I would procure poetical Composures full of Piety, and such as may have a Tendency to advance Truth and Goodness, to be published, and scattered into all Corners of the Land. There may be an extract of some, from the excellent *Watts's* Hymns. "Massachusetts Historical Society Collections" (7th series), VIII, 242.

Mather's comment is of particular interest as suggesting that ballad sheets were circulating freely at this early date.

GREENWOOD'S bless'd Translation

   This was apparently Thomas Greenwood of Cambridge, who died in 1720.

Th' Eastern Peace not lost

   With the Indians.

THE MERCIES

Of the YEAR, COMMEMORATED:

A SONG for Little CHILDREN IN NEW-ENGLAND.

December 13*tb* 1 7 2 0.

[1]

Heaven's MERCY fhines, *Wonders & Glorys* meet;
Angels are left in fweet *furprize* to fee't.
The *Circle* of the *Year* is well near Run
Earth's-*Conflagration* is not yet begun.

[2]

Heaven fpares the *Bulwark* of our *Peace*, King GEORGE;
Our CHARTER holds; and *Privileges* large.
Our GOVERNOUR and SENATORS can meet;
And Greet, and *Join* in Confultations fweet.

[3]

Though *Great* our *Lofs* in GREENWOOD's blefs'd Tran-
Yet well fill'd *Pulpits* blefs the *Little Nation.* [lation;
New Churches Gather'd; Th' *Eaftern Peace* not loft;
And *Satan's* overthrown with all his Hoft.

[4]

Sicknefs from Diftant Lands Arrives, and Fears;
JEHOVAH in the *Mount* as oft *Appears.*
Contagion ftops with Precious *Captain* GORE;
How *Great* our *Lofs*? But *Heav'n* will draw no more.

[5]

Tho' ripening HEAT came *late*, yet *Froft* held off,
We Reap the *Harveft*, and have *Bread* enough.
Provifion's dear, Goods high, Bills low, Cafh none;
And yet the *Suffering Tribe* is not *Undone.*

[6]

A *Miracle!* That Ocean-Seas of Sin,
Have not prevail'd to let a *Deluge* in!
That Earth's upheld to bear the heavy Load!
Adore the *Grace* of a *Long fuffering* GOD!

[7]

Some Vices in the Church not yet fubdu'd;
Old Barren Vines and Trees, not yet down hew'd.
Sinners, not fent to their Deferved Place;
A YEAR is added to their DAY of Grace.

[8]

The Fugitive may be returned home;
The Foe to GOD, a Favourite become:
Who have no fhelter from Thy Jealous Eye,
JESUS! for fhelter to thy Wounds may Fly.

[9]

The *whole Years fpace* for Faith, Repentance, Prayer;
The *Moft* have not improved well, I Fear:
Look then, *with broken Hearts*, upon your ways;
And fee, your *Future Lives*, JEHOVAH Praife.

PSALM CVII *left Part.*

TRANSLATED by the Reverend

Mr. *Ifaac Watts*

And by him Intitled,

A *Pfalm* for New-England.

[1]

When GOD provok'd with daring Crimes;
Scourges the madnefs of the Times,
He turns their Fields to barren Sand,
And Drys the Rivers from the Land.

[2]

His Word can Raife the Springs again,
And make the wither'd Mountains Green,
Send flowry Bleffings from the Skies;
And Harvefts in the Defart rife.

[3]

Where nothing dwelt but Beafts of Prey,
Or Men as Fierce and Wild as they,
He bids th' Opprefs'd and Poor Repair,
And builds them Towns, and Cities there.

[4]

They Sow the Fields, and Trees they Plant,
Whole Yearly Fruit, fupplies their Want.
Their Race Grows up from fruitful Stocks;
Their Wealth Increates with their Flocks.

[5]

Thus they are Blefs'd. But if the, Sin,
He lets the Heathen Nations in;
A Savage Crew invades their Lands;
Their Princes Dye by Barbarous hands.

[6]

Their Captive Sons, expofs'd to fcorn,
Wander unpityed and Forlorn,
The Country lies unfenc'd, untill'd;
And Defolation fpreads the Field.

[7]

Yet, if the humbled Nation mourns,
Again His Dreadful hand, He Turns;
Again He makes their Citys Thrive;
And bids the Dying Churches Live.

[8]

The Righteous, with a Joyful Senfe,
Admire the Works of Providence:
And Tongues of Atheifts fhall no more,
Blafpheme the GOD that Saints Adore.

[9]

How Few with Pious Care, Record,
Thefe wondrous dealings of the LORD?
But Wife Obfervers ftill fhall find,
The LORD is Holy, Juft and Kind.

F I N I S.

No. 85

EARNEST EXPOSTULATION IN THE NAME OF THE GREAT & GLORIOUS GOD WITH THE INHABITANTS OF THIS LAND, ESPECIALLY THE RISING GENERATION, 1739

[The American Antiquarian Society]

SIZE, 8 by 11 inches. In 1739 Samuel Kneeland and Timothy Green had a printing house in Prison Lane, corner of Dorset's Alley.

There appears to be no overwhelming disaster which gave occasion for this entreaty to righteousness. The record of storm, fire, pestilence, and other so-called "judgments of God" is not more impressive for 1739 than for other years. The present author merely reflects the spirit of contemporary evangelical preaching incident to the Great Awakening.

The Nations I drave out,
> Meaning the Six Indian Nations, of course.

My holy Sabbaths
> In August, 1739, Governor Belcher had issued a Proclamation regarding Sabbath observance. This suggests that there had been some unusual laxity heretofore.

To visit you with Sicknesses,
> If the author has in mind the sicknesses of the current year, he may be alluding to the smallpox which was epidemic in Rhode Island and in South Carolina during 1739. He may, however, be speaking only in general terms.

What Seas consume, what Wars destroy
> England had declared war on Spain, August 19, 1739.

1788 March 20

Earnest EXPOSTULATION

In the Name of the great & glorious GOD with the Inhabitants of this Land, especially the Rising Generation.

O Earth' Earth Earth attend,
The mighty GOD hath spoke
Why will you still offend 'gainst (me?
Why will you me provoke?

Have not I waited long,
upon a sinful Land,
But still my Calls they do refuse,
and spurn at my Command?

I've try'd you many a Year,
my Judgments you have seen,
But yet you've not return'd to me,
though afflicted you have been.

I've laid my gentle Hand
upon you many a Time,
Yet from my Ways and Judgments still
perversly you decline.

Ungrateful Sons of Men,
your Fathers I have shown
The Way into this Wilderness,
And gave it for their own,

The Nations I drave out,
not by your Arm or Bow;
it 'twas my Might deliver'd you
from th' fierce insulting Foe.

When raging Infidels
inclos'd you round about,
sent mine Angel speedily
to chase and drive them out.

Till I a noble Vine
your Fathers planted here,
Protected and supported them
'midst all Distress and Fear.

Till they had taken Root,
and mightily had grown,
Abundance of this pleasant Land
you planted have and sown.

But O ungrateful Sons,
what are you now a doing,
Forsaking of your Fathers God
and seeking your own Ruin.

Long after you I've call'd,
and for your Fathers sake,
Have not departed quite from you,
nor yet my Cov'nant brake.

With tender Pity I,
your great Distress have seen,
And in the Mount of sore Distress,
your stedfast Friend have been.

I've sent my Messengers
who faithfully did warn
This sinful and rebellious Race,
unto me to return.

But to their earnest Call,
you've stop'd and clos'd your Ear,
Tho' they've besought you in my Name
and in my awful Fear.

My holy Sabbaths which
your Fathers highly priz'd
Are dreadfully prophan'd by you,
and wickedly despis'd

With holy Reverence,
they did adore my Name,
Which you their sinful wicked Sons
most awfully prophane.

And now behold my Hand
is out against you still,
Because in wicked Ways you walk,
contrary to my Will.

My Thunders you have heard,
my Tempest you have seen,
And other Judgments which so long,
upon this Land have been.

Under your crying Sins,
the Earth hath trembling stood,
And over you the Heavens like Fire,
I meant it for your Good.

But you've provok'd me still,
to Heav'n your Sins have reach'd
But yet my strong consuming Arm
against you I've not stretch'd.

Your tender Children dear,
on them mine Hand I've laid,
But wherefore doth the Lord contend?
who hath the Injury made?

And now again I send
mine Angel through the Land,
To visit you with sickness,
Which you can't withstand.

O what can you expect
a People near to God,
If you will not obey his Word
nor hearken to his Rod.

Distressing Judgments still
may fast upon you come,
Till in his hot and fiery Wrath,
he utterly consume.

A vile rebellious Race
unworthy and forlorn,
Who all Reproofs and all Rebukes
despise contemn and scorn.

Haste now to the Old World
and see what God did there;
And let it fill your guilty Souls
with trembling Dread and Fear

Secure and safe they were,
and confidently stood,
Till they were swift consum'd away
by a destroying Flood.

Away to Sodom now
a solemn View there take,
A famous City in one Day,
the next a burning Lake.

See Jerusalem for their Sins,
tho' a People nigh to God,
Drave out and cast away from him,
hated, despis'd, abhor'd.

If on the green Tree such
prodigious Judgments come,
How will the dry Tree fire and flame,
destroy, consume and burn.

But not to go so far,
the daily 'counts we hear,
Are 'nough to fill a thinking Soul
with trembling Dread and Fear.

Of Europe's Tempest Storms,
Destructions they have made,
What Seas consume, what Wars destroy
and Fire in Ashes laid.

And see who of you dare
to stand it out 'gainst GOD,
Who alone destroys, and who consumes
by his all powerful Word.

Repent, repent O Land,
why will you stand it out,
Against the great eternal GOD,
till he shall drive you out.

Of all your fine Possessions
which he to you hath given,
And leave you not a Name nor Son
under the Copes of Heaven.

And give your Land at once
he did that of Isr'el,
To Strangers and to Foreigners
to take, possess, and dwell.

To Earthquakes and to Plagues
to Pestilence and War,
Till for your vile Transgressions
you all consumed are.

Note, It is earnestly desired that Parents would teach these Lines to their Children in the Fear of the LORD.

FINIS.

BOSTON: Printed and Sold at the Printing House in Queen-Street over against the Prison. 1759.

No. 86
BUY THE TRUTH, AND SELL IT NOT [1764]

[The Massachusetts Historical Society]

Size, 10⅜ by 14⅞ inches. The only clue to the date of this sheet is that in 1764 the same verses were issued by William Goddard of Providence, Rhode Island. (Cf. Ford, 1310.) The cut was different. It represented an open Bible, placed in the center of the heading. The colophon was as follows:

Providence: Printed in the Year 1764, by particular Request of a worthy honest old Gentleman, who is zealous for the Cause of Truth, and anxious for the Welfare of his Fellow-Creatures.

Such verses continued the colonial traditions for the instruction of youth. There is another broadside issue, of 1731, which borrows the Janeway-Mather title, "A Token for Children, That they may know to avoid the Evil, and chuse the Good." (Cf. Ford, 596.) Its theme is apparent from the closing lines,

> Children! May these few Lines you move,
> Christ to embrace, while young;
> You'll ne're repent that you have read,
> Or I have writ this Song.

Still another, undated, is called "The Parents Pious Gift, Or, A Choice Present for Children." This admonition takes the form of a "Dialogue betwixt a Religious FATHER and an Extravagant SON. . . . It being an excellent Pattern for all Young Persons to set before them, in our present Sinful Times." As might be expected, it concludes with a parental victory in argument.

BUY THE

TRUTH,

AND

SELL IT NOT.

AS I did walk, I heard a talk,
    which founded in my ear;
Come foolish Youth and buy the truth
before it be too dear.
The price may rise, your season prize,
    and to my voice attend;
For this I say, the market-day
    may quickly have an end.
Its worth is great, I do intreat
    you therefore now give heed,
The same to buy most speedily,
    a purchase 'tis indeed,
Which if you gain, you'l soon disclaim
    the best of earthly pleasure.
You'l see earth's joys are foolish toys,
    and but deceitful treasure.
The pearl of price, and paradise
    are thine, if thou get truth,
'Twill raise thee high to dignity,
    and make thee a glorious Youth.
'Twill clean thy heart, whoe'er thou art
    from all thy evil ways,
And set thee free from misery
    and bondage all thy days.
'Twill set a crown of high renown
    for ever on thy head,
And make thee sing like birds i'th' spring,
    whose wings with joy are spread.
It doth excel the rich beryl,
    The onyx and the saphire,
Rubies rare can't with it compare,
    no, nor the gold of Ophir.
This bargain then do you young men
    resolve with speed to buy,
That in your choice you may rejoice
    to all eternity.
But you'l say, What (dear friend) is that
    which we for truth must give;'
'Tis ev'ry lust which leave you must,
    and holy you must live.
Self-righteousness, I do confess,
    you must part with also;
Yea, and in fine, whate'er is thine
    with speed you must let go:
Do not delay, time will not stay,
    but take my good advice;
Whate'er you see the terms to be,
    come strait unto the price.
For I do fear 'twill soon grow dear,
    it much runs in my mind;
Or be so rare, you'l scarce know where
    God's precious truth to find.
Satan doth strive for to revive
    each cursed heresy,
And tries his wit to counterfeit
    the same continually.
That scarce do, you hardly know
    within a little while,
Truth's lovely face, from errors base
    and heresy most vile.
Men day and night begin to flight
    God's holy truth also;

Thee graceless be, and hate I see
    both it and conscience too.
For which things sake, God soon will make
    the price of truth to rise;
Its precious worth for to hold forth
    i'th' midst of enemies.
They don't believe, neither receive
    what truth doth now declare;
But to condemn, and it contemn,
    and that too ev'ry where:
But let such know, their overthrow
    and ruin is at hand,
Their day doth end, and God will send
    truth to some other land;
Who joyfully, of certainty,
    will it indeed embrace,
When such shall howl, and much condole
    in Hell their woful case.
Dear lambs beware, there is a bear,
    and other evil beast,
In ambush lies, and by and by
    on you they think to feast.
O watch, don't sleep, besure to keep
    awake continually,
Again I say, watch night and day,
    for ruin great is nigh.

The Child's Instructor.

O Child most dear incline thine ear
    and hearken to God's voice;
His counsel take and it will make
    God's angels to rejoice.
Be not like those, which grace oppose
    and give their mind to play;
But let thy mind be well inclin'd
    in seeking wisdom's way.
Learn in thy youth God's holy truth,
    Christ's blessed cross to bear;
And so shalt thou, though hated now,
    in Heaven have a share.
Don't lie nor swear, to steal don't dare
    O fear such grievous evils;
For such must die, and in Hell lie,
    with damned Souls and Devils.
In a right way thou must obey
    thy Father and thy Mother;
'Tis also right in God's dear sight,
    to love Sister and Brother.
Let no vain pleasure, nor earthly treasure
    thy Soul seek and desire;
For those things know, God will o'erthrow
    with his consuming fire.
Spend all thy days in righteous ways,
    God's holy name to hallow;
That at the last thy days being past,
    a blessed end may follow,
And though thou die, and in grave lie,
    yet raise Christ will thee make;
And Angels sent thee to attend,
    and into's Kingdom take.

Where thou shalt rest, with Saints the best
    to all Eternity,
And have the Crown of blest renown,
    God's name to magnify.
That thou with Christ, in paradise,
    for ever mayest dwell;
Thus do thou may, both night and day,
    and so good Child farewell.

The Second Part.

O Then remember God above,
    vain way do thou not take,
But learn betimes the Lord to love,
    who did thee form and make:
For Sin the Lord doth greatly hate,
    his nature is so pure,
That those he doth abominate,
    which can their sins endure.
Let Sin therefore to thee appear
    to be the vilest thing,
And labour Christ to love most dear
    that did Salvation bring.
And by all means see thou do strive
    against all youthful Lust,
Lest Sin do in thy Soul revive,
    remember die thou must.
On earth thy days will be but few,
    like as the swallow flies,
Or like unto the morning dew
    doth pass when sun doth rise.
So doth thy days, thy months and years
    make haste to fly away,
Much like the blossom that appears,
    and quickly doth decay.
Or like the flower in the spring
    which is for beauty rare.
Or as the birds in summer sing,
    I thee to them compare;
The glory of the flowers fail,
    the summer ends also;
The birds do then themselves bewail,
    and know not what to do.
The blossom withers soon away,
    like Jonah's gourd 'tis gone,
So thou sprout'st up and shall not stay
    thy life will soon be done.
Consider then, young men I pray
    the time which is to come;
Remember well thy dying day
    and dread the day of doom.
There is no help, but thou must die,
    alas, but that's not all;
Beyond the grave's eternity,
    God will to judgment call.
The Trump will sound, the dead to wake
    before Christ to appear,
The wicked then will dread and quake
    the Sentence for to hear.
Reform from sin, therefore with speed
    all evil ways defy,
That so thy soul may then be freed
    from Hell and Misery

SOME POETICAL THOUGHTS ON THE DIFFICULTIES OUR FORE-FATHERS ENDURED IN PLANTING RELIGIOUS AND CIVIL LIBERTY IN THIS WESTERN WORLD [After 1765]

[*The John Carter Brown Library*]

SIZE, 14¾ by 11⅛ inches. In all probability, this is a Connecticut, possibly a New Haven imprint, since the conditions described concern New Haven quite narrowly. The allusions to the policies of Lord North, as still effective, suggest a pre-Revolution date of composition, and yet the reference in Part II, Stanza 12, to an incident of 1765 as "Some years ago," would seem to indicate that at least four or five years had elapsed since the Stamp Act agitation. Certainly the verses were written before the outbreak of actual warfare, and since they constitute an appeal rather than a record, it is probable that they were printed at the time such admonition was necessary. The cut is an attempt to represent the first day in New Haven history, namely, the assembling of the colonists, newly arrived from Boston, in their first religious service, held on April 15, 1638, under a great oak tree. The gathering was the occasion for a sermon by John Davenport, one of the religious leaders of the colony. (Cf. the allusion to this scene in Part I, Stanza 12.)

28. *Which did the king's great fury raise*,
   Not entirely accurate. The king was on Daniel's side. Dan. 6.16–24.

Part II, 10.
Thus from Lord North, there does come forth
   The present tense is significant as suggesting a pre-Revolution date. The allusion to ships and men in the following stanza would apply to Boston conditions prior to the Massacre of 1770.

12. *Some years ago . . .*
   This would seem to be quite clearly a reference to the mission of Jared Ingersoll, representative of the New Haven colony at the court of King George in 1765. After working with Benjamin Franklin to prevent the passage of the Stamp Act, Ingersoll accepted an appointment as Stamp Distributor for the colony. This action aroused the indignation of his townsmen, who, upon his return to New Haven, faced him with threats, burned him in effigy, and on September 19, 1765, forced him to resign the office.

20. *There is a number in this land*,
   Probably a reference to the strong Tory element in New Haven itself.

27. *Will be like Judas in disguise.*
   At the time of the resentment against Jared Ingersoll, much was made of the fact that his initials corresponded to those of Judas Iscariot. The present allusion to Judas, however, appears to have no such significance.

SOME POETICAL THOUGHTS
On the DIFFICULTIES our FORE-FATHERS
endured in planting Religious and civil LIBERTY,
In this Weſtern WORLD.

With a few HINTS on the preſent STATE of AFFAIRS.

PART I.

WHEN our fore-fathers were oppreſt,
In their ſettle native land,
Then in their minds they could not reſt,
Until a method they had plan'd,

How to remove unto ſome grove,
Or to enjoy their liberty,
Thus they did form themſelves into
Into religious ſociety.

Thus they did put themſelves into
A method for them and their friends,
To find a place where they might go,
Where they might all obtain their ends.

Thus they did bear, as doth appear,
For there was a place in Providence
Provided for ſuch as they were
In honeſty and innocence.

The place that now they had in view,
Was over the great ocean wide,
And how to gain a paſſage thro'
They ſought to God to be their guide.

Who orders all that is above,
And alſo in this world below,
We are protected in his love,
And thus we gain'd our paſſage thro'

Thus we have gained our paſſage,
Into a place where we may reſt;
Let us give him praiſe which is his due,
That we may be forever bleſt.

Now we are come unto the ſhore
Where we have longd for to be,
Which ſatiſfies our hearts much more
Than all the Indies we might ſee.

Now let us ſing to God our king,
Who hath preſerv'd us o're the ſeas,
Now with our hearts our tributes bring,
Thro' faith and works that do him pleaſe.

Now we have ſung his praiſes here,
Upon this happy happy ſhore;
Let love abound as in his fear,
When we recal his mercies o're.

Now let us not forget him who
Has been ſo gracious and ſo kind;
Let's conſtant with him anew,
And keep his mercies freſh in mind.

Thus happy we under the tree,
Began the worſhip of our God,
None to moleſt, thus happy we
Attending on his holy word.

Upon the firſt day of the week,
After that we arrived here;
Now of our God we freely ſpeak,
We eſteem one day above a year.

When we was in our native land,
We was oppreſt with popery,
But we are now a feeble band,
Our God he hears us when we cry,

Which gives us free acceſs to him,
As in and through his only Son.
'Tis not a fancy or a dream,
The victory that he has won.

Thus we eſteem what we enjoy
Above the things we left behind,
Nor Britain's glory doth annoy,
Nor fruſtrate our peaceful mind.

Thus happy we, with bleſſings free,
Both with our wives, alſo our ſons,
Our daughters in equality,
Alſo our deareſt little ones.

Now we are bleſt above the reſt,
Of all Great Britain's richeſt heirs,
Thus we have travell'd to the weſt,
So we remain the Almighty's care.

So was our father's happy here,
While they continued in the truth,
Their language was in praiſe and prayer,
Both in their old age and their youth.

But O how awfully we've ſtray'd
From the good path our father's trod,
Nor kept the faith in love and pray'd,
But gone counter to his word,

Which is a rule for us to walk,
In civil and in ſacred things,
Therein we are taught to live and work,
Both for our princes and our king.

Thus we have ſtray'd from the Lord,
By not obeying his commands,
Now he doth threaten us with the ſword,
Both in Great Britain, and theſe lands.

But 'tis to be hoped in this land,
There's yet ſome heroes to be found,
That prays to God with heart and hand,
And with ſalvation ſhall be crown'd.

So notwithſtanding that our king
And parliament, and nobles rage,
He that doth rule in every thing,
Can eaſily their wrath aſſwage.

By ſacred writ in times of old,
When very few was to be found,
That ſerv'd and fear'd the Lord to hold,
So as to pray the bleſſings down.

When kings of old did ſet up gold,
And brought all nations thereunto,
Then did thoſe heroes appear ſo bold,
They to the image would not bow.

When muſic all did for them call,
To bow unto that image there,
They did not fear before them all,
Who was there God they did declare.

Which did the kin's great fury raiſe,
He cauſ'd the furnace to be heat,
The boldeſt men thus in a rage,
Did caſt thoſe heroes into it.

But O thou condeſcending Lord!
That God in whom they did believe,
Amidſt the furnace he appear'd,
Them from the fire he did relieve.

But when the king look'd in the fire,
For to behold there what was done,
He ſaw the three ſafe and entire,
The fourth appear'd like God the Son.

Now when the king ſaw what was done
Unto thoſe three that was preſerv'd,
A firm decree he made therefrom,
No other god there ſhould be ſerv'd.

Now we that are the offspring from,
Such happy men as doth appear,
Now let us put ourſelves in form,
That we be the Almighty's care.

Now we are call'd from Britain's ground,
Both by our king and parliament,
Let heroic boldneſs now confound,
Requeſts to us they do preſent.

Thus let us proſecute thoſe things
As for our right it doth appear,
It ſhall confound princes and kings,
Truſt in our God and do not fear.

Now we are happy in our choice,
So let us act our minds as free,
Let us go on with heart and voice
As the true ſons of liberty.

Thus I've compos'd theſe few lines,
To ſpeak of former and latter things,
Come all that are of peaceful minds,
True ſubjects to princes and kings.

PART II.

Now as we are under ſuch reſtrictions from Great Britain, as both appear unconstitutional, the proceedings are as ſmooth by a Congreſs generally conceded to by moſt of this continent, tho' oppoſed by ſome.

THE freemen general of this land,
Do proſecute more things that are
Of great importance and doth demand
Speedy and prudential care.

But theſe are a few that doth not view,
What our fore fathers did poſſeſs,
Will not thoſe good things purſue,
Propoſed by our own Congreſs.

But they go counter to theſe men,
Who are true ſons of liberty,
Nor do appear what they pretend,
But ſtruggle for the victory.

While others are for love and peace,
Virtue and truth and piety,
Their oppoſition doth increaſe,
Therewith they will now comply.

Altho' the ſons of liberty,
Do proſecute thoſe things that are
For love and peace and harmony,
Their condeſcention is moſt rare.

We wait, we long with great deſire,
To ſee thoſe happy, happy days,
When we ſhall meet with love entire,
To ſing his praiſes and his praiſe,

So long as we are diſagreed,
The houſe divided cannot ſtand,
So let us take all care with ſpeed,
To dwell in love with heart and hand.

That we might ſhare among the reſt,
Thoſe towns that's in America,
From North to South, from Eaſt to Weſt
Our homage to our God we'll pay.

To him we'll ſeek, on him we'll wait,
Hoping for deliverance from
That victory and diſmal fate,
That gathers round us like a ſtorm.

Thus from Lord North, there does come
Repeated ſtokes of tyranny,   forth
Thus in his fury and his wrath,
He ſays the coloneſt ſhall comply.

Now he doth ſend both ſhips and men,
To bring us under his command,
Thus doth his fury now extend,
Both in Great Britain and this land.

Some years ago, two ſad, it ſo,
Did effect us doth appear,
Or agent went to him alſo,
This great ſabale for to rear.

Thus with his ſword he went on board,
With graceful face he did appear,
Altho' his truſt was in the Lord,
They hoiſted ſail, the wind was fair.

He was preſerved o're the ſeas,
And ſafely he was there convey'd,
The counſel preſented to him did pleaſe,
By him our cauſe it was betray'd.

Into the hands of him that would
Bring us all under tyranny,
Thus 'tis ſuppos'd, it was for gold,
That was preſented to his eye.

The ſum that was ſix hundred pounds
Of ſterling money and alloy,
The ſight of which did him confound,
His faith and truſt it did deſtroy.

Thus he deſerted the truſt and cauſe
His agency it did demand,
And he went counter to our laws,
So he became a counterband.

Thus he was our pretended friend,
But prov'd himſelf our greateſt foe,

We fear theſe things will prove the end
Of his moſt fatal overthrow.

Now all you that will ſecond him,
And perſonate him in your hearts,
Let juſtice now take place and bring
Into the place of their deſerts.

There is a number in this land,
Who ever do pierce the air,
They form themſelves into a band,
There wills they have they do declare.

True they do go in their diſguiſe,
As the true ſons of liberty,
But they are known by their true ſize,
The ſons of light do them deſpiſe.

But O the madneſs of theſe men,
That will go on and ſtop their ears,
Againſt themſelves and their children,
The truth of this doth now appear,

So are the ſeeds, from bitter weeds,
In as conſtant age as minerd,
Thus by their practice and wicked deed,
Their deſtruction they have procur'd.

But oh to them that have thus ſtray'd
From the true light and liberty,
Proviſion now is for you made,
On happy terms if you comply.

Thus we invite you with delight,
With all our hearts and minds at eaſe,
Thus we do aim to walk upright,
As the true ſons of liberty.

And now to thoſe who do oppoſe,
The privilege that now comes forth,
Tho' they'll dwell under the roſe,
Moſt bear the fate with great lord North,

That doth pretend for to be a friend,
Unto our king and nobles wife,
Like Abſalom we fear the end,
Will be like Judas in diſguiſe.

Now come all you that will be true,
Unto the things you do profeſs,
That let us go on and thus purſue
The doings of our own congreſs.

Which doth appear both plain and clear,
A method for us in this land,
So let us go on with courage rare,
Tho' we are but a feeble band.

Tho' things look diſmal thick and dark,
Great oppoſition doth appear,
From our fore-fathers let us remark,
Truſt in our God and do not fear.

To Rulers of New-Haven town,
Under the preſent ſtate affairs,
Let equity and truth abound,
We ſhall be bleſſed and our heirs.

Now you that are inhabitants,
Within theſe bounds, let's live in love,
Let male and female with their preſents
With loyalty theſe things approve.

Now to the lawyers and merchants too,
Let not your minds go to exceſs,
But keep thoſe things always in view,
Appointed by our own congreſs.

Now to inholders of this town,
And all that's fall upon the ſeas,
Now let good order now abound,
As love and friendſhip ſhall increaſe.

Now to the farmers that till the ground,
Go on with a prudential care,
Let equity and judgment abound,
And God will crown the enſuing year.

O that ſome heroes might go forth,
And preach the goſpel as of old,
Viewing the ſouls that are more worth,
Than thouſands of ſilver and gold.

No. 88
A DIALOGUE BETWEEN DEATH AND A LADY [Before 1775]
[The American Antiquarian Society]

SIZE, 8 by 12 inches. The date is conjectural, but it could not have been later than 1775, as the Heart and Crown imprint still remains unchanged. The sign became the Bible and Heart after that date. For other issues of verses under this same title, cf. Ford, 3058–3061, 3096. The John Carter Brown Library possesses another issue, not listed by Mr. Ford. It was printed at Windham, and has a different cut. Death, holding a scythe in one hand, is about to hurl his dart at the lady with the other. The imprint is later than the one here reproduced, as printing in Windham dates from 1791. These verses may originally have been issued on the occasion of the death of an individual, as the "Dialogue between Flesh and Spirit," included above (p. 43), but the "Very suitable for these Times" of the present issue, suggests that this particular sheet was intended rather as a timely reminder of mortality than as a funeral tribute. There are no allusions to events which make possible the dating of the verses.

Dives
> The Latin word for rich(man), occurring in the Vulgate, Luke 16, and therefore taken commonly as the name of the rich man in the parable. *NED.*

A DIALOGUE BETWEEN Death and a Lady.

Very suitable for these Times.

Death.

FAIR Lady lay your coftly Robes afide,
　No longer may you glory in your Pride;
Take Leave of all your carnal vain Delight,
I'm come to Summon you away this Night.

Lady.

What bold attempt is this, Pray let me know
From whence you came, or whither muft I go;
Shall I, who am a Lady yield or bow,
To fuch a pale fac'd Vifage, who art thou?

Death.

Do you not know me? Well, I'll tell you then,
'Tis I that conquer all the Sons of Men;
No Pitch of Honour from my Dart is free,
My Name is *Death*, have you not heard of me?

Lady.

Yes, I have heard of you time after time,
But being in the Glory of my Prime,
I did not think that thou wouldft call fo foon,
Why muft my Morning Sun go down at Noon?

Death.

Talk not of Noon, you may as well be mute,
This is no time at all for to difpute.
Your richeft Jewels, Gold, and Garments brave,
Your Houfes, Lands they muft new Mafters have,
Though thy vain Heart to Riches was inclin'd,
Yet thou, alas! muft leave them all behind.

Lady.

My Heart is cold, I tremble at the News,
Here's Bags of Gold if thou wilt me excufe,
And feize on thofe, thus finifh thou the Strife,
With fuch who are aweary of their Life.
Are there not many bound in Prifon ftrong,
In bitter grief of Soul have languifh'd long.
From all would find a Grave a Place of Reff,
From all their Grief in which they are oppreft?
Befides there's many with their Hoary Head,
And Palfie Joynts, by which their Joys are fled,
Releafe thou them whofe Grief and Sorrow's great,
And fpare my Life to have a longer Date.

Death.

Tho' they with Age are full of Grief and Pain,
While their appointed Time they muft remain,
I come to none before my Warrant's feal'd,
And when it is they muft fubmit and yield:
I take no Bribes, believe me, it is true,
Prepare your felf to go, I come for you.

Lady.

Death, be not fo fevere, let me obtain,
A little longer Time to live and Reign;
Fain would I ftay, if thou my Life wilt fpare,
I have a Daughter Beautiful and Fair,
I'd live to fee her Wed, whom I adore;
Grant me but this and then I'll afk no more.

Death.

This is a flender frivolous Excufe,
I have you faft, and will not let you loofe;
Leave her to Providence, for you muft go
Along with me whether you will or no.
I *Death* command great Kings to leave their Crown,
And at my Feet to lay their Scepter down;
If unto Kings this Favour I'll not give,
But cut them down, can you expect to live
Beyond the Limits of your time and fpace?
No, I muft fend you to another Place.

Lady.

You learned Doctors now exprefs your Skill;
And let not Death of me obtain his Will;
Prepare your Cordials, let me Comfort find,
My Gold fhall fly like Chaff before the Wind.

Death.

Forbear to call, their Skill will never do,
They are but Mortals here as well as you.
I give the fatal Wound, my Dart is fure,
'Tis far beyond a Doctor's Skill or cure.
How freely can you let your Silver fly
To purchafe Life, rather than yield to die:
But while you flourifh'd here in all your Store,
You would not fpare one Penny to the Poor.
In all your Pomp the Poor men then did hate,
And like rich *Dives*, fcourg'd them from thy Gate;
But tho' you did thofe whom thus you did fcorn,
They like to you into this World were born;
Tho' for your Alms they did both cringe and bow,
They bore GOD's Image here as well as you.
Tho' in his Name their Suit to you they make,
You would not give one Penny for his fake;
My Lord beheld wherein you did amifs,
And calls you hence to give Account for this.

Lady

O heavy News! Muft I no longer ftay?
How fhall I ftand good God, in thy great Day
Down from her Eyes the dying Tears did flow
And faid, there's none knows what I undergo
Upon a Bed of Sorrow here I lie,
My carnal Life makes me afraid to die,
My Sins, alas! are many great and foul,
Which have deformed my immortal Soul;
And tho' I do deferve the righteous Frown.
Yet Pardon, Lord and pour a Bleffing down.
Then with a dying Sigh her Heart did break
And did the Pleafures of the World forfake.

　Here we may fee the High and Mighty too,
For *Death* he fheweth no Refpect at all,
To any one of high or low Degree,
Great Men fubmit to *Death* as well as wee,
Tho' they are gay, their Lives are but a Span,
A Lump of Clay, fo poor a Creature's MAN.

Sold at the Heart and Crown in Cornhill, Boston.

No. 89

OPPRESSION: A POEM, OR, NEW-ENGLAND'S LAMENTATION ON THE DREADFUL EXTORTION AND OTHER SINS OF THE TIMES [1777]

[The New York Historical Society]

SIZE, 7¾ by 13¾ inches, with margins considerably trimmed. The exact date is unknown, but the theme *extortion* would suggest composition in 1777 or 1778, when this evil was the subject of much disaffection among the colonists, and the topic of many a sermon. The same cut was used on a sheet entitled "Predictions for the Year 1783," printed by Ezekiel Russell. (Cf. p. 193, *infra.*) It is probable that Russell also issued the present sheet. *The Diary of William Pyncheon of Salem* (Boston, 1890) contains various items relative to the conditions described in these verses. Typical entries are as follows:

May 16, 1777. (P. 31).

. . . Bought half a cord of wood, and am now richer in wood than 39/40 of the whole town, having part of two loads by me! We crawl about and exist, but cannot be said truly to live. It is said we have full enjoyment of our liberty, but where is the proof of it?

June 30. (P. 33).

. . . Broadcloth said to be £ 6. 3.4. per yard, and scarcely any to be had. B. tea at 7 and 8 dollars per pound.

July 22. (P. 34).

. . . Mob at Salem demand sugar, and the stores are open.

July 23. (P. 34).

. . . The ladies rise and mob for coffee; cart it and the owner, Boylston.

Mar. 8, 1778. (P. 52).

Tradesmen and salary-men grumble at the countrymen's extortion, and threaten to join the Regulars against them.

Mar. 24. (P. 52).

. . . Grumbling at the extortion of the farmers, the blunders of politicians and legislators, the ambition and selfishness of the ministry and of the demagogues, badness of the times, etc., etc.

Nor [are] we yet alarmed, to Gospel Regulation;
F[or are] not men's desires . . .
[The] stronger are his wishes, . . .
[For there's] no skilful Physician . . .
[A more] destructive poison . . .
If there's [a combination among the sons of men,]
If Sea-ports first oppressed, [the County mayn't abuse,]
Let all with [protestation] abhor for to oppress,
We are loth to be held [short] to Laws of our own making.
Who promises Salvation [in all Transgressions.]

OPPRESSION
A POEM.

Or, NEW-ENGLAND's LAMENTATION, on the dreadful EXTORTION and other Sins of the Times. Being a serious EXHORTATION to all to repent and turn from the Evil of their Ways, if they would avert the terrible and heavy JUDGMENTS of the ALMIGHTY that hang over AMERICA at this alarming and distressing Day.

COME all you Friends to Goodness, I pray you to attend,
I'll tell to you a Story on which you may depend,
If you will not believe it, I think you must be blind,
When it appears so evident to every serious mind.

There wants a Reformation throughout AMERICA,
And deep Humiliation, for it's a sinful day;
But how can we desire, or look for better times,
So long as we aspire to multiply our crimes!

The Law has been despised, the Gospel trampled on,
And we have been surprised by powerful Briton;
But they can go no farther than the length of their chain,
JEHOVAH is their Master, who can their Power restrain.

But while we are complaining of England's Usurpation,
Iniquity is reigning throughout this Northern Nation;
So bad is our behavior, we grieve the Holy Spirit,
And if we slight our Savior, we cannot Heaven inherit.

We seem quite unconcerned about our souls salvation,
Nor are we yet alarmed, to Gospel Regulation;
The house of Saul grows stronger, as David's house grows weaker,
And Satan will reign longer, if we are such self-seekers.

His kingdom is maintained and strengthened by sin,
By some the building's framed, and others drive the pin,
New England's Sons will venture to travel in the dark,
And do refuse to enter the New-Test ment Ark.

A storm of wrath is proclaim'd, a flood will surely come,
And overtake the strongest, and drown the wicked one;
Altho' they fly to mountains, and hide themselves in rocks,
Of wrath there is a fountain to sweep the mountain-tops.

If we will not take warning, we must go down to hell,
Who like delight in scorning the great IMMANUEL;
Whose arms are always open, and bids us welcome there,
And shews the greatest token of love and friendship dear.

We have had publications, from the OMNISCIENT ONE,
A promis'd habitation, prepared by his Son;
At this Fountain of Treasure men might forever dwell,
But they refuse such pleasure, and damn themselves to hell.

'Tis very melancholy to hear of so much cheating,
To see men trick and jolly while they are over-reaching;
But fish delight in water, for that's their element,
And if men are not cheating they cannot be content.

Extortion has been used too much for to relate,
The Poor have been abused for to increase estates;
When Extortion's increasing, and greedy Muckworms crawling,
By such unlawful Fleecing the Public Wealth is falling.

Extortioners and Tories, which of them is the worst,
One brings us a fair story, the other a blunderbuss,
And openly presents it, a musket or a gun,
The other acts more secret, and murders ten to one.

We need not much admire that there are such commotions,
Are not men's desires unbounded as the ocean?
The more a man possesses, the more he really craves,
The stronger are his wishes, voracious as the grave,

Man's no skilful Physician can easily invent,
His destructive poison by long experiment,

Than some Merchants and Farmers in every State and Town,
Oppression and Extortion make up their second compound.
If there's any intimation going round to every State,
To ruin State and Nation, let us all turn out them straight;
If Sea-ports first oppressed, the Country may rest at ease,
Tho' Evil the first thinks easy, does we not excuse.

Let all with detestation abhor this vile oppression,
Nothing exalts a nation so much as righteousness;
We are not so enlighted but we may live so fast,
If Christ is so much slighted GOD will continue a war.

We have an invitation to save ourselves and lands,
To practice invocation for this is God's command,
We hope to have favour then, yet from the Savior turn,
If there's no reformation New England is undone.

GOD gives us plain direction how we may come to see,
And live in good subjection unto our Maker's Laws;
But we are so impolite, and there are such out-breakings,
We are loth to be held out to Laws of our own making.

If we had just conceptions of sin which so abounds,
Should follow God's directions and tread corruption down;
Without much pains or labor we may know our duty,
And do by all our Nabors, as we would be done by.

This law is just and equal, we cannot it deny,
'Twill prove so in the sequel of life where we shall die,
If we believe the Story found in the Gospel Plan,
No one can enter glory that's a dishonest man.

Since God has given us reason let us use it for him,
And not commit high treason against the King of Kings;
Who is our Lord and Master, and him we ought to own,
He is our rightful Sovereign, and to him we belong.

New England has been sick, and many a one have dy'd,
We've buried Father Goodchace, and rock'd Mother Price,
Faith is now languishing, Repentance given over,
Without a good Physician these two cannot recover.

Charity fast is cooling and Virtue faints away,
Ignorance is prevailing, but Knowledge goes away;
Profaneness is in fashion, Religion loses ground,
Holiness is decreasing, Covetousness abounds.

Sincerity is wanting, Sagacity is fled,
And Wisdom lays expiring, and Piety is dead;
When Mercy is forsaken, Dishonesty's elected,
Justice and Truth condemned, Morality rejected.

How beautiful and god-like, delightful it is to see
Princes and People walking in Love and Unity;
Remembering their Maker, whom they are bound to love,
And to be wise as Serpents, and harmless as the Doves.

If we would be forgiven and live in Peace and Rest,
Be Favorites of Heaven, and be forever blest,
Then let us all be willing at this appointed Day
To be just in our Dealings, and do as we would say.

Behold the Invitation of GOD ALMIGHTY's Son,
Who promises Salvation to all,
Let every Son for LIBERTY bow down to sinful town,
Accept the Invitation to an Immanuel Crown.

No. 90

A NEW TOUCH ON THE TIMES, WELL ADAPTED TO THE DISTRESSING SITUATION OF EVERY SEA-PORT TOWN [1779]

[*The New York Historical Society*]

Size, 8⅛ by 12¾ inches, with margins trimmed. The date of these verses cannot be fixed accurately. The conditions described would fit equally well any one of the years 1776 to 1780. The sufferings of the women and children in Marblehead during this time had been severe in the extreme, and had at various times been the basis of appeals for relief. It is probable, however, that the verses were written after the conditions described had been long endured. Mr. Ford lists the piece under 1779. (No. 2161.)

For they are gone the ocean wide,
    Many of the men of Marblehead were in the marine service.
[F]or which we [can't] get any ease,
[F]or they are gone to work for [us,]
Wan't it [for th]em we now should starve,
To go thro' the world how can we [do,]
For times they sure grow worse and [worse,]
For money is not worth a pin,
    Many of the soldiers had been paid in Continental notes which had depreciated to less than half of their face value.
Takes 20 weight of sugar for two foot of wood,
    Shortage of fuel was one of the chief causes of suffering in Marblehead during this time, and many buildings and fences were torn down and burned to supply the lack. The situation was investigated by a legislative committee in 1780, and tax reductions made by way of adjustment.
By means of which we shake [the head,]
All we can get it is but [rice,]
And that is of a wretched [price.]
[N]othing now-a-days to be got,
To put in ket[tle or in] pot.

A NEW
TOUCH ON THE TIMES.

Well adapted to the diftreffing Situation of every Sea-port Town.

By a DAUGHTER OF LIBERTY, living in MARBLEHEAD.

OUR beft beloved they are gone,
We cannot tell they'll e'er return,
For they are gone the ocean wide,
Which for us now they muft provide.
  For they go on the roaring feas,
For which we can't get any eafe,
For they are gone to work for nae
And that it is to fill our purfe.
  And to fill our houfes too,
What more could we then have them do?
They now do more than we deferve,
Wan't it for them we now fhould ftarve,
Starve then we fhould and perifh too,
And without them what could we do?
  We muft do as well as we can,
What could women do without man,
They could not do by night or day,
Go round the World and that they'll fay
  They could not do by day or night,
I think that man's a woman's delight,
It's hard and cruel times to live,
Takes thirty dollars to buy a fieve.
  To buy fieves and other things too,
To go thro' the world how can we do,
For times they fure grow worfe and worfe
I'm fure it finks our fcanty purfe.
  Had we a purfe to reach the fky,
It would be all juft vanity,
If we had that and ten times more,
'Twould be like fand upon the fhore.
  For money is not worth a pin,
Had we but falt we've any thing,
For falt is all the Farmer's cry,
If we've no falt we fure muft die.
  We can't get fire nor yet food,
Takes 20 weight of fugar for two foot of wood,
We cannot get bread nor yet meat,
We fee the world is nought but cheat.
  We cannot now get meat nor bread
By means of which we fhake our head,
All we can get it is but rye,
And that is of a wretched

And as we go up and down,
We fee the doings of this town,
Some fay they an't victuals nor drink,
Others fay they are ready to fink.
  Our lives they all are tired here,
We fee all things fo cruel dear,
Nothing now-a-days to be got,
To put in kettle nor in pot.
  Thefe times will learn us to be wife,
We now do eat what we defpis'd,
I now have fomething more to fay,
We muft go up and down the Bay.
  To get a fifh a-days to fry,
We can't get fat were we to die,
Were we to try all thro' the town,
The world is now turn'd up-fide down.
  But there's a gracious God above,
That deals with us in tender love,
If we be kind and juft and true,
He'll fet and turn the world anew.
  If we'll repent of all our crimes,
He'll fet us now new heavenly times,
Times that will make us all to fing,
If we forfake our heinous fins.
  For fin is all the caufe of this,
We muft not take it then amifs,
Wan't it for our polluted tongues
This cruel war would ne'er begun.
  We fhould hear no fife nor drum,
Nor training bands would never come
Should we go on our finful courfe,
Times will grow on us worfe and worfe.
  Then gracious God now caufe to ceafe,
This bloody war and give us peace!
And down our ftreets fend plenty then
With hearts as one we'll fay Amen
  If we expect to be forgiv'n,
Let's tread the road that leads to Heav'n
In thefe times we can't rub along.
I now have ended this my fong.
    MOLLY GUTRIDGE compofitic
  Be fure it is no unpofition.

No. 91

PREDICTIONS FOR THE YEAR 1783

[*The John Carter Brown Library*]

Size, 9½ by 13¼ inches. The Essex Street printing office, near the Liberty Stump was that of Ezekiel Russell. As these verses would have had no sale other than at the time to which they apply, it may be assumed that they were printed around New Year's Day, 1783.

Bickerstaff
> A pseudonym used by Benjamin West, a mathematician, in his Boston Almanacs, issued from 1763 to 1793.

Peace lead the front
> The British evacuated New York, November 25, 1782. Peace was not formally ratified until September 3, 1783.

loobies
> Awkward, clownish fellows.

Louid'rs
> A gold coin issued from the reign of Louis XIII to Louis XVI. Early in the century, about 1717, it had been valued at 17*s*.

Pistereens
> An American name for a small silver coin current at this time.

[*And bawl, "take me! for I'm a better bunch!"*]
We wade in cacavilla, port, [*and claret,*]

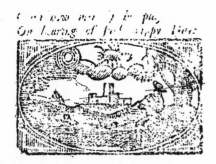

PREDICTIONS

FOR THE

YEAR

1783.

THE GAY YOUNG MUSE salutes the opening
year,—
PEACE lead the front! and plenty bring the rear!
Felicity shall glitter all compleat,
And silver, gold, and jewels, pave the street.
We slump in saphires, emeralds and rubies,
All men grow wise for who are wit-lings and
loobies:
View far and wide, with wonder, and behold,
Trees bloom in silver, and mature to gold;
Whene'er in groves we seek the rural shades,
Ripe crowns drop down by millions on our
heads;
No more in fields we walk o'er weeds and
greens,
But tread on Louid'rs and pistereens;
In plumbs of pearls and garnets, we discern all,
The stones pure gold, and dimonds every
kernal;
Brocades, and cambricks, keep us always hot,
Cold pinch no more, and winter be forgot:
When round the chimney roars our social
mirth,
Carbuncles blaze on each refulgent hearth.
The iron pots and spits of every scullion,
And wooden cans, and earthen bowles a bullion,
But now our opulence is thus compleat
You ask, " What shall we do for drink, and
meat ?
What drink and meat ?—See! show'ring down
the skies
Chesecakes, cold hams, plumb-puddings, and
mince-pies!
Each wind of Heaven o'er all the ground shall
spread
Tarts, custards, and plumb-cakes, and ginger-
bread;
Partridge and pasty smoke, where'er we look,
With every sauce contriv'd by every cook.

Pigs, ready roasted, run along the street,
And grunt, and squeak, and squeal, " come eat!
come eat!
Beef a-la-mode, endu'd with language, cries,
' You're welcome, gentlemen, pray take a flice,
Grapes, cluft'ring forward, one another
And bowl, take me for the better of the
For liquor, what profusion I never spare it,
We wade in cacavilla, port, and claret,
Sterling madeira, burgundy, and sack,
And all the gutters run with frontinac:
Hills shall be honey combs, the ocean ale,
Whipt-cream shall snow, and sugar plumbs shall
hail,
Drink springs spontaneous, fit for every lip,
Grog, punch, raw-rum, and hyson-tea, and flip,
Soups, syllabubs, ragouts, and frigassees,
And nature change to chickens and green pease,
How ? All things gems, all gold, all drink, all
food too ?
I own 'tis somewhat crouded: But pure good tho'.
'Tis transport all, all by inchantment plan'd!
Fair fairy-fields, and laughing lubber-land.
Thus we, all fun, while faithful FRENCH
defend us,
Titter and giggle at our INDEPENDENCE.

Stop! GAY YOUNG MUSE! be serious ere we
part,
And let me speak a language to your heart:
You, in your moral breast the answer find;
Can such vain bubbles bless the immortal
mind ?
This fallen earth can hold no happiness,
Bliss was not made for such a world as this
You draw perdition in with every breath,
Sin, sorrow, and old age, disease, and death:
Leave madmen o'er the illusive scenes to roam,
Seize thou thy raptures in a world to come.

Sold at the Printing-Office in ESSEX STREET, near LIBERTY-STUMP.

No. 92
AS THE PIECE DEDICATED TO THE YOUNG GENTLEMEN HAS MET WITH A KIND RECEPTION, THE AUTHOR WOULD ADDRESS HER OWN SEX, JUNE 10, 1786

[The Boston Athenaeum]

SIZE, 6½ by 16¾ inches. The Liberty-Pole address identifies this as probably an imprint of Ezekiel Russell. The piece dedicated to the young gentlemen has not survived.

Bellona

    The Roman goddess of war.

Columbian Daughters' skill

    The future fame of America in all directions was one of the themes of the hour.

descry

    Apparently in the sense of *reveal*.

Vacuna's soothing charms

    A Sabine goddess who presided over the works of the garden and field.

and save a sinking land

    Cf. this concern for the future of America with similar sentiments in the verses entitled "Home Industry," p. 199, *infra*.

As the Piece dedicated to the young GENTLEMEN has met with a kind Reception, the Author would addrefs her own SEX in the following manner ; hoping it will have the like Acceptance with the young LADIES who are under the Tuition of the feveral SCHOOL-MISTRESSES in this State, more efpecially in the Town of BOSTON.---Compofed June 10, 1786.

THE early lark falutes the vocal groves,
  With warbling fongs the mufick fweetly roves,
The fun's prolifick rays illumes the fkies,
With fmiling accents bids young Ladies rife.
  See, by the clock, the Semptrefs waits for you,
Rife, like the plants, fed with nectarine dew ;
With elevation feize the balmy gale,
This will abide when other riches fail.
  Minerva her profufe endowments fends
To her induftrious and beloved Friends.
Bellona now unlocks her magazine,
And to the Ladies comes with graceful mein.
  As facred volume gives the needle praife,
So would my pen attempt its worth to raife ;
When the fair Princefs to the King is brought,
Her fnowy raiment fhall be needle wrought.
  Succeeding ages will your virtues tell,
Your genius *Egypt*'s Nymphs fhall far excel,
Accomplifh'd Nuns with fhame their works will hide,
Columbian Daughters' fkill extends fo wide.
  The virtuous Woman may defy the cold,
She cloathes herfelf in fcarlet, wrought with gold ;
Lives by induftry in her native land,
With the production of her frugal hand.
  Wifdom with prudence dwells, and daily finds
Witty invention to improve your minds ;
Be all attention, like the filken worm,
Left giddy fancy all your art deform.
  The cyprefs texture which with care you view,
Your flender ftate of youth refembles true ;
As lily white will foon defcry a foil,
So reptile vice will all your virtues fpoil.
  Your pattern oft you mark with anxious eye,
That criticks may no fault nor blemifh fpy ;
What panick tremor foon invades your frame,
When negligence expofes you to blame.
  The many puzzling turns you have to wind
Are far more ftrait than your untutor'd mind ;
What roving paffions harbour in the breaft,
Dear bought experience can the truth atteft.
  If once *Vacuna*'s foothing charms you hear,
Her firen notes will foon inchant your ear ;
Drones in the winter are not kept alive,
Left they fhould be a nuifance in the hive.
  Will curling vines, trees, plants, or bloffoms grow,
Unlefs fome pains the Gard'ner will beftow ?
Can folded hands their fweet refemblance fpread ?
Will dormant needles draw the flender thread ?
  No brilliant rings fuch fingers fhould adorn,
Who treat induftry with apparent fcorn ;
Nature moves on her wheels for your fupply,
And will you let your talent buried lie ?
  Exert yourfelves and fave a finking land,
It is by you that we muft fall or ftand ;
If prudence and difcretion guide your ways,
Ages to come fhall fpeak it to your praife.
  Inroll'd among the famous and the wife,
Your virtues fhall like precious odours rife ;
In diftant lands your mem'ries will be bleft,
Who broke the galling chains that long oppreft.

Sold next LIBERTY-POLE. 1786.

No. 93
A LINE TO THE MODERN LADIES
BY JOSEPH HOPKINS
[*The Pennsylvania Historical Society*]

SIZE, 7⅝ by 12¾ inches. There is no certain clue to the date of composition or printing. Nor can the author be identified with certainty. He may have been the Joseph Hopkins mentioned in the *French and Indian War Rolls for Connecticut, 1755–1757*, as serving in the Company of Captain Lee of Farmington in 1757. ("Collections of the Connecticut Historical Society," IX, 210.) This may or may not be the same Joseph Hopkins whose marriage to Ann Smith, Farmington, Connecticut, March 18, 1762, is included in *The Early Marriage Records of the Hopkins Family in the United States* (William Montgomery Clemens, New York, 1916, p. 6). The name also occurs elsewhere. But whoever may have been the author, the verses represent a typical example of the numerous appeals to women to forsake their vanity in the interest of their souls' welfare. The sheet probably belongs to the last quarter of the eighteenth century.

A Line to the Modern LADIES:

Found among the Writings of

JOSEPH HOPKINS,

Late of FARMINGTON, deceased.

LADIES, can you in Conscience say,
Your useless costly fine Array,
As Tossels, Topnots, flow'ry Stuffs,
Jewels and Rings, and heaps of Ruffs:

With Paints, Expence, and spending Time,
Can be slipt o'er, and thought no Crime?
Can you procure those things of Cost,
And say no Time nor Money's lost?

Can you spend Months to curl your Hair,
And Years to fix the Clothes you wear?
Can you spend all the Sabbath Morn,
Your Dust and Ashes to adorn!

Nor all the Morning read and pray,
Nor once think 'tis an holy Day?
And think it is no Thing of weight,
That you come into Church so late?

At length into the Church you gether,
With here a Tossel, there a Feather:
With many other Nacks and Nicks,
That I judge took you Hours to fix.

One Practice more among the rest,
With which you Ladies are possest;
Pray let me mention just this one,
Then I'll dismiss you, and will done.

When you together happ' to meet,
Tea for to drink, and Food to eat,
Without a Thought that GOD hath giv'n,
Or thinking all you have's from Heaven.

Heedless you set yourselves to eat,
And thus contemptuously treat
Him who hath given present Food,
Who is the Author of all Good.

And what's more Heaven-daring still,
Is when you've eaten to the full,
You bless not God, return no Thanks,
But fall to playing of your Pranks.

By telling Fortunes by an Art,
Which none but Satan could impart,
Pretending by the Dregs of Tea,
To tell of any Destiney.

Your Fortune tell in this or that,
Which only youthful Lusts excite,
Setting your Passions all on Fire,
And rousing up impure Desires:

Which serve to draw the Mind from good,
In Disobedience to your GOD.
Ladies, I now to you appeal,
What Spirit doth those Things reveal?

Can you think God who is Most High,
Is pleased with such Vanity?
And freely to you intimates,
The Thing which in his Heart he hates.

You can't, I'm sure, then you must own
Your Art is from the wicked One.
What! be familiar with the Devil,
It is both wicked and uncivil.

Remember when you eat and drink,
Whatever do, or ever think,
You are oblig'd by Laws of Nature,
To glorify your great Creator.

Consider well your bold Offences,
And know the dreadful Consequences;
For Thoughts, Words, and all such Actions
You finally must make Retraction.

Sure there's a Day which soon will come,
In which all Souls receive their Doom;
See that your Doom is not, *Depart*,
For practising the Devil's Art.

HOME INDUSTRY, THE MOST DIRECT ROAD TO NATIONAL PROSPERITY [After Oct. 14, 1794]

[*The Boston Public Library*]

Size, 9 by 11¼ inches. The margins have been trimmed. These lines present both paraphrase and quotation of selected lines and passages from Colonel David Humphreys' *A Poem on Industry*, Philadelphia, October 14, 1794. The selections are made chiefly from the latter half of the poem. Doubtless many of the newspaper appeals for support of native manufactures during the late nineties likewise had their inspiration from Colonel Humphreys' eloquent arguments, for "Home Industry" was one of the themes of the hour. But it is to be feared that the author of so dignified a volume would scarcely have been pleased with the well-meant efforts of the present compiler, who wisely withheld his name.

What mighty elements advance the plan;
While fire and earth obey the master's call,

Then true utility with taste allied,
Shall make our homespun garbs our nations pride.
See wool the boast of Britain's proudest hour,
Is still the basis of her wealth and power;

In every vale, on every hill, the fleece!
And see the folds with thousands teeming, fills,
With flocks the bleating vales and echoing hills,
Ye harmless people, man your young will tend,

Him nature form'd with curious pride, while bare,
To fence with finery from the piercing air,
This fleece shall draw its azure from the sky,

HOME INDUSTRY,

The moſt direct road to National Proſperity.

SAGES conven'd from delegating States,
Who bears the charge of unborn millions fates,
From early ſyſtems ſtates their habits take,
And morals more than climes a difference make,
Then give to toil a bias, aid his cauſe
With all the force and majeſty of laws ;
While you preſide in uſeful arts direct,
Create new fabrics and the old protect.
Lo ! at your word. ſubdu'd for wondering man,
What mighty element advance the plan ;
While fire and ſpoey the maſters' call,
And water labours in its forceful fall ;
Teach tiny hands with engin'ry to toil,
Cauſe failing age o'er eaſy taſks to ſmile ;
Firſt let the loom each liberal thought engage,
Its labours growing with the growing age ;
Then true utility both tied allied,
Shall make our homeſpun garbs our nations pride.
See wool the boaſt of Britain's proudeſt hour,
Is ſtill the baſis of her wealth and power ;
From her the nations wait their wint'ry robe,
Round half this idle, poor, dependant globe,
Shall we, who foiled her ſons in fields of fame,
In peace add glorious triumph to her name !
Shall we, who dar'd aſſert the rights of man,
Become the vaſſal of her wiſer plan !
Then rous'd from lethargy, up ! men ! increaſe,
In every vale, on every hill, the fleece !
And the folds with thouſands teeming, fills,
With flocks the bleating vales and echoing hills,
Ye harmleſs people man your young will tend,
While he for him your coats ſuperfluous lend
His future form'd with curious pride, while bare,
To fence with faſt from the piercing air,
This fleece ſhall ſhew it's azure from the ſky,
This drink the purple, that the ſcarlet dye ;
Another where immingling hues are given,
Shall mock the bow with colors dipt in heaven ;
Not guarded Colchis gave admiring Greece
So rich a treaſure in its golden fleece.
To toil encourag'd, free from tythe and tax,
Ye farmers ſow your fields with hemp and flax,
Let theſe the diſtaff for the web ſupply.
Spin on the ſpool, or with the ſhuttle fly.
But what vile cauſe retards the public plan !
Why fail the fabrics patriot zeal began !
Muſt nought but tombs of induſtry be found,
Proſtrated arts expiring on the ground !
Shall we of gewgaws gleaning half the globe,

Diſgrace our country with a foreign robe ?
Forbid it int'reſt, independence, ſhame,
And bluſh that kindles bright at honor's flame !
Should peace, like ſorcery, with her ſpells controul,
Our innate ſprings and energies of ſoul ;
To you Columbian dames, my accents call,
Oh, ſave your country from the threatened fall !
Will ye, bleſt fair, adopt from every zone,
Fantaſtic faſhions noxious in your own ?
At wintry balls in gauzy garments dreſt,
Admit the dire deſtroyer in your breaſt ?
Oft when nocturnal ſports your viſage fluſh,
As gay and heedleſs to the halls ye ruſh,
While tiptoe ſpirits buoy each graceful limb,
See down the dance the lovely fair one ſwim ;
Her own neat needle work improves her bloom,
Cloth'd in the labours of Columbia's loom.
Of ſavage life "know ye the bitter fruits,"
'Tis ſavage indolence the man imbrutes,
From induſtry the ſinews ſtrength acquire,
The limbs expand, the boſom feels new fire,
Unwearied induſtry pervades the whole,
Nor lends more force to body than to ſoul ;
Hence character is form'd, and hence proceeds
The enlivening heat that fires to daring deeds :
Then animation bids the ſpirit warm,
Soar in the whirlwind and enjoy the ſtorm.
But ſloth begets ſervility of ſoul,
Degrades each part, contaminates the whole ;
And taints in torpid veins the thickening blood,
Like the green mantle on a mire of mud.
Where convents deal the poor their daily broth,
See charity herſelf encourage ſloth !
Though helpleſs ſome, more lazy join the troop,
And healthful beggars ſwell the ſhameful group.
Will heaven benignant on thoſe nations ſmile,
Where ſloth and vice are leſs diſgrace than toil !
With opiates drunk, in indolence reclin'd,
Unbrac'd their ſinews, and debauch'd their mind.
Can crowds turn'd cowards, ſelf eſteem retain,
Or long unſpoil'd of freedom's gifts remain !
'Tis by the lofty purpoſe, deſperate deed,
Of men who dare for liberty to bleed,
By long endurance, fields with crimſon ſtain'd,
That independence won, muſt be maintain'd.
What Rome once virtuous was, that give us now,
Stateſmen and warriors awful from the plow.
Then ſhall Columbia know at length,
In toil, not GOLD, conſiſts our nation's ſtrength.

NEW YEAR'S GREETINGS

No. 95
A NEW YEAR'S WISH, FROM THE LAD, WHO CARRIES
THE *POST-BOY & ADVERTISER*, JAN. 1, 1760

[*The Pennsylvania Historical Society*]

SIZE, 6½ by 10½ inches. The *Boston Post-Boy & Advertiser* was established August 22, 1757, as the *Boston Weekly Advertiser*. It was published by Green and Russell, who added their name to the title January 1, 1759. At the time this broadside was issued, the full title of the paper was *Green & Russell's Boston Post-Boy & Advertiser*. Green and Russell's connection with the paper ceased in 1773, and it discontinued publication in 1775.

Led thro' a Scene of Blood, a dreadful Year,
    The Siege of Quebec had ended September 18, 1759.
Wolfe lends his Arm
    Wolfe had been killed in the battle. Cf. the ballad, p. 129, *supra*.

A

New Year's Wifh,

from the Lad, who carries

The Poft-Boy & Advertifer.

LED thro' a Scene of Blood, a dreadful Year,
What glorious Conquefts to our View appear ?
In Afpick's fcorching Plains our Thunder roars,
And *Afia* trembles for her diftant Shores :
Gallia's, Germania's cluft'ring Legions prefs,
But *Europe* Wonders at our great Succefs :
Nor *Britifh* Valour is to us unknown,
WOLFE lends his Arm, and Conqueft is our own.
O may the dawning Year full-fraught with Joy,
Bring Peace, bring Health, fo prays your faithful Boy :
May ev'ry Bleffing in Succeffion rife,
And new Joys bloffom, when the old One dies ;
May happy News by every Wind be blown,
And Heav'n's felected Bleffings deluge down :
May ev'ry Paper caufe of Joy difplay,
For this I'll run : But let me humbly pray,
Make by your Bounty, *this my happieft Day.*

BOSTON, JANUARY 1, 1760

No. 96

THE NEWS-BOY'S CHRISTMAS AND NEW-YEAR'S VERSES, HUMBLY ADDRESS'D TO THE GENTLEMEN AND LADIES TO WHOM HE CARRIES THE
BOSTON EVENING-POST,
DEC. 31, 1764

[The Pennsylvania Historical Society]

SIZE, 7 by 11¼ inches. The *Boston Evening-Post* was a continuation of the *Weekly Rehearsal*, and dated from August, 1735. It was printed by Thomas Fleet, whose two sons continued it after his death in 1758. After 1775 the sign was changed to the Bible and Heart. The Heart and Crown sign dated from 1731.

He search'd the Earth and Air and Skies,
For all the Curiosities,

> So did every printer of a newspaper. The eighteenth-century public frankly admitted its interest in the curious and the spectacular, and there is hardly an issue of the press which does not report some marvel of nature, if only a three-foot cucumber, or a calf with two heads.

May the Noise of War henceforth cease,

> Peace had not been concluded in the French and Indian Wars until 1763, a year before this date.

THE
News-BOY's
Christmas and *New-Year's* VERSES.

Humbly Address'd

To the Gentlemen and Ladies to whom he carries the *Boston Evening-Post*, published by T. & J. FLEET.

THE *Boy* who Weekly Pads the Streets,
With all the fresheft *News* he meets,
His Miftresses and Masters greets.

The flying Year is *almoft* paft :
Unwearied Time, which runs fo faft,
Has brought the welcome Day at laft.

This Time of Joy to all Mankind,
Your *News-Boy* humbly hopes to find,
The Bounty of each generous Mind.

Christmas and *New-Year*, Days of Joy,
The Harveft of your Carrier Boy,
He hopes you'll not his Hopes deftroy.

But cheer him as he trips along,
And kindly liften to his Song,
Which runs fo fmooth in Rhime, ding, dong,

He begs you now to re-explore,
His Zeal to pleafe you heretofore,
That may be never thought of more.

The great Events which mark'd the Year,
Whofe final Hour approaches near,
Within his *Papers* did appear.

He fearch'd the Earth and Air and Skies,
For all the Curiofities,
That Time produces as it flies.

How often has he run or flew,
Loaded with all the NEWs he knew,
And given all he had to You.

He ran, he flew from Street to Street,
Thro' Winds, & Storms, & Snow, & Heat,
And never fpar'd his Shoes nor Feet.

To pleafe, he fpar'd no Toil nor Pain,
Nor now the Labors of his Brain,
Let him not Toil nor fing in vain.

He by Experience woful knows,
When Fancy's Current's almoft froze,
Verfe hardly from low fpirits flows.

But when the chearful Heart's at Eafe,
As freely as the Weftern Breeze
It plays, and never fails to pleafe.

And 'tis afferted by the Wife,
That *Wealth* and *Spirits* fympathize,
And with each other fall and rife.

If fo, what pure poetic Fire
His generous Patrons may infpire,
By filling up his Pockets higher !

And, fince they can, he hopes they will,
Infpiring Zeal to pleafe, and Skill ;
With *New-Year's Gifts* his Pockets fill.

This is his only Day of Gain,
To cheer a tedious Year of Pain,
Oh let his Hopes not prove in vain.

Let him who in an humble Sphere,
Has ftrove to pleafe you all the Year,
Your *Favor* now and *Bounty* fhare.

Then will your humble News-Boy fing,
And pray,---God blefs great George our *King!*
Long from his Reign may Bleffings fpring.

May the Noife of War henceforth ceafe,
And Britifh Realms be hufh'd in Peace,
And Wealth and Happinefs increafe.

May nothing Britain's Peace annoy,
May *New-Year* prove a Year of Joy,
To every honeft Man---and Boy.

The *News-Boy* hopes you ne'er may know,
The want of *Something* to beftow,
And richer for your *Gifts* may grow.

December 31. 1764.

No. 97
THE CARRIER OF THE *BOSTON-GAZETTE*, TO HIS CUSTOMERS, JANUARY, 1766
[The Pennsylvania Historical Society]

SIZE, 5½ by 12¾ inches. This was the *Boston-Gazette and Country Journal*, established April 7, 1755, and continued with various changes of title until September 17, 1798. This sheet was printed until April 20, 1775, by Benjamin Edes and John Gill, and after that time by Benjamin Edes alone, and with his sons. Throughout the Revolution it was identified with the cause of the patriots. Beginning with the issue of January 1, 1770, the vignette of the present heading was altered in accordance with the bolder patriotic sentiment of the hour. The new cut represented the figure of a woman, crowned and equipped with shield and scepter, in the act of liberating from a cage a bird which flies out over a skyline in which there are as many churches as dwellings. This emblem was retained until the sheet discontinued publication in 1798.

'Tis past! 'Tis gone! th' important Day has fled,

  The Stamp Act had been passed by Parliament on March 22, 1765, to take effect November 1, 1765. It is this latter date to which the present author refers. The act was not repealed until March 18, 1766. Cf. p. 131, *supra*, for the verses recording the Boston protest of August 14, 1765.

The Carrier of the *Boston-Gazette*, to his Customers.

A NEW-YEAR'S WISH.

'TIS paft ! 'Tis gone ! th' important Day * has fled,
    When *Tyrants* wifh'd to ftrike fair FREEDOM dead.

Permit me, then, GOOD SIR, with Heart fincere,
To wifh you happy in this welcome Year ;
That Men and Bufinefs may be freed from Chains,
And each one happy with his honeft Gains.
May LIBERTY, and FREEDOM ! O bleft Sound !
Survive the Stab, and heal the deep'ned Wound ;
May *Tyrants* tremble ! and may *Villains* fear !
And fpotlefs JUSTICE, crown the happy Year.
May *GEORGE* the Great, with open'd Ears and Eyes,
Obferve our *Injuries*, and hear our *Cries* ;
Redrefs the Grievance ; and vouchfafe to give
Joy to us FREEMEN, who like BRITONS live.
The early News, with hafty Step I'll bring ;
And loudly blefs Great *GEORGE* the Britifh King.

But——Let me now experience your Regard ;
Beftow fome Trifle for my paft Reward ;
For in the Year that's gone, I doubly ftrove,
To *warn* you *timely*, and deferve your Love.
I told you, *wicked Men (and trembled at the Fact)*
Combin'd to curfe us, with that curfed § Act :
So let my Time be fpent in Days to come,
To tell AMERICA her threaten'd Doom.
Or otherways ! which *Heaven* grant I may,
With *youthful Eyes*, behold the joyful Day
When GOOD, on GOOD, from an almighty Hand,
Shall blefs each *Briton*, in this happy Land :
Then fhall my glad'ned Heart with Joy proclaim,
The *Voice* of FREEDOM, FREEDOM's lofty Name.

[N. B. No *Stamp Paper defired.*]

---

* *Nov. 1, the Day for the Stamp-Act to take Place.*
§ *The STAMP ACT.*

No. 98

VERSES FOR THE YEAR 1790, ADDRESSED TO THE GENEROUS SUBSCRIBERS OF THE *NEW-YORK WEEKLY MUSEUM*

[The New York Historical Society]

SIZE, 8½ by 10¼ inches. Issued January 1, 1790. The *New-York Weekly Museum* was a continuation of the *Impartial Gazetteer and Saturday Evening Post*, which had been established May 17, 1788, by Harrison & Purdy. They changed the name September 20 of that year. This sheet is an excellent illustration of the New Year's greeting as a challenge to the printer's originality and neatness of workmanship.

Verses *for the* Year *1790*.

Addreſſed to the *Generous Subſcribers* of the

NEW-YORK WEEKLY MUSEUM,

Wiſhing them a Happy New Year.

ONCE more awake the ſtrain of grateful praiſe,
  Accept your votary's humble annual lays;
To you my Patrons—'m in duty bound,
To ſerve while life runs its continual round,
Collecting every ſubject worth a ſingle line,
Apollo's notes—ſung by the ſacred nine.
What's done in foreign climes freſh come to hand,
Array'd in order—in the MUSEUM ſtand.
From Heſper's ſilver flood-gates (from the ſtar,
That ſhoots its pale and glimmering rays afar)
To old Oceanus off I ſend the muſe,
To bring the cream—the beſt of all the news;
Swift-footed Hermes, trips acroſs the maiо,
Viſits the cabinets of France and Spain;
From thence to China, where he leaps the wall,
That's fifty cubits high, nor dreads the fall.
He viſits Pekin—peeps into their ſchemes,
And finds ſome more abſurd than madmen's dreams.
With twiſted rod he cleaves the nether ſkies,
And ſwift to London and St. James's flies;
Next to the Houſe of Commons—reads the bill,
Where ſullen Juſtice ſat with ſtumpy quill—
Inebriate Faction, hoodwink'd reel'd along,
And leering Folly ſang Deception's ſong.
Hermes returns, and brings the pond'rous mail,
And bids fair Freedom's preſs the truth reveal.

No doubt you've wonder'd whence we had our news,
While you our WEEKLY MUSEUM did peruſe;
Therefore to ſatisfy my Patron's anxious thought,
I aroſe this morning—and the muſe I ſought,
Long e'er the ſun awoke the new born day,
I ſtood prepar'd to ſtrike th' accuſtom'd lay.
I rang'd the types, ſtraightway to work I went,
To pleaſe my Patrons—was my chief intent;
And now preſent the offering of my muſe,
Though ſmall the gift—pray don't the ſame refuſe.
With it I wiſh you all an *Happy Year*,
Content of *mind*, with plenty of *good cheer*;
And as the year rolls on its annual round,
May *Health* and *Peace* within your doors be found.
May ſmiling *Fortune* all your ſteps attend—
May *Heaven* all your wiſhes ſtill befriend—
May conſcious *Virtue* in your boſom blaze,
And ſweet *Contentment* crown your *happy days*.

  With due ſubmiſſion now I take my leave,
Soon as your GENEROUS BOUNTY I receive,
For which with grateful heart I'll thank moſt fervent,
And am with due reſpect—

your humble ſervant.

  The PRINTER's DEVIL.

No. 99

THE VERSES OF THE NEWS-CARRIER, OF THE *DAILY ADVERTISER*, TO HIS CUSTOMERS, ON THE NEW YEAR, 1790

[*The New York Historical Society*]

SIZE, 8⅛ by 12⅞ inches, with edges trimmed. Included as another example of the elaborate decoration common to verses of this sort late in the century. The *New York Daily Advertiser* was first issued April 6, 1785. Under various titles it continued to be published throughout the century.

Chapel
    Apparently the name of the "news-carrier."
Yet like a cert[ain] bard of Britain's isle,
A Laureat call'd,
    Thomas Warton was poet laureate at this time. He died May 20, 1790.
Had clos'd my ey[es]—t[hen] lo! I 'gan to nod,
And in a dream [meth]ou[ght] a form drew near,

Remind the friends of [great] Columbia's cause,
That still my name s[hould cl]aim their just applause,
The first e'er [jo]in'd to happy fed'ral laws:

carman
    A man who drives a car; a carter, carrier.

Nor tea, no[r toast,] nor dainties could avail,
Before you [hea]rd my Advertising t[a]le.

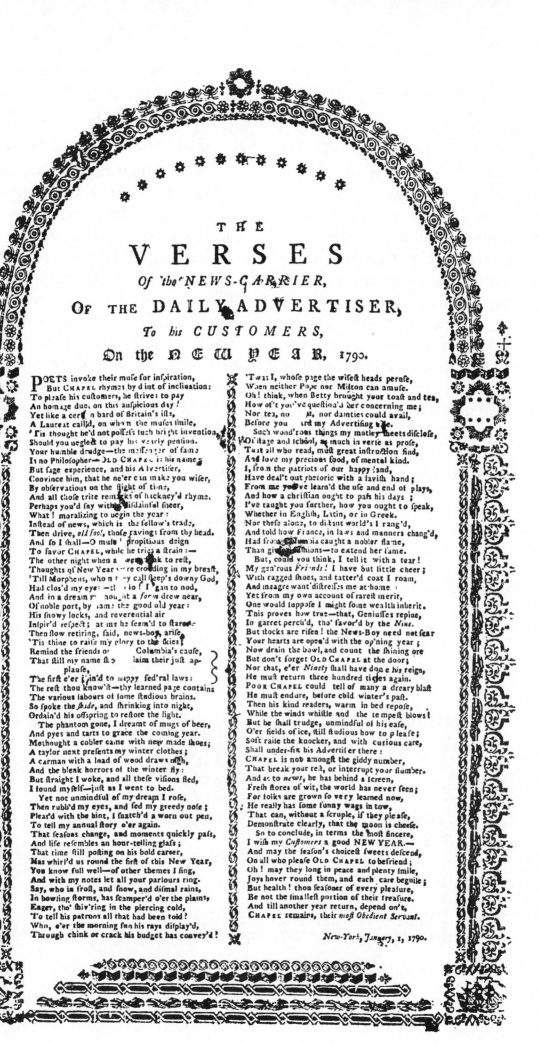

THE
VERSES

Of the NEWS-CARRIER,

OF THE DAILY ADVERTISER,

To his CUSTOMERS,

On the NEW YEAR, 1790.

POETS invoke their muse for inspiration,
But CHAPEL rhymes by dint of inclination:
To please his customers, he strives to pay
An homage due, on this auspicious day!
Yet like a certain bard of Britain's isle,
A Laureat call'd, on whom the muses smile,
'Tis thought he'd not possess such bright invention,
Should you neglect to pay his yearly pension.
Your humble drudge—the messenger of fame
Is no Philosopher—OLD CHAPEL is his name;
But sage experience, and his Advertiser,
Convince him, that he ne'er can make you wiser,
By observations on the flight of time,
And all those trite remarks of hackney'd rhyme.
Perhaps you'd say with a disdainful sneer,
What! moralizing to begin the year:
Instead of news, which is the fellow's trade,
Then drive, *old fool*, those ravings from thy head.
And so I shall—O muse! propitious deign
To favor CHAPEL, while he tries a strain :—
The other night when I went ?? to rest,
Thoughts of New Year were crowding in my breast,
'Till Morpheus, who ?? ?y call sleep's downy God,
Had clos'd my eyes—?? ?io ! I 'gan to nod,
And in a dream ?? ?ou?ht a *form* drew near,
Of noble port, by ?ame the good old year:
His snowy locks, and reverential air
Inspir'd respect; at me he seem'd to stare
Then slow retiring, said, news-boy, arise,
'Tis thine to raise my glory to the skies!
Remind the friends of Columbia's cause,
That still my name ?? ?laim their just applause,
The first e'er ?in'd to happy fed'ral laws:
The rest thou know'st—thy learned page contains
The various labours of some studious brains.
So spoke the ?ide, and shrinking into night,
Ordain'd his offspring to restore the light.

The phantom gone, I dreamt of mugs of beer,
And pyes and tarts to grace the coming year.
Methought a cobler came with new made shoes;
A taylor next presents my winter clothes;
A carman with a load of wood draws nigh,
And the bleak horrors of the winter fly:
But straight I woke, and all these visions fled,
I found myself—just as I went to bed.

Yet not unmindful of my dream I rose,
Then rubb'd my eyes, and fed my greedy nose;
Pleas'd with the hint, I snatch'd a worn out pen,
To tell my annual story o'er again.
That seasons change, and moments quickly pass,
And life resembles an hour-telling glass;
That time still posting on his bold career,
Has whirl'd us round the first of this New Year,
You know full well—of other themes I sing,
And with my notes let all your parlours ring.
Say, who in frost, and snow, and dismal rains,
In howling storms, has scamper'd o'er the plains,
Eager, tho' shiv'ring in the piercing cold,
To tell his patrons all that had been told?
Who, e'er the morning sun his rays display'd,
Through chink or crack his budget has convey'd?

'Twas I, whose page the wisest heads peruse,
When neither Pope nor Milton can amuse.
Oh! think, when Betty brought your toast and tea,
How oft you've question'd her concerning me;
Nor tea, no ?t, nor dainties could avail,
Before you ?rd my Advertising tale.
Such wond'rous things my motley sheets disclose,
Of ?tage and school, as much in verse as prose,
That all who read, must great instruction find,
And love my precious food, of mental kind.
I, from the patriots of our happy land,
Have deal't out rhetoric with a lavish hand;
From me you've learn'd the use and end of plays,
And how a christian ought to pass his days ;
I've taught you farther, how you ought to speak,
Whether in English, Latin, or in Greek.
Nor these alone, to distant world's I rang'd,
And told how France, in laws and manners chang'd,
Had from Columbia caught a nobler flame,
Than give ?hions—to extend her fame.

But, could you think, I tell it with a tear!
My gen'rous *Friends!* I have but little cheer;
With ragged shoes, and tatter'd coat I roam,
And meagre want distresses me at home ;
Yet from my own account of rarest merit,
One would suppose I might some wealth inherit.
This proves how true—that, Geniusses repine,
In garret perch'd, tho' favor'd by the *Nine*.
But stocks are risen! the News-Boy need not fear
Your hearts are open'd with the op'ning year ;
Now drain the bowl, and count the shining ore
But don't forget OLD CHAPEL at the door;
Nor that, e'er *Ninety* shall have done e his reign,
He must return three hundred times again.
POOR CHAPEL could tell of many a dreary blast
He must endure, before cold winter's past.
Then his kind readers, warm in bed repose,
While the winds whistle and the tempest blows!
But he shall trudge, unmindful of his ease,
O'er fields of ice, still studious how to please;
Soft raise the knocker, and with curious care,
Shall under-fix his Advertiser there :
CHAPEL is not amongst the giddy number,
That break your rest, or interrupt your slumber.
And as to *news*, he has behind a screen,
Fresh stores of wit, the world has never seen;
For folks are grown so very learned now,
He really has some funny wags in tow,
That can, without a scruple, if they please,
Demonstrate clearly, that the moon is cheese.
So to conclude, in terms the most sincere,
I wish my *Customers* a good NEW YEAR.—
And may the season's choicest sweets descend,
On all who please OLD CHAPEL to befriend;
Oh! may they long in peace and plenty smile,
Joys hover round them, and each care beguile;
But health! thou seasoner of every pleasure,
Be not the smallest portion of their treasure.
And till another year return, depend on't,
CHAPEL remains, their *most Obedient Servant.*

New-York, January, 1, 1790.

PETER JARVIS, TO HIS FRIENDS AND PATRONS, WISHING THEM A HAPPY NEW YEAR

[*The Pennsylvania Historical Society*]

SIZE, 7½ by 13⅜ inches. Three other issues are extant for Peter Jarvis, cabinet maker of 76 Newbury Street, Boston. The first, issued in 1787, announces his wares. The second, issued in 1798, and entitled "The Supplications of Peter Jarvis," details his increasing infirmities, and politely asks "a mite for aged Peter." At that time he gave his age as "verging on threescore and ten." The present issue is undated, but since Peter makes less of his infirmities, the sheet may be earlier than 1798. For the two other Jarvis issues, cf. Ford, 2496, 2857.

The blacksmith's greeting may serve as another example of the newsboy's appeal for donations extended to other callings. The few such specimens which survive display amusing incongruities in their increasing elaborateness from year to year. There is, for example, in the John Hay Library of Providence, a neat Boston imprint of 1832, adorned with a heavy border of medallions and entitled "The Scavenger's Address to his Employers." The sheet is further adorned with a cut showing the scavenger's wagon drawn by two horses, and the scavenger and his assistant in action. The last stanza reads,

> Now hand us out a little cash,
> And we will come and take your trash—
> And wish you free from ev'ry pain,
> Till a NEW YEAR comes round again.

So enterprising a scavenger might possibly have chosen for himself a less humble calling.

No. 101

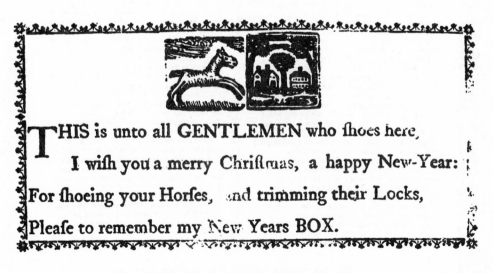

THIS is unto all GENTLEMEN who ſhoes here,

I wiſh you a merry Chriſtmas, a happy New-Year:

For ſhoeing your Horſes, and trimming their Locks,

Pleaſe to remember my New Years BOX.

PETER  JARVIS,

TO HIS FRIENDS AND PATRONS,

WISHING THEM

A HAPPY NEW YEAR.

YE who, around the focial winter fire,
Participate in all your hearts' defire :
Who find in all your dealings, profit, clear,
With bleffing upon bleffing ev'ry year :
To whom, connexions, friends, and fortune's given,
And all the kindly legacies of heaven.

Around in little groups, your little bairns
Share the enjoyments, which your labour earns ;
In cheerly paftime, pleafant chat and glee,
Dancing the little prattlers on your knee ;
You who through all the feafon's " changing fcenes,"
Thus find true pleafure in your ways and means ;
You who thus know what feelings to afford,
To you my heart appeals, and to your God !

Think of the aged, the infirm, and poor,
Nor drive the helplefs ftranger from your door ;
Hear his petition !—give him a relief,
Prevent misfortune, and inhibit grief ;
Strengthen his hopes with lenient, lib'ral good,
And be your recompence, his gratitude.

Accept all HONEST PETER can impart,
The warmeft wifhes of his grateful heart ;
That yours may ever be, without alloy—
Peace, Friendfhip, Profit, Pleafure, Love, and Joy.

Yours, moft affectionately,

PETER JARVIS.

INDEXES

INDEX OF TITLES AND FIRST LINES

Index of Titles and First Lines

INDEX OF NAMES

This Index includes names of authors, subjects, and printers of the broadsides reproduced, and also names of contemporary persons mentioned in the Introductory Note and in the editorial comment. Names occurring in the text of the broadsides and in quoted material are not included.

Index of Names

Mather, Increase, cited, 68
Maverick, Samuel, 44
Mein, John, 134; acrostic on, 135
Milton, John, xxi
Minot, Captain John, 6
Minot, Lydia, xx, 6; verses on, 7
Mode, Magnus, 92; verses on, 93
Montgomery, General Richard, 128, 146; verses on, 147
Morton, Nathaniel, cited, xix, 20
Mullins, Priscilla, 14

Newell, Thomas, diary quoted, 54, 100
Newland, Jeremiah, 66
Nicholas V, Pope, xvii
North, Lord, 184
Norton, John, xix, 10
Noyes, Nicholas, xix, 18, 20, 28; verses by, 21, 29

Oakes, Urian, xxi
Occom, Mr. Samson, 98; verses by, 99
Oliver, Andrew, 130
Ormsby, John (also Ormesby and Amesby), 84, 90; verses on, 85

Packcom, Reuben, verses by, iv
Paine, Thomas, xxiii, 128; verses by, 129
Paul, Moses, 98
Paulding, John, 156
Pearson, Captain, 154
Peck, Abiezer, 122; verses by, 123
Peck, Samuel, 122
Penhallow, Samuel, quoted, 114
Pepperell, General William, 118
Philip, King, xxii, 8, 12, 16, 112, 164
Phillis, Mark and, 86; verses on, 87
Phillis (Wheatley), 48; verses by, 49
Phoebe, 86
Pidgin, Parson, xxv
Pitcher, Nathaniel, 32; verses by, 33
Pitt, William, the Elder, 130
Plummer, Jonathan, xx, xxv
Prescott, Colonel (William), 142
Preston, Captain Thomas, 44
Prince, Thomas, 66
Purdy, Harrison and, printers, 208
Putnam, General Israel, 146
Pyncheon, William, diary quoted, 72, 188

Quarles, Francis, xxi
Quincy, Major, 82

R., E. [Elisha Rich], 144; verses by, 145
Reiner, John, 10–12; verses on, 11
Revere, Paul, 44, 96
Richardson, Ann, 90; verses on, 91
Richardson, Ebenezer, 94, 96, 134; verses on, 95, 97
Richardson, John, 90; verses on, 91
Rivers, Captain, 116
Robinson, Mrs. Hannah, 32
Rogers, John, 82
Rowe, John, diary quoted, 44, 90, 96; mentioned, 54
Russell, Ezekiel, printer, 48, 56, 57, 59, 74, 76, 78, 106, 146, 170, 188, 192, 194
Russell, John, printer, 66

Saint Clair, General, 58, 150
St. John, Peter, of Norwalk, 42; verses by, 43
Schuyler, General (Philip), 146
Seccomb, John, 162; verses attributed to, 163
Seider, see Sneider, 96
Sennet, John, 90, 102
Sewall, Hannah, 28, 30, 32; verses on, 31
Sewall, Rebekah, 26–28; verses on, 27
S. S., see Sewall, Samuel, 161
Sewall, Judge Samuel, diary quoted, xix, 12, 17, 18–20, 22, 24, 26–28, 160, 174; mentioned, 30, 32; verses by, 161, 175
Shephard, Rev. Thomas, xix
Shirley, Governor William, 118
Shute, Governor Samuel, 114
Smith, Ann, 196
Smith, Elizabeth, 90, 102
Sneider, Christopher, also Seider, 94, 96
Sprout, Hannah, xxv
Starr, Comfort, 38
Starr, Nathan, 38; verses on, 39
Stetson, Cornet Robert, 32
Stetson, Isaac, 17, 32; verses on, 33
Stetson, Mary, xx, 17, 32; verses to, 33
Stetson, Robert, xx, 17, 32; verses to, 33
Stone, Rev. Samuel, 20
Swan, Captain, 136
Sylvester, Joshua, xxi

Thomas, Elisha, 108; verses on, 109
Thomas, I., and H. W. Tinges, printers, 114, 115
Tilton, Daniel, xxii, 114; verses on, 115
Tilton, Jacob, xxii, 114; verses on, 115
Tinges, H. W., I. Thomas and, printers, 114, 115
Tinkham, Amasa, 170
T., B. (see Tompson, Benjamin), 27

[223]